WINNING DIRECT RESPONSE ADVERTISING

FROM PRINT THROUGH
INTERACTIVE MEDIA

SECOND EDITION

Joan Throckmorton

FOREWORD
by
Thomas L. Collins

Printed on recyclable paper

NTC Business Books
a division of *NTC Publishing Group* • Lincolnwood, Illinois USA

Library of Congress Cataloging-in-Publication Data

Throckmorton, Joan.
    Winning direct response advertising : from print through
interactive media / Joan Throckmorton. —2nd ed.
        p.   cm.
    Originally published: Englewood Cliffs, N.J. : Prentice-Hall,
c1986
    Includes index.
    ISBN 0-8442-3428-1 (alk. paper)
    1. Advertising, Direct-mail.   2. Direct marketing.   I. Title
HF5861.T47   1997
659.13'3—dc21   96-40856
                                                    CIP

659.133

5/00 MT

Published by NTC Business Books, a division of NTC Publishing Group
4255 West Touhy Avenue
Lincolnwood (Chicago), Illinois 60646-1975, U.S.A.
Manufactured in the United States of America.

7 8 9 0 BC 9 8 7 6 5 4 3 2 1

*This book is dedicated to all those who
believe in the interactive selling process and the
marketing it embraces—Direct Marketing.*

CONTENTS

**Chapter 5   Nurturing Creative Concepts:
How to Sharpen Your Creative
Judgment and Grow a Concept`   129**

Chapter 6   Creating the Direct Mail Package   175

Chapter 7   Deathless Prose   217

Chapter 8   A Gallery of the Good Stuff   **251**

Chapter 9   How to Create Winning Print Ads   **317**

Chapter 10 At Last — Creating for Broadcast
                   and Digital Interactive Media   **349**

About the Author

Ms. Throckmorton is a direct marketing specialist with over 30 years' experience. She now heads up her own marketing and creative consultancy in Pound Ridge, New York.

Prior to establishing her direct response advertising agency in New York City in 1970, she was associated with such major publishers as Time Inc., Cowles Communications, Inc., Doubleday & Company, Inc., and American Heritage.

While at Time Inc., she was associated with the former *Life* magazine where she helped introduce the first major Time Inc. book, *The Life Picture Cookbook*. She also worked on *Sports Illustrated* and later became Assistant to the Chairman of the Board of Time Inc.

At Cowles Communications, she helped set up the first merchandise and service operation for *Family Circle* and *Look* magazine subscribers. She ran her own promotion business in Mexico City, Mexico, in the early 1960s.

Since 1970, Joan Throckmorton, Inc. (formerly Throckmorton Associates, Inc.) has worked on significant direct marketing projects for a broad variety of clients in consumer publishing, merchandising, and services and in business services and products.

Among these clients are Hewlett-Packard, General Electric, McGraw-Hill Publications Company, AT&T, American Express, IBM, Citibank, Rodale Press, Inc., Meredith Corporation, Time-Life Books, and Viacom International, Inc.

Ms. Throckmorton was a member of the board of directors of the Direct Marketing Association, Inc. for six years; she is a former member of its executive committee and the long-range planning committee. She was one of the founding members of Women's Direct Response Group, now called Women in Direct Marketing International, with chapters across the United States and abroad. She is a member of the Women's Forum, Inc., New York and the International Women's Forum.

She has been a national speaker at direct response advertising organizations across the country and abroad and at a variety of the Direct Marketing Association's national conferences and conventions. Under the sponsorship of the DMA she currently co-conducts a seminar entitled "Direct Marketing to the Mature Marketplace" and has, for over 10 years, conducted the creative seminar "Winning Direct Mail."

In 1976 she was selected as one of the top 100 Corporate Women in America by *Business Week* magazine. In 1986 she was named The Direct Marketing Woman of the Year by the Women's Direct Response Group, Inc. In 1987 she received the Silver Apple Award from the Direct Marketing Club of New York. And in 1996 she received the Edward N. Mayer, Jr., Award for Educational Leadership from the Direct Marketing Educational Foundation.

Acknowledgments

In this new edition of *Winning Direct Response Advertising* I want to acknowledge all those talented writers and designers from whom I drew my inspiration.

Some of the finest direct response writers in America are represented in these pages—as well they should be. I know they will inspire you as they did me.

But I also want to acknowledge my debt to all the others—those many who couldn't be included here. I went back over 20 years of direct mail samples as preparation for parts of this new edition and I was deeply moved and impressed.

What marvelous work we've been doing! Granted I had saved only what I considered the best. But—WOW—we did some wonderful stuff over the last two decades. Some of the older direct mail from the late 1970s and early 1980s was particularly impressive.

If I had to pick a Golden Age of Direct Mail, I'd say it was then. A staggering collection of great letters—to inspire and remind me how great letters can be . . . envelopes that insist we open them. Bright, bold, and brassy brochures. We dared a lot, too—a lot more, perhaps —in those days. Our leads, our teasers were compelling. We were friendlier, more relaxed in our tone (more professional, that is), more polished.

What was it that made the works from the seventies and eighties so appealing, so strong? More creative freedom? Certainly there was less "computer" and a lot more USPS freedom in price and abilities to do unusual things without massive cost penalties.

Then again, perhaps it was new people discovering a new direct marketing for the first time, just as now our focus is changing to an even newer direct marketing—digital interactive marketing. And we'll have "new" people all over again, discovering still new forms and new freedoms. Welcome!

FOREWORD

Joan Throckmorton is part of a long tradition—but a rather short list—of treasured advertising mentors. She carries on a tradition begun by Claude Hopkins and John Caples in the 1920s and advanced by Victor O. Schwab and Maxwell Sackheim in the 1950s . . . David Ogilvy and Rosser Reeves in the 1960s.

Perhaps I am prejudiced because of my own background in direct marketing, but it seems to me that most of the best and most useful books about how to do advertising have been by direct marketing practitioners.

Rosser Reeves is the one exception that comes to mind. His *Reality in Advertising* (1960) is still found in the marketing section of many bookstores today, and rightly so. His rigorously logical concept of the Unique Selling Proposition forced its way into the language of advertising the way his headache-remedy commercials forced their way into our minds.

I would not count David Ogilvy as an exception because he always said that he learned so much from the direct marketers and so often paid tribute to their knowledge of what motivates consumers. So I think of him as one of us.

But apart from Ogilvy and Reeves, there has been surprisingly little written about how to create good "general" or non-response advertising. My suspicion about the reason for this is that without the yardstick of response to tell them how close they are coming to the mark, image-makers don't really know what will be successful and what will not. The aim becomes to tickle the client, win the award, and get lucky. This has led to some horrific disasters as well as great successes. And little is learned from the disasters to help them avoid a similar disaster the next time.

My own personal mentor was my first boss—Victor Schwab of Schwab & Beatty. His classic book, *How to Write a Good Advertisement,* was recently republished and still deserves careful reading.

It began as a way of promoting the agency. It was not a question of doing so in competition with other mail-order agencies, because at that time there almost weren't any others. But Schwab, like so many direct marketers before and after him, felt frustrated that the lessons learned from observing mail-order responses were being blithely ignored by the rest of the advertising world.

So he began running little five-inch advertisements in the *New York Times,* each one devoted to making just one point about "How to Write a Good Advertisement."

Later all of these ads were collected and reprinted, first in a full-page newspaper ad and then in a little book, which soon became a bigger, more detailed book.

What Schwab was teaching about good advertising contributed greatly to my own education as a young copywriter. He, in turn, had surely learned an enormous amount from his one-tme bosses, the incomparably brilliant copywriting team of Maxwell Sackheim and Harry Scherman. They had founded and operated the agency under the name of Sackheim & Scherman and then, when they became too busy running their Book-of-the Month Club, sold the agency to two young employees named Vic Schwab and Bob Beatty.

But so much has happened since then that entirely new guidance is required today.

For instance, in those days, there was no mail-order advertising on the radio. (And I say "mail-order," because mail was about the only way to order directly and have delivery made to your home or office.) The first major use Schwab & Beatty made of radio was when they invented, to the best of my knowledge, "support" advertising, spending half a million dollars a year on radio commercials which said, "Watch for your letter from *Reader's Digest.*"

Oh, yes, we also ran a brief saturation campaign on the radio every November for a client known as "the wrong Victor Schwab"—so called because his name, believe it or not, was Victor I. Schwab, not Victor O. Schwab. Every year he ran pre-Christmas mail-order commercials offering three maps for $1, and sold millions of maps that way. It was almost the only mail-order success on radio at the time that I can recall.

Although there was some direct mail, it was by no means the giant industry that it is today, and the agency would create direct mail for a client almost as a grudging favor because it was not commissionable.

When commercial television came along in the early 1950s, the primitive ancestors of the infomercial producers made their appearance. They were literally Atlantic City boardwalk pitch men (I say "pitch men" because I don't recall ever having seen a pitch woman) who simply faced the television camera and recited their spiel for half an hour. In their crude way, they had their own finely honed skill because, like mail-order practitioners, they too had learned by observing what made people respond and buy. But they were soon driven off the air until the advent of cable television opened up air time for their comeback in far more sophisticated form.

"Media strategy," in those days, consisted mostly of testing the most promising magazines and newspapers and continuing to use the ones that had proven to be most profitable.

The idea that brand advertisers might use direct-response advertising to identify promising prospects by name and address and then use that information to establish a continuing relationship by direct mail was unthinkable. By far the most important reason for this, of course, is that we were not yet able to use the power of the computer to store and retrieve such information in a way that was economically feasible.

Lever Brothers did stumble on the capability of direct response to maximize response to sales promotion offers.

They were planning to offer a new premium in exchange for box tops (today it would be package barcodes): "a pair and a spare of nylon stockings." They came to Schwab & Beatty and asked us to use direct-response methods to find the best way to present the offer. We prepared eight jumbo postcards, each one wording the offer a different way, and they mailed them in equal quantities to a large number of in-house names.

The difference in response between the weakest postcard and the strongest was startling, perhaps as much as five to one. The headline on the strongest postcard said, "Our Way of Saying Thanks to the Millions of Women Who Use Lever Brothers Products."

The entire winning copy panel was then printed on the back of hundreds of millions of Lever Brothers cartons.

You would think this would have ushered in a new era of scientific copy testing by brand advertisers. But you would be wrong. The mind-set of orthodoxy was too strong to be undone by the facts. Lever Brothers never again conducted such an experiment, and neither did any other brand advertiser (with the possible exception of some of the fortunate brand advertisers who were clients of David Ogilvy). And even today it is still almost unheard of for a brand advertiser to split-test promotional advertising, as we did for Lever Brothers at Schwab & Beatty, or to split-test product appeals, as Ogilvy tells of having done for Dove Toilet Bar. But the capability is not only still there, today it has been greatly enhanced by the sophisticated skills of database marketing.

I mention all this only to make the point that direct response advertising is a whole new world today and we need a Joan Throckmorton to guide us through it. And only Joan had the keenness of mind, the patience, the experience, and the tenacity to undertake the whole job.

We direct marketers have a secret weapon which taught us almost everything we have learned. That secret weapon is grounded in the same scientific method that medical researchers use to test a new pharmaceutical drug cure or remedy, the double-blind test in which the new drug is tested against a placebo in statistically significant numbers.

Our version is the split-run test, in which two or more advertising approaches are given absolutely equal exposure and the coded responses from each are counted and compared.

By confining the difference between the ads to one variable—the headline, the illustration, the offer, the price, even one word in the headline—we can make amazingly precise discoveries, and apply those discoveries to future efforts.

The result has always been a kind of process of evolution toward a more and more effective creative effort. When one would receive an elaborate sweepstakes mailing from *Reader's Digest,* one of the most zealous practitioners of testing, it might be the end product of literally half a hundred tests leading up to it.

The sad truth is that in many ways, except in direct mail, this scientific method is often falling by the wayside. There is a new generation of advertising client that makes decisions by committee, and I have always been convinced that smart people make dumb committees. And there is a new generation of young creative people with no response experience. They often not only don't know what makes advertising work better—they don't realize that they don't know. All this leads to an unfortunate mind-set: "We already know what needs to be said and done, so why test?" This conclusion is often arrived at through the misuse and misinterpretation of focus research.

But Joan Throckmorton has been around long enough to have personally seen, experienced, and used the electrifying power of split-run testing many times, and she has been a brave voice crying in the wilderness for testing, testing, and more testing. Long may she be brave.

Her book is a product of this experience with scientific testing. She is not telling you what she thinks. She is telling you what she *knows*—and you had better listen if you want to get the most advertising bang for the buck!

Today we stand at the threshold of an extraordinary new medium, global interactive advertising on the World Wide Web of the Internet. It is so different from everything that has gone before, you might understandably jump to the conclusion that none of the old rules apply. But if you do, you will be making a mistake.

Joan Throckmorton wisely shows how the eternal verities of direct response—of empathizing with and listening to the customer, of developing a relationship with prospects and customers built on trust—have been operative in every new medium as it emerged. And advertising on the Web will be no exception.

Remember what David Ogilvy taught us:

"When I write an advertisement, I don't want you to tell me that you find it 'creative.' I want you to find it so interesting that you buy the product."

But already, on the Web, we are seeing advertisers make the same mistake they have made so often in the other media: focusing on being "creative" rather than making you want to buy the product.

They could profit from the wisdom that Joan Throckmorton brings to this book, and some of the smartest ones will.

THOMAS L. COLLINS

co-founder, Rapp & Collins
Executive Editor of
the monthly newsletter,
Maximarketing Insights

INTRODUCTION

Why You Should Read This Book

This is the second edition of *Winning Direct Response Advertising* and, although it sets down the same basic tenets as the original book, you'll find it has many new examples and new views as well as much about our electronic media as they affect direct response advertising

The creative basics don't change; how we ap-ply them does change. From a direct mail package to a Web site on the Internet is a technological revolution indeed. But our tactics of persuasion, our pleas to change the hearts and minds of our prospects and customers remain much the same.

This is a book for creative people or those people who are involved, one way or the other, in the creative process in direct response advertising.

Aha! you say—creative people—that means *writers*. Sure it does, and *Winning Direct Response Advertising* is for direct response writers (or aspiring writers), but it will also prove helpful for others whose jobs touch on the creative process:

- Creative directors who must work with their staff to develop good advertising

- Managers who must judge their agency's creative work or the work of their own promotion departments

- Marketers who are in charge of developing advertising plans

- Product managers and corporate directors who work with market planning

- Artists and art directors who work with copywriters (and just about everyone else on the creative team)

- Broadcast and electronic communicators in all forms of audio/visual media

- Large companies, small companies, and individuals who wish to enter the field of direct marketing

Not only will this book enable writers to do a far better job in all forms of direct response advertising, but it will help management—in businesses large and small—to better understand what must go into good direct response advertising and how to work with creative people. There are several fine books that can help individuals and companies entering direct marketing today, but this book uniquely enables them to participate in, evaluate, and judge good creative development and direct response advertising as a whole.

This book will also help managers and supervisors encourage greater quality and creativity in direct response advertising. It will assist creative directors in guiding their creative people—artists as well as copywriters—to higher levels of direct response advertising.

As for you writers—take heart. This book gives you the solid basics of direct response advertising—and then some. It offers you a sound grounding in technique: the formulas, rules, and rules for breaking rules. Equally important, it will guide you through the creative process from beginning to end and set you on the way to creative reasoning. This is an area that will be crucial to your career—to your own creative growth and development. Once you master this aspect of direct response advertising, you will understand not only the fundamentals, but the heart and soul of direct marketing. You will be prepared to chart your own future, whether it be master craftsperson and creative star, or creative director and leader of others.

And what a future this can be today as the 20th century turns into the 21st century and a new electronic age lies before us! No one —absolutely no one—is in a better position to take advantage of all the opportunities it presents than you are, as a direct marketer!

Whether you want to focus on direct mail, print, broadcast, or other electronic media, direct marketing's inroads in the 1980s and 1990s have placed it in an undisputed position of leadership in the world of interactive advertising.

More and more major services and products are demanding response and measurement from their advertising investments; the marketing focus has shifted totally away from production and sales to customer cultivation and fulfillment. The customer is king or queen and good customer relations are the culmination of our marketing goals.

Customer relations, of course, have been the basis of all direct response advertising for as long as it's been practiced. How lucky we are to be a part of it today.

Understanding and mastering the creative principles of direct response advertising can put you way ahead in electronic advertising, marketing, public relations, and sales promotion. (Not to mention the fact that it will help make you a stellar direct marketer.)

As our ability to communicate one-to-one and persuade people to act and to enable them to do so *immediately* grows, selling directly to the prospect or customer will predominate. Personal persuasion, the role of the salesperson, will lead effective advertising communications. And with this, those of us who practice sound direct marketing principles will be able to lead the professions of persuasion.

CHAPTER ONE

A NEW WORLD OF OPPORTUNITIES FOR YOU

Into the 1970s most business people called it *direct mail*. Then it became known as *direct marketing*. More recently the term *direct response* has taken hold, and now it's in the vanguard of one-to-one marketing. But whatever you call it, direct response advertising is big business today and a keystone of all marketing for two simple reasons: properly executed, it works, and it is measurable, so you *know* when it's working.

The changes in terminology reflected the changes in perception. Few, if any, business people call direct response *junk mail* anymore. Why? Because of its accountability. It also enables the seller to talk directly to a potential customer and to be able to track the outcome of that "conversation." In addition, it is flexible. It can be used in combination with any kind of media, not just print. Whatever the medium—print, broadcast, or electronic—direct response advertising enables you to talk to your customer and measure the results in tangible sales units and dollars. Accountable advertising in an era of cost-conscious marketers and CEOs: no wonder direct response has gained respect!

That newfound respect can be seen in the numbers. During the 1950s and 1960s, direct marketing (or direct mail) was a relatively small part of the total advertising and marketing landscape. But by the mid-1990s direct marketing sales were nearly $1 trillion, and total spending on direct marketing in all media was more than $124 billion, more than 50 percent of all U.S. advertising expenditures. Another interesting change is in agency billings. In the mid-1980s only two direct response agencies were billing more than $100 million. A decade later, more than five U.S. direct response agencies were billing more than that amount in *international billings alone,* and three agencies had total billings of nearly a billion dollars.[1]

More Than Ever: The Need for Creative Leaders

At this stage you might be asking yourself, "All of this is very interesting, but what does it have to do with me?" The answer is simple: Big business has found out that, to be effective, direct response advertising needs good creative managers *and* creators. That's where you come in.

Creativity is at a premium.

In New York City in the 1990s, surprising as it may sound, one free-lance direct response copywriter received upwards of $300,000 in royalties in a single year for several successful direct mail promotions. Another top writer asked for and got over $25,000 to write *one* direct mail promotion. Still other writers received bonuses of $20,000 and more from companies when their promotions won out over other promotions they tested against.

Meanwhile, at major direct response agencies in cities such as New York, Boston, and Chicago, full-time creative director jobs at $100,000 to $250,000 plus are not unusual; there are frequently positions open for polished copywriters at $50,000, $75,000—even $90,000 for a top financial copywriter; and the best-paid corporate direct response writers, working in promotion departments of major direct marketing companies, can go as high as $110,000 to $135,000. (Note that corporate perks are *extra!*)

In a profession that can measure response to its advertising, and that uses database targeting and relationship-building techniques, the ability to understand, supervise, and execute winning direct response advertising pays off big. Proven top performers are treated royally, because time after time they help ensure the profitability of the businesses that hire them.

If there is so much money to be made as a top creative performer, why aren't hordes of people trying for these jobs? They are. Many new people do keep pouring in claiming to be direct marketing experienced, but most come and go without making much of a name for themselves or proving very much. Top jobs frequently go unfilled, free-lance stars continue to ask for large fee arrangements without challenge, and more and more competent direct response advertising professionals are going for those free-lance dollars.

So, why the shortage of talent? Explosive industry growth is one reason. All of this expansion takes people. In the creative area it takes marketers and product managers, promotion directors, creative directors, copywriters, copy chiefs, artists, designers, and art directors. And the people most desperately needed and hardest to find are those managers, marketers, directors, and creators with a solid understanding of the underlying creative principles of direct response advertising. Another reason for the shortage of talent is that until recently, there were few places to learn the principles of creative direct response advertising other than "in the trenches" of on-the-job experience.

Although the first direct mail agencies were founded in the early 1900s,[2] as direct response became a more acceptable form of advertising a number of specializing agencies sprang up. Schwab and Beatty, Inc. was founded in 1928; Altman, Vos and Reichberg, Wunderman, Ricotta and Kline, Rapp and Collins, and Stone and Adler followed in the 1950s and early 1960s. As a consequence, demand grew for good creative practitioners, but there were very few creative leaders or teachers beyond the original masters: John Caples, Tom Collins, Martin Baier, Bob Stone, the late Max Sackheim, the late Vic Schwab, and the late Edward N. Mayer, Jr.

This situation did not correct itself, but allowed, instead, a sort of free-lance "star" system to build up in the 1960s and 1970s—the kind of system that can develop only in a creative vacuum. By the 1980s it consisted of some twelve to fifteen or so creative stars or free-lancers who asked top dollar and worked for agencies and clients alike across the country.

As direct marketing continued to grow, experienced creative writers remained scarce, and today we have a similar situation. However, there seems to be a new level of competent free-lancers coming up and moving to join the stars in a business that can easily support all it can get. Big direct response agencies who develop their own talented creative people are largely responsible for training such free-lancers, who later opt for greener pastures.

In 1965 the Direct Marketing Association (DMA) established an Educational Foundation that now offers broad programs and services for both educators and students across the country. There is a Center for Direct Marketing at the University of Missouri, Kansas City, and one at New York University. Direct marketing courses are offered at a broad variety of colleges and universities including Boston University, Syracuse Newhouse School of Communications, the University of Cincinnati, and Alabama State. But for this to have an impact on the situation, direct marketers may have to wait a few more years, until the first wave of direct response students begins to make waves in the success pool.

In a sense, direct marketing today represents a massive growth area with few qualified creative leaders in relation to its size and still fewer accomplished teachers with a sound, pragmatic background in the basic fundamentals. Four outstanding leaders who have shepherded today's educational programs through some 30 years of development and are largely responsible for today's achievements are

Bob Stone, former chairman of Stone and Adler, who continues as a leading author and teacher in direct marketing; Martin Baier, former senior vice-president of Old American Insurance Company, who wrote the first teaching text and directs the Block School program at the University of Missouri; Nat Ross, former vice-president of Lincoln Graphic Arts, who developed and nurtured the N.Y.U. School of Continuing Education's direct marketing programs over the last 30 years; and John D. Yeck, Partner, Yeck Brothers Group, who has devoted his talents, time, and heart to the DMA's Direct Marketing Educational Foundation, Inc. as trustee and chairman for over 28 years.

The need for sources of formal training becomes even more critical as direct marketing is "mainstreamed" into more and more corporate programs. Traditionally, writers were expected merely to sit in a cubicle, take assignments, and ask few questions. Experience was the writer's and the art director's primary teacher. The creative department as a whole was given little information and was continually left out of the marketing process. When they were let in, no one gave them training in using marketing tools. People who supervised or bought creative work—or actively developed creative work—were often not privy to marketing formulas or the most basic of statistics. On the other hand, few marketing people were trained to understand or judge good creative work. It's amazing we survived at all.

This disastrous situation has changed considerably today. Marketers understand and participate actively in the creative function as do creative people in the marketing function. In the most productive situations they work together as a team. Marketing requirements are overlaid on creative basics and the result is structured creative strategies and tactics—the first steps to successful promotions.

The standard marketing plan deals with sales goals. The creative strategy, an important part of the overall marketing strategy, deals with the development of winning promotions. The two areas must interrelate, and while the creative strategy relies heavily on the big plan, neither can succeed without the other. What's more, the creative strategy cannot be successfully developed without full input from the creative people—the writers, artists, art directors, creative directors—as well as the product managers and the marketers.

Product and marketing people need guidelines for helping creative people do their best. A creative person must request and receive the marketing cooperation that allows him or her to develop true creative concepts. The goal of this book is to make sure *you* know exactly what you need, where to find it, and how to use it in whatever role you have.

Successful Direct Response Advertising: Discovering the Secrets, Learning the Rules

The term *creative talent* is an appropriate but, in some respects, unfortunate phrase. It carries with it a certain mystique. Your training in direct response advertising and the development of your creative talent are further compounded by this mystique, perpetuated by practitioners of direct marketing who often profess that years of experience are required before one is initiated into the mysteries of their profession.

What are these mysteries of direct response advertising? In truth, there are none. But there are a lot of secrets—secrets of direct marketing that only a relatively small number of people seem to understand, or share, or know how to put into practice. Those without solid direct response advertising training, without a clear understanding of the rules, techniques, and concept development—the secrets—can neither teach nor practice confidently or successfully. *You* are going to learn the secrets in this book.

Perhaps the best-kept secret of all is that there's no need for you to fail in direct response advertising! No marketing director, product manager, creative head, or copywriter need ever sponsor a "bomb" or create a dismal direct response promotion—not when you know the initial creative steps to follow. These are proven first steps that you can apply to a project to give you a solid idea of success or failure even before any copy is written. Protect yourself if you need to when these steps show the red light. Top creative stars turn down projects when their red lights start flashing. You can learn how to judge for yourself as these stars do..

Next, there is no excuse for you ever to produce direct response advertising that is not professional and, consequently, measuredly successful.

Good direct response advertising that pays out in dollars-and-cents sales can be executed if you understand the techniques, rules, and procedures, how to apply them professionally, and when to break the rules. You can take control of the basics to develop effective direct response advertising.

Finally, you can also learn the "secret" principles for executing direct response winners—advertising that beats out all comers!

In any situation that deals with accountable advertising, the advertiser is able to test your advertising against the best going ad or direct mail package or television commercial. This testing is a continual process in good direct marketing, and the winners—the direct response promotions that consistently beat the competition—also have their secrets.

Here's where top creative talent comes into play. When you study the techniques of the pros, understand the rules they live by, and appreciate the kind of creative reasoning that goes into their direct response promotions, then you'll be ready to move out and develop your own stable of winners.

You may wonder, "Why doesn't everyone in direct marketing do this?" Successful direct marketers *have* done this, and they are always looking for others who can, who are willing to learn how.

Remember, there are few teachers to produce new leaders; few professionals to set down the steps that need to be followed; few creative people who even understand the disciplines required in creative concept development.

And no one yet has placed these steps or stages squarely before the door of the creative function in a form that creative people can recognize and use—until now. In *Winning Direct Response Advertising* you have at your fingertips both the technical and the creative equipment you need.

Your Requirements

Once you break down the marketers' doors, learn the planning secrets, and help develop creative strategies that will work, how do you develop the skills and talents to carry the strategies through to winning promotions?

Possibly one more reason for the lack of top creative people in direct response advertising today is the heavy demands it makes on the skills and talents of its professionals. To begin with, creativity here is not pure inspiration. It is not "intuitive" or something you sense "innately" or any other way. It is something that can be taught and learned.

More than any other form of advertising, direct response advertising requires you to have a diversity of talents and skills. These skills can be acquired; the talents can be honed; the systematic procedures and tested techniques can be assimilated.

YOU MUST BE A TECHNICIAN

First, in addition to being artistic or creative, you also have to be a technician. Because direct response is filled with creative guidelines and tested do's and don'ts, over 50 percent of your basic work falls under various groups of rules. There are, for example, rules for cold prospecting, rules for customers, and rules we can call "The Big No-No's" (or "Big Yes-Yes's"). You will have to incorporate certain of these rules and formulas and adapt certain guidelines as you plot every piece of direct response advertising copy and build your sales message.

YOU MUST BE AN ARTIST

Second, as an artist, you have to visualize—*see* your creative product as it develops and convey your visual concept to your designer.

YOU MUST BE AN
ADVERTISING COPYWRITER
AND A SALESPERSON

Third and fourth, you need the skills of an advertising copywriter and a salesperson. These two are tied closely together when it comes to basic writing requirements, but there's a discernible difference between them, and two different temperaments are involved. One is the dream-builder and sizzle-seller who uses words and pictures to make a person long for things he or she never knew they needed. The other is the fast-talking circus barker, the typical traveling sales-man who wants your money now—the sale-closer.

You need a combination of the two because in direct response advertising, in one way or another, you must ask for the order (or at least for a response, an inquiry). Advertising that merely "influences" or gives the recipient a better feeling about a product or service or creates a brand awareness is not a focus for direct marketers.

As a direct response writer you have to entice, cajole, promise wealth, health, and happiness—all for a very special price *if* the cus-tomer "acts now." You have to advertise *and* sell. And as does any good salesperson, you have to know your selling points well and anticipate questions in advance. You must know your customer well, too. If your customer has one question unanswered, your entire sales talk is wasted and you lose that customer.

You also have to understand how a good salesperson makes the sale. You have to have a feeling for sales and a feeling for your typi-cal customer. What's more, you have to develop your sales dialogue for each product all alone, without the use of role playing or other interactive selling techniques or actual trial-and-error practice on real customers. This takes imagination!

On the other hand, you'll be expected to be a good, solid adver-tising copywriter—one who knows how to position the product, to extract benefits from features, to build images using the right words and pictures. You have to make your point and develop your selling proposition with the efficient use of words and phrases that people will relate to.

YOU MUST BE AN ACTOR

We now have four skills for you to apply in your role as a direct response advertising creative person—the skills of the technician, the skills of the artist, the skills of the salesperson and the skills of the advertising copywriter. One more role or skill should be added; it grows logically out of the other four.

You will also need the skills of an actor. In writing the all-impor-tant letter in the basic direct mail package, you as a creative person seldom write as exactly who you are. You must become other people at the same time. You must identify with them, and as you assume their roles, you must be credible. You must sound like them, talk like them, feel the way they feel and know the things they know as you address your prospect market. And, of course, as this other person, you must empathize with and understand their needs and desires.

You may be thinking, "Anyone can write a letter from a magazine publisher or an insurance executive or a merchant. Just put the name and title at the end." But that doesn't work—unless you want to sound like a faceless technician with neutralized, no-appeal copy. Each magazine publisher must reflect the tone of his or her product. Each insurance executive should have her own style and, certainly, every good direct response merchant has a distinct personality, from Richard Thalheimer of Sharper Image to Amos Pettingill of White Flower Farm to Lillian Vernon of Lillian Vernon. Without this personality or point of view and voice, you will write flat and faceless copy. Mediocre stuff. Sausage.

A top writer knows that insurance executives don't sound like lingerie saleswomen, nor do they express themselves in the same words or use the same expressions or describe their product in the same glowing terms. And many professions have their own "lingo" or jargon. To sound credible to your prospect, you have to get into the skin of the person signing your letter, the logical spokesperson.

What's more, you have to put yourself in the place of the prospects in the group you're addressing. You have to understand this market's motives, aspirations, dreams, drives, and desires. And, above all, you must have respect and consideration for the people who make up this market.

So you need one more skill—the skill of speaking as someone else; the skill of the actor. You must speak in another's voice, or *the voice people would expect that speaker to have.* In each case, you have to learn to sound the way the customers or prospects imagine you *should* sound.

For example: Almost all of us can hear and readily recognize the differences between the voice of the football sportscaster and the voice of the minister speaking from the pulpit. They don't sound the same. Close your eyes and listen. You can *hear* the difference right now if you try.

Your job is to listen to different spokespeople and understand what makes that difference so that you can recreate it—recreate it and direct it to a specific market with its own personality. So now we add "actor" to your list of needed skills, right under copywriter.

Which leads us to the next requirements . . . .

Three Important Personal Qualities: Curiosity, Imagination, and Discipline

So far, we have talked about the skills you need to excel in direct response advertising. You also need three important personal qualities: curiosity, imagination, and discipline.

CURIOSITY

Right under "actor" comes curiosity—a very necessary, most important quality on which the five skill areas must balance. Supporting curiosity are imagination and discipline.

Curiosity is vital to artistic temperament and to the development of highly tuned skills, largely because no advertising copywriter can work in a vacuum. Curiosity gives you a storehouse of input to draw on when you need it, particularly if you are working on letter writing or dialogue for broadcast.

How do you start your mind-expanding curiosity, get it going? First you listen to dialogue. *You eavesdrop.* Every passing conversation has something to tell you. On any given day you might learn how a busy career woman complains about her dry cleaning bill, how a threadbare old man inquires about a grocery purchase, or how a clerk in a bookstore presents new books. You can get a small idea of trivia and lingo from two adolescents on a park bench, or you can sense the loneliness of an out-of-town traveler as he or she strikes up a conversation with a waiter.

Curiosity also means asking questions and reading newspapers, magazines, journals, and books that you wouldn't ordinarily read. It means surfing the Internet and interacting. It means wanting to know how people feel about things—like asking a college freshman about world affairs or quizzing a senior citizen on the national debt. It means watching a broad assortment of television programs, especially things you haven't seen before. It does not mean escape reading or mindless TV viewing or radio playing or TV as background.

The quality of your curiosity also contains something I call your *Renaissance Quotient (R.Q.).* Beginning in the fifteenth century, the Italian nobles set the standards for the Renaissance Quotient by looking into a vast diversity of things. Wealthy, enlightened Italians spent their lives exploring and delving into the arts and sciences—everything then known to man—*just for the sake of knowing.* (Remember Leonardo da Vinci—painter, inventor, engineer!) Today, a high Renaissance Quotient usually means having a marvelous rampant curiosity about many aspects of life—a very important attribute for you to develop if you're aspiring to top status in any area of advertising. (It'll also make life a lot more fun for you, while you're at it.)

Curiosity is particularly important for you here, however, because of that unique "actor" aspect of direct response that requires you to speak as an expert on all sorts of products and services in someone else's voice, directly to their prospect market.

Your R.Q. or curiosity factor helps you be a versatile spokesperson who is conversant with all sorts of markets. It helps you understand how people (customers) feel, the values that are important to them, the things they enjoy, how they *sound* or talk, their particular lingo or accent. Writers who don't really care about these things will most likely have a tough time developing the all-important creative skills of dialogue writing—they may even end up as mere technicians—if they lack curiosity.

IMAGINATION

Curiosity leads logically to imagination, which visits your mental storehouse to select and shape the fruits of your curiosity into something great and grand and beautifully, appropriately, creatively moving. Imagination grows from your desire to know when you imagine beyond what you know, utilizing your experiences. It enables you to create something meaningful and compelling for others from all you've observed and learned.

Imagination is a critical quality for everyone who plans to develop artistic skills of any kind, be it composer, writer, painter, wood carver, chef, architect, or direct response writer.

DISCIPLINE

Last and equally important of the three qualities you need is discipline. This is your ability to develop your curiosity and your imagination, then put them to work productively—and keep on doggedly working and polishing and reworking. Call it determination or sheer devotion, but in direct response advertising you need a lot of it. As Tom Collins, the former creative head of Rapp Collins Worldwide, says, "Advertising is hard!"[3] and, as you can see, direct response advertising is no exception.

But take heart. By mastering direct response advertising you assure yourself of a good future with many opportunities and growth options. It equips you to move into all other forms of advertising and promotion as well.

David Ogilvy, the renowned former chairman of Ogilvy and Mather and an early supporter and user of direct marketing, claims that the disciplines of direct response advertising are invaluable. "This elite corp . . . knows more about the *realities* of advertising than anybody else."[4]

You'll Be Tested!

Before we get too far along, now is a good time for you to decide how you feel about being tested. Remember, direct response advertising is accountable. If you're lucky and working for a smart company, everything you do will be tested. This may seem a little unnerving at first, but ultimately, your ability to do winning promotions will make your reputation. And give you highs. Exhilaration! Confidence! (But not without testing!)

If you stick with it, you will actually learn to love testing. You'll know the rules, you'll understand how to practice them professionally, and you'll be eager to prove yourself through your work—and win.

Speaking of winning—please bear in mind that there are two kinds of winning in our business. The promotions that win awards are not always the promotions that win tests. Everyone likes awards. But if winning awards is all you want, keep reading, then plan to stay with a company or ad agency. Top creative stars are very well paid, not because they win awards but because they win tests and win over and over, making money for their clients.

It will prove most helpful in learning to write direct response copy if you are now writing advertising copy, or have some experience writing or experience in advertising or marketing. And if you are presently writing direct response copy, so much the better.

Direct response advertising desperately needs more creative talent, but up until now no one has shown potential stars how to go about it. Although you can find quite a few books that offer fine instruction and rules on writing good copy[5] and lots of hot tips for copy improvement, there are very few guideposts to follow in developing good, solid professionalism-cum-creativity in direct marketing today.

This book intends to point the way, act as your mentor—teaching you . . . pushing you . . . challenging you . . . encouraging you. Its job is to give you the tools, the instruction, and the guidance—even the inspiration—you need to cultivate your creative skills and determine whether direct response advertising wealth and fame are ahead for you.

You *can* become a better creative person (one who understands writing a little more), and you might come away with a very solid, profitable lifetime profession—a profession you enjoy and even love. Try it. And try hard. Remember, direct marketing needs you, too.

Some Basic Terms and Ideas

As you saw in the opening of this chapter, things have changed and are continuing to change at a dizzying speed. Even the name of the industry itself has changed. Under these circumstances, it's probably a good idea to begin with working definitions of basic terms and ideas.

WHAT IS DIRECT MAIL?

It's easy enough to describe direct response magazine and newspaper advertising as well as direct response radio and television ads. You've seen these ads many times and, no doubt, recognize them for what they are with their obvious coupons and toll-free numbers. You can't miss infomercials or catalogs either. But direct mail needs clarification.

Coming from the outside with clear vision and perspective, you're liable to think that the term *direct mail* itself is somewhat redundant.

After all, what is more direct than a message from one person to another? Even a piece of mail addressed to "Occupant" or "Boxholder" goes direct to someone in a particular place. Electronic or otherwise, mail *is* direct. Can it be *more* direct? If anything, isn't direct mail as we know it somewhat *less* direct?

If you have spent most of your business life in direct marketing, the term *direct mail* is perfectly acceptable; direct marketers, when questioned about the term, give no valid reasons for it. Homer J. Buckley started it all back in 1902.[6] No one objected to it then, and I suspect no one wants to change it at this stage.

So for your sake, bear in mind that *mail* is a letter from mother to son, husband to wife, banker to client, doctor to patient, friend to friend, while *direct mail* is a promotion or communication from an institution, company, or business to a group of people—sometimes hundreds of them or thousands or even millions!

Direct mail means postcards, self-mailers, folders, corrugated boxes, jiffy bags, tubes, booklets, envelopes large and small—anything that goes through the U.S. Postal Service as a package.

A *package* in this business is a term used to refer to a mailing unit's contents or components. Components mean an outer envelope, *always* a letter (one of our BIG rules), almost always a reply form or card, sometimes a brochure, and often other things such as stamps or stamp sheets, postpaid reply envelopes (or business reply envelopes), samples of one sort or another, buck slips (short messages on small papers to emphasize a selling point or a deadline, or to add "news"), and lift letters (brief *second* letters or notes that we'll be discussing in Chapter 4). Figure 1–1 shows a basic direct mail package.

A package can also be a *self-mailer*—a large, folded piece of relatively heavy paper that combines letter, brochure, and order card on one sheet without a real envelope. Be wary of self-mailers, however. Because of their economies, they have a strong appeal for many new direct marketers. Although hundreds of professionals have tested them in the past, they have been consistently successful *only* for business conferences, seminar announcements, and business books and reports. Times are changing, however, and more and more people are working harder and harder to *make* them work due to soaring costs of paper and postage. Success stories are building; perhaps people are getting accustomed to self-mailers and resistance is wearing down. Perhaps no one is testing carefully. If you must do a self-mailer, be sure to try to incorporate all of the elements shown in Figure 1–2.

WHERE DO NAMES COME FROM?

Where do we get the names to send letters to hundreds, thousands, even millions of people? First know this: names (in all cases) come

FIGURE 1–1 A Basic Direct Mail Package

XYZ COMPANY
Address • City, State, Zip

BULK RATE
U.S. POSTAGE
PAID
COMPANY NAME

John Longname
Address
City, State, Zip

Outer Envelope

ORDER FORM

YES Bene. E quali sono le tue impressioni sull citta? E' molto bella pero mi sembra che non. Marco, ti presento mia cugina Carla. Lei e americana. Molto lieto di conosceriea, signorina. Il piacere e mio. Pero diamoci del tu. Ti dispiace? Niente affaftto. Da quanto tempo sei a Roma? Sono qui gia da una settimana. Gia da una settimana? Allora, che cosa hai fatto di bello durante questo tempo? tue impressioni sull citta? E' molto bella pero mi sembra che non. Marco, ti presento mia cugina Carla. Lei e americana. Molto

John Longname
Address
City, State, Zip

Order Form

NO POSTAGE
NECESSARY
IF MAILED
IN THE
UNITED STATES

BUSINESS REPLY MAIL
FIRST-CLASS MAIL   PERMIT NO. 0000   CITY, STATE

Postage will be paid by addressee

XYZ COMPANY
Address
City
State, Zip

Business Reply Envelope

LIFT LETTER

Dear Reader,

Marco, ti presento mia cugina Carla. Lei e americana. Molto lieto di conosceriea, signorina. Il piacere e mio.

Pero diamoci del tu. Ti dispiace? Niente affaftto. Da quanto tempo sei a Roma? Sono qui gia da una settimana.

Gia da una settimana? Allora, che cosa hai fatto di bello durante questo tempo? Sono andata in giro per la citta, ho visitato alcune chiese e ho fatto un po' di shopping.

Bene. E quali sono le tue impressioni sull citta? E' molto bella pero mi sembra che non. Marco, ti presento mia cugina Carla. Lei e americana. Molto lieto di conosceriea, signorina. Il piacere e mio. Pero diamoci del tu.

Ti dispiace? Niente affaftto. Da quanto tempo sei a Roma? Sono qui gia da una settimana. Gia da una settimana? Allora, che cosa hai fatto di bello durante questo tempo?

Lift Letter

LETTERHEAD
Address • City, State, Zip

Marco, ti presento mia cugina Carla. Lei e americana. Molto lieto di conosceriea, signorina. Il piacere e mio. Pero diamoci del tu. Ti dispiace? Niente affaftto. Da quanto tempo sei a Roma? Sono qui gia da una settimana. Gia da una settimana? Allora, che cosa hai fatto di bello durante questo tempo? Sono andata in

Dear Reader,

Marco, ti presento mia cugina Carla. Lei e americana. Molto lieto di conosceriea, signorina. Il piacere e mio.

Pero diamoci del tu. Ti dispiace? Niente affaftto. Da quanto tempo sei a Roma? Sono qui gia da una settimana.

Gia da una settimana? Allora, che cosa hai fatto di bello durante questo tempo? Sono andata in giro per la citta, ho visitato alcune chiese e ho fatto un po' di shopping.

Bene. E quali sono le tue impressioni sull citta? E' molto bella pero mi sembra che non. Marco, ti presento mia cugina Carla. Lei e amer

Letter

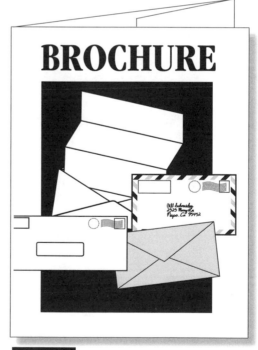

BROCHURE

Brochure

FIGURE 1–2   A Basic Self-Mailer

XYZ COMPANY
Address • City, State, Zip

Teaser headline to get you in!

John Longname
Address
City, State, Zip

Address Side: Teaser with Address

Take this little quiz!

Marco, ti presento mia cugina Carla. Lei e americana. Molto lieto di conosceriea, signorina. Il piacere e mio. Pero diamoci del tu. Ti dispiace? Niente affatto. Da quanto tempo sei a Roma? Sono qui gia da una settimana. Gia da una settimana? Allora, che cosa hai fatto di bello durante questo tempo? Sono andata in giro per la citta, ho visitato alcune chiese e ho fatto un po' di shopping. Bene. E quali sono le tue impressioni sull citta? E' molto bella pero mi sembra che non. Marco, ti presento mia cugina Carla. Lei e americana. Molto lieto di conosceriea, signorina. Il piacere e mio. Pero diamoci del tu.

Back of Fold: Involvement "Test"

What our Celebrity is saying…

Marco, ti presento mia cugina Carla. Lei e americana. Molto lieto di conosceriea, signorina. Il piacere e mio. Pero diamoci del tu. Ti dispiace? Niente affatto. Da quanto tempo sei a Roma? Sono qui gia da una settimana. Gia da una settimana? Allora, che cosa hai fatto di bello durante questo tempo? Sono andata in giro per la citta, ho visitato alcune chiese e ho fatto un po' di shopping. Bene. E quali sono le tue impressioni sull citta? E' molto

Q's & A's

Marco, ti presento mia cugina Carla. Lei e americana. Molto lieto di conosceriea, signorina. Il piacere e mio. Pero diamoci del tu. Ti dispiace? Niente affatto. Da quanto tempo sei a Roma? Sono qui gia da una settimana. Gia da una settimana? Allora, che cosa hai fatto di bello durante questo tempo? Sono andata in giro per la citta, ho visitato alcune chiese e ho fatto un po' di shopping.

What ordinary people are saying…

Marco, ti presento mia cugina Carla. Lei e americana. Molto lieto di conosceriea, signorina. Il piacere e mio. Pero diamoci del tu. Ti dispiace? Niente affatto. Da quanto tempo sei a Roma? Sono

Marco, ti presento mia cugina Carla. Lei e americana. Molto lieto di conosceriea, signorina. Il piacere e mio. Pero diamoci del tu. Ti dispiace? Niente affatto. Da quanto tempo sei a Roma? Sono

Marco, ti presento mia cugina Carla. Lei e americana. Molto lieto di conosceriea, signorina. Il piacere e mio. Pero diamoci del tu. Ti dispiace? Niente affatto. Da quanto tempo sei a Roma? Sono

Inside First Fold: Celebrity Endorser, Q and A, Testimonials with Photos

FIGURE 1–2 A Basic Self-Mailer (Continued)

Benefit to consumer headline!

LETTERHEAD
Address • City, State, Zip

Dear Reader,

Marco, ti presento mia cugina Carla. Lei e americana. Molto lieto di conosceriea, signorina. Il piacere e mio.

Pero diamoci del tu. Ti dispiace? Niente affatto. Da quanto tempo sei a Roma? Sono qui gia da una settimana.

Gia da una settimana? Allora, che cosa hai fatto di bello durante questo tempo? Sono andata in giro per la citta, ho visitato alcune chiese e ho fatto un po' di shopping.

Bene. E quali sono le tue impressioni sull citta? E' molto bella pero mi sembra che non. Marco, ti presento mia cugina Carla. Lei e americana. Molto lieto di conosceriea, signorina. Il piacere e mio. Pero diamoci del tu.

Ti dispiace? Niente affatto. Da quanto tempo sei a Roma? Sono qui gia da una settimana. Gia da una settimana? Allora, che cosa hai fatto di bello durante questo tempo?

Sono andata in giro per la citta, ho visitato alcune chiese e ho fatto un po' di shopping/ Bene. E quali sono le tue impressioni sull citta? E' molto bella pero mi sembra che non. Marco, ti presento mia cugina Carla. Lei e americana. Molto lieto di conosceriea, signorina. I l piacere e mio. Pero diamoci del tu. Ti dispiace? Niente affatto. Da quanto tempo sei a Roma? Sono qui

Full details

Marco, ti presento mia cugina Carla. Lei e americana. Molto lieto di conosceriea, signorina. Il piacere e mio.

Pero diamoci del tu. Ti dispiace? Niente affatto. Da quanto tempo sei a Roma? Sono qui gia da una settimana.

Gia da una settimana? Allora, che cosa hai fatto di bello durante questo tempo? Sono andata in giro per la citta, ho visitato alcune chiese e ho fatto un po' di shopping.

Bene. E quali sono le tue impressioni sull citta? E' molto bella pero mi sembra che non. Marco, ti presento mia cugina Carla. Lei e americana. Molto lieto di conosceriea, signorina. Il piacere e mio. Pero diamoci del tu.

Ti dispiace? Niente affatto. Da quanto tempo sei a Roma? Sono qui gia da una settimana. Gia da una settimana? Allora, che cosa hai fatto di bello durante questo tempo?

Call to action...NOW!

una settimana? Allora, che cosa hai fatto di bello durante questo tempo? Sono andata in giro per la citta, ho visitato alcune chiese e ho fatto un po' di sh

Detach and mail today!

ORDER FORM

YES Bene. E quali sono le tue impressioni sull citta? E' molto bella pero mi sembra che non. Marco, ti presento mia cugina Carla. Lei e americana. Molto lieto di conosceriea, signorina. Il piacere e mio. Pero diamoci del tu. Ti dispiace? Niente affatto. Da quanto tempo sei a Roma? Sono qui gia da una settimana. Gia da una settimana? Allora, che cosa hai fatto di bello durante questo tempo? tue impressioni sull citta? E' molto bella pero mi sembra che non. Marco, ti presento mia cugina Carla. Lei e americana. Molto

name
address
city
state zip

Inside Spread: Response Coupon, Illustrations, Letter from President, Full Details, and Call to Action

on *lists* (lists of names). These lists are generally handled by *list brokers* who quite literally do the brokering or act as middle agents for the *list owners* and those who desire to *rent* the names.

You rent names that are most representative of the defined market you wish to reach. But you start out by testing first; that is to say, you rent and mail in small (minimal) quantities until you are sure that the particular lists are productive for you. Someone may ask you how many names you are mailing: this is the total count of your mailing—its overall size.

If someone asks, "What lists are you using?" he or she wants to know the specific categories or sources from which you are drawing your names or your test markets. There are magazine subscriber lists, catalog buyer lists, good lists, bad lists, unavailable lists, lists to barter or exchange—all kinds of lists of names. Here are a few that you should know:

House lists, or internal customer lists, are sometimes called simply your "database." These are the best lists, certainly, because your own customers are always the finest prospects for additional purchases from you. Both business and consumer direct marketers work hard to develop and maintain these customer or house lists.

Rental lists are lists of names that you rent for a specific number of uses—usually a one-time use—from the list owner or list broker. (You generally cannot *buy* lists for unlimited use.) Some subcategories of rental lists are mail order buyer lists and compiled lists, which are described below.

Mail order buyer lists are lists of people who have responded to a wide variety of direct marketing media: catalog customers, magazine subscribers, and direct mail purchasers, inquirers, and trial acceptors.

Some direct marketers are wary about renting out their own lists (their database) at all; some rent out only inactive or former customers; none will rent to outright competitors. Those who do rent out their lists enjoy considerable net income from such rentals.

Compiled lists are lists of like or similar people: lists of doctors, lawyers, and other professionals, for example, or lists of wealthy people, people owning cars, people living in specific geographic or demographic areas, people belonging to special-interest groups and societies. There are even lists of people selected by lifestyles and psychographics or cohort groups! There are lists of businesses and services of all kinds, too, broken out by SIC classification, job titles, size of company, employee numbers, business volume, and so on.

Traditionally, lists of current *mail order buyers* will generate nearly twice as much response as compiled lists of unqualified people or companies (i.e., with no previous purchase history) with only business titles but no individual names, or households addressed simply as "Occupant." However, compiled lists of purchasers from dozens of sources (warranty cards, solo mail, ride-alongs), combined with mail order customer files, created large databases in the 1990s. If properly matched to or overlaid on a house list or database, these lists can provide mailers with a relatively effective, broad range of prospects with considerably more quality than standard compiled lists.

Whatever their quality, there can be no direct mail without lists and no good lists without valid names, titles, and addresses—and no *sure* lists without list testing.

IS ALL DIRECT MAIL ALIKE?

Direct mail comes in lots of different colors and sizes. It covers both products and services and it goes to consumers and business prospects. Although it always asks for a response, sometimes this response is no more than a request for information or approval for a salesperson to call—or it may work to create a favorable impression that in the long run will result in a major sale.

Let's summarize the different types of direct mail here, as they will affect you in your creative role:

Consumer mail is generally the more colorful or promotional form of direct mail and represents a wide variety of products and services directed to specific consumer markets. It is sent out in large quantities, using outer envelopes, a letter, brochure, and reply card and therefore makes wider use of third-class postage based on its weight requirements (well over one ounce). Consumer mail goes to the home and is frequently directed to the woman in the household, although this is changing, based on the proliferation of two-income families. The focus of consumer mail is purely the professional salesperson (in one guise or another) speaking to the amateur about the salesperson's area of expertise.

Business mail, or business-to-business communications, frequently have a smaller market and a far larger per-capita budget than consumer mail.

Business mail often consists of a series of direct mail letters or an initial mailing with several follow-up mailings or calls, while consumer mail usually tries to close a sale or get a commitment in one effort. (Actually, the price of the product or service determines this. In both markets, higher-priced products often require standard two-step promotions or several mailings and follow-ups as opposed to one.)

The primary objective of business promotion is sometimes less to make a sale than to create good will or elicit an evidence of interest—a request for more information—thus gathering qualified prospects for sales calls or futher promotions, and for building the database. This makes an individual promotion harder to evaluate.

It is far more difficult to pinpoint and reach your prime customer or decision maker in business-to-business mail than it is in consumer mail for the following reasons:

- More than one person in a company is often needed to make a major decision, so decision makers at two or three levels of influence must be reached.

- The names you need are frequently not available without expensive research and/or in-house list development costs, so most business names are merely title-addressed on compiled lists—"Purchasing Manager," X Corporation.

- Your promotion will be screened in most businesses by mail-room personnel and/or secretaries. When you mail only by title, it is very difficult to get past the screeners, who are liable to throw out "unimportant" or third-class mail.

- Sometimes, if you have the names and addresses, it makes sense to even send your mailings to the prospect's home.

Your major appeal to business prospects will often differ from the appeal to consumer prospects because in most cases a business prospect is being asked to make a decision that will not directly benefit him or her personally. A consumer, on the other hand, is buying or considering something for herself or the family.

These differences between consumer and business mail are significant, but the similarities will far outweigh the differences for you as a creative person.

I stress this here, because much has been done to separate practitioners of business and consumer direct mail. Trade groups in direct marketing divide themselves into business groups and consumer groups; they say they are one or the other, but you should not do that. As a creative person, you can be both.

Once you understand the minor differences, you must remember that business men and women are also consumers—and they are human beings. You write and create direct mail for human beings—not for business versus consumer categories. Don't let anyone label or limit you here. Ultimately, of course, you may gain more experience in one area than the other, but why not go for both now?

The same important rules, formulas, and guidelines apply to both businesses and consumers. The research requirements are no different; creative concept methodologies (Chapter 5) work roughly the same for one market as for the other. Your writing guidelines (in Chapters 6 and 7) apply to both.

Anyone who argues with this is saying that a good creative person doesn't know the difference between a highly promotional consumer package and a business letter to a big industrial client. I think you do—or will after reading this book.

CAN THE SAME PERSON MARKET DIFFERENT PRODUCTS AND SERVICES?

I'd also like to put to rest some major reservations on products and services (and fund raising, while we're at it). Over the course of a long career in direct marketing, people have asked me if I was a "financial services" specialist or if I knew how to "do insurance letters" or "fund raising." If I answer "yes," they feel comfortable. If not, they are concerned about my abilities to do something "so specialized."

Many financial and insurance mailings circulating these days could use an infusion of creative people with a fresh approach. There's not a good creative person who couldn't handle them, regardless of his or her background. But pigeonholes and prejudices persist.

Granted, there are some definite legal no-no's and specific lingo and small print that you'll have to digest in each area. But as long as you do your homework (which includes studying the competition closely), this shouldn't hold you back. As for fund raising, some of the top product professionals in our business slide easily into all sorts of successful fund-raising letters without a thought.

You may encounter many noncreative types along the way who like to surround their areas of direct marketing with an aura of mystery; don't let them discourage you or deter you from a worthwhile experience. If you're good at products, you'll be good at services, and at fund raising. And vice versa.

HOW DOES DIRECT RESPONSE ADVERTISING FIT INTO INTEGRATED ADVERTISING?

As direct marketing grows and its influence spreads, integrated advertising is fast becoming very important to direct marketers. And why not? If one frog croaking makes a noise, imagine one hundred of them. If one small message creates a small image (or a limited image), imagine what thousands of similar messages, all with the same theme, can do.

The definition of integrated advertising is a little more complicated, however, and it can change depending on who's speaking. General agency people, for example, usually see it as "speaking with one voice in all media"—every single medium from billboards to hang tags. They see it as a massive branding or image-building effort, a campaign where every element works toward the same end.

When you add direct marketing or direct response advertising, which is often the case today, a major problem may pop up. For us direct marketers to be truly accountable, to get the greatest measured response, we have to lead off our selling message with strong benefits (more about this in Chapter 5). If we don't, quite simply, we cannot motivate our prospects to act. But to do this, branding or image/awarenesss advertising must sometimes take second place to (or work alongside) our benefits.

Often, the general agencies fail to understand this (something that will never happen to you once you finish this book). And if these agencies push the point, rather than working with the direct response arm, benefits can be subordinated to the branding message and the direct response portion of the integrated campaign will surely flop.

Good, solid integrated advertising that recognizes the requirements of our bottom-line approach represents some the strongest, most effective advertising around. The communications are synergistically integrated to build awareness while getting response. You can expect a lot of growth in this area. Keep your eye on it.

Your Creative Potential

This self-test will help you evaluate and expand your creative abilities. Check off the answers that describe you. Don't spend much time mulling over the subjective questions, but check the answer that seems to fit you best on first thought. Try to finish all 26 questions within seven minutes.

Add up your cumulative score here. _____

1. Do you ever watch TV programs that you don't ordinarily watch, just to see what other people are watching?

   ☐ Yes (3)   ☐ No (1)

2. Check the boxes at the right to indicate whether you read the following magazines regularly, irregularly, or not at all.

	Regularly	Irregularly	Not at All
Prevention	☐	☐	☐
Cosmopolitan	☐	☐	☐
Playboy	☐	☐	☐
Condé Nast Traveler	☐	☐	☐
Ladies' Home Journal	☐	☐	☐
Car and Driver	☐	☐	☐
S.I. for Kids	☐	☐	☐
Essence	☐	☐	☐
Audubon	☐	☐	☐
Victoria	☐	☐	☐
Smithsonian	☐	☐	☐
The Atlantic Monthly	☐	☐	☐
Esquire	☐	☐	☐
Food & Wine	☐	☐	☐
The Nation	☐	☐	☐
Vanity Fair	☐	☐	☐
U.S. News & World Report	☐	☐	☐
Allure	☐	☐	☐
Modern Maturity	☐	☐	☐
Vibe	☐	☐	☐
Spin	☐	☐	☐
YM	☐	☐	☐
Utne Reader	☐	☐	☐

   Score 3 points for "regularly," 2 points for "irregularly," and 0 for "not at all."

3. Have you ever ridden a rollercoaster?

   ☐ Yes (3)   ☐ No (1)

4. Do you know what's #1 on the Fiction Bestseller List?
   ☐ Yes (3)   ☐ No (1)

5. On the Nonfiction Bestseller List?
   ☐ Yes (3)   ☐ No (1)

6. Do you know who's at the top of the music charts this week?
   ☐ Yes (3)   ☐ No (1)

7. Can you name today's hottest music group?
   ☐ Yes (3)   ☐ No (1)

8. Have you watched *Nick at Night* on cable?
   ☐ Yes (3)   ☐ No (1)

9. How about MTV?
   ☐ Yes (3)   ☐ No (1)

10. Do you eavesdrop on other people's conversations?
    ☐ Yes (3)   ☐ No (1)

11. You see a poor man in rags on a cold day; unshaven and without a coat, he's huddled in a corner reading *The Wall Street Journal*. Do you feel inclined to make up a story about him?
    ☐ Yes (3)   ☐ No (1)

12. A young, attractive couple is seated near you in a restaurant. He's talking, but while he talks you notice that a tear rolls down her cheek. Do you:

    ☐ continue your conversation with your companion. (1)

    ☐ try to figure out what might be happening between them while your companion speaks on. (2)

    ☐ get up and throw your glass of wine in the man's face. (3)

13. As you wait for a salesperson, a middle-aged couple next to you is buying a product from him. They cannot agree. The woman seems to dominate the conversation. Do you:

    ☐ look at other items on display. (1)

    ☐ make a mental note of their decision and agree/disagree with the final choice. (2)

    ☐ make up a story about the man and woman. (3)

14. Do you solve tough problems in the shower/shaving/brushing your teeth?

    ☐ Yes (3)   ☐ No (1)

15. Do you daydream?

    ☐ Yes (3)   ☐ No (1)

16. Do you have fantasies?

    ☐ Yes (3)   ☐ No (1)

17. Do you like to:

Travel	☐ Yes (2)	☐ No (1)
Explore ruins	☐ Yes (2)	☐ No (1)
Climb mountains	☐ Yes (2)	☐ No (1)
Cross-country ski	☐ Yes (2)	☐ No (1)
Sail	☐ Yes (2)	☐ No (1)
Birdwatch	☐ Yes (2)	☐ No (1)
Sailplane or glider	☐ Yes (2)	☐ No (1)
Kayak or canoe	☐ Yes (2)	☐ No (1)
Snorkel	☐ Yes (2)	☐ No (1)
Scuba	☐ Yes (2)	☐ No (1)
Hike	☐ Yes (2)	☐ No (1)
Camp	☐ Yes (2)	☐ No (1)
Take long walks	☐ Yes (2)	☐ No (1)

18. Do you like to read?

    ☐ Yes (3)   ☐ No (1)

19. Do you write poems, stories, or articles (whether or not they've been published or even read by anyone)?

    ☐ Yes (3)   ☐ No (1)

21. Have you studied anthropology or archaeology?

    ☐ Yes (3)   ☐ No (1)

22. Do you spend more than 2 hours a day watching TV?

    ☐ Yes (3)   ☐ No (1)

23. Do you subscribe to an online computer service like Prodigy, CompuServe, America Online?

    ☐ Yes (3)   ☐ No (1)

24. Are you on the Internet?

    ☐ Yes (3)   ☐ No (1)

25. Can you imagine what it would be like to be 16 years old again? Can you picture the clothes you'd wear, the three things you'd like most to buy, how you'd feel about music, food, exercise, college and your future career, money, dating, AIDS?

    ☐ Yes (3)   ☐ Sort of (2)   ☐ Hardly (1)

26. Now, think what it's like to be 65. Imagine the kind of a place you'd live in. The car you'd own. How do you feel about food, your health and America's health care issues, Social Security, politics, retirement, your family? Can you imagine what it's like to visit your grandchildren, have time on your hands, or be chronically ill?

    ☐ Yes (3)   ☐ Sort of (2)   ☐ Hardly (1)

After answering all questions, put each score in the left-hand column, then add up your scores for a grand total.

EVALUATION

If you scored from 110 to 170, you have an active, imaginative mind that explores and pries and tries almost everything. Your creativity is a constant source of entertainment and a joyful companion.

If you scored 90 to 109, you, too, have an imaginative mind and a great potential for creativity. Just give your imagination a little more head—experiment with new viewpoints and new experiences. Go kite flying in the spring! Or to the Orient!

If your score falls between 75 and 89, your mind needs a diet—one that's filled with light and airy flights of imagination, bubbling daydreams, champagne, lawn parties, yachts in the Aegean, treks through the Himalayas, safaris in darkest Africa. Get cracking!

Under 75? Put down this book. You should be pumping iron!

Go over this self-test again for a reminder of the many ways you can exercise your brain cells every day. Work them well. Let your curiosity build your reserves of knowledge and experience—a storehouse for your imagination. This exercise will serve you well as you create winning direct response advertising.

Notes

1. *Economic Impact: U.S. Direct Marketing Today,* The WEfA Group, October 1995, courtesy of the Direct Marketing Association, Inc., 1120 Avenue of the Americas, New York, N.Y. 10036-6700. "Top DR Agencies Boost 1994 Billings, Says DMA Annual Survey" *DM News,* August 14, 1995.

2. Buckley-Dement, founded in Chicago in 1905 and Dickie-Raymond, established in 1921. Source: *Fact Book on Direct Marketing,* 1984 edition (New York: Direct Marketing Association, Inc., Publications Division, 1984) p. 6.

3. Edward L. Nash, *Direct Strategy/Planning/Execution* (New York: McGraw-Hill, Inc., 1982), p. 231.

4. David Ogilvy, excerpted from *Confessions of an Advertising Man.* Copyright © 1963 David Ogilvy. Reprinted with the permission of the author.

5. John Caples, *Tested Advertising Methods* (Englewood Cliffs, N.J.: Prentice-Hall, 1974). John Caples, *Make Your Advertising Make Money* (Englewood Cliffs, N.J.: Prentice-Hall, 1983). David Ogilvy, *Ogilvy on Advertising* (Crown Publishers, 1983). Ed McLean, *The Basics of Copy: A Monograph on Direct Marketing* (Ryan Gilmore Publishing Co., Inc., 1975).

6. Nat Ross, "A History of Direct Marketing," *DMA Factbook* (1984).

INDISPENSABLE TOOLS

Those of you who are new to direct marketing will soon realize that there are lots of things that are good to know and some things that are absolutely essential.

For the "nice-to-knows" there are lots of books that will help you get a sense of the business overall. The roles and importance of distribution channels, database, fulfillment, media buying, pricing strategies, numbers, ratios, equations, model building, product selection, ROI: all these and many other things are useful and important to know. But for your life as a successful creative, knowing about them isn't a life-or-death proposition.

There are other things that you virtually can't live without if you are going to thrive—and maybe even just survive—as a direct response creative person. You must understand and digest them if you hope to arrive at a point where you plot your own creative course and make your own creative determinations.

Contrary to some beliefs, your creative work begins long before you develop a copy platform, put one word on paper, or plan a mailing format. You need to start much earlier in the marketing process unless you want to be at the mercy of others' thinking.

At the start you'll need the abilities to understand and evaluate the basic marketing premises that underlie every assignment you undertake. Otherwise, you're at the mercy of the marketers, and so is your reputation. Although you don't really need to follow the details of probability charts or handle long-range planning, here are the essentials that you truly cannot live without if you want to be confident and succeed in direct response advertising.

Are You Getting the Big Picture? Are "They" Sending It?

There will be, or should be, solid reasoning behind every assignment you are given. Assignments don't "drop out of the blue" as one-shot communication efforts. Something has gone before (except in the case of a new product introduction); something will follow.

From the start, you need to know where your assignment fits in the big picture, and most good marketing people will be happy to tell you. You'll do well to come prepared with questions of your own, just to make sure. You need to understand how the marketers see the overall promotion and its effects, and how they set their objectives. The following questions will help get you started:

- Why do the marketing people feel direct marketing is appropriate for the product or service?

- Why has one specific medium been chosen over another (say, direct mail instead of TV)?

- Is this project part of a campaign, or one in a series of promotions?

- Does it make sense to pre-announce the promotion? To follow it up with additional promotions?

- Have they considered a media mix?

- Does the project have a realistic budget? (No one seems to work with abundant funds these days, but some allocations are ridiculous. You'll learn to sort these out as you go along, with a little production experience.)

- Are their outcome expectations reasonable? (This is *not* one for you to ask them, but to ask and answer for yourself. It takes some experience to do this well, but you'll have solid evaluation guidelines to start you off in just a few pages.)

The Basic Law of Creativity and Its Premises

Once you have the big picture, you can deal with the function and purpose of direct marketing as a whole. On the surface, that may seem simple. But some things are so basic and so close to us that we run the risk of losing sight of them as we adjust our vision to more complicated aspects of the marketing process—we can't see the "trees" for the "forest." This happens every day with experienced marketers, and they pass it right on to the creative people.

To make sure *you* don't lose sight of these essentials, you need the *Basic Law of Creativity* for direct marketers. Follow me through it, digest it, make it part of your basic equipment. It will help you begin your climb toward success.

The Basic Law of Creativity is this: *Whatever you say, however you say it, however you present an offer, first ask, "Does this make sense to the customer?"* The five premises of this law are your foundation for successful direct response advertising. If you don't carry this Basic Law in the back of your head, you'll be starting out on an important creative journey without a spare tire. Sooner or later, maybe not this week or next, it will catch up with you.

THE FIRST PREMISE: WE'RE HERE TO GET A CUSTOMER

The first premise of the Basic Law of Creativity deals with the function of direct marketing itself.

As direct marketers we're not here primarily to make a sale; we're here to get a customer.

Sales are important, of course. But our focus must be on the *lifetime value* of the customer—*repeat* sales rather than merely the value of a single sale. And to have that, you need a customer relationship.

Some marketers use a form of advertising that I call "response" advertising. Response advertising goes directly to customers, who respond to the promotion via coupon redemption or electronic means such as telephones and computers. But generally response marketers do not record customer names and information to establish a database. Therefore, this type of marketing is sampling, or coupon redemption, or sales promotion. It is *not* direct marketing.

To capture a customer or prospect, you must capture customer data in a database so that you can build a relationship based on a growing knowledge of the customer and his or her habits. Once you have this, you're ready for the second premise.

THE SECOND PREMISE: SET UP A POSITIVE DIALOGUE

The second premise deals with developing the customer relationship: *We set up a positive dialogue with our customers via direct response techniques. Through this dialogue we constantly test and measure to determine what "pleases" or appeals to the customer.*

Smart direct marketers understand that they are dialogue marketers. Establishing a dialogue is, in fact, the essential characteristic of direct response marketing, whether it is by mail, phone, or computer.

Here is a sample of dialogue between a marketer and a customer: See if you can hear it.

> "Dear Reader: Here is an exciting new product. Act now and you can receive it . . . ." "Yes. Send me . . . and charge it to my VISA card . . . ." "Thank you for your order. Here's a special offer for new customers and our new fall catalog . . . ." "I want to exchange the green skirt, size ten for a size twelve . . . ." "We have a green plaid blouse that matches your skirt on a private customer sale right now . . . ."

And so it goes—on and on.

If you want to keep your customers buying, ask them what they want. What could be more sensible, once you have a database of customers by name and address, than to test and measure their likes and dislikes?

You learned in Chapter 1 that this is a profession in which you will be tested, because the results of your work can be measured. It is important to point out here that you will also be responsible for alternative advertising methods.

The direct marketers with whom you work will test media and markets and products. You will participate with constant creative testing. You'll be expected to test entire ads or promotions, copy concepts or approaches, creative devices, format changes, premiums or other offer variations, and graphics.

Your job is to discover the strongest appeals, the most compelling presentations, the most involving formats through testing, or by talking to the customers and prospects.

Direct marketers gain wisdom from their customers. Customers will tell us what we want to know, if we test carefully and scientifically. (Scientific testing can be summarized in two brief sentences: Test only one thing at a time. Test in quantities or numbers of customers that are statistically valid and can therefore be projected.)

Your customers will even tell you when they've had enough or when a product needs to be changed. And certainly, they will tell you when they are unhappy or disillusioned. Remember, what's best for your customer is ultimately best for you.

THE THIRD PREMISE: THE CUSTOMER IS ALWAYS RIGHT

The third premise is that the customer is always right, in the old-fashioned sense.

Customer service is an important aspect of our business. Properly treated, the customer will continue to tell us reliably not only what to sell, but when to sell, how much to sell, and the best offer to use.

Certainly all marketers should know this. But no one is equipped to demonstrate it better and more precisely than direct marketers, because direct marketers were the first to develop and utilize customer records (the database) to establish a productive customer dialogue or an ongoing, repeat purchase history. We should know so much about our good customers that we can put the average retail sales clerk to shame!

In addition to customer history, a well-run operation will record when an order was received, when it was shipped, how it was shipped, when and how it was billed and paid for. This is known as *fulfillment data*—the complete history of order processing—and it is part of customer service.

If order processing, or fulfillment, does its job, customer inquiries and complaints can be kept to a minimum and handled promptly and positively when they occur. If it doesn't do its job, a good customer may be lost, not just to one direct marketer, but often to direct marketing as a whole.

THE FOURTH PREMISE:
LISTEN TO THE CUSTOMER
FIRST

Not every marketer *does* put the customer first. Sadly, some very big manufacturing companies have come to direct marketing with a "quota-driven" approach, rather than using "customer-driven" marketing. The marketer may say, "We have to sell 100,000 of these widgets by spring. Find more customers. Roll out the advertising, cut the prices!" rather than saying, "Find out how the customer will react to the new widget. What can he or she tell us about price preferences that will increase sales volume?" And so we have the fourth premise:

When we listen to the customer first, we can make money with considerable confidence. We can analyze customer information and learn not only where we are, but also where we can logically expect to be over the years ahead.

Marketers in every kind of direct marketing—magazine subscriptions, book clubs, continuity programs, catalogs, third-party mailings—not only have extensive testing programs all along the line, but also have established formulas based on consistent behavior of specific customer groups. Good direct marketers use these formulas to calculate the *lifetime value* of their customers, not just as a group, but specific customer segments. Marketers develop computer models based on these formulas and use them to draw up their long-range marketing plans.

Each magazine, book club, or catalog modifies or adapts the formulas to its own customer groups, of course, and no two are exactly alike. Knowledge of these formulas and models are not critical to your creative well-being, but if your Renaissance Quotient (see Chapter 1) is high, ask your marketing people about them.

THE FIFTH PREMISE:
MAINTAIN YOUR
CREDIBILITY

The fifth premise is critical to your creative development. You know by now that the customer is pretty sacred in this business—or should be. *You* must take an active role in developing and preserving the integrity of the customer relationship.

Nothing must destroy our credibility with the customer. The customer takes us very seriously. The customer listens to us. The customer remembers.

Sounds a little corny, doesn't it? Well, so do "A penny saved is a penny earned," "The best things in life are free," and "Too soon old and too late smart!" These are all old-fashioned adages—proverbs. They live on.

In direct marketing this premise is foundational. Every time we forget it or ignore it, we suffer.

You, as a creative person, get the last opportunity to hold fast to this premise. It may not happen often, but many managers and marketers, in their enthusiasm to structure a plan, neglect the very people the planning is intended to reach. Their objectives, goals, and quotas take over and they lapse a little in terms of customer credibility. They may say, for example, "Who's going to remember that this is our *sixth* Final Sale this year?" And frankly, even we creatives can get too lax and begin to lose our credibility.

The Basic Law of Creativity comes in here. It was established to help you help all those managers and marketers, and also help you help yourself sort out the real story from all the hyperbole.

Making Sense to the Customer

The Basic Law of Creativity bears repeating: *Whatever you say, however you say it, however you present it, first ask, "Does this make sense to the customer?"*

As you proceed through your creative development in the pages of this book, you'll have opportunities to apply this law at several important stages. Neglect it, and you risk failure. Use it, and you'll be a step closer to successful direct response advertising.

It may seem obvious that things have to make sense. Yet, too many direct response marketers have gotten short-sighted on this point today. The industry needs more questioners and you should be among them. If you aren't, you might try futilely to sell something to customers, realizing that you aren't making sense or that you aren't being honest. This attempt may lead to some unsolvable creative problems, including writer's block.

Our customer base is growing and evolving right along with direct marketing. Customers now buy jewelry, expensive collectibles, boots, cosmetics, fine clothing, and furs—even cars—through direct marketing. They are better educated and more sophisticated than customers of twenty years ago. They have more money to spend. They are also more demanding and more skeptical.

You have to be pretty good to sell to today's customers, so make sure before you even begin that you won't be forced to shake their credibility or try something on them that *you* don't believe in yourself. For example:

- Don't proclaim a "BIG" sale every few weeks, or say "Last Chance" too often, or you'll end up getting no response—like the boy who cried "Wolf!" too often.

- Don't shout "Hurry" when a magazine subscription still has six months to go. (There are other things you can say to motivate your subscriber.)

- Don't tell a customer how important he or she is to you when your database doesn't even contain the customer's gender or first name.

- Don't exclaim "This invitation is not for everyone," when "Official Invitation No. 1,318,149,975" is printed on the reply card.

- Don't promise something on your outer envelope or in a headline that you can't immediately substantiate in the copy that follows. Customers get mad, and so would you.

- Don't try to hype a weak offer with deceptive phrases and weasel words.

These are all obvious no-no's—at least they should be. But making sense to the customer, or failing to do so, can also be seen in far larger ways that pertain to the basic rules of direct marketing.

In addition to failing to ask, "What did we say to the customer *last* time?" and "Based on what we said, will this make sense?" some practitioners ignore major rules such as "Always call to action or ask for the order after your sales story," or "Always start your sales message with benefits for the prospect." Here are three situations that illustrate these points. (More examples will come in succeeding chapters.)

SOME OFFERS THAT DIDN'T MAKE SENSE

Inviting Members to Quit. The first example is a nationally known record club that had a joining offer of thirteen recordings free to new members, with a commitment to purchase eight additional recordings over the following three years. Members who fulfilled their commitment were free to leave the club any time thereafter. The club's marketers found, however, that many of their members failed to purchase often, or at all, once their initial commitment was fulfilled.

To deal with this problem, the marketers decided to try to get members who had fulfilled their commitment to *recommit.* They tested many incentives but, finally, the most effective offer proved to be the same offer the members had accepted originally: thirteen *more* free records if they would recommit for eight more purchases over the next three years.

Then came the question of how to approach the members with this offer. The marketers decided to remind the members that it represented the initial joining offer, repeated. Because it seemed obvious that members couldn't *rejoin* while they were still members, the club wrote and asked the members to quit!

The headline read:

You are invited to cancel your membership—and then receive 13 albums FREE!

The letter began:

Dear Preferred Member:

Remember way back when you first decided to join the Club? What prompted you to do so? Undoubtedly it was the lure of getting a sizable number of albums all at once, at practically no cost! . . .

Well, how would you like to relive that exciting moment once again? . . . .

If you tell us to, we'll cancel your present membership and then send you 13 albums of your own choice . . . . Nothing for you to pay . . . .

In exchange . . . you simply re-enroll in the Club and agree to buy 8 selections at regular club prices, in the coming three years.

A close friend of the author, who is not a direct marketer, had been a perfectly happy member of this record club. He'd finished his commitment and continued to buy through the monthly mailings. When he received the promotion suggesting that he quit and rejoin, he thought the club had lost its mind. He was both confused and angry, certain he was being "taken." He did not respond to the offer and has since stopped buying completely from the club.

The above-mentioned promotion is an example of smart marketers dealing intelligently with real problems, but they were so intent on solving *their* problems that no one—right down to the copywriter—ever stepped back and asked, "Will this make sense to the customer?" Figuratively, you could say they neglected to invite the customer to their meeting. And *that* is a big no-no.

Nothing to Do . . . No Place to Go. The second example comes from a major American automobile manufacturer who mailed sophisticated, computerized letters to prime prospects for a new sports car.

The four-color brochure was exciting and the letter was an invitation to test drive the new car, but nowhere in the entire mailing was a phone number or address given! If the customer didn't know the address of a local dealer, he or she had to look it up in the phone book. And that, somehow, didn't make sense after they had just received a *personal* invitation from the general marketing manager himself. A toll-free telephone number to call "headquarters" for the nearest dealer (or a computer-generated listing of local dealers) would have paid off in many more test drivers!

Forgetting the Customer. The final example is a really big no-no from an Italian publisher for a magazine bearing his name. (This alone should indicate a potential problem.) The advertisement— shown in Figure 2–1, was a full-page direct response print ad in *Fortune* magazine.

As you look at the ad you'll see that the word "you" is strangely absent. It is used only in the third paragraph and once again near the end of the ad. This is the first big mistake and symptomatic of the major problem.

The headline and all the copy describe the new magazine in glowing terms. The page is filled with facts and figures regarding the remarkable publication. It's like a self-centered movie star talking about herself at a cocktail party—arrogant and boring.

This advertisement breaks a primary rule: "Don't tell me about yourself. *Tell me what you can do for me!*" Break this rule at your peril. (A lot more about this later.)

SOME OFFERS THAT DO MAKE SENSE

The Double Postcard. Just as some direct response advertising can fail to make sense to customers and prospects, so other advertising seems to go out of its way to be both reasonable and logical to customers.

The double postcard (or "turn-around document") is a particularly fine example of this. These double-postcard mailings (used initially by Ziff-Davis Publications and *Newsweek* to solicit magazine subscriptions) make sense to both the prospect and the publication.

For the publication, they are economical to mail. For the prospect, they state simply (to paraphrase the offer), "You are busy. Why bother with lots of details. Here's a good offer for a publication you know. Tell us if you're interested at this time."

This works well when the publication is a nationally-known magazine, because the majority of the recipients know this product. It also works well when the magazine is a special-interest publication that is repeatedly promoted to a core group of individuals who are prime prospects because of their known interests.

Some ten years ago the double postcard worked well for a few magazines. Today you see it more and more. Does it work better than a direct mail package? Well, sort of. You see, as postage and paper costs continue to rise for publishers and other direct marketers, direct mail is becoming expensive. And even when the double postcard gets a lower response than a direct mail package (as it often does), the postcard may still be more economically feasible on a cost-per-order basis.

Figure 2–2 is a good example from *Inc.* magazine (a magazine for small business executives). The card was sent to known top executives of small companies who had already received several other,

FIGURE 2–1   *FMR:* **A Self-Centered Ad**

more extensive and detailed promotions. Without this prior editorial "sell," however, heavy reliance on double postcards can be dangerous. Some publishers have reported poor upfront pay up as well as poor renewals from their respondents.

FIGURE 2–2 *Inc.:* **A Double-Postcard Promotion**

Inc. Free Copy Reservation Card

☐ **Yes!** I'd like to sample the next issue of Inc. I understand that I'll also receive Inc.'s *Guide to Small Business Success*—FREE—just for trying Inc. If I like my free issue, I can subscribe at 47% off the cover price. I'll get a full year (12 issues in all) of Inc. for just $19—plus I'll also get my Inc. Soft Briefcase AND my Inc. Micro Card Calculator—free with my paid subscription.

   If I don't choose to subscribe, I'll return your subscription bill marked "Cancel." The free issue and *Guide to Small Business Success* will be mine to keep. But I will owe nothing at all.

652 28309426 06CM6

Name	Title	06CM6
Sheldon Satin		
Company		
Sheldon Satinassc		
Address		
1175 York Ave		
City	State	Zip
New York,	N. Y.	10021

Inc.'s regular subscription rate is $25.

TO RECEIVE YOUR FREE ISSUE, JUST TEAR OFF HERE—AND MAIL THIS POSTPAID CARD—TODAY!   **CR20**

R.R. LaPointe
P.O. Box 9091
Boston, MA 02205

Attention Postmaster:
If Undeliverable Please
← **Return To This Address**

FIRST
CLASS
POSTAGE
PAID
INC.
MAGAZINE

Sheldon Satin:

Good news!
You've been selected
to receive a compli-
mentary issue of Inc.

Please accept by re-
turning the attached
postpaid card at your
convenience.

With so much to gain
-- and nothing to
lose -- shouldn't you
at least take a look
at Inc.?

First Class Presorted

CAR-RT SORT ✳✳ CR 20

Name	Title	06CM6
Sheldon Satin		
Company		
Sheldon Satinassc		
Address		
1175 York Ave		
City	State	Zip
New York,	N. Y.	10021

‖‖‖‖‖‖‖‖‖‖‖‖‖‖‖‖‖‖‖‖

Clear and Credible. The ad in Figure 2–3 from Lands' End is a beautiful example of making sense to the customer. The ad is low-key, but crystal clear and credible in telling the customer or prospect exactly everything he or she needs and wants to know without hyperbole.

How easy it would have been to use unbelievable "hype" such as, "Here, Now—The World's Best Shirt!" Instead, Lands' End opted for a more modest and credible statement that implied they are constantly striving for perfection but aware that nothing in this world is perfect or *the* best. The take-outs around the shirt do much to reinforce their headline and make sure you don't miss the important features.

These examples from Lands' End and *Inc.* demonstrate a creative approach that was formulated by asking "Will this make sense to our prospect? What have we said before? What questions or problems can we put to rest for our customers with this mailing or ad? Are we being consistent? Is this in keeping with the image we wish to convey? How will it strengthen and improve our image in the eyes of our good customers and prospects?" In short, does this make sense to the customer?

Now—on to your next essential: Research.

Laying the Groundwork for Success: Research and Testing

Creative people are constantly changing their selling hats—from software to beer to cars to spaghetti sauce. That's why most successful advertising types have a strong Renaissance Quotient. They're constantly trying out new services, learning about new products and markets. It's one of the nice things about being in advertising. If you have that R.Q., this is one part of the job that is so exciting that it hardly warrants being called work—and certainly not something as forbidding-sounding as *research*. But that's exactly what research is: learning about products and markets.

Research offers you opportunities for marketing insights that no other source can give. Because of this, as important as research is in general advertising, it becomes far *more* important to creative people in direct response advertising. Here's how.

YOUR SECRET WEAPON: MEASURABILITY

Direct response is a measurable form of advertising, so if your product or service isn't absolutely new to its market, you can obtain some very exciting insights with test research.

Any marketer worth his or her salt in direct response advertising keeps extensive and clear records of testing history. And this testing history can provide you with a lot of help, if you enjoy being a bit of a detective. For example, you can test lists and media, offer, and format, as well as test current offers against previous successful efforts, known as *controls*.

FIGURE 2–3   Lands' End: A Clear and Credible Print Ad

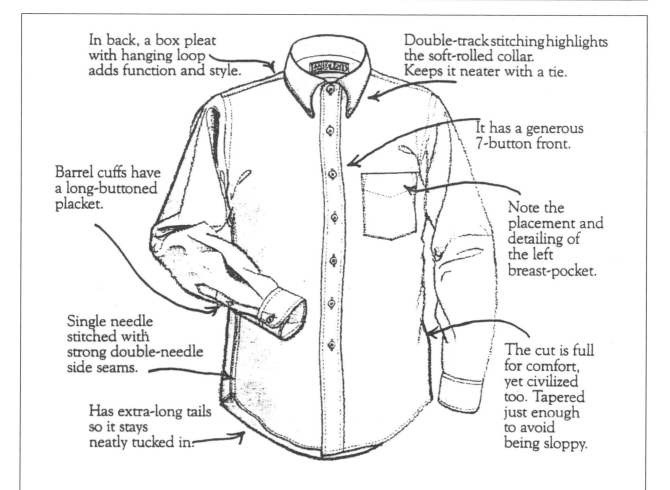

In back, a box pleat with hanging loop adds function and style.

Double-track stitching highlights the soft-rolled collar. Keeps it neater with a tie.

It has a generous 7-button front.

Barrel cuffs have a long-buttoned placket.

Note the placement and detailing of the left breast-pocket.

Single needle stitched with strong double-needle side seams.

The cut is full for comfort, yet civilized too. Tapered just enough to avoid being sloppy.

Has extra-long tails so it stays neatly tucked in.

We set out to make the world's best buttondown. This one comes close. At $25.

This is the Hyde Park—the latest addition to our impressive Oxford Collection, featuring both shirts of 100% cotton and our Lands' End reverse cotton blends.

Check it out feature for feature, beginning with the knowledge that it's made of imported 100% cotton Oxford. Heavier. More densely woven for a nicer drape. It launders better, resists wrinkles; best of all, it wears longer than normal.

For those of you interested in more specifics, we've provided this step-by-step "tour" of the shirt—available in pink, ecru, blue, maize, helio and white solids, as well as stripes and tattersalls, too.

Why make so much of a single shirt? We may have told you more than you ever wanted to know about a shirt. But only to make a point about the Lands' End philosophy of doing business.

It is a simple philosophy really:
First, *quality.* Then, *price.* And always, always *service.*

A quality item at a reasonable price represents a Lands' End value. Anything less is someone else's ballgame—not ours. What's more, every item we offer you— from soft luggage to sweaters to snow wear to shoes—is unconditionally guaranteed.

of fine wool and cotton sweaters, Oxford button-down shirts, traditional dress clothing, snow wear, deck wear, original Lands' End soft luggage and a multitude of other quality goods from around the world.

We don't ask you to trust us, just try us. Mail the coupon for a free catalog. Better still call our toll-free 800 number, 800-356-4444. 24 hours a day (except Alaska and Hawaii call 608-935-2788).

☐ **Please send free catalog.**
Lands' End Dept. W-08
Dodgeville, WI 53595

Name_____

Address_____

City_____

State_____Zip_____

Or call Toll-free:
800-356-4444
(Except Alaska and Hawaii call 608-935-2788)

List and Media History. If media testing history is available to you, see if you can also get an accurate picture of the *list history.* Ask what lists of names are rented regularly because they consistently respond or "pull" well for the particular product or service. (Lists are databases of names from different sources—mail order buyers, magazine subscribers, association members, professionals—that are rented, not sold, for a one-time use in a mailing.) This can tell you a lot about the prospect market.

For example, if the following lists did exceptionally well for your product—subscribers to *Esquire, GQ, Runner,* and *Executive Fitness Newsletter* plus Eddie Bauer catalog buyers—you might assume that you have an affluent, young to middle-aged male executive market with strong interests in health and fitness.

List test responses for lists of names that *did not* respond well are also informative. If, for example, *Field & Stream, Car and Driver,* and *Rod & Gun* subscriber lists all responded poorly for your product, this may be because your males are upper middle class, conservative, and affluent with little interest in the workings of fast cars or in hunting and fishing. This knowledge helps to familiarize you with the market you'll be talking to. Of course, this list testing history should be compared with the product's market as it is described to you by the marketers.

List test history can also indicate possible shifts in the market or changes in the product perception as new lists become productive and old lists fall away into marginal profitability.

Space ads in magazines can be an indicator of your market as well. For example, targeting the affluent male market described above, you can easily pick the three or four best magazines for your ads based on the magazines' subscriber demographics. This also works in reverse. If the magazines work well for you, so will their subscriber lists, and so may other lists that work for each magazine in its own subscriber prospecting if you can find out what they are.

Offer History. Another valuable kind of research will be the offer test history. Price, of course, is a part of the offer. But good offers also take into consideration premiums, involvement devices (such as tokens or stamps), guarantees, and trials. Some markets respond better to one offer than another, while certain products require certain offers to remain competitive.

Information on what worked well in the past and what didn't can give you a good idea of what offers to recommend and what to avoid, as well as ways to make your current offer even stronger. For example: Your market may be a greedy bunch that needs a lot of premiums, or they may respond to razzmatazz and color, or they may have a passion for tokens and other involvement devices, or they may even hate free books.

Format History. Another valuable source of information is the format history. Is a brochure important in direct mail? Does it pay to include extra flyers or promotional materials? Is an order card important, or will a simple 800 number do better? Must you always use a jumbo envelope? How successful has each format been up to now? Find out whenever you can.

The Control. One of the most important areas to study is what direct marketers call the *control.* The control is the current direct mail promotion, ad, or TV commercial that out-pulled all the others. Good direct marketers constantly test against their control to develop still stronger promotions, or replacements when the old control begins to slip. It is important to ask about the control history as part of your initial research. (After all, if you do not, you just might reinvent a previous control without realizing it!)

The control history should give you a nice little pile of direct mail promotions (ads, videos, or whatever), along with data sheets showing when each promotion was control, for how long, which one beat what, controls that were later retested (and, possibly, reinstated), controls that were hard to beat, and so on.

The losers in the control history also have a story for you. (The only thing worse than reinventing a wheel is reinventing a *square* wheel.) In some cases, it may be easy to see why a mailing was a loser. In other cases, it's not easy to figure out why one failed where another succeeded. The control history may tell you something useful about the market and your product or service, and it can surely give you ideas on what to do or not to do with your own promotion.

I was recently lucky enough to be able to study over five years of winning and losing mailings from a new client. The results were unexpected but consistent and forced me to reverse my entire creative attitude regarding the client's market. It kept me from jumping in and repeating the mistakes of the past.

You can also learn from testing results on such things as seasonality (the best time of year for promoting the product), the use of four-color versus two-color printed pieces, and so on. You must ask for this information in many cases. Not everyone gives much importance to test results, unfortunately.

Altogether, good testing history can be an invaluable guide. "Good" testing history, by the way, assumes that the testers have tested only one thing at a time in statistically valid list groups *and* have taken into consideration the *quality* (as well as the *quantity)* of the prospects or new customers brought in by one test versus another—their ability to continue to purchase or renew the relationship. (An offer that increases initial response by "giving away the store" dilutes net response and is a costly way to prospect.)

CLIENT CONFIDENTIALITY
AND TEST RESEARCH

If you're an outsider, working for an advertising agency or as an independent free-lancer, don't be surprised if the client feels wary about sharing test information with you. Direct marketers are notoriously protective of their test results. After all, the best direct marketers put a fortune into testing and learning and applying what they learn. Research is a major corporate investment and a most valuable asset. Why should they risk sharing their breakthroughs and discoveries with competitors?

There is more industry-wide cooperation among companies today than there was in the past, but this does not extend to sharing statistics from current test results or the response to a current promotion. Direct marketers are pretty smart about knowing when to share information and when not to.

So if you're not on the payroll, you may encounter some resistance to divulging test results. You may be told, "You don't need to know that." or, "That's not important to you." or, "No one's ever asked for *that* before." Don't be put off! It is important and you *do* need to know it—if you're going to do professional work.

If they don't have the information you need, protect yourself by making it clear that having no testing history to refer to puts you at a disadvantage.

If they do have it, but won't divulge it, here's one way of enlisting cooperation. Rather than asking for actual response, ask them to index response rates for you. For example, say the marketer has run a seven-part test as follows:

A - Control Package
B - Control Package with Premium
C - Control Package with Special Brochure
D - Control Package with Free Trial
E - New Creative Package 1—Control Offer
F - New Creative Package 1—Premium Offer
G - New Creative Package 2—Control Offer

Assign 100 as the score for the control and ask that everything else be scored relative to the control. In the list below, for example, although E, a new creative package, barely beat the control (A), it moved ahead considerably when the premium was added (F). Package G, meanwhile, did poorly against the control. And both the special brochure (C) and free trial offer (D) actually decreased response.

	F-105	D-99
	B-103	C-94
	E-101	G-90
Control	A-100	

You may have to give a little and sacrifice pure accuracy in using such rankings. Do it anyway. It will still serve your purpose—and it will show that you're working in good faith, on the same team.

NONTESTERS AND RESISTERS: A DANGER TO THEMSELVES

I've described optimum situations of companies that believe in testing, and keep a testing history. Strangely enough, with all of the potential customer data available, some companies (mostly newcomers to direct marketing) still refuse to test. They just don't understand the principles of successful direct response marketing!

One of the worst examples of this was a major financial institution that, when asked about testing, told me they had no need to test. Here's how they figured it: they knew exactly what percentage of response they needed from their prospects. They had calculated the "lifetime value" of a customer perfectly. So I was told, "Why test? We're getting the 1.5 percent response we need."

When you come face to face with most nontesters, here's what they usually tell you: a) There's no time. b) There's no budget. or c) The market's too small.

Sometimes they give one reason, sometimes another—or all three. What this really tells you (since none are valid excuses) is that there's no management commitment to testing. This is bad news.

Testing does require a small budget to get started. (But then, the budget grows as testing quickly demonstrates its benefits.) Tests also take time, so careful advance planning is needed. As to market size—you can always test, no matter how small your market. Certainly the tests must be carefully structured to protect their statistical validity. But there are nearly half a dozen books on how to accomplish this.

For your sake, I hope you don't get mixed up with nontesters. At least not intimately. You won't learn much. Neither do they.

PRODUCT RESEARCH

It's vitally important for you to be familiar with the product or service. After all, you are the salesperson. You're not just creating awareness advertising.

Top direct response writers who are promoting subscriptions by direct mail read at least one to two years' worth of the magazine; when selling products, many writers will buy or borrow the product, use it or sample it, try it out on family and friends, and visit the manufacturer. They also study the competition. This includes reading the competition's advertising, so they can be sure to go it one better. Examining competitors' advertising may, in fact, be the most valuable way to get started.

You'll want to know how the marketers perceive a product or service, too—how they position it. What is the "branding" statement? Ask questions and listen.

Try to determine why the company is particularly qualified to make or offer this product or service. (You may find ideas here for a story that helps establish credibility.) Ask for a history of the product or service, how and why it came about. (More ideas.)

How do the various principals (owner/founder/editor) describe their product and its benefits? Do they agree with the marketers? How do they perceive the competition?

Don't trust yourself entirely to the marketers when you're doing product research. Some of your most valuable input may come from others (designer/inventor/builder/the competition), and from your own relationship to the product or service itself.

The Market

You will want to know as much as possible about the people to whom you'll be "talking," and you'll get a good start by reviewing a media history. You will also want a clear primary (and secondary) market profile from the marketers. (If anyone fudges on this, consider it a dangerous sign.)

Nat Ross, a great teacher and one of the founders of direct marketing education, says, "Our culture changes every hour. Our biology has remained the same for millions of years." This means you'll need full demographics, geographics, and psychographics as well, where they are available. Your marketing people must have a precise knowledge of the market, based largely on an analysis of those customers already in the database, and they should willingly share this with you.

In business-to-business direct response advertising, rather than get into demographics and psychographics, you'll want to pinpoint the decision maker or makers. This is very important when more than one person may be involved in making the buying decision. (In a family where a decision requires more than one person, your selling proposition won't change as long as all members of the family are included in the market profile.) In big business purchases decision makers may have different areas or levels of interest, requiring different advertising approaches.

For example, your sales message to the president of a company or the head of a division would not be the same message you'd send to the engineer who might actually use your product—or to the purchasing agent who might approve the equipment purchase. Each of these people has different interests and different responsibilities. Sometimes you'll have to communicate with each separately before you get an opportunity to make a sale.

As you'll see more fully later on, to proceed you need a clear customer picture (whether it's pinpointing the decision makers in the corporate structure or defining your market's lifestyles). As a matter of fact, without a good market definition, no one can succeed in this customer-driven form of marketing.

ANOTHER SECRET WEAPON:
PERCEPTION TESTING

In this form of marketing in which customers call the shots, it's one thing to know who this customer is and still another to understand how this customer or prospect *already* perceives the product or service, or the company that is offering it.

Information on market perceptions, if you can get it, is your most valuable research in developing a strong, convincing dialogue with the customer or prospect. This information is not always available, of course, but there are three places to look for it. Try them and you may discover a pot of gold (or a pot of problems):

Customer Correspondence and Telephone Calls. Direct marketers aim at developing a dialogue with customers and prospects. See if you can listen in on this dialogue. Chances are, you'll pick up new impressions of the customer and how he or she perceives the product and/or the company.

Every direct marketer has a fulfillment and customer service area where customer inquiries, complaints, and requests (that are not simple orders) come in. Borrow records of as many of these different kinds of correspondence or conversations as you can for review. These records may give you some valuable insights. They will certainly do so if there are problems that you should know about.

For example, several years ago a large Midwestern mail order company was having an unusual problem with nonpayment and customer cancellations on a certain product line. Before repromoting the line, the company decided to do some customer research by reviewing cancellations on the product. An extensive study of hundreds of customer letters indicated cancellations and failures to pay were based largely on a broad misconception regarding the product line and its performance.

This was not evident at first. Few, if any, customers came right out and stated the problem, if indeed they understood it. Only after listening to the tone, the words, and the phrases used to justify cancellation did a pattern emerge. Once the problem was known, the company devised a clear, creative solution. The product was repositioned and its benefits were clarified in the promotional material.

Focus Groups. A *focus group* is a scientifically planned discussion group of ten or twelve people, all prime prospects or users of a specific product or service, led by a professional interviewer, who follows an outline. The participants are encouraged to candidly voice their opinions on the product or service that is being marketed. The leader keeps things going and on track.

Good marketers are wary of overinterpreting focus groups, because they know that a small, intimate group of individuals cannot give a good reading on quantitative product appeal (or how many people will or will not buy the product or service). They also will not give a clear indication of the strength or weakness of the actual direct mail, print, or broadcast promotion. But by using four or more focus group from different geographical areas marketers can and do get a pretty good picture of how their prime prospects might respond to the features and benefits of the product or service, why they would purchase it, and what impresses (or does not impress) them about it.

For you, a focus group can be a gold mine of ideas. Smart creative people jump at an opportunity to observe (unseen behind a one-way window) a focus group in action, or, as a second choice, to listen to or to view a tape recording of the focus group conversation.

The dialogue of the focus group can almost write your copy! It can also show you dangerous areas or weak places in the product or service where your copy will have to work hard to make its points. And if you listen carefully, you may even pick up a "thread" or theme running through the groups that can give you an entirely new creative approach. (There is a fine example of this in the following section.)

Sure, there's a lot of useless talk, but when the participants get "turned on" they'll say things you might never think of—and in an ingenuous style that you might never develop alone.

It's not unusual for a smart copywriter to pick up several big headlines, copy leads—even entire creative approaches—just by listening to a good focus group.

Be sure to ask about focus groups when you start your project research. Your timing may be good and you may be in luck!

Telephone Interviews. Professional direct marketers know that there is no true mystery in direct response advertising. There is a reason for everything. But sometimes explanations are hard to come by.

For example, suppose that in a regular customer mailing, many customers fail to respond. The mailing is so far below its expected or budgeted return that it looks suspicious. After checking to make sure all mail was delivered, a smart marketer may turn to the telephone and ask customers if they received the promotion and why they did not place orders. Only a dozen or so of these calls are needed to yield valuable information.

If you encounter a situation in which basic research is scanty, and there seems to be a customer problem, you might suggest that the marketers consider first taking the proposition to a customer sample by phone—a sort of quick-and-dirty way to determine whether your promotion is likely to succeed.

You'll find this particularly helpful when you're asked to resurrect, or reactivate, a dormant customer group with a new promotion. Those customers may be gone, moved away, apathetic; they may even hate the company. If there's doubt, often all it takes is fifteen to twenty customer calls to get a reading.

At this point you may wonder how you got bogged down with all this research and testing business. You were promised creativity—and all I've done is pile on caveats about data gathering. But I also promised you no failures, right? And you can't succeed without research, the big picture, and the Law of Creativity. The following section gives two examples that show you the power of research and testing in ensuring direct marketing success.

Testers Who Leave the Pack Behind. If you watch your mailbox carefully (a good habit to get into), you may notice something strange. Many of our popular mass market and special interest magazines have been forced into using the double postcard we described earlier—forced, due to ever-rising postage and production costs. But look! A few magazines seem to be expanding the size and complexity of their direct mail prospecting—and making a bundle with these expanded promotions. (Testers just don't do things over and over—or even more than once—if they're not making money with them.)

Better publications? Not necessarily. Better promotions is more like it. And I beg you to follow closely these promotions, and the companies that test them, wherever they go. You'll learn more from them than from any book (except, of course, this book).

For example, take the Meredith Corporation with over 15 magazines (including *Better Homes and Gardens* and *Ladies' Home Journal*) and some 40 special interest publications. The Meredith Publishing Group believes in focus group sessions to keep current with their customers and to fully understand *why* people are purchasing each of their titles.

Naturally they do this on a publication-by-publication basis. During several such focus groups for *Golf for Women* the circulation people picked up a thread—a real creative opportunity well worth a test.

They already knew that women wanted instruction on improving their golf game. But then they found that women were competitive and ultimately wanted to be as good as men. In fact they often expressed a desire to beat men at golf!

Meredith tested this concept with an outer-envelope color photograph (on a 9-by-12-inch jumbo envelope), showing a woman in front, victoriously sinking a putt, while her partner (a man) is brought to his knees in anguish (see Figure 2–4). The copy reads, "How Sweet It Is! When I sank the putt that beat him, I had to pick my husband up off the green!"

FIGURE 2–4 *Golf for Women:* **A Creative Approach Generated by a Focus Group**

Source: Courtesy of Meredith Publishing Group

This new approach lifted response by over 30 percent. All thanks to focus groups. You may wonder how many companies even bother with focus groups for ongoing publications. Well, the smart publishers, the ones you'll keep up with, do.

And here's a breakthrough in format testing from Rodale Press, Inc. (See Figure 2–5.) It takes real creativity to test from a scrawny double postcard or even from a standard direct mail package to a 16-page, four-color, 8 1/2-inch by 11-inch mini magazine with a cardstock, saddle-stitched bind-in. The promotion for *Men's Health* magazine is filled with action leads and heads and lots of exciting color picture spreads, and it works!

We call the format a "magalog." It's expensive to develop and costly to produce and mail. How can it possibly pay off? Testing. Smart testing. It shows how to spend more to get more—rather than pull back, defeated and spend less to get less and less.

And right now these "magalogs" (I assume you've figured it's a combination of the words "magazine" and "catalog") are working well for several newsletters and self improvement courses, books (of all things) and some magazines. "Magalogs," like television's "infomercials," seem to be feeding a prospect need for long sales messages in direct response. Subject to change. Keep testing. More later (see Chapters 4 and 10).

Your Early Payoff— Making It All Worthwhile

If you've ever wondered why top creative people always end up good, better, or best *but never worst*, here's your answer: they know when (and how) to bow out or say "No thank you" (or tactfully suggest a little remarketing).

There's a primary rule for creative stars and other winners that says "Take no dogs." If the product or service concept is elusive, if the market is hazy, if benefits aren't clear and credible, if you can't get all the information you need—no amount of fine writing will help.

Make this *your* rule, too. Why should your name be leashed to a preordained "dog?" But how can you be sure it is a dog—and how do you explain this to others without making enemies or losing your job? It's one thing to say "No" as a free-lancer, quite another to do it as an employee or an agency. The free-lancer is able to take the easy way out. (He or she can say there's a conflict or no time left in the schedule.)

You, on the other hand may have to explain your reservations clearly and constructively to a boss who is expecting the work to be done, or to a team that's raring to move ahead.

To do this effectively, it's good business if you can demonstrate your concerns by testing out the proposition. Once you know how

FIGURE 2–5   *Men's Health Magalog:* **A Breakthrough in Format Testing**

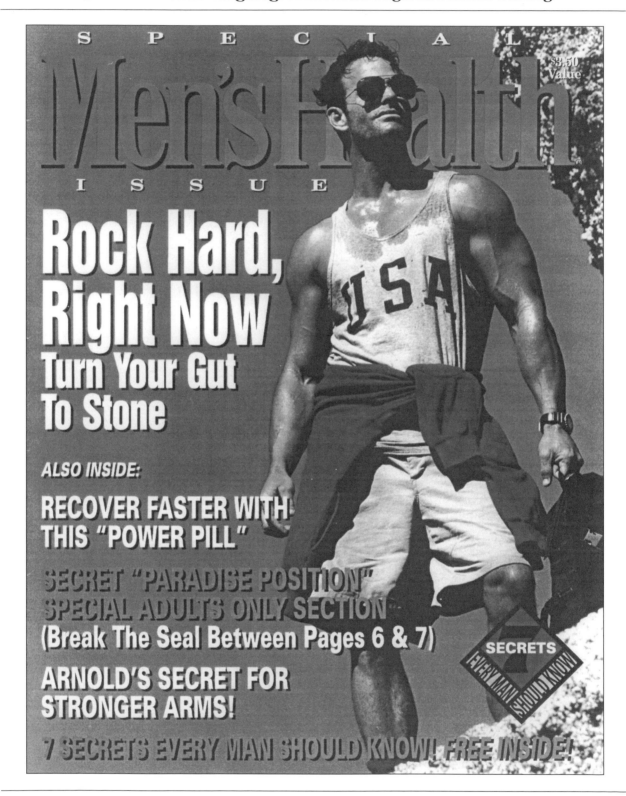

Source: Courtesy of Rodale Press, Inc.

Most good magalogs, like this one, try to look like magazines.

to do this little exercise, you'll know when your assignment is sound or when it's time to blow the dog whistle. You'll also know how to explain it all impartially and positively. (And maybe come up with some positive recommendations for modifications.)

Testing Your Selling Proposition

Before you even accept the fact that a creative piece of direct response advertising is required or desirable, you have to be comfortable with the basic selling proposition. You have to be sure it's sound. Here's how you do this:

- *First,* how is the product or service described and how is it positioned in the market? (What is its branding statement?)

- *Second,* what is the offer? What is the objective of the offer? More than one objective?

- *Third,* what is the market definition or description?

- *Fourth,* is this a single promotion or part of a "big picture?"

  - How does it fit in the marketing plan?

  - Has the plan been thought through, covering all bases? (Ask what happens if the prospect does this? What if he or she does that? Then what?)

- *Fifth,* apply the Basic Law of Creativity.

  - Does this product or service sound reasonable?

  - Why is the product targeted to this market?

  - Will this product make sense to this customer market?

  - What is the competition's proposition?

  - What are your product's advantages?

  - Is the offer solid?

  - Will you feel comfortable offering this to the defined market?

  - Is there another market?

TRY YOUR HAND AT A FEW EXAMPLES

Here are some examples to help show you how this works. (Try to decide each one for yourself before looking at the analysis; it's good practice!)

1. *Example*: Your product is a book club on home care, maintenance, and improvement. It offers two new selections every month, plus dozens of bonus or special books. The books are hard to find, as few book stores offer such a wide variety of home improvement publications.

The club can be positioned as an exclusive service for those who are interested in all aspects of home improvement (including do-it-yourself). The joining offer is three books for a dollar, with no membership commitment. The initial market is 500,000 subscribers to a home improvement magazine.

ANALYSIS: On all counts, the book club sounds like it might be a reasonable project. The big point here is that the books are "hard to find," making it a fine candidate for mail order (as opposed to something that could be found in every local drugstore). It has a clearly defined market; it is a unique club aimed at that market; it is going out with a popular (and proven) book club offer. It also offers a partial market for testing and concerns a subject that has attracted much interest over the past few years. It is timely.

2. *Example*: You're asked to help a new magazine that will be the first magazine ever to focus on "work." It will deal with unusual jobs that people do, new job opportunity areas, examples of successful workers from all kinds of jobs, and so on. The subscription offer is one year for fifteen dollars. The initial market is entrepreneurs, professionals, graduating college students, American Express cardholders.

ANALYSIS: You study the product and find that the magazine concept is poor. "Work" is much too broad and amorphous a topic for a magazine. Because it means something different to everyone, it won't make sense to anyone. As a result, there is no targeted or efficient way to reach its market (no real market to target). The entire concept should be reworked. (Just try and write the first paragraph for the magazine. It's practically impossible.)

3. *Example*: Your assignment is to offer several luxury liner cruises to the customer list of a large travel agent. The cruises last sixty days and thirty days. They are the finest luxury cruises offered. The prices are competitive but on the high side. The promotion's job is to generate inquiries for the agent. It will mail to customer lists of which 50 percent are over age fifty-five.

ANALYSIS: You agree that the idea is a good one, but over 50 percent of the agent's customers are under fifty-five years of age. A sixty-day cruise (or even a thirty-day cruise) is something few executives and few families (with one or two working members) could afford in terms of time.

You recommend cutting the list in half, using only those over fifty-five who are both affluent and retired (those who show an active travel history). You also suggest mailing to outside lists with older, affluent demographics.

4. *Example*: A famous sports supplies company with a reputation for good quality at high prices asks you to design a mailing for 200,000 catalog customers.

It has been losing a considerable amount of customer business in its shoe and boot division over the last year because its products (although of the finest quality) are priced considerably higher than the competition.

The company wants you to announce a permanent one-third percent price decrease to its customers on almost all the major shoe lines. They see this as a big new promotion.

ANALYSIS: At first it sounds like a good idea, but then you shake your head and decline. Although they have the right product and market, this cannot make sense to the customer. A sale is one thing, but you need solid reasons for a major price cut. Without a good solid, explanation, it will certainly appear that the company has been overcharging its good customers all along!

5. *Example*: A manufacturer of office equipment wants to establish a customer base of mail order buyers. He has a large, elaborate catalog filled with his product lines. He wants to get this catalog to the proper decision makers at small and medium-sized businesses. Since this is his first entry into direct marketing, he's not sure exactly how much appeal the products will have or at what business level the appeal will be strongest. He would like you to do a direct mail test to find this out, using lists of small to medium companies.

ANALYSIS: If the product lines are attractive and competitively priced, you accept the assignment, but with the stipulation that he consider inquiry generation in small space or print advertising first. Then use direct mail on qualified prospects who request the catalog, because

- the catalog is too costly to send out to unqualified prospects
- the market is ill defined.

A lead-generating print ad in several large business publications is the most economical way to build a list and to determine the market composition and size.

This may sound a little tricky, but once you start applying your proposition-testing formula to your own work, backed up by your big picture and research, you'll see how easy it is to walk others through this with you. It's your best defense when you see a danger signal popping up, because it approaches the problem logically and removes you from the stigma of personal prejudices.

You can save yourself time, and maybe even reputation, if you move through the research process and into this test of your proposition humming, "Take no dogs." Be a skeptic—until you feel comfortable. Now's the time to do it—not later.

Using Test Research

Let's say you've been asked to do a test mailing for a big, nationally known travel magazine called *Sunrise*. You've asked for test history and you've been given the following seven mailings, along with their indexed ratings. You can assume all were properly tested and all went to the same or similar markets. What is your conclusion from the history? What formats and offers might you suggest for your new test based on this?

***Package 1—Current Control*: Index 100.** This was a jumbo package (9" × 12") offering a year's subscription for eighteen dollars (billing later) and the ability to cancel on the first bill if not satisfied. The letter was two pages, back and front. The brochure was four-color, showing magazine covers, life size, and many large pictures from the magazine. There was an order card, a token, and a postpaid reply envelope.

***Package 2—Test 1*: Index 91.** This was also a jumbo package and it had the same offer as the control. However, it contained a short, one-page letter and the brochure was filled with many more colorful pictures than the control but they were reduced in size. There was no picture of magazine covers in the brochure. The order card had a token. There was a postpaid reply envelope.

***Package 3—Test 2*: Index 107.** This package was identical to the control, except that the offer included a small calculator as a premium.

***Package 4—Test 3*: Index 99.** This package was identical to the control except that there was no token on the order card. And there was no postpaid envelope. The order card itself was postpaid.

***Package 5—Test 4*: Index 94.** This was a four-color package measuring 6" × 9" (outer envelope). Inside was the same letter as in the control, a slightly smaller version of the control brochure, the control offer, and a reply card with token and postpaid reply envelope.

***Package 6—Test 5*: Index 103.** This package was identical to the control, except that instead of a token there was a stamp that had to be affixed to the order card. No postpaid reply envelope was included, but the order card itself was postpaid.

***Package 7—Test 6*: Index 89.** This package was identical to the control except that there was no cancellation guarantee after receipt of the first issue.

CONCLUSIONS

1. Jumbo (9" × 12") packages seem to do best with this market.

2. The use of a premium (or at least a calculator premium) raises response considerably.

3. Long descriptive copy is preferable to shorter copy.

4. Large, attractive pictures seemed to have more appeal than a large number of smaller pictures. Readers liked the many large pictures in the magazine itself and these were most representative of the product.

5. Use of a token is not justified.

6. A stamp seems to be an effective involvement device.

7. The clause allowing cancellation on first bill is very important to response.

Based on these indications, you'd be playing it safe to consider a new test package that incorporated:

- A jumbo format.

- A calculator premium.

- A four-page letter and brochure with large, colorful pictures.

- A stamp that has to be affixed to a postpaid order card.

- An offer that allows cancellation on first bill.

References

Martin Baier, *How to Find and Cultivate Customers Through Direct Marketing* (Lincolnwood, Illinois: NTC Business Books, 1996)

Bob Stone, *Successful Direct Marketing Methods, Sixth Edition* (Lincolnwood, Illinois: NTC Business Books, National Textbook Company, 1997) see also Bob Stone, *Direct Marketing Success Stories* (Lincolnwood, Illinois: NTC Business Books, 1996)

Edward L. Nash, *Direct Marketing Strategy, Planning, Execution, Third Edition* (New York: McGraw-Hill, Inc.)

Edward L. Nash, *Database Marketing: The Ultimate Marketing Tool* (New York, McGraw-Hill, Inc., 1992)

Dick Hodgson, *The Greatest Direct Mail Sales Letters of All Time, Revised Edition* (Dartnell Corp., 1985); see also, Herschell Gordon Lewis and Carol Nelson, *World's Greatest Direct Mail Sales Letters* (Lincolnwood, Illinois: NTC Business Books, 1996).

All of the above are available from the Direct Marketing Association's Publications Department.

DIRECT RESPONSE TECHNIQUE: PROVEN FORMULAS AND KEY SALES GUIDELINES

Direct response advertisers used to use the sink-or-swim method to train creative beginners. They would hand creative assignments to new writers with little or no previous training, and only after their first chilling plunge would comments be forthcoming: "You never start a letter with . . . ," "Don't ever put the whoozis before the whazzis," and so on.

Take heart. Today things are better. For one, you now have some good books on direct marketing and almost all of them offer solid guidelines to producing effective direct response advertising. As a matter of fact, you will find an amazing number of rules, guidelines, formulas, and do's and don'ts for creative promotion in general. They appear regularly in trade publications such as *DIRECT, The Magazine of Direct Marketing Management; DM News; Direct Marketing; Catalog Age; Folio;* and the Direct Marketing Association's *Manual,* its monographs, and its newsletters.

Every time direct marketers move into new media, such as the telephone and broadcast, and now the Internet, new rules and formulas spring up. If you try to follow everything, you might even begin to feel a little overwhelmed. You could take your first plunge and sink right to the bottom, weighted down with iron-clad rules and formulas.

Technique Is Essential

Is direct marketing composed predominantly of do's and don'ts, instead of pure creative panache? Is it advertising that eschews intuition and inspiration in favor of rules and formulas?

You bet it is! And as a matter of fact, you could find it quite comforting. You'll know exactly what to do. You have rules to help you keep your head up. In a form of marketing that tests everything, creative guidelines will evolve and rules will proliferate. Finally someone will start to record all these rules in one place.

These rules are not invented by marketers. The customers dictated them by saying, "All things considered, this is what makes me respond."

As people change with the times, so the appeals to which they respond change and must, therefore, be constantly checked and adjusted. The result is a vast body of shifting knowledge made up of years of experience, testing, and retesting.

In direct response advertising this vast body of knowledge is called *technique*, and you can't put one word to paper without it.

All right. You've heard that before, but this is creative progression. Here's where you are on the scale.

- You're honing your creative skills and letting your imagination grow.

- You've made the Basic Law and its five premises yours.

- You know your research requirements and refuse to take "no data" for an answer.

- You're protected from failure because you can test your selling proposition.

Now you're ready for the big "T"—technique. *Some professionals claim that 75 to 80 percent of direct response advertising is technique, and that the balance is creativity!*

This may be a bit of an exaggeration, but even if good direct response advertising is only *50* percent technique and 50 percent creativity, technique is essential to your success as a competent direct response creative person.

You can't be a professional without mastering the big T simply because this amalgam of formulas and rules represents a vast body of direct marketing experience, and ensures that you repeat the successes rather than the mistakes of the past.

Eventually your own experience in applying these formulas and rules (often to the point where your application is automatic and unconscious) qualifies you to break the rules from time to time—but not until you have a reasonably long and intimate relationship with them. (More about this later.)

The Formulas

Formulas are all-encompassing structures or frameworks for the entire direct response promotion, whether it is a direct mail package, a newspaper ad, a television commercial, or an interactive electronic promotion. They tell you what your promotion must accomplish and how it should do this, in logical progression from start to finish.

You have several formulas to choose from, because a lot of people like to write them. Some formulas pertain to all direct response advertising, others concentrate on direct mail.

First, there is *P-P-P-P*, created by Henry Hoke, Sr.[1] P-P-P-P has four steps:

Picture: Get attention early in the copy to create desire.
Promise: Tell what the product or service will do; describe its benefits to the reader.
Prove: Show value, backed up with personal testimonials or endorsements.
Push: Ask for the order.

Another formula is William Steinhardt's *A-B-C Checklist*.[2]

*A*ttain attention.
*B*ang out benefits.
*C*reate verbal pictures.
*D*escribe success incidents.
*E*ndorse with testimonials.
*F*eature special details.
*G*ild with values.
*H*onor claims with guarantees.
*I*nject action in reader.
*J*ell with postscript.

One of the most popular and widely used formulas is called *AIDA* (pronounced like Verdi's opera).

A - Attract Attention.
I - Arouse Interest.
D - Stimulate Desire.
A - Call for Action.

AIDA is the broadest in application and will carry you through years of good direct response writing. There is, however, something to be gained from each of them, so use what makes you comfortable. Most people know AIDA simply because it is easy to remember.

The best way to digest a formula is to practice by applying it to existing promotions. AIDA is easily demonstrated in direct response ads, so you may want to start there. Figure 3–1 shows AIDA applied to a print ad for the *New Yorker*. (Note that in the *New Yorker* ad the coupon is on the left-hand side. The ad was designed with a coupon on the right-hand side as well as on the left-hand side, as it is here,

FIGURE 3–1 *The New Yorker:* **AIDA Applied to a Print Ad**

Attention

Interest

Desire

Action

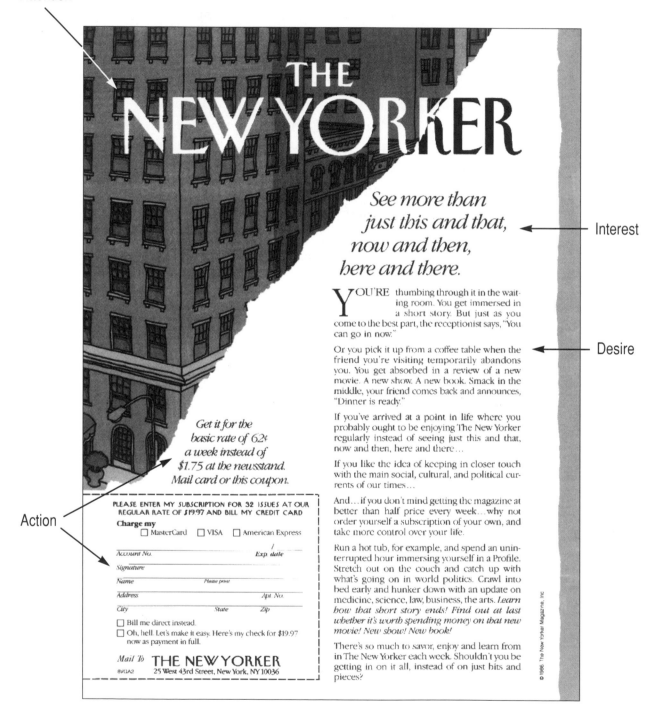

so it could appear on either right or left hand pages in the magazine. This allows it to take last-minute advantage of unsold ad space on any page and still maintain the integrity of the coupon. It's a big No-No to allow a coupon to run on the inside or "in the gutter" where it's next to impossible to remove.)

Every time you come across a direct marketing promotion, try applying one of the formulas. Sometimes, by the way, the formulas may not fit. If this happens, you can be pretty sure the ad didn't work either.

As you move along, you'll become more and more expert at spotting good or effective direct response advertising. And you may be surprised at the number of promotions that could clearly have been improved by following AIDA or another formula.

The best examples of successful formulas are the promotions you see repeated over and over. As everything is measured, the promotions that keep running are obviously the ones that keep getting strong response.

Four Key Sales Guidelines

In conjunction with the formulas, you have the Basic Law with its five premises that work for you in all media. Applying these, use the following sales guidelines to help you as a copywriter to create a salesperson's presentation. These guidelines will be explained in depth in the following sections of this chapter.

> *Establish Credibility:* Present the seller and explain why he or she is qualified to make this offer. (Would you buy a used car from this person?)
>
> *Get Involvement:* This means use "you" and sing the benefits provided by the product or service. It could be a song titled "You, You, You."
>
> *Motivate Your Prospect:* Tell the customer why he or she should act *now*, not later. (Most prospects who put it off never return.)
>
> *Structure a Strong Offer:* Unless your product is unique, you'll need all the competitive ammunition you can muster.

Then apply the Underlying Law: Don't let anyone convince you a promotion makes sense if it doesn't!

These guidelines as well as the rules and guidelines for direct mail packages are just too important to miss. Of all the things the customer has taught direct marketers, these are the most important. (You will find further guidelines and checklists from others who have gone before at the ends of Chapters 4 and 7.)

GUIDELINE 1: HOW TO ESTABLISH AND MAINTAIN CREDIBILITY

You can't establish a relationship with a prospect or sustain a dialogue with a customer without credibility. This is true in all areas of direct response advertising and in all media. If prospects or customers don't believe in you or in your company and product, forget it. No need to worry about benefits, involvement, motivation, or offer.

Once you've got credibility going for you, maintaining it is largely a question of constantly applying the Basic Law. Be consistent. Make sense.

But how do you start? How do you go about *establishing* credibility?

Imagine you've knocked on a stranger's door, holding a wonderful product (or service) with honest-to-goodness values. The first question the prospect asks is, "Who are you?" *not* "What do you have there?"

Once you've identified yourself satisfactorily and the prospect shows an interest in your product, the next question is "What qualifies you (or your company) to make this product?"

If you've done your research, as described in Chapter 2, you should be able to answer these questions, quickly and effectively, right? *Wrong.*

If it were only as simple as that! Here's the curve. There's credibility and there's credibility. How you handle it depends largely on the company or person you represent. And to whom you are speaking.

It sounds convoluted, I know. But here are some examples that will clear it up.

With *customers*—people who know you and have purchased from you or dealt with you in the past—there are a few very simple but important rules. In short: *Don't treat customers like prospects.* To get the strongest response from your customers, identify yourself up front—on the outer envelope. Let them know that you perceive them as a "valued" customer (and it certainly never hurts to tell them that inside your outer envelope is a "special customer offer.")

Prospects are a different matter. They should be treated as you would treat a stranger. But here's where it can get complicated: say, for example you ring a stranger's doorbell wearing the uniform of the local telephone company, and your truck, clearly marked, is out in front. Will anyone ask, "Who are you?" Of course not. You've established an instant identification that carries with it all the trappings of the telephone system, good and bad. You carry its image around on the side of your truck and the front of your shirt. It opens a lot of doors. (So does the identification that goes with the Good Humor truck, the local grocery, UPS, FedEx, the post office. All are operations that are known, familiar.)

But now imagine for a minute the prospect's response if you ring that bell wearing a gray suit and a black hat and carrying a small black case. You'd better be fast—and convincing—when the prospect asks, "Who are you?"

In direct response advertising (and most particularly in direct mail) you'll have to deal with this all the time because *you go out to the prospect;* the prospect is not referred to you. This means you must establish credibility in every element of your package, beginning with the outer envelope.

Often you'll represent a nationally known and respected operation. More often, you'll probably represent someone or some company that does not command immediate recognition and, consequently, credibility. Each situation has its guidelines for establishing credibility. In some cases, it's a question of degree.

To illustrate this let's take an example of two extremes—a large company with instant credibility (such as AT&T, Sears, IBM, or American Express) and a little-known, small company such as Sam's Suit Company.

Direct response advertising from well-recognized, big companies must attempt to humanize the cold, impersonal image and *maintain* credibility by setting their particular "corporate" tone throughout, while Sam's Suit Company must fight to *establish* credibility and stature. (It must answer the question, Why is it qualified to do what it promises?) And then it must go on to *build* credibility in every part of the mailing.

Major U.S. Corporation	**Sam's Suit Company**
1. Recognition	1. Recognition
• Instant logotype identification	• No "recognition" factor
• Company image immediately conveyed	• Need to establish company in the prospect's mind, explain, corporate policy, years in business, size
	• Good photography helpful (Example: Our new warehouse and fulfillment center, pictured here)
2. Spokesperson	2. Spokesperson
• President or chairman not credible unless he or she is addressing the soundness of the company's stock	• Needs president, chief executive, or owner— the person most logically to be trusted, most credible

(Continued)

Major U.S. Corporation	**Sam's Suit Company**

Major U.S. Corporation

- Must be a department or service executive (marketer, salesperson, engineer), preferably a peer of the prospect
- *Someone with whom the reader can identify*

3. Guarantee
   - Expected as part of the corporate image

4. Testimonials
   - Needed only for an unusual new service

5. Endorsements
   - If used at all, must be carefully chosen to represent product, market, and corporate image (Big companies are often wary of "personality" endorsers)

6. Tone of Promotion
   - In accord with corporate image; but a friendly and accessible tone is suggested for the letter so the prospect feels he or she has someone to relate to in the big company (A me-to-you approach)

7. Offer
   - Conservatively stated proposition

Sam's Suit Company

3. Guarantee
   - Absolutely necessary
   - Must be clear, carefully worded, strong, and visually reinforced with equally strong graphics

4. Testimonials
   - Very important, but must use real people with real names (Photographs help)

5. Endorsements
   - Helpful if the endorser is credible and has a good image in the company's marketplace

6. Tone of Promotion
   - Strong, confident, and straightforward in the style that best represents the company image
   - Strong, persuasive selling is acceptable

7. Offer
   - Strong sell with absolute satisfaction guaranteed
   - Use of motivators and incentives wherever possible

As you can see, there's quite a difference in the optimum requirements for the two companies. The little company has to prove its right to do business. The big company has to show that it is warm and human and not too big to care about individual customers.

GUIDELINE 2: HOW TO CREATE AND SUSTAIN INVOLVEMENT

The best way to get people involved in a promotion is to concentrate on the "you." What wonderful attention-getters and attention-holders the following are:

"Enough of me. Let's talk about *you*."
"Tell me, Mr. Jones, what did *you* think of the movie?"
"My, what lovely eyes *you* have, Miss Smith."
"Take this test to see how *you* rate in attracting the opposite sex."
"Have I got something for *you!*"
"Can *you* answer these important questions?"

We all like to talk about ourselves; express opinions; see how our skills, knowledge, or abilities stack up; receive compliments; and learn about things that will benefit us, please us, and fulfill our needs, wants, and desires. You can categorize involvement by benefits-to-you, questions, quizzes, and flattery, but it's so much more—and more exciting—that that.

Here is a secret: To be a top creative person, in every job you take on, think of the many ways to say, "let's talk about you," and *use them all!*

This is particularly important in the direct mail letter, where you speak directly to your prospect or customer. Use "you" generously; use "I" sparingly. And remember, your readers are human; we all like to be stroked.

Most professionals will tell you that the best way to stroke the reader is by promoting benefits (and we'll deal with this in detail in the next two chapters). This is true, of course, *but don't stop there*. How else can you sidle up to your prospects? Can you ask them some questions? Give them some quizzes? Flatter them or talk in terms of their perceived self image ("Congratulations—you're bright, healthy, fun-loving, and you enjoy good books!")? Make them smile? Have some fun? Why not, as long as it makes sense and relates to the subject? But remember, to do this well, you must know your market well. If they are customers, you must know how they have been treated by the company in the past, what has gone before.

How else can good direct marketers create involvement? Give your prospect something fun to do. Gimmicks or involvement devices work. Here are ten involvement commands:

Insert token	Scratch the panel	Choose the color
Peel off the seal	Lift here	Fill in here
Paste stamps here	Detach here	
Check the box	Initial here	

FIGURE 3–2   Involvement Devices

Used properly, such involvement devices can increase your response because humans enjoy lifting, peeling, and pasting, especially during the act of ordering. It's fun. And it's participatory. Figure 3–2 represents a group of involvement devices at work on order cards.

The token, which is now over 35 years old, is still one of the most effective devices you can use—and it is particularly good in book mailings and magazine subscriber marketing. (Research has shown that it has special appeal to affluent, well-educated readers! Hmmm?)

Use it if you can link it to the offer and, graphically, with the product. And if you can personalize your token (laser your prospect's name on it), so much the better; a token that's personalized is far more important and valuable (less likely to get tossed). (See Figure 3–3.)

Stamps are even older than tokens and can be used in much the same way. (Another way is the stamp *sheet*, from which your prospect makes a selection.) Peel-off stamps or seals can also go out affixed to the letter or even to the outer envelope. ("Peel off and affix to your order card.")

FIGURE 3–3 *Southern Living:* **A Personalized Token as an Involvement Device**

The peel-off token is used frequently in the "Yes-No" offer (or "Yes-No-Maybe" offer). The "Yes-No" offer is supposed to enhance appeal and credibility by implying that if you don't say "Yes" or "I accept" you say (or you imply) "No" so that "someone else can be given this opportunity."

To impart true credibility some creative folk insist that a space for "No" be supplied as well as a space for "Yes." Others who are more practical decline to pay for "No" responses and allow only a space for "Yes." Don't try to figure this out—insist on testing if it comes up. There are two schools of thought here and you don't want to join either of them yet. (See Figure 3–4.)

Speaking of joining, we Americans are great joiners, so it'll come as no surprise to you to learn that instant membership recognition from nonprofit fund raisers such as Smithsonian, The Nature Conservancy, and the National Trust for Historic Preservation works very nicely. They all include a "membership card," computer personalized and ready to use, as the part of the reply form that respondents "tear off and keep." (See Figure 3–5.)

FIGURE 3–4A *Bon Appetit:* **A Solo "Yes" Token as an Involvement Device**

If your product's smell is a big selling point, scratch-and-sniff fragrant inks can play a role in your promotion if you're promoting a sweepstakes, prizes or "mystery" gifts, a scratch-off covering on winning numbers, and clues to decipher offer you still more involvement devices.

A sure involver is a bulked-up outer envelope. So how about adding a nice fat pencil (to use in answering the "Tough Questions" inside). Fat or lumpy outer envelopes work by stimulating curiosity— "What could be in here?" And quizzes create involvement!

A truly unusual involvement device is shown in Figure 3–6. It could *only* be conceived and successfully tested by a serious tester. It is a small outer envelope attached to the back of the primary outer, the mailing envelope. It asks the prospect to "Open Me First" and contains a postpaid merchandise return label *for the product that is promoted inside the mailing envelope.* Copy inside the little envelope asks

> "Why are we giving you the attached label . . . even before you send for the book?"

FIGURE 3–4B *Hippocrates:* **A Token Choice as an Involvement Device**

FREE EXAMINATION.

To signal your willingness to examine a copy of HIPPOCRATES, simply peel off the "YES" sticker on the outside of the envelope and place it in the space at right. Then detach the card and mail it in the postage-paid envelope provided.

NO OBLIGATION.

You'll be able to see for yourself. Read each enlightening article. Weigh every articulate commentary. Learn not just the *what* of health and medicine, but the *why*. And how it relates to *you*.

Then, if you decide not to subscribe, you're under no obligation whatsoever. Simply write "cancel" on our bill. You've spent nothing. You owe nothing. And the FREE issue is yours to keep.

THE MAGAZINE OF HEALTH & MEDICINE

PICK ONE

PLACE "YES" STICKER HERE

YES. Send me a sample issue of HIPPOCRATES to examine at no cost or obligation. Bill me later at the special introductory rate of $12 for one full year (five additional issues). That's a savings of 50% off the regular rate. If not delighted, I can cancel, owe nothing, and keep the issue free.

PLACE "NO" STICKER HERE

NO. Give my free preview copy to someone else.

PLACE "MAYBE" STICKER HERE

MAYBE. Send me the current issue at no risk, obligation, or commitment. If I decide to subscribe, I'll let you know by paying the bill I'll get later. If I don't want HIPPOCRATES, I'll just write "cancel" across the bill, owe nothing, and keep the issue – absolutely free.

```
********** CAR-RT SORT ** CR20
JOAN THROCKMORTON
1175 YORK AVENUE
NEW YORK, NY 10021

67301346408 0FAX
```

HURRY! Only a limited number of FREE issues are available.
HIPPOCRATES, P.O. Box 56878, Boulder, CO 80321-6878

Good question. Seems like they're putting the proverbial cart before the horse. Who would even *test* such a crazy, expensive thing? Rodale Books. And it was tremendously successful. It continued to make money for them for several years. Rodale Books, by the way, was (to the best of my recollection), the first to add the postpaid merchandise return label to their guarantee. A very inexpensive dramatization of *free returns* that increased response *without* increasing returns, simply because it removed one more objection for the fence-sitters.

In all of these cases, you should test to make sure response is increased sufficiently to cover the increased costs of such involvement devices.

When you use check-off boxes, fill-ins, tear-offs, and the like it's also important to remember this: your prospect may be confused by too many choices or options. If the options create confusion or result in indecision, you may lose the order.

FIGURE 3–5   A Membership Card as Involvement through Instant Gratification Device

FIGURE 3–6A   Rodale Books: An Unusual Envelope Involvement Device

FIGURE 3–6B   (Continued)

Rodale Books
Emmaus, PA 18049

WHY ARE WE GIVING YOU THE ATTACHED LABEL —A POSTAGE-PAID WAY TO RETURN OUR BOOK —EVEN BEFORE YOU SEND FOR IT?!

Because when we say 15-day free trial, we mean it!

If, after 15 days, you're not completely satisfied with THE ALLERGY SELF-HELP BOOK (described within) you can mail it back to us *without paying a cent.*

But we're so confident that this landmark guide will help you discover *and control your symptoms,* we're willing to "bet the postage" that you'll want THE ALLERGY SELF-HELP BOOK to have and to use for many years to come.

To get your copy, simply mail the postage-paid card inside!

↙ DETACH AND SAVE THIS RETURN LABEL ↘

FROM:

_____

_____

_____

CLASS:

SPECIAL FOURTH CLASS RATE—BOOKS.
RECEIVING OFFICE COMPUTE POSTAGE DUE.
ADD 20¢ MERCHANDISE RETURN FEE.

TOTAL:

MERCHANDISE RETURN LABEL

PERMIT #1   EMMAUS, PA 18049
RODALE PRESS INC. 33 E. MINOR ST.

NO POSTAGE
NECESSARY
IF MAILED
IN THE
UNITED STATES

POSTAGE DUE UNIT
U.S. POSTAL SERVICE
EMMAUS, PA 18049

Tests have shown that two options are acceptable (a one- or two-year subscription, a gold or green recipe box). More than two options may create inertia through indecision. You walk a thin line here between the fun of involvement and the fear of indecision. For this reason, many direct marketers are shying away completely from choices-as-involvement today and keeping it simple.

In some magazine solicitations marketers have found a continued interest in playing with stamps and tokens, but a decided fall-off in response when prospects are asked to choose or check boxes, or add information, signatures, or initials. What could this be saying about our society? About our inability to act? Our love of dumb tokens? It says one thing for you—this is an area in which you'll want to move carefully and test, test, test.

GUIDELINE 3: THE CALL TO ACTION—HOW TO OVERCOME THE DREAD DISEASE, INERTIA

The final command of all direct response formulas is "Action!"

The opposite of action is inertia. All your smooth phrases, benefits, tokens, and stamps amount to nothing if you can't get your prospect to take the final step and respond. Once he or she puts your promotion aside to consider it at a later time, you're pigeon-holed—and few promotions that get pigeonholed ever fly again.

Several techniques to prevent inertia should be considered even under the best promotional circumstances. You can count on them to be effective if you use them honestly. These techniques are *limited offer; limited supply; a deadline;* and *a free gift.* Actually, they are used all the time by good salespeople, who capitalize on the very human fear of losing out on or missing a hot opportunity.

The word "free" itself is probably the greatest motivator (or incentive to respond) in all direct response advertising. The phrase "free gift," although redundant, is even stronger. Some top copywriters hesitate to take an assignment without the word "free" in the offer. It can be important for you, too. We'll talk more about this later when we build the offer.

If you are going to test a deadline, two measures should be considered: (1) It must be close enough to incite the prospect to act; and (2) it must be sufficiently far off to allow the promotion to reach the prospect and to give the prospect enough time to respond. About four to five weeks from your *drop date* in third-class direct mail is considered tight but right, taking into consideration third-class delivery time. With first-class delivery, you can easily lop off a week or more.

"Limited offer," a weaker form of "deadline," *implies* that this is the only chance and that it may not be repeated. I find that if legalities prevent you from claiming that the offer can't be repeated, you can always make the implication with, "I just don't know when we can offer this to you again," or a similar phrase.

As for "limited supply," here's a good example of human psychology: A hairbrush distributor was offering his product at a 50 percent savings in small space ads. Almost all prospects ordered only one brush. He added the headline "Strictly Limited—Only Two Per Customer," and immediately over 45 percent of his orders doubled in size. Of course, "limited supply" also implies that you could run out, so "To avoid disappointment, don't put this off" is another common use of the technique.

You will also want to employ action words and phrases to combat inertia (like "let us know now," "hurry," "act now," "don't delay," "send your answer by return mail," "call today," and so on). And you may want to vary your tone a little by speeding up the rhythm or pacing at the end of your letter, using very brief sentences and paragraphs with lots of action phrases on the last page. It is also important to give your order form or coupon a valuable look that urges, "Process me now."

A little of this rousing motivation goes a long way, however; and you should concentrate here on the causes of inertia so you'll never be guilty of *slowing down your own response rate.* (What a horrible thought!) There are three major mistakes to avoid—and even top professionals have to watch out for these.

The first response-slowing mistake is a lack of full information regarding your product or service (all the benefits in the world can't prevent inertia if your prospect still needs to know one tiny little bit more about the product—such as whether or not the product is over eight inches high).

The second response-slowing mistake is a general lack of clarity regarding the offer. "Clarity" means a lot more than stating the full sales story clearly and including all the features and benefits. A lack of clarity can mean a cloudy guarantee or complex offer terms. (*You* can understand it, and so can the marketing director, but does it really make sense to your prospect? Try it out on the cleaning man or the delivery girl.) A lack of "clarity" can also mean too many check boxes and choices. As you saw with involvement devices, when your prospect or customer can't make up his or her mind, inertia sets in.

To compound the problem, people just don't read very carefully. (This is no surprise.) As the old saying goes, you have to tell them what you're going to tell them, then tell them, then tell them what you've just told them. In direct mail this in itself is good enough reason to have the letter and the brochure (if you have one), as well as the order card or order form, all repeat the offer *and* the major selling points or benefits. Wherever your prospect starts in, it will all be there, as clear as one-two-three.

Which leads to the third mistake—lack of ease of response. *Make it easy* is, or certainly should be, a rule. Put the prospect or customer name and address on the reply form for starters. This is a tested and proven response enhancer and one of the reasons so many direct mail outer envelopes have windows. Today, however, computer capabilities are to the point where dual or multi addressing is not cost-prohibitive and personalization can appear on the outer envelope, the reply card, the letter, and so on. But *always personalize the reply form* no matter what your format. You'll find more detail on this in the next chapter.

Another facilitator of response is the postpaid reply card (the business reply card or BRC) or business reply envelope (BRE). No good direct marketer asks a prospect or customer for the order without one or the other of these. When there's no BRE, you'll find the reply form carries the BRC on the back. And if confidential information, such as credit card data, is requested, *always* enclose a reply envelope.

GUIDELINE 4: HOW TO DEVISE A COMPELLING OFFER

These three basics—credibility, involvement, and a call to action—interrelate and contribute to the fourth: a compelling offer. The ability to develop and creatively present a strong offer will be critical to your success in all forms of direct marketing. You simply cannot create involvement and motivate your prospect in this competitive world without a strong offer.

Of course, strong offers are not important if you are the only one on the block with an unusual product that everyone wants. But how often is that going to happen—and how long will it last?

Of course you are responsible for creative material, and as a creative person you rarely control the offers. This unfortunate situation is precisely why I'm dragging you into "offer."

You must be able to spot a weak offer. You owe it to yourself. If you *can't* recognize a weak offer, you'll prepare a promotion that, no matter how good it is, it will dive for the circular file.

Thanks to your research, you should know immediately whether your offer is highly promotional, barely competitive, or trouble ahead. Equally important, *you must know how to make recommendations for strengthening the offer.* And that's what you'll pick up here. A lot has been written on this, but I've set down those most important elements for creative people like you.

When it comes to price and other major financial decisions, there is not much you can do about weak offers and noncompetitive pricing other than to clearly point out what the competition is offering—and the powers that be should know this anyway.

But offer is not just price. Price is only part of the offer. And there are a lot of creative ways you can make a dull or barely competitive offer much stronger. Such creative offer structuring can make a large difference in response—as much as 100 percent difference! For example, one bright direct marketer took an offer that provided a 100% money-back guarantee for the first 30 days and turned it into a 30-day FREE trial. This tested out to more than double response without hurting pay-up!

The Offer Composition

In addition to the product or service itself, your offer is composed of the price, the credit or payment terms, the commitment, the guarantee, the response motivators and incentives, and any other conditions.

Terms may be set legally, or they may merely reflect the competition in a particular business, but for established products and services, most of the offer's terms have been carefully tested and retested. (New products have a lot of testing to do.) The terms represent the commitment on both sides, the agreement. ("If you do this, we'll do that.") For example:

- This catalog purchase may be made by cash or credit card. There's an extra charge for shipping and handling and 5 percent discount for cash. Returns are accepted if received within thirty days of delivery, and so on.

- When the prospect joins the book club he or she gets four books for three dollars with the understanding that the prospect will also purchase at least four club selections over the next two years. Every purchase is also worth member bonus points. Every month or so the member will receive an announcement, and so on.

- When the prospect enters a subscription to this new magazine, he or she will be billed after receipt of the first issue. He or she may cancel and owe nothing (and keep the first issue) by simply writing "cancel" on the invoice and returning it, and so on.

STRENGTHENING YOUR TERMS

You'll want to go over all your terms carefully to find out where changes can be made (tested) and where they can't. If it's a new offer, you'll probably have much more latitude. Look for ways to enhance credibility, build involvement, and create motivation to act.

One major way to build credibility that should be in every offer as one of its basic terms is the guarantee. If someone tosses you an offer without a guarantee, put one in. If your offer already has a guarantee, see if you can strengthen or dramatize it. If it's a new product, don't even consider letting it out without one. For example:

- *Strong:* If for any reason you're not satisfied with your magazine subscription, just let us know and we'll promptly refund all monies due on unmailed copies.

- *Stronger:* If for any reason, at any time during the first year of your magazine subscription, you're not completely satisfied— just let us know and we'll promptly refund your initial payment *in full.*

- *Strongest:* 100% Money-Back Guarantee. (Add this headline to the above.)

Another important aspect of the terms is payment. It's unlikely you'll get heavily involved with this, but it's good to understand what's available to help you further evaluate your offers as they come along.

- "Bill me later" represents optimum terms. Response can rise 30 percent or more with this credit option. It is extended primarily to customers with an established credit standing; or it is confined to magazines, club plans, and financial services (all things that can be suspended if payment is not made). Its most effective expression is "Send No Money" or "Pay Nothing Now."

- Credit card charges (usually a choice of two or three cards) are used by most mail order companies.

- Installment billing is common for large-ticket items. Some bright companies even offer $25 to $30 books on installment terms.

- Check or cash offers are increasingly rare and sometimes encouraged with cash payment incentives.

Usually, several options are included (such as "bill me later" or "payment enclosed" or "credit card"). Wherever you can, work to effect ease of payment. And remember, next to "free," the best terms are, "Send No Money" and "100% money-back guarantee."

DETERMINING THE OBJECTIVE OF YOUR OFFER

Before you get too tangled in the terms of your offer, however, you might find it helpful to reestablish your objectives.

Step back from the product, stretch, relax, and ask yourself, "What is the offer out to accomplish?" To get new subscribers? To get business inquiries? Or do you simply want the prospect to buy something?

Here are some possibilities:

- Make a purchase
- Subscribe to a publication
- Join a program (book or record club)
- Enter a continuity agreement (to buy a series of products over a period of time)
- Accept a trial
- Make an inquiry for more information
- Make a contribution (fund raising)
- Become a regular customer (make repeat purchases)

If your perspective is clear and you're feeling especially creative, you may be able to strengthen your offer right at this point by combining two objectives:

- Instead of one purchase, how about adding something to motivate repeat purchases. ("A $5 credit coupon comes with your purchase to apply to future purchases!")

- Instead of just an inquiry or a trial offer, perhaps you could combine the two. ("Send me the gidget widget for 30 days' free examination under your unconditional guarantee," or, "Send me more information on your new gidget widget.")

Caveat—this offer combination deals with *objectives* only and must be kept to the original product or service. To attempt to sell two or more additional items at the same time will hurt your original offer objective.

SELECTING AN OFFER

If you have your druthers—and who knows, you *should* be called in to help develop the offer—what kind of prospecting offer should you favor? (Yes, there is one right answer!)

If you said "Free," or "Premium" offer, you are right! (Remember, some top copywriters won't take on a highly competitive product without a freemium/premium.) Even if you don't have a premium, there are still opportunities to capitalize on "Free" (see below). Of the seven broad offer categories described here, the premium ranks number one in testing to acquire new customers.

1. *The Offer with Premium:* A premium can do wonders for a lackluster offer; use it to motivate response to trial offers, to increase order size in mail order, or to generate inquiries and sales leads.

There are three big caveats, however: First, if the premium overshadows the product or service, you may get a lot of takers but few stickers. Premiums do build response (they can even double it), but often the new customers are only bargain hunters who fall away quickly. Second, premiums are habit-forming. There's a saying, "Premium sold means premium renewed" in future promotions. Once you've started, your customers logically come to expect it every time you go back to them. Third, premiums must be tested if they're not highly-related "paper" products. Stories are legion of sales *lost* solely because the prospect didn't want or like the premium!

For example, the business premium in Figure 3–7, an executive desk set, is a prime example. Worse still, it was shown on the outer envelope so the prospect could make an instant decision ("Yuk!") and toss it without ever opening the envelope. A BIG no-no!

To avoid forming bad habits in consumer and business-to-business direct response, try to encourage selection or development of a premium that is closely related to the product or service you are promoting. Some of the best premiums are booklets, videocassettes,

FIGURE 3–7   Toshiba: A Premium Offer That May Have Lost Sales

CD-ROMs, demonstrations, or surveys that directly relate to the product or service and, therefore, help you by qualifying respondents and reinforcing the need for your product or service.

In business it may also be something that can be used in the office or at home, such as a tape recorder, a calculator, or a portable phone. Consumer premiums can cover a wide range of products including mystery gifts, which always seem to have appeal.

Note: With "bill me" terms, expensive premiums are often sent out only when the invoice is paid; low-budget, highly related premiums most often go out with the product or service before payment for the order is requested.

Do not overpromote the premium at the expense of your main product's selling story. The premium belongs *with* the offer, every time the offer is stated. It is *not* the offer.

2. *Introductory Offers:* These can be trial offers or sample offers— or one-time joining offers, and can often utilize the powerful "free" ("Free Trial," "Free Preview").

a. *The Charter Offer:* If you're launching a new magazine, newsletter, or other subscription publication be sure to structure a charter offer. Subscribers signing on during the early months of the publication will be called Charter Subscribers, entitled to the lowest going rates (in perpetuity), first word, and best price on new projects and publications for as long as their subscriptions continue without interruption. This may not sound like much to you, but this offer alone can make a full one percent difference in response. Charter offers have an unceasing appeal—so far.

b. *Trial, Preview, or Sample Offers:* Here's where you try to get your product into your prospects' hands at all costs, under the assumption that they will be pleased and impressed enough to purchase. Trial offers usually have low prices or (in the case of subscriptions) a shorter term or subscription period and low price.

With 100 percent money-back guarantees, there is less and less sampling these days, except with magazines that have a "first issue free" offer. This has been the most productive offer for publishers despite its drawbacks. Such free sampling offers tend to generate at least 30 percent to 50 percent more response than regular offers when the "free" is heavily promoted; they also generate nearly the same percentage of additional bad pay or "cancels." It pays to test.

Newsletters can be promoted by sending out several sample issues; it's an inexpensive way to get the product into the hands of the prospect. Some smart promoters shy away from this, however, as few specific issue samples can live up to the broader promises of the promotion regarding the overall subscription.

3. *Club and Continuity Plans:* Book and record clubs and collectors' groups have joining offers that require significant commitment. Some of them ship product automatically every month or so until you cancel ("Til Forbid"); sometimes the purchase of one book "entitles" the customer to preview future books without obligation; others ship unless you tell them not to ("Negative Option"); and still others ship only when you say "yes" ("Positive Option"). These are offers you won't be able to change, as they are carefully tested and even more carefully worded—often by the legal staff. You can police them for clarity, however, as they do tend to run on. When premiums are used (which is often, with such joining offers), you can shine with your contribution.

4. *Sale or Discount Offers:* Here are the good, old-fashioned savings promotions, based on the notion that all the world loves a bargain (save $50, 30 percent off, all products on this page reduced 25 percent, use this coupon to get $10 off any product, etc.).

It's common practice to have regular sales for mail order customers when there's a reason—time of year, specific holiday, anniversary, back-to-school sale, or warehouse clearance. These sales work if there's an established retail price against which the sale price is compared, and you can often do some nice footwork on price comparisons.

Consider this offer for a monthly magazine that sells for $3.50 on the newsstands: "Your Price, only $17.50 for one year!" This can be compared with the newsstand cost (12 Issues, $42.00) and the regular subscription price (12 issues, $35.00). "Your price is half the regular subscription price!"

There's really a lot you can do with your offer when you apply a little testing and creativity to the basic bargain or sale statement. For example: One large publisher found that $1.50 payable monthly was a more appealing offer than $18.00 a year and that 12 issues for 99 cents per issue was more effective than 12 issues for $11.97. The new price was only a few cents cheaper but response increased 10 percent!

See what you can do with this sales challenge: Let's say you're selling wigs (yes, wigs) and you are able to give $15 off on any one or all of three popular wigs that ordinarily retail for $45 each.

How many promotional offers can you come up with here? *Answer:*

a. One-third off on any of these wigs

b. Save up to $45 (buy three at one-third off each)

c. Buy two wigs and get a third wig FREE!

d. Get a graduated discount on the wigs that lets you *save more* the more you buy *plus* get a FREE wig brush with each purchase of two wigs or more.

Which of these offers are the stronger and why? The two strongest offers are "c," because it has the magic word, "free," and "d" because it has the magic word *plus* a premium and discounts.

Can you come up with another offer enhancement here? "Who needs more than one wig?" you may wonder. No one, probably, until you put a "limited" in the offer. And so you have: "Purchase Limited—only 2 to a customer!" And up goes response.

Also, in case you wondered how we got the wig brush premium offer squeezed in here (a highly related premium), we did it by daring to ask "If $15 off is feasible, why not lessen the discount a bit with a graduated discount and spend a little on a good premium for an offer that has both discount and premium?" Be inventive!

If you've got a good price story, feature it, and feature it creatively. Embellish it with guarantees and a premium where you can. Use the magic word "free." Make comparisons. State your savings in different ways. "Limit" your product. Add a deadline. Dramatize a significant savings with a big, ritzy "savings coupon." And keep with it! Your offer is getting stronger at every step.

Your price—how a penny can make the difference! A word about numbers here: Most direct marketers (and magazine publishers in particular) find that

- There are price breaks above which there is real consumer resistance.

Good	Not Good
$9.99	$10.00
$49.99	$50.00
$99.99	$100.00

- Odd numbers are more credible than even.

Good	Not Good
$7.97	$7.90
$2.77	$2.80
$5.59	$5.50

To carry this even further, many publishers believe in "the law of the seven." That is, prices that end in 7 (and, if possible, also have another 7 in the first or second number) get a greater response than simple odd number pricing. For example, $7.97 is stronger than $7.99! None of this is conjecture—it is the result of years of repeated testing.

Here's another tested shaker: One top tester found that on installment payments "three for $7.98 each" tested better than "three for $7.32 each." The customer didn't notice a difference, but the total selling price increased almost $2.00! (Try this net gain on 150,000 sales.)

You have been carried outside your area of required expertise at this point only so you can throw in a 99¢ or a 97¢ now and then, when you have the opportunity. You may even help your client or employer make a small fortune on pocket change! Most good direct marketers (and fortune tellers) already understand all about this.

5. *Sweepstakes Offers:* Advocates of sweepstakes claim they can raise order response up to 100 percent. Maybe so, but the power of the sweepstakes is so strong, that I marvel anyone remembers what they've ordered after they respond, other than a chance at a dream.

Whatever your R.Q. (Renaissance Quotient) on sweepstakes, here are a few important offer aspects to remember.

- A sweepstakes is a form of an *offer*.

- This offer has two parts: the sweepstakes is the overpowering one, and then there's your basic product or service offer, which is really what it's all about.

- You probably know (by virtue of pure bombardment) that you "need not order anything to win." That's a fact in every legal sweepstakes. Yet people *will* order anyway just to be safe. To encourage this, some sweepstakes have two reply envelopes—one for orderers and another for nonorderers. The entry-with-order is hyped on the reply form and made to look more official (as though it has a better chance to win). This sort of thing obviously contributes to the belief that it's necessary to order (even though the small print says it is not).

- Although you cannot legally combine the sweeps offer and your main offer, see if you can get your prospect to combine the two mentally in ways other than "fear of not winning." For example, lobby to get a sweepstakes that is themed to tie in with your product, or that has product-related prizes. Or, you might try for a sweepstakes name that incorporates the name of your product or service or its theme. In addition, fight hard to keep enough space in the sweepstakes package to present and sell your product or service properly.

6. *The Inquiry Offer:* This is most common in business-to-business direct mail, although it has been used for unusually large-ticket consumer purchases and services such as homes, cars, loans, and financial planning assistance.

The objectives here are to prequalify the prospect (a) for a sales call or visit, (b) for a more elaborate promotional mailing, or (c) for a prospect visit to a showroom, office, or plant. It is often called a two-step promotion, as it works to make sure that only the strongest, best qualified prospects receive step two: an expensive direct mail promotion or an equally expensive sales call or visit.

All steps should be carefully thought through by the time you get involved, but this is a good place for you to apply the Basic Law to the inquiry and be sure the progression will make sense to the customer or prospect.

For example:

- Be sure to include a toll-free 800 telephone option.

- Use price and other terms solely as a qualifier in the first step (the offer itself comes in at step two).

- To discourage unqualified "voyeurs" you might also want to build in some qualifiers such as requesting "title, company name and address, function, and SIC code," or asking for a dollar or two to cover postage, etc.

7. *Fund Raising:* Fund raising offers are a breed apart. The prospect benefit is a good feeling, based on responding to a perceived need—whether to aid starving children or rainforests or a politician who will "save" the people. Ostensibly, people contribute for altruistic reasons, expecting no tangible reward. (The underlying reason for political contributions is good government.)

There are several things to remember when you formulate a fund-raising offer:

1. People must perceive a clear and imminent need to give—a strong reason to contribute *now.*

2. They must be encouraged to "give all they can," while being told that "no amount is too small."

3. Prospects need to be told *how* to contribute and *what their contribution will do* as well. (Here—and only here—choice can be a plus. In some cases, established levels of giving are absolutely necessary. Rather than create inertia via indecision, several choices can encourage response. A choice can also be encouraged by graphically encircling the contribution "needed.")

4. Today, many nonprofit groups use "membership" and "membership benefits" (a newsletter or magazine) as well as related premiums or token gifts for contributors (bumper stickers, tote bags) as discussed earlier in this chapter.

Look over the seven offer types for a minute. How about combining them? A lot of direct marketers do all the time. Try to combine two or even three if you can. For example:

- A business inquiry solicitation with a premium
- A straight purchase offer with option for more information
- A charter offer and a free sample issue
- A club offer with a discount or savings offer
- A fund-raising offer with membership and a premium

This gives you more opportunities for strengthening your offer. Compelling offer structuring can't be passed off lightly.

COMBINING YOUR OFFER WITH MOTIVATORS AND INVOLVEMENT DEVICES

Look how far you've come already.

- You have an offer that is clear and easy to understand.
- You have defined objectives and have developed an offer with more than one objective.
- You have an offer that combines other offers for strength (premium offer, joining offer, sale or discount, inquiry).
- You have credibility with a strong guarantee.
- You have attractive financial terms.
- You use numbers and price comparisons promotionally.

Now use your creative tools—the motivators and involvement devices! Here's where you hark back to the basics of involvement and motivation.

Fear of losing out:

- Offer deadlines (limited-time offer for enrollment or membership)

- Limited supply

Pure fun of involvement (devices that let the prospect participate):

- Tokens to insert
- Labels or seals to peel off
- Stamps to lick and paste
- Colors to choose
- Boxes to check
- Panels to scratch
- Space to initial
- Perforations to tear

A FEW SECRETS ON DRAMATIZING YOUR OFFER

Don't forget your designer here. In addition to an important-looking order form, graphic dramatizations with a savings coupon, a "FREE" or a "YES" peel off—all help strengthen your offer. Even the way a token is used. For example: try a win-win offer (if yours has a choice of price, prize, or term). Make both responses "Yes" so the customer wins wherever the customer puts the token. (See Figure 3–8.) Or take a $20.00 savings on an introductory offer and put it on a separate "value" certificate that's personalized and includes a certificate number and cut-off date. Omaha Steaks has been doing this successfully for over 5 years. (See Figure 3–9.)

Have fun, but please remember to use caution on choices. Moving a "yes" or "free" token is one thing. Asking your prospect to decide between three alternatives is quite another. Play it safe! Test!

You have now covered the Four Key Sales Guidelines, as well as the Basic Law and its premises, and I hope you've noticed how they interrelate and overlay. To have a strong offer, for example, you need credibility, involvement, and motivation. You can't have motivation without involvement. You won't get involvement without establishing credibility. And you won't have any of this, of course, without the Basic Law: Make sense to the customer.

Now, on to the specific direct mail guidelines!

Notes

1. Martin Baier, *Elements of Direct Marketing* (New York: McGraw-Hill, 1983), p. 306.
2. Ibid., p. 308.

FIGURE 3–8 *Forbes:* **A Win-Win Response Device**

FIGURE 3–9 **A Personalized "Value" Certificate**

DIRECT MAIL: HOW THE PROS DO IT

Once you get involved and start testing and learning with professionals—you won't want it to end. Rules and guidelines are always changing or being modified as times and people change. This is exciting stuff, and vitally important to you as a creative person.

For example, top writers use wonderful secrets and tricks to get the direct mail envelope opened. And much, much more, my friend. You're going to learn *why* people open envelopes and *how* envelopes are perceived—as well as all the tools you need to create a winning direct mail package on your own.

This chapter tells you how to develop envelopes, letters, and brochures—things that haven't been adequately covered before. Maybe no one considered that writers need to know these things— maybe they assumed you'd pick them up on your own. One thing is certain, however—knowing these techniques and understanding the how and why of them puts you ahead of the pack in creating successful direct mail promotions.

Why Start with Direct Mail?

Why not start with electronic interactive selling—isn't it more glamorous, more fun? Or broadcast? Or print ads? Why mail?

If you feel that way, even a little, I'm going to do all in my power to prove to you that direct mail is every bit as exciting . . . far more complicated and more challenging and more fun than any other medium in the world!

Starting anywhere else is like building a house without a foundation . . . jumping without a parachute or high diving when you can't swim (not only dumb, but impossible to conceive). You're right, I feel strongly about this, because quite simply, direct mail is the learning ground that unlocks all the creative secrets.

- It embodies the majority of all direct response technique—all the formulas and nearly all the rules.

- It is not confining—not limited to 60 seconds of air time or an 8" × 10" page.

- Its format is flexible—a letter, a postcard, a folder—even a box.

- It is a pure one-on-one communication—the only other medium that can make this claim at present is the telephone, and its cost and flexibility can't compare with direct mail.

- It is discreet and highly efficient because of its precise ability to target its market, and it is therefore the most effective medium for serious testing.

- The direct mail letter itself is a true test for the direct response writer. It initiates dialogue with the prospect; it maintains dialogue with the customer.

So when we talk about rules, we're going to concentrate on direct mail first. The big rules that apply to all direct response marketing are best represented here. The specific rules for other media will fall easily into place in later chapters.

Guideline 1: Get the Envelope Opened

In a way, *get the envelope opened* is the first creative rule of direct mail, for obvious reasons. If the outer envelope doesn't get opened, nothing else matters much. (Notice that we call the envelope the "outer" envelope, because there's often an "inner" envelope or Business Reply Envelope, or BRE. The BRE is generally a postpaid envelope used to return an order form or an order card that doesn't carry return postage. A card that has a postpaid side is a BRC or Business Reply Card. See Chapter 3.)

The outer envelope may prove to be your greatest challenge, because no matter how carefully you plan, one small detail can make a big difference. Sometimes it's the paper stock . . . sometimes the size of the envelope or the type . . . sometimes it's the use of color . . . sometimes it's *one word* in the teaser copy or the promise . . . sometimes it's what I call "mailbox ennui"—just too much stuff for your prospect to assimilate.

I have polled literally hundreds of professionals regarding effective envelopes over the years, and the constant disagreement over successful envelopes still amazes me. Many direct marketers have trouble spotting or understanding winners and losers! Perhaps we're too close and too analytical. Certainly most envelopes take a chance—and you do, too, until you can distinguish between the winners and the losers.

To get your outer envelopes (or folders, self-mailers, or boxes) opened, it's important to consider what makes people open some envelopes, and throw others away. Today's mailboxes are crowded with envelopes competing for your prospect's dollar.

First, your envelope must *gain attention*. What will make it stand out? You can certainly get attention with an oversized envelope in bright colors. Because of the postage surcharges on these jumbo outers, fewer people are using them right now, so it's a good time to test. But size and color are not enough—many of your prospects have had their fill of big, bright envelopes. Your real job is to create positive involvement—fast (see Chapter 3, Guideline 2), and to do that, you'll have to do one of two things: your envelope will get opened 1) if it gains immediate positive recognition or 2) if it arouses significant curiosity.

GAIN IMMEDIATE RECOGNITION

First, it is important that you understand both the positive and negative aspects of recognition. For example, all of the following statements indicate recognition, but the recognition is positive in some cases and negative in others:

"Wow, a check from Dad!" (Positive)

"A letter from my wife!" (Positive)

"A new offer from my favorite book club!" (Positive)

"The phone bill." (Sort of positive)

"Ugh. Who needs an encyclopedia?" (Negative)

"No need to bother the boss with this kind of mail." (Negative)

In some cases corporate recognition is a plus: 1) when the prospect is already a customer (This is a rule—use it!), 2) when the company is well known and respected—it has credibility, and 3) when the envelope itself is fully personalized, carries first-class postage, and looks very important. (This is the best way to do business-to-business mail, if you can afford it.)

You can see that recognition has its good and bad sides, however. Negative recognition may cause your package to be discarded. Imagine Sam and his suit company from Chapter 3. Printing "Sam's Suit Company" on the outer envelope would allow a prospect to make an immediate decision without opening the envelope. The customer might think, "I don't know who Sam is and I don't want a suit!" . . . Toss! This is a big no-no.

And here's where direct marketers go crazy. They use all sorts of involvement devices and disguises to prevent such negative recognition.

Since you may have few opportunities to bask in the unqualified positive recognition of "Wow, a check from Dad!" you'll want to concentrate on the second strong form of involvement, curiosity.

You have lots of possibilities when trying to get positive recognition. Some of the tried-and-true old standards follow.

AROUSE SIGNIFICANT CURIOSITY

The Important Envelope. A disguise technique used in business when recognition may have a negative effect is the important envelope. The goal is to make the envelope look impressive or important enough to get by the mailroom, or whoever screens the prospect's mail, by averting negative recognition and arousing curiosity. ("Hmm, looks important. Looks first class. Maybe I'd better keep it for the boss.")

The Envelope That Carries a Promise. In consumer and business direct mail, perhaps the most popular way to arouse curiosity is to make a strong promise. A promise on your outer envelope can be as simple as "You are invited . . ." or as complex as "Respond to this special 50% off introductory offer by April 30th and get a FREE Gift." You can set down one big benefit, "How to regain the vitality of youth . . . see inside" or lay out the three basics of your package right on the outer envelope:

"A Special FREE gift offer (offer)
that can bring you (involvement)
the vitality of youth (big benefit)
—from the world-reknowned Smith Company" (credibility).

As sophisticated as we all are about direct mail, the promise of something free is almost always the best bet, however you use it. Remember, *premium on the inside rates a FREE on the outer.* So if you have it, flaunt it.

The Questioning or Challenging Envelope. You can hook the curious by asking a question ("Hard boiled eggs, bedroom slippers, and oil tankers. How are they going to affect your income? See inside.") or by making a challenging statement ("Only one person in four will qualify for this opportunity. See inside.").

The Tell-It-All Envelope. This one pulls no punches. It immediately states exactly what's inside. Just by opening it, the recipient becomes a qualified prospect. In many cases, particularly business-to-business, this can ensure that it gets to the right person and gets opened. But a word of warning: Make sure first that it's a killer of an offer, something so strong no qualified prospect could refuse. Or they just may refuse to open the outer at all because of negative recognition.

The Mysterious Envelope. In consumer advertising when third-class postage is used, or when the name of the company is not well known or known at all, you may want to consider developing an outer envelope that teases the recipient, that uses copy and/or art and format to tickle the imagination and arouse curiosity without a direct promise of any kind.

This might be an envelope with a distinctive look and a simple return address with a very well-known name. ("Now, why is Harvard writing me?") Or you might start an exciting story on your outer, to be finished inside. Or state simply, "The favor of your reply is requested," leaving the prospect to wonder what kind of invitation might be enclosed. Or put one large, attention-getting word in two-inch letters across the entire envelope.

The Blind Envelope. The ultimate teaser is something called a blind envelope. It is called "blind" because it carries virtually no identification. ("What—who might this be?")

Use it very carefully for blind envelopes sort of cheat. They try to involve the prospect without qualifying him or her (For example, "If you are a gardener," qualifies the prospect) and without setting down a promise (such as "A free book offer . . . "). Blind envelopes therefore run the risk of disappointing, or even irritating your prospects. ("You jerks—you tricked me into opening this!") On the other hand, I must tell you that *blind envelopes do work.* So by all means, don't hesitate to test them.

Aside from making copy promises and sending out teasers, you also arouse curiosity by the way you use envelope format, paper and color, personalization, and postage.

Let's stop a minute. I've slipped in some involvement tools on you. We've been building a pyramid from top down and it goes something like this.

Effective envelopes
get attention (AIDA)
via involvement (Key Guideline 2)
through recognition or curiosity/promises
using copy/format/personalization/postage/art/die cuts/folds/
perforations/distinctive stock.

By now you're no doubt getting a good idea why recognition is *not* the key route for you as a direct marketer. Not always, anyway.

CONSIDER MORE THAN
PURE COPY

Positive recognition, you'll remember, is most often given to the pure personal letter, hand-addressed on pale blue stock or hand-typed on a fine white #10 business envelope—both with a first-class stamp. Of course, in business, it's also a corner card that identifies a company or professional firm with whom we already do business. There's no fighting in the mailbox among these fine aristocrats.

Your challenge falls outside this sacred arena among all those other outer envelopes hustling and scrounging—and sometimes even cheating—for attention. Get that envelope opened!

In business-to-business competition you must rise with dignity and importance above the rubble and get past the guardian at the gate, be it mailroom clerk or secretary, nurse or assistant—and you'll need more than pure copy to do it.

In consumer competition you must shout when the others whisper, whisper when the others shout—and out-guess them all with a shining, deathless, delightfully compelling appeal that cannot—just cannot—go unopened. Again, it is much more than just copy.

As a copywriter you must understand how to use three tools creatively to arouse curiosity: format, personalization, and postage.

Format. Envelopes come in all different sizes but due to U.S. Postal Service regulations and budgetary limitations, much of your work in third-class mail may be confined to only three or four sizes: the #10 envelope (4 1/8" × 9 l/2"), the 6" × 9", the 6 1/4" × 11 1/2" and the jumbo envelope (9" × 12"). The jumbo is my favorite because it always seems to work—so far. But it is costly, so careful testing and alternative size tests are recommended when you try it.

If you're not on a budget and can travel first class, you are free to choose from small envelopes (minimum size, according to USPS, is 3 1/2" × 5") to a monarch (3 7/8" × 7 1/2") up to the jumbo, and all variations in between. (Permissible maximum envelope sizes vary somewhat between first-class and third-class mail.)

But remember, third class allows you nearly 3 ounces for its lowest price, first class gives you only *one* ounce. That's not enough paper for a full sales story!

A business-to-business envelope should look important and businesslike. That doesn't mean, however, that it can't go to a jumbo size or use a colored or kraft stock.

To attract attention with your consumer-directed outer, you'll also want to consider colored stock and die cuts (or windows) in your envelope that show graphics from the brochure or a token from the order card. Or you may want a four-color drawing or photograph right on the outer. Or, if everyone else in the mailbox is shouting, you may want to whisper with a plain white envelope and just one or two strong words in heavy type. (They'd better be strong, though.)

Other packaging devices you could choose include all-plastic envelopes or polybags (which many mailers have stopped using due to ecological considerations) and snap packs—envelopes with "tear here" flaps that pull down to open "windows." Some envelopes even self-destruct. This is where copy, art, and production come together to determine what can be done and how far you can go within the budget.

But remember—all of these choices are your *tools*. They are a means to an end. You have a story to tell. It starts on the outer envelope. You must make sure that the tools work for you to tease or start your story and *get the envelope opened*.

Addressing and Personalization on the Outer Envelope. The least effective form of addressing is a label addressed to "Occupant" or "Boxholder," stuck on the outside of an envelope. The *most* effective form for direct marketers is a hand-typed or laser-printed address (three or four lines) to the individual with a full title (Ms., Mrs., Mr., Dr., and so on).

Every other form of addressing falls in between, as will most of your work. Budget and production will again largely determine which end of the spectrum you work in, but here are some things to remember:

Few direct marketers can afford the luxury of hand-typed (word processed) outers (unless you have a very classy, big-ticket promotion).

Response is always stronger if the order form goes out already filled in with the prospect's name and address. (Remember "Offer" in Chapter 3.) Computer-personalized reply forms are a popular way to do this. Computerized labels or printout name-and-address strips are affixed to the form or, of course, you can laser right to the form. The name and address then show through a "window" (or die cut) on the outer envelope. This enables the mailer to use one address form instead of double-addressing (on both the order card and outer envelope). This is particularly popular with low-budget jobs and test mailings where rented names are set up on computer tape, presorted in Zip sequence for mail delivery, and affixed to order cards in sequence.

More and more frequently, however, outer envelopes, order cards, letters, and even business reply envelopes can all be economically computerized within one package. As it becomes less expensive, good computer personalization will be used more and more, so it's important for you to understand it and to understand that there are times to use it extensively and times to use it sparingly. The least you should expect today (if your envelope is to do its job), is addressing to the card or reply form with a window outer.

Postage. To understand postage, you have to understand a little of the economics of postage. After all, postage can take up 30 percent or more of your total direct mail budget! If you have a high R.Q., check the Direct Marketing Association's *Statistical Fact Book*.[1] Here are three major points to remember:

- First class is just about double the cost of third class postage. (You get certain discounts for presorting or separating your mail when you mail in quantities in both groups.)

- First class with its much higher cost is priced by the ounce, while third class allows you over three ounces right up front at its much lower rate. (One ounce of first class is more than double the cost of three ounces of third class.) By the time you read this, of course, things may have changed, but with all the recent postal increases the relationship between first and third class has remained relatively constant.

- At some point you pay the piper for those third-class advantages, however. Third class mail gets third-class travel. It is segregated from first class; it seldom rides as well and, most important, it travels like a snail—and unevenly. Sometimes it's slow; usually it's slower; often it's slowest. And it's hard to predict. A third-class letter can go from Long Island, New York, to San Francisco in 6 days or 16 (and sometimes a lot more). Sometimes, too, third-class mail is misplaced or deliberately "lost."

People notice postage. A standard #10 envelope with a first-class stamp has a better chance of getting opened than does a standard #10 with a third-class indicia (or preprinted permit with postal number). And it gets there faster and more surely. However, a precancelled third-class stamp has a pretty fair chance against the first-class stamp on a white envelope. It's worth a test.

In consumer communications, where third-class is popular because of the savings, you have to learn to use it well. The plain #10 envelope with a third-class indicia doesn't stand much chance against a 9" × 12" jumbo envelope with the same indicia plus four-color photography and strong involvement copy.

If you are clearly promotional—don't just sit there. Use promotional tools to create involvement and stimulate curiosity, teasing the prospect into opening the envelope.

In consumer direct mail, a first-class letter can be effective and is worth testing if it fits the budget and the product's image *and* if the message is short. To use first-class postage on an envelope that is obviously and blatantly promotional is a waste of money.

Because business-to-business mail is usually screened, as I've said your objective is to create something that the screener will be afraid to throw away or decline to throw away because of its implied value. Postage helps. However, since Pitney Bowes' first-class metered mail looks very much like its third-class cousin, the difference narrows. Secretaries and mail rooms don't or can't read the meter carefully. This is well worth testing.

The advantages of first-class and third-class postage are continually being argued. This is an area where you must test unless your market and product clearly require one or the other. (Mass appeal products that drop millions of pieces of mail at a time always mail third-class because of the immense savings.)

When considering postage in relation to format, it's smart to apply the Basic Law. "What will make sense to your prospects or customers?" What will look "right" or logical or interesting to them? For example: If you must use third-class postage (and most of us must), try a Pitney-Bowes meter for a serious, businesslike approach and use a preprinted indicia for a clear consumer promotion with color art and pizazz and/or a big copy teaser on your outer.

If you can justify first-class postage—and if you're blessed with a stamp—keep your outer envelope pure and pristine with only a return address and possibly a "faux" hand-typed name above that. If it's first-class Pitney-Bowes, you might want to call attention to it by stating something "official" like "First-Class Mail" on the envelope itself. It may sound corny, but it helps.

The outer envelope should always be in keeping with the tone and appearance of the direct mail package as a whole. If your market is sophisticated and your product is high-brow, your message and the format that carries it should be sophisticated. (Remember the Basic Law.)

A small change in your envelope can and will affect your entire mailing. So, go carefully here; *test that outer and any changes.* And, please, don't try to be cute or clever or funny on your outer—not until you're very, very good. Spend a lot of time. Think it through and never cheat by promising something outside that you don't carry through on the inside.

This is a lot of envelope business to digest all at one sitting, but here's something that can help you. Every day when you collect your mail, before you open the envelopes, test them out. Set aside the ones you open on pure recognition (bills, letters from friends and family). Then look at the rest and rate them.

First, knee-jerk-evaluate them on pure appeal. The envelope stopped you . . . it intrigued you . . . it said "open me" . . . it said "toss me." *Now* analyze your feelings. Why did you respond as you did? What about the envelope made you feel the way you felt? What did it do to catch your attention? How did it succeed (or fail) in involving you through copy promises, teasers, and involvement devices? Now open it up. Look at the offer. Was the outer honest? Could you have devised a stronger outer?

After a week or so, this evaluation process becomes automatic and very valuable, because you're applying and learning and remembering—and getting some good ideas for future use while you're about it.

Now before you move on from the envelope to the letter, let's look at some winning outer envelopes.

SOME WINNING ENVELOPES   ***The Curiosity Arousers.*** The first two examples in Figure 4–1 are all-time winners and still going. And the other two proved irresistible in their own right. (Admit it, you'd certainly open them!)

FIGURE 4–1   Four Curiosity-Arousing Outer Envelopes (Condé Nast, Colonial Williamsburg Foundation, Brooklyn Botanic Gardens, *Mother Jones*)

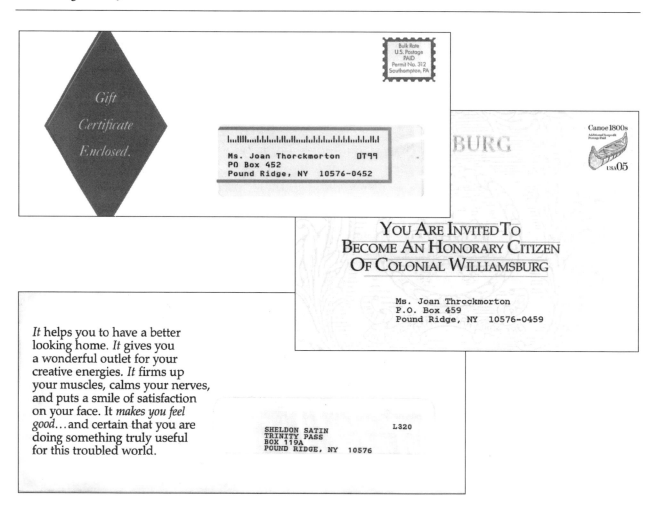

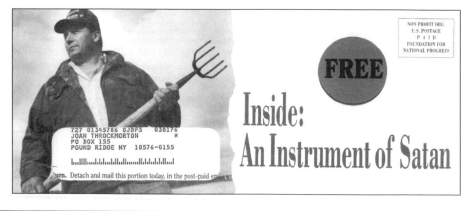

The Office Curiosity Arouser and the Totally Personal. In certain kinds of office situations, the "routing" envelope in Figure 4–2 insists on being opened. The second envelope in Figure 4–2 is totally personal; it looks hand-typed or word processed, and it has a stamp and no further identification. This will get opened in *every* situation, business and consumer.

FIGURE 4–2   Two Envelopes That Are Sure to Be Opened (*Direct Marketing Market Place* and Georgetown Publishing House)

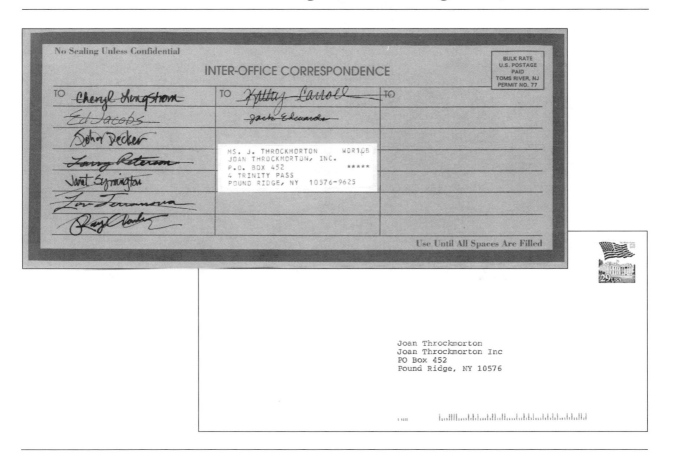

The Dual-Purpose Involver. The ingenious solution shown in Figure 4–3, a dual-purpose involver, is ideal when you have limited funds and two products for a similar market, such as horse lovers.

The Wild Question Catcher. The big and brassy (9" × 12") and "blind" outer shown in Figure 4–4 does three things right: It raises curiosity with a question bound to create interest. (How will they get out of *that* one?) It offers the involvement of peel-offs, "Yes. No. Maybe." And it states, "The favor of your reply is requested"—a proven response helper.

FIGURE 4-3   A Dual-Purpose Involver (*Practical Horseman* and *Performance Horseman*)

FREE/RSVP

If you ride English-style, open this envelope. (Otherwise, see other side.)

FREE/RSVP

If you ride Western-style, open this envelope. (Otherwise, see other side.)

FIGURE 4-4   A Wild Question Catcher

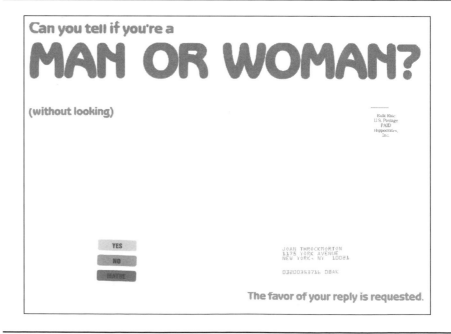

Can you tell if you're a

MAN OR WOMAN?

(without looking)

YES
NO
MAYBE

Bulk Rate
U.S. Postage
PAID
Hippocrates,
Inc.

JOAN THROCKMORTON
1175 YORK AVENUE
NEW YORK, NY   10021

The favor of your reply is requested.

FIGURE 4–5 *Bottom Line:* **An Envelope Change That Restored a Control**

A Simple Envelope Change That Can Restore a Control. The top envelope in Figure 4–5 ran many years as the outer for the control. When this winning package began to wear out and lose its "pull," the second envelope took over and gave the package over four more years of life. This also works in solid-color outers; a new color alone can restore the package's pull.

Guideline 2: Use the Voice of the Logical Spokesperson

Remember that one of the first guidelines for your creative efforts is credibility. I talked about using the most credible spokesperson. Hand in hand with credibility goes *tone* or voice—or., you might say, establishing the "voice of the logical spokesperson."

Not everyone in our business does this well, and some don't even bother. Their letters are signed simply J. Smith for X magazine or B. Jones for Y company.

If you really believe in direct response as dialogue marketing, however, you simply can't support such bland anonymity. Every

direct mail letter should come from *someone* (even a pseudo someone), the person who, in the customer's mind, is logically suited to
make the offer.

What's more, you, as the writer, will find it much easier to
develop your dialogue *if you know who you are.* Imagine being
shoved out in front of an audience to make a spontaneous presentation on a new product without knowing who you are supposed to
represent. (Manufacturer, inventor, salesperson, user—what's your
point of view?) A salesperson does not present like an inventor or
sound like a consumer. Your tone in presentation will be largely
determined by the kind of person you are speaking for and by the
prospect audience to whom you are speaking.

To determine who you are, first define your audience. You'll
want to know what kind of individuals, what kind of families make
up your market. In the case of business-to-business markets, for
example, you could be addressing two or even three levels of decision makers. You don't want to talk to the corporate division head or
president in the same tone as the purchasing manager or chief engineer, so you might want to use a different executive as your
spokesperson to represent the company *at each level.* You must
check out the audience—you've done your research, of course (see
Chapter 2)—then select your logical spokesperson or persons.

Once you decide who you are, develop that individual's point of
view and stick with it. Sound the same throughout the letter. (If you
start off like Don Imus, don't end up like Deepak Chopra.) *Sound
the way your readers think you should sound.*

For example: A business executive writing to other business men
and women will be serious and to the point; a doctor writing to "colleagues" will sound technical and authoritative; a sportswear and
camping catalog owner might sound like a friendly camper who
understands the outdoors; a cookbook author will sound like a person who enjoys good food and understands cooking methods; a
fashion designer will use the terms and jargon of flair and style when
describing clothes. And, interestingly, an editor or publisher of a
magazine should *sound like the magazine,* adopt the style of the
magazine, when he or she describes it.

What does this role playing do for you, the creative person? First,
it enables you to dramatize, to set up an imaginary dialogue in your
head before you even start writing. Act out your sale with your imaginary prospect. Empathize with your spokesperson. Now empathize
with one individual in the spokesperson's market. Back and forth.
One on one. *You're writing dialogue!*

There are many logical spokespersons—real people—who
have become legends in mail order, such as J. Peterman of The
J. Peterman Company, Lillian Vernon of Lillian Vernon, Amos
Pettingill of White Flower Farm, and Richard Thalheimer of Sharper
Image, to name a few.

You don't have to immortalize the boss, but you should know who you are speaking for if you're going for continuity with credibility. And if you're working for a small company—what's wrong with using the boss?

So get the envelope open and set the tone . . . and now let's do the letter.

Guideline 3: The Elements of a Successful Letter

You've now arrived at the center or heart of the direct mail package: the letter. You must first focus on getting the letter to the right market with the strongest offer coming first; then creativity kicks in.

Letters come in all shapes and sizes. A letter can be one paragraph, one page, four or eight pages. It can be a postcard, or a note, or an 8 1/2" × 11" page. You'll find letters in "packages" as well as part of all other direct mail formats from postcard to shipping carton. You'll find two-line letters and even ten-page letters. In some cases, you may find that all you need is two paragraphs or two sentences—for example, on a double postcard.

Whatever format it takes, *always include a letter.* This is important for you to understand, because a few Philistines who claim you don't always need a letter have crept into this business. Letters are important. *They start a dialogue.* They help establish a relationship. They increase response. Ignore them at your peril. The letter is the most important part of the package besides the outer envelope. (Because your outer envelope doesn't get opened, your letter will not be read.)

By the way, as you move ahead in direct response advertising you're going to hear a lot of negative comment about long letters. It generally goes like this: "No one reads a four-page letter." "Long letters are old-fashioned. Today's readers want a short, one-page message."

Don't believe it! The customer or prospect who's interested needs all the facts. You're a salesperson, remember. You have to present these facts and even if it takes eight pages, the true prospect or customer will stay with you happily, as long as you're telling a good story and presenting a case that appeals. (The only person you'll bore is the one who is clearly *not* your prospect.)

So how long should a letter be? *As long as necessary to get the story across.* Follow this rule, write a good tight letter, and anyone who says it's too long is either a Philistine, or no prospect for your product, or both. In keeping the letter tight, consider the product and market first. If it's a product for *doers* (and a market of doers) work to keep the letter as short as possible. If it's a product for *readers*, don't worry. Business letters, especially if they're inquiry seekers, can afford to be short and tight because the *message is short*—"Send for more information."

Some products or services naturally demand long letters; self-improvement programs or financial information services can regularly support letters up to *sixteen pages.*

Letter-writing, more than any other medium or media segment in direct response advertising, is loaded with rules. Sink-or-swim on the letter is unforgivable. You can't jump off the dock or wade to your ankles without getting tangled up in a network of guidelines.

Before we examine this network, let's review the basic elements of a successful letter by examining what the letter must accomplish—every time—all by itself. Again, it's important to remember that sometimes it does this in a few sentences and sometimes it takes eight pages.

All right. What does go into a letter? Your big benefits, your offer, your qualifications, other benefits, all the features, involvement devices, and motivation to respond all belong there.

Figure 4–6 shows a framework that relates the seven major elements of the letter to each other in descending order. The first four frames—the offer, major benefits, involvement, and credibility—are grouped together. You've already seen how three of the outer frames work together to create the initial impact of every piece of direct response advertising: *Offer for you—with benefits to you—equal involvement from you.*

FIGURE 4–6   The Framework for a Successful Letter

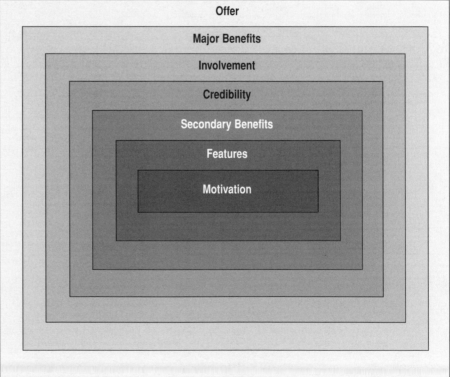

That's how you start to gain attention. But before you can say "free" or "50 percent off," credibility also comes in. (Who are you? What qualifies you to make this offer?) Credibility can even outdo the other three if it's offered in the form of a well-known corporate logotype on the letterhead.

What's more, offer, involvement, and benefits can all *precede* the letter, if you decide to put them on your outer envelope (see Chapter 4). When your prospect opens the envelope, the letter should immediately take over the same theme, embellish it with secondary benefits and features, then add motivation to act. Your letter must contain or complete the seven elements shown in Figure 4–6 in one form or another. That's your structure or formula.

Now how do you go about writing your letter? To begin with, no matter how long or short it is, your letter should *look like a letter*. It should have indented, short paragraphs, underlines, and marginal notes—a variety of visual devices to make it easy to read, spacious, and friendly. In other words, *it should be designed*.

You are not trying to fool your prospect into thinking you've typed a letter, by the way—you are flagging him or her that someone is speaking. You are producing a familiar, friendly format conducive to a one-on-one dialogue to which your prospect will relate. In these days of short attention spans and lazy eyes, you are also designing something the eye will love, cling to, return to over and over should it be interrupted or distracted. (You'll find an example of the right way to design a letter in Chapter 7.)

TEN STEPS TO A PROFESSIONAL LETTER

- Know where your offer goes in a four-page letter?
- Know what a Johnson box is and when to use one?
- Where do "nuts 'n' bolts" go?
- How about the P.S.?

In less than five minutes you will know the answers to these questions, and that will put you ahead of 50 percent of the striving direct response beginners.

Let's start on page one and work our way through a standard two-to-four-page letter.

1. Your offer *must* go on the first page and on the last page, near the end. If you bury your offer and big benefit, you lose your prospect right off the bat!

2. The offer can go in your letter copy, first paragraph, or in a Johnson box on page one. A *Johnson box* is a sentence or two preceding the salutation giving the high points of the offer. Originally it was centered on the page right under the letterhead and surrounded by a border of typed asterisks. The Johnson box was invented by a

great direct mail letterwriter, Frank (you guessed it) Johnson. Frank devised this "box" because he's a fine storyteller. He likes to start right off in the first paragraph of his letter and carry the reader along with a totally involving sales story. Frequently there is just no way to fit the offer in the first page without ruining a good story. The Johnson box is his compromise, to get the offer on the first page. It gives him flexibility and it works. And it's been working for others, in one form or another, ever since.

3. The first page should also have a letterhead and a salutation. (Sometimes the letterhead can be moved to the last page at the bottom, if you're using a big Johnson box, lots of lead-in copy, and/or a picture at the top of page one.) *Always* use a salutation. This is a letter. When you can't personalize here, many writers choose "Dear Reader" or "Dear Friend." "Dear Valued Customer" is always good for customers if you're not using full personalization. And often you can personalize to the prospect's job, profession, or hobby, depending on the lists you are using (Dear Architect, Dear Fellow Bird Lover, Dear Collector, Dear College Graduate). One salutation to women 18 to 34 years old went like this: "Dear Career Woman, Professional Person, Wife, Sweetheart, Mother, Economist, Gardener, Cook, Interior Designer, Chauffeur, Buyer of Most Consumer Goods—Friend." A salutation can be used to give recognition ("we know who you are") and to establish shared interests and respect (Dear Fellow Gardener, Dear Concerned Citizen).

In fact, even if you do have good personalization, some of these reader-friendly salutations are far more powerful in establishing a relationship than the cold, impersonal "Dear J. H. Throckmorton" or "Dear John Sample."

4. Your *very first paragraph* must grab your prospect by the eyelashes—and hold on! The first few lines of your letter will determine the success of the letter itself. Why? Because almost everyone starts reading there. You want to make sure their eyes continue from the first line through the first paragraph to the second and on.

5. Whether you use a Johnson box or not, don't end your first page with a period. Try to break your thought and entice the reader to turn the page. (You know what I mean: "She looked up fearfully and saw the curtain move. Suddenly . . . over please.")

6. Between the opening and the close of your letter (whether it's one page, two pages, four, or whatever) you'll be working your benefits, then adding all features and reinforcing credibility (if need be). And this can mean such things as a list of features, customer testimonials, descriptions with specific examples (specifics sell), and always "you," "you," "you."

7. Before closing, go back to your big benefit and major selling points once again, and tie them in with your original lead to frame your message.

8. In the wrap-up just before you close, state the full details of your offer. It's part of your call to action. In this section you should restate the offer, emphasize haste, and provide an easy way to respond. It is called "Nuts and Bolts."

9. If you use involvement devices, motivators, and incentives (premiums and deadlines in particular), be sure to bring them in up front *and* when you wrap up in Nuts and Bolts.

10. Please don't think that direct response copywriters are absent-minded just because many, if not most, good letters carry a P.S. It's just another rule or technique that always seems to work. *People read the P.S.*

Even when the first few lines of the letter itself can't hold on to the reader, the P.S. offers another chance. This makes it a good place to repeat an important selling point or to pop in a new or different benefit. The P.S. helps catch the reader's attention and once more *guide him or her back to the body of the letter.* I can't prove to you that it always works, but, like chicken soup—it can't hurt.

We have now covered the basics of letter-writing, but there'll be even more technical guidelines as we move along. Some important ones are included in the Exercises at the end of this chapter and at the end of Chapter 7. Remember, some of these guidelines and rules can be twisted or broken from time to time, but only if you're *very* good and already adept at using them!

EXCERPTS FROM THREE WINNING LETTERS

Figures 4–7 through 4–9 show some winning direct mail letters. In Figure 4–7, notice the Johnson box, the lead-in, and the short paragraphs. Read the copy and enjoy. Figure 4–8 shows a super successful, super-big 21" wide (open) and 17" deep letter. Notice the one-sentence paragraphs, salutation, and the offer illustrations with the Johnson box. Lots of take-outs, underlines, short copy, and an old-fashioned Johnson box made the letter in Figure 4–9 a *Smithsonian* winner.

Guideline 4: When and How to Use a Lift Letter

It's time for you to meet one of the most valuable friends you can have in developing a direct mail package—the lift letter. And it does just that; reliably, consistently, dependably it can "lift" response for you almost every time, if you use it correctly. Bless its heart.

We'll start with a word of history, because the lift letter has actually evolved over the years, and you'll find this helpful in understanding and using it.

Back in the 1960s, the Greystone Press, a company that handled mail order book sales, did a promotion that added a second, shorter letter to the other direct mail components. The second letter was

FIGURE 4–7 *Southern Living:* **A Winning Letter Using a Johnson Box, Lead-in, and Short Paragraphs**

GOOD NEWS! It's never too late to start! Now you can stop — perhaps reverse — the harmful effects of your family's high-fat eating habits. With mouthwatering, scrumptious recipes so good it's hard to believe they're good for you!

INTRODUCING

THE LOW-FAT WAY TO COOK

The Newest Cookbook from SOUTHERN LIVING BOOKS!

YOURS TO TRY FOR 30 DAYS FREE!

Dear Friend:

Are we alone? You and me?

I think it's best you keep what you're about to read away from your family -- at least for now ...

You'll have plenty of opportunities to break the news to them later.

Like after they've polished off your Beef Tenderloin au Poivre, Creamy Garlic Potatoes, and Minted English Peas.

Or perhaps while they're waiting for seconds of your Chocolate Layer Cake with Creamy Chocolate Frosting.

News? At some point you'll probably want to tell them that everything they've been ooooohing and aaaahing about has been low-fat, heart-healthy, and good for them!

Because -- here's the great part! -- if you don't tell them, they'll never suspect a thing!

(Come to think of it, maybe you don't ever have to tell them!)

over please ...

-- 2 --

Now, thanks to THE LOW-FAT WAY TO COOK -- you can have your cake and eat it, too!

Doctors have been telling us for years to "watch what we eat." "Everything in moderation." And "eat more fruits and vegetables."

But more recent evidence is straight to the point. And more frightening.

Now they tell us that while calories, sodium, and cholesterol are still worth watching -- the real enemy is fat!

Fat in our food not only makes us fat, it can lead to heart attacks, strokes, even cancer! And a high-fat dinner could put you at risk the very next morning!

The good news is that switching to a low-fat diet can help reverse clogged arteries and perhaps save your life! Even after just one meal!

And now, thanks to the dietitians and nutritionists at SOUTHERN LIVING BOOKS, you can make the switch to a low-fat diet and never miss a thing! The fat's out! The flavor's still in!

Now, you can learn the secrets of turning dangerous, high-fat favorites into luscious low-fat lifesavers! All in THE LOW-FAT WAY TO COOK!

Over 450 mouthwatering, kitchen-tested, can't-believe-they're-good-for-you surprises. Plus 30 great menus that put it all together!

All "yes-yes's" -- not a single "no-no!"

Here are out-of-this-world entrees like ...

Beef Burgundy. Garlic Flank Steak. Marinated London Broil. Roasted Rack of Lamb with Bordelaise Sauce.

Crispy Oven-Fried Chicken. Spicy Chicken Casserole. Chicken Cacciatore. Turkey Tetrazzini. Hearty Braised Quail.

Fantastic Fish like ...

Crabmeat Imperial. Shrimp Scampi. Oven-Fried Catfish. Snapper Veracruz. Blackened Amberjack.

Tangy Grouper Sandwiches. Salmon Croquettes with Mustard Sauce. Lobster Thermidor. Vegetable-Topped Flounder.

-- 3 --

And crowd-pleasing pastas like ...

Fettucine Primavera. Greek-style Cappellini. Vegetable Lasagna. Italian Rotini Casserole. Macaroni and Cheese.

Plus rices, soups, salads, sauces, breads, breakfasts, sandwiches, appetizers, and more!

Desserts, desserts, desserts!

Over 40 in all, like ...

Chocolate Swirl Cheesecake. Frosted Chocolate Brownies. Old-Fashioned Banana Pudding. Lemon Meringue Pie.

Summer Blackberry Cobbler. Creamy Vanilla-Almond Custard. Chocolate Cream Pie. Key Lime Cheesecake.

Creamy Vanilla Mousse with Blueberry Sauce. Grand Marnier Souffle with Bittersweet Chocolate Sauce. And more!

Wish you could? Well now you can!

With THE LOW-FAT WAY TO COOK, you can eat what you thought you couldn't. Enjoy what you thought was excess. And splurge on what used to be sinful! It's almost too good to be true!

Best of all, we've done your homework for you. So all you have to do is cook! Eat! And enjoy!

No searching the health stores for odd ingredients. You'll find what you need in your local grocery store.

No complicated conversions or measurements to calculate. You'll find complete nutritional information for every recipe!

Switching to low-fat eating couldn't be easier!

Every recipe tasted and tested so you can cook with confidence!

You never have to worry about how each recipe will go over. Because we've tried them all -- we guarantee they're great! So you can share these luscious low-fat lifesavers with family and friends knowing you'll win raves and compliments! And you can keep your low-fat secret to yourself!!

We'll show you how to add flavor the natural way, using fresh herbs and spices and flavorful vegetables to replace the fat.

over please ...

-- 4 --

Also in THE LOW-FAT WAY TO COOK -- informative, even vital, information about fat and its dangers, kitchen utensils that help you cook the low-fat way, preparation tips, low-fat cooking short-cuts, how to shop for low-fat groceries ... read labels ... modify those high-fat recipes currently in your recipe file. Plus much, much more!

Preview THE LOW-FAT WAY TO COOK for 30 days FREE and get a FREE GIFT ...

SEND NO MONEY. Simply mail the enclosed Free Preview Reservation Card in the postage-free envelope. We'll rush your new cookbook to examine free. Read it. Learn from it. And cook a few recipes while you're at it. (See if your family can tell they're low-fat!)

FREE GIFT. We'll also send you a super-accurate, easy-to-use desktop calculator, just for looking. If you like THE LOW-FAT WAY TO COOK, you can keep the book and pay the direct-from-the-publisher price of $19.96 in four easy monthly installments of just $4.99 each, plus a nominal amount for shipping and handling. If, however, at the end of 30 days you decide not to keep the book, simply return it without obligation. And keep the free calculator -- no matter what!

THE LOW-FAT WAY TO COOK is part of an exciting new series from SOUTHERN LIVING BOOKS called Today's Gourmet. If you decide to keep it, you'll be entitled to preview future cookbooks as they are published with absolutely no obligation to buy.

So act today! Isn't it time you started cooking the new low-fat way? It will help your family look better. Feel better. And live longer. And the sooner you get started, the better! Mail now!

Sincerely,

Dianne Mooney

Dianne Mooney for SOUTHERN LIVING BOOKS

P.S. Remember, you get to keep your FREE GIFT no matter what! It's a special desktop calculator that we know you'll really like! And it's yours free when you mail the card!

P.P.S. Win $50 Cash! If your reply is among the first 50 we receive by mail, you'll win $50 cash! Hurry! Mail today!

FIGURE 4–8   *Prevention:* **A Successful Super-Big Letter**

PREVENTION

FREE

May we send you a FREE sample issue of PREVENTION and a FREE BOOK?

(They're <u>both</u> yours to keep with no obligation, of course.)

Dear Health-Conscious Friend,

Many doctors now believe that the most powerful remedies on Earth do NOT come from a pharmacy.

They come from a <u>farm</u>.

They come from the <u>sea</u>.

They come <u>direct</u> from Mother Nature.

And you'll find them all in your FREE book, <u>PREVENTION's Guide to Mother Nature's Miracle Cures</u>.

On page 3, you'll see how a secret ingredient — in ordinary eggs — actually DIMINISHES AGE LINES AND WRINKLES!

On page 10, you'll discover a common (and delicious) food that <u>captures</u> the cholesterol in your body and carries it out.

      By adding this food to their everyday diets, one group dropped their cholesterol levels 20 percent in just 21 days! (For a 250 cholesterol count, that translates into a huge, 50-point drop!)

On page 4, you'll discover which FITNESS FOODS can add lean, new muscle to a woman's body <u>without exercise</u>!

And on page 9, you'll see how a simple salad of carrots, cucumbers and lettuce may help women reduce their risk for breast cancer a whopping 50 percent.

OVER 250 SAFE, DOCTOR-PROVEN HEALING SECRETS

These astounding natural cures are so effective, yet so safe, many doctors now "prescribe" them for their patients (and <u>themselves</u>).

There are over 250 new health secrets in <u>PREVENTION's Guide to Mother Nature's Miracle Cures</u>. These are the health secrets your doctor may have never told you about. These are the natural antidotes that heal your body like no medicines can.

(over, please)

FIGURE 4–9 *Smithsonian:* **A Good Letter Using Take-outs and Underlines**

CONGRATULATIONS! You've been selected for FREE membership in the SMITHSONIAN.

I hope you enjoy the FREE basil seeds I've enclosed. Just a small "thank you" for reading this letter. Plant immediately or throughout 1995!

```
*********************************
*                               *
*   You may now join America's national
*   museum, the Smithsonian Institution ...
*
*   ... and receive a FREE MEMBERSHIP for
*   SIX MONTHS -- including SIX FREE ISSUES
*   of SMITHSONIAN magazine -- when you
*   accept a half year at the regular rate.
*                               *
*********************************
```

6 FREE ISSUES

Dear Member-Elect:

I think I know something about you.

You have above-average intelligence and a wide range of interests.

You work hard -- you're always on the go.

And, alas, you have little time for relaxing -- but when you can wind down, you like your entertainment to be intellectually stimulating.

Am I right? If I am ...

... then welcome to the club. You belong in that select group who are members of the Smithsonian National Associates. Sounds fancy, but here's what it really means:

You'll get member DISCOUNTS — vacations that don't cost an ARM & A LEG —

You can shop at beautiful Smithsonian museum stores with a 10% - 20% discount -- in person or by catalog.

You can shake up your life with members-only tours and vacations at low cost. Take trips near or far, short or long -- great experiences and warm memories guaranteed!

Best of all, you'll receive 12 colorful and engrossing issues of SMITHSONIAN magazine. Each one an adventure ...

and a SUPER MAGAZINE

... to a great museum, a small corner of nature -- back in history and far in the future. It's hard to describe. You meet fascinating people and extraordinary animals. You laugh. You wonder. Your mind bends.

If you've seen SMITHSONIAN magazine before, you may be ready to subscribe right now. But if you're in the dark about what to expect,

next page ...

folded and carried teaser copy on its outside that said "Please *do not* open unless you have already decided *not* to send for . . . ." (Curiosity being what it is, you can be sure most prospects opened it.)

This second letter was not from the person who signed the longer letter. In this case, it was from the publisher, Paul M. Greystone, and it began, "As the publisher of this encyclopedia I am puzzled. Frankly, I do not understand why *everyone* does not send in for free Volume 1 . . . ." The writer went on to express amazement that everyone would not take advantage of this exciting, no-risk offer. It ended by urging the reader to reconsider.

And scores of readers did so—every time the little letter was used. Some of us called it the "Frankly, I'm puzzled" letter, but it was no puzzle why and how this brought in additional response:

1. It allowed a second promotional point of view.
2. It strengthened the credibility of the offer.
3. It permitted new benefits, or different selling points, to be highlighted.

After Greystone, "Frankly, I'm puzzled" was used effectively by dozens of astute practitioners. By the 1970s Time-Life Books began using a version undersigned by their publisher. (The Editor wrote the main letter.) They called it the "Publisher's Lift Letter" (or Pub Lift Letter), because it carried a message from the publisher. This was only the beginning of the lift letter's evolution. Other voices, other points of view were added. Celebrities or individuals who contributed to the Time-Life Books series were used in lift letters to provide a particular point of view regarding the excellence of a specific book or series (for example, they told how the unusual photography was executed, how carefully recipes were checked out in the test kitchens).

From here on, the lift letter, as it became widely known in the late seventies, was a no-holds-barred approach. Anything was feasible for testing, and most sensible creative utilizations struck responsive gold.

Outer teaser copy varied from "Open only if you don't plan to respond" to "Open only after you've dropped your order card in the mail," or "Read this side if you've decided to respond, read the other side if you've decided not to respond," or "Here are three more good reasons to respond now," to almost anything that "teased."

The lift letter can come from any logical person with a strong, promotional point of view, including an editor, a customer service supervisor, a museum director, or a happy husband. (Happy husband? Yes, speaking for his wife's new cookbook.)

Think of the lift letter as a sort of *second* salesperson; a young sidekick who goes around with the older salesperson (the main letter) and helps out with his or her own separate little sales routine.

Some say the lift letter has been overused and has, therefore, lost its effectiveness (i.e., its lift). In fact, it has been misused rather than overused. Using a lift letter for the sake of being cute or presenting a charming point of view that doesn't directly reinforce or enhance the sales message is misuse, and it may even detract from the main message. Hold back. Don't use the lift letter frivolously. Use it well and it will "lift" for you, too.

It is my sincere hope that you will learn to love the lift as I do. It will solve many of your letter-writing problems by giving you a good stage for a big selling point that just doesn't fit in the main letter. It will enable you to introduce a new point of view and change your character (and your tone) a little. It will give your package more interest and strengthen your offer. It can also be one of the most enjoyable parts of the promotion if you use it creatively. (Frankly, *I'm* puzzled that more writers don't add a lift letter.)

Guideline 5: When and How to Use a Brochure

The statement, "A brochure is nice—if you can afford it," is not rational, yet people say this all the time. Brochures aren't *nice*. They are either absolutely necessary or absolutely unnecessary.

A brochure's mission is to dramatize the benefits and illustrate the features of a product or service. Please don't expect it to do a lot more than this for your product. This *is* a lot.

Brochures are *not* necessary

- When you have a product or service with features that don't require illustration, such as a newsletter or newspaper.

- When you have a product so well known that it doesn't need visual description for most prospects—like *Time* or *Newsweek* magazines, or the customer's expiring membership or expiring subscription to whatever.

- When you have a business-to-business promotion geared to *qualify prospects by creating inquiries* for "more information." "More information" will include the expensive brochures, charts, and diagrams.

- When you have the ability to write so well that your description does a *better* job than words and pictures because you can create a mental "framework" that lets your prospect move into a picture in his or her mind, draw upon his or her own imagination! This works best when you're selling services like travel and entertainment, or self-improvement books and programs that help individuals achieve goals and aspirations. It doesn't work if you're selling widgets.

Brochures are *necessary* almost all other times—and you cannot afford to go without them.

A word of caution. Brochure (or "folder" or "flyer" or "booklet" or "broadside") shouldn't mean just pictures and words. A brochure can be represented by a game board, a travel folder, a life-size shot of a table spread with food, a miniature magazine that fits in the palm of your hand, a page "torn" from a book, a sales kit or manual, a printer's proof sheet. It can be all four-color photography or two-color charts and graphs and columns of words and lists of figures—particularly in financial promotions.

How you see your brochure is limited only by your creativity and cost constraints. Creativity and cost constraints are unlikely bedfellows, however, so in most cases (particularly in consumer advertising) you'll have to hold your soaring imagination to a piece of paper that folds nicely into a #10 or 6" × 9" or 9" × 12" outer envelope.

Brochures generally call for standard paper weights as well—and efficient paper sizes and logical folds. Learn about all of these from your art director and production specialists before you plunge ahead with plans for a design that exceeds your budget and production's capabilities. (More about this in Guideline 6.)

By the way, this does not mean that a reasonably priced, simply folded brochure is the only way to go. Careful testing has enabled the Meredith Publishing Group to increase response significantly with larger, more dramatic brochures for modestly priced products. Their first breakthrough is shown in Figure 4–10—a giant 22" by 25 1/2" four-color brochure in a 9" × 12" mailing package for a single $14.95 book, offered with a free gift!

Aha—but there's more to it than just size; look at the pictures and headlines—benefit-laden dramatizations that made this brochure a clear winner. The payoff strategy behind the three-fold format, according to Ellen DeLathouder, director of creative services for the Group and a top creative writer as well: "To gain access by promising personal fulfillment through the use of single, large images highlighted with emotive benefits, while the large center spread covers the tangible benefits. It's a form of psychographic tracking."

WHEN TO PUT A COUPON IN YOUR BROCHURE

Every piece in your direct mail package has a job to do. The brochure, order card, and letter have to work together, but they must also stand alone. No one is exactly sure how many prospects read which first and why, but it is definitely established that our society is composed of order-card-first readers as well as brochure-or-letter-first readers.

Think about it this way: Good prospects are often tempted to *save* the brochure or pass it on to a friend. This can generate more business and enable one direct mail package to reach two prospects or more. But for this process to work, creative people must include a coupon *with an offer* on the back of the brochure itself. This is hard

**FIGURE 4–10   Some Selected Panels from a Dramatic Brochure for an
                Inexpensive Product**

FIGURE 4–10 (Continued)

"How did you think of that?"

Make the Most of Your Talent

Cross-Stitch! Sugar Plums! Knit & Crochet! Start your make-ahead Christmas today!

To home-test* the First Edition of CHRISTMAS AT HOME for 21 days risk-free and have your free bonus gift rushed into your hands, **send no money now**. Simply slip the token in your R.S.V.P. card and return in postpaid envelope right away!

*Details of offer in letter.

YOUR 100% "GLITTER AND CRUMBS"
Guarantee

If for any reason you decide not to keep your new book, you can send it back within 21 days (even if there's glitter and crumbs between the pages), and owe nothing. No questions from us. No apologies from you. You can even keep your bonus gift!

53-501

Now the secret of a glorious Christmas is yours –

How to get a jump on the holidays, play Santa in creative new ways, and still stay within a budget you can afford...

NEW!

New CHRISTMAS AT HOME is a feast for your talents! And, a practical way for you to create the Christmas you've always dreamed about — way ahead of time (when you can still enjoy every single minute). It's a book only true Christmas lovers can fully appreciate, a book only the experts at BETTER HOMES AND GARDENS. could have put together.

Which of your make-ahead decorations will be passed on for generations?

NEW!

Better Homes and Gardens
Christmas At Home

FIGURE 4–10   (Continued)

th one **GREAT** ideabook!

Which of your make-ahead gifts will family members and friends swoon over?

Exquisite cardinal quilt, an heirloom wall hanging to treasure year after year.

Cross-stitched stockings, delightfully detailed.

Exotic vinegars for an exotic gift.

A little floss and a few materials add a superb holiday card holder.

Wooden egg angels, surprisingly easy

Whimsical nativity, made from scraps

Ribbon rosettes and handmade tassels look that's inexpensive to create.

Country Angel, too heavenly for words!

- Brilliant fine enamel paper!
- Beautiful color photos of each project!
- Original designs (68 in all)!
- Scrumptious kitchen-tested recipes (36 in all)!

You have a First Edition copy of new CHRISTMAS AT HOME reserved in your name. May we send it to you for a 21-day, no-risk home tryout?

(See letter for details.)

Crafts Galore!

Ready To Make No Matter What Month It Is!

- Cross-Stitch • Duplicate-Stitch • Quilting • Crochet • Knitting
- Scherenschnitte • Spool Art • Ribbon Art • Painted Woodcrafts
- Dried Arrangements • Topiaries • Easy-Do Projects for Kids
- Plus, Recipes! Recipes! Recipes!

Complete materials lists, step-by-step how-tos and color photos guarantee

Festively giftwrapped Chutney-Cheese Ball, warm wishes from your kitchen.

Duplicate-stitched sweater, holiday pretty!

Advent tree, uniquely adorned with Christmas wreaths.

Old latex gloves get recycled into finger puppets.

Which nifty, easy-do crafts will give your children hours of fun?

Festive Christmas ornaments made from kitchen sponges.

Yummy candy cars to assemble on a rainy day.

Plastic vinyl tubing and little candies make up these colorful tree trimmings.

Easy hole-punched paper dot Santas over blown-out eggs.

Check out your "glitter and crumbs" guarantee on back!

to do when you're testing several different offers on the order card, as you'll also have to repeat those offers on the brochure coupon (and then make sure the right brochure is enclosed with the right order card!).

Today, with prices subject to frequent testing and changing, direct marketers often develop generic brochures that can be economically printed in one large batch and used over and over in a variety of packages because they do not spell out the offer at all. They refer the reader to the order card instead. As you get to understand printing costs, you'll see that this is often a necessary economy. On the other hand, something is lost by it.

Try to test the brochure coupon whenever the cost is not prohibitive. It can bring you a serendipity of extra (unbudgeted) orders. How Many? The better your offer, the better your serendipity.

YOUR BROCHURE
REQUIREMENTS

Whether it stands alone, or limps a little without its offer, the brochure must work with your other components.

1. If it does nothing else, it must *dramatize* the benefits.
2. It must use all the basic techniques applied in the letter to do this: big benefits/credibility/involvement/motivation.
3. It must illustrate the features. (Here's where every single bit of basic information and detail goes—detail that reinforces the letter's sell and answers all possible questions.)
4. It must create its own tone. A golden-tongued orator or a folksy cook may speak in the letter, but the brochure is neutral ground—a credible straightforward presentation without the intimate or impassioned one-on-one dialogue of a letter.
5. It must *track*. If you don't know what "track" means, you can probably guess. Just envision your prospect at the "gate" of the racetrack. This is your cover. A good brochure leads the prospects gently around the curves and corners to the first fold, then to the next spread, then right down the home stretch to the finish line (inside spread).

Instead of wandering aimlessly, unfolding, and turning the paper (and how many times have we all gotten lost in the maze of a poorly-designed brochure?), your prospect moves along with your message in pictures and words—following closely as the story develops—right up to the grand finale in the center spread. That's tracking!

SOME HELP
ON ILLUSTRATION

In any talk of brochures, you're liable to run into arguments on illustration. Some art directors swear by photography, others stick to drawings or commercial illustrations. A few (and they have to be very good) combine the two effectively.

Here are some thoughts when you're confronted with illustration decisions:

1. Most art directors prefer good four-color photography. Color photography works particularly well for

food and cooking	"picture" publications
travel	hard goods
gardening	soft goods
sweepstakes	entertainment

2. But drawings have a place, too, and every art director has opinions here. I suggest you consider drawings for

- Light and heavy industrial machinery

- Technical product details or enlarged areas

- Shots that are expensive and difficult to set up (aerial views; groups of buildings; large groups of people, children, or animals; period pieces and historical settings)

- Mood shots (to express strong feelings of sentiment, mystery, horror, nostalgia, and fantasy)

- People pictures when you are only showing one or two people.

3. Your illustrations show your product's major benefits and features and, if it is appropriate, they show the product in use as well. For example: If it is a service such as a travel program, show people enjoying a ship or a plane (the product or service at work), then show specific pictures of planning the trip, destinations, and featured places on the itinerary. Services, are more easily shown in use than are products, as use itself is part of the benefit structure of services. If the product is a sewing machine, for example, show the benefits (all the clothes it made), and possibly some close-up shots of important features. Showing the product at work is not appropriate here; it will add nothing to your story as motion or moving parts obviously cannot translate to still photography.

4. People illustrations in direct response advertising can make or break your story. Photography has a stronger impact, but offers more dangers than drawings in big benefit situations. People often identify readily with people shown in benefit illustrations, drawings, and cartoons. On the other hand, given one or two close-up photographs showing real people and benefits, many may refuse to identify and say, "That's not *me*. My family doesn't look like that!" or "I'm not even married!" or "I'm not *that* old," and so on.

When you use a wide variety of photographs, with different people groupings in benefit situations, your prospects are more likely to identify with them, and photography in such cases is preferable. If you have room for only one picture, be careful. Your prospect must be able to identify with the benefit dramatization.

For example: A major book club with broad appeal to both men and women tested two different benefit presentations. One presentation showed a large photograph of a "family" reading together. There was a father, a mother, and two children. The other used a cartoon drawing of a nondescript but pleasant man reading. The cartoon worked better. Moral: When you can't photograph all the types that make up your prospect market (or aren't sure what they all are), try drawings, sketches, or cartoons that anyone and everyone can and will relate to without saying, "That's not me . . . this isn't real."

5. If your illustrations aren't self-explanatory and don't have headlines, make sure they have strong captions. *Captions get read.*

6. Push hard for color. Your alternative to four-color is two-color, which is fine for many financial services and business promotions. In some cases, if you must compromise, two-color can even be used for soft goods, hard goods, and travel—but not for food! We know four-color improves response, but you won't be able to quantify this precisely until you test with and without it. Most professionals, when including a brochure, opt for four-color if their product needs it.

ORGANIZING YOUR
BROCHURE COPY

In creating direct mail packages, direct marketers tend to overlook guidelines and assistance in developing brochures. They get lost in the excitement of outers, letters, and order cards—and many direct marketers probably never sit down and really analyze the brochure.

This may happen because the brochure's job is tough and thankless. In addition to dramatizing the benefits, it must list all features without leaving out one detail or specification; it must anticipate and field all questions. An effective brochure is the result of good research and organization. Creating can be grueling work. It can also be enjoyable. Here are some techniques to help you organize and present a brochure, and to make this task more enjoyable.

- A "standard" brochure uses headlines and illustrations to guide your prospect through a logical story from benefits to features— from *what* it will do for you to precisely *how* it will do this.

- The main headline restates your big benefit(s).

- The secondary headlines point up secondary benefits and features.

- Your first block of body copy usually starts with a broad, overall benefit sell.

- Use lots of subheads to hold the reader and pull the waverer back into your body copy.

- Use "throwover" heads at the bottom of each spread to help tracking and to guide your reader (for example, "See other side for your special offer" . . . "To Get Your Free Copy— Return the Enclosed Card—Today!").

- Your back cover is a good place to restate your offer and/or to dramatize your guarantee.

Organize your data and make it more interesting with these graphic devices:

- Use takeouts around the photograph or drawing of your product to illustrate features and benefits.

- Use the question-and-answer technique—the best way to anticipate sales resistance and dissolve it.

- List benefits numerically, using the old countdown method.

- Line your features up in a column and bullet them.

- Include a boxed-off section of testimonials (with pictures, if you have them).

- Add charts and graphs to dramatize the numerical aspects of your story (for example, to show how compound interest works or to chart financial growth).

Good prospects will want all of your information, but they'll take it better if you sugar-coat it where you can. And remember, if you enjoy bringing it together, they'll enjoy tracking through it with you! The brochure in Figure 4–11 shows many of these graphic devices.

Guideline 6: How to Win on Cost-per-Order

In the past, most creative people didn't have to worry about cost per order (CPO). Back then, when a creative team was asked to do test packages to beat the control, they were usually told not to worry about cost, just be creative. If the new packages got more responses than the old control, the costs could always be honed down by gradually testing production efficiencies. Gross response or pull was all that counted. When you won—you *won*.

That's not the case today. Thanks to the high cost of getting into the mail, every package is judged by its cost in relation to its pull, not by its pull alone.

Marketing managers are also apt to challenge their creative people on the *cost per thousand,* or *CPM*—the cost to produce, print, obtain lists, label, insert, stamp, and mail a thousand packages. In direct response marketing, printing, lettershop (the place that prepares and inserts all components, addressing, batching, and mailing them), lists, and postage are all estimated in terms of thousands produced. That is to say, each of your components is costed out by the thousand, postage is added in by the thousand, then list rental and lettershop are plugged in—still by the thousands. Look at it this way: $300M equals $.30 per piece, $500M equals $.50, and so on.

FIGURE 4–11   Layout for a Dramatic Brochure Spread

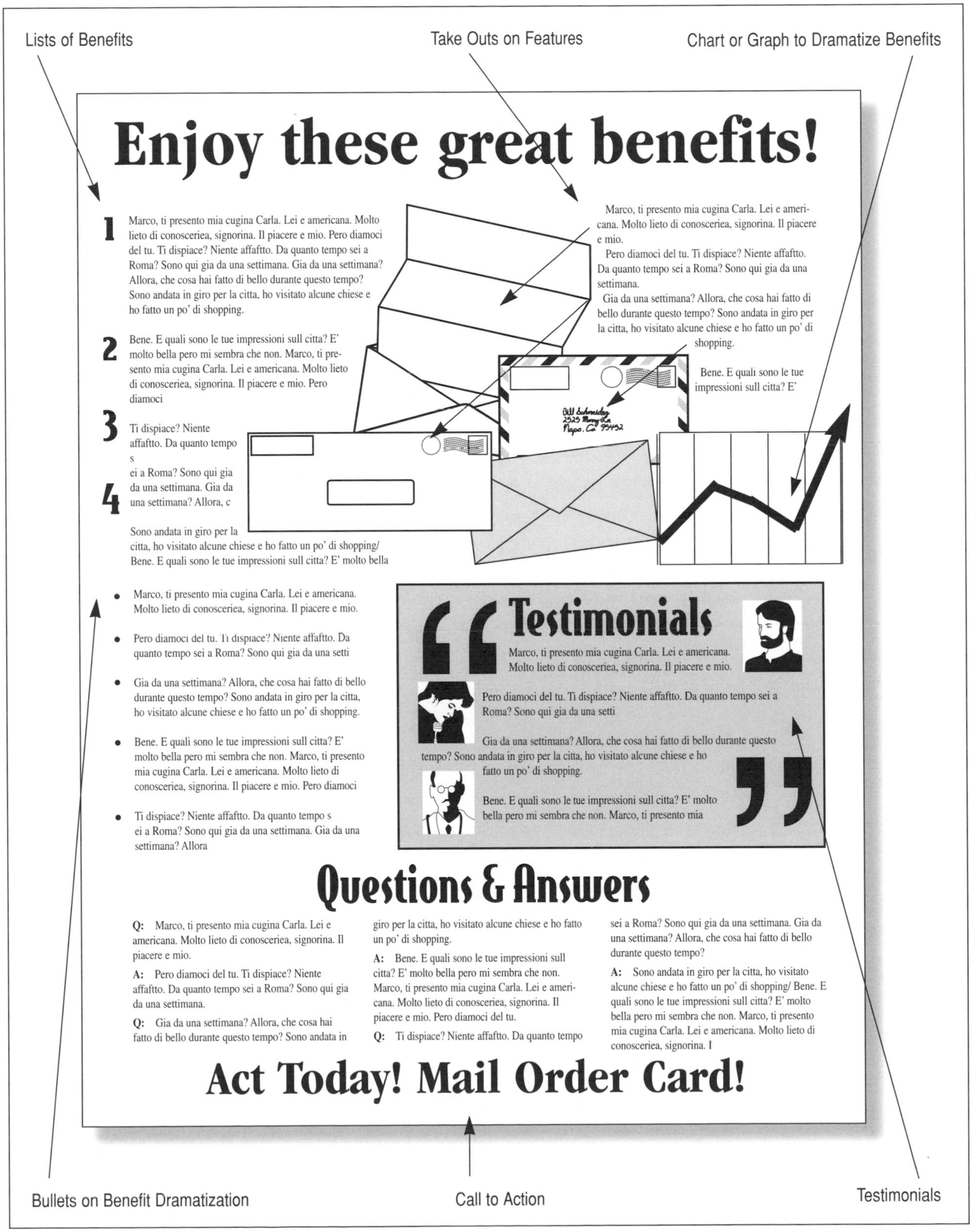

Lists of Benefits   Take Outs on Features   Chart or Graph to Dramatize Benefits

Enjoy these great benefits!

1 Marco, ti presento mia cugina Carla. Lei e americana. Molto lieto di conosceriea, signorina. Il piacere e mio. Pero diamoci del tu. Ti dispiace? Niente affaftto. Da quanto tempo sei a Roma? Sono qui gia da una settimana. Gia da una settimana? Allora, che cosa hai fatto di bello durante questo tempo? Sono andata in giro per la citta, ho visitato alcune chiese e ho fatto un po' di shopping.

2 Bene. E quali sono le tue impressioni sull citta? E' molto bella pero mi sembra che non. Marco, ti presento mia cugina Carla. Lei e americana. Molto lieto di conosceriea, signorina. Il piacere e mio. Pero diamoci

3 Ti dispiace? Niente affaftto. Da quanto tempo s ei a Roma? Sono qui gia da una settimana. Gia da una settimana? Allora, c

4 una settimana? Allora, c

Sono andata in giro per la citta, ho visitato alcune chiese e ho fatto un po' di shopping/ Bene. E quali sono le tue impressioni sull citta? E' molto bella

- Marco, ti presento mia cugina Carla. Lei e americana. Molto lieto di conosceriea, signorina. Il piacere e mio.

- Pero diamoci del tu. Ti dispiace? Niente affaftto. Da quanto tempo sei a Roma? Sono qui gia da una setti

- Gia da una settimana? Allora, che cosa hai fatto di bello durante questo tempo? Sono andata in giro per la citta, ho visitato alcune chiese e ho fatto un po' di shopping.

- Bene. E quali sono le tue impressioni sull citta? E' molto bella pero mi sembra che non. Marco, ti presento mia cugina Carla. Lei e americana. Molto lieto di conosceriea, signorina. Il piacere e mio. Pero diamoci

- Ti dispiace? Niente affaftto. Da quanto tempo s ei a Roma? Sono qui gia da una settimana. Gia da una settimana? Allora

Marco, ti presento mia cugina Carla. Lei e americana. Molto lieto di conosceriea, signorina. Il piacere e mio.

Pero diamoci del tu. Ti dispiace? Niente affaftto. Da quanto tempo sei a Roma? Sono qui gia da una settimana.

Gia da una settimana? Allora, che cosa hai fatto di bello durante questo tempo? Sono andata in giro per la citta, ho visitato alcune chiese e ho fatto un po' di shopping.

Bene. E quali sono le tue impressioni sull citta? E'

" Testimonials "

Marco, ti presento mia cugina Carla. Lei e americana. Molto lieto di conosceriea, signorina. Il piacere e mio.

Pero diamoci del tu. Ti dispiace? Niente affaftto. Da quanto tempo sei a Roma? Sono qui gia da una setti

Gia da una settimana? Allora, che cosa hai fatto di bello durante questo tempo? Sono andata in giro per la citta, ho visitato alcune chiese e ho fatto un po' di shopping.

Bene. E quali sono le tue impressioni sull citta? E' molto bella pero mi sembra che non. Marco, ti presento mia

Questions & Answers

Q: Marco, ti presento mia cugina Carla. Lei e americana. Molto lieto di conosceriea, signorina. Il piacere e mio.

A: Pero diamoci del tu. Ti dispiace? Niente affaftto. Da quanto tempo sei a Roma? Sono qui gia da una settimana.

Q: Gia da una settimana? Allora, che cosa hai fatto di bello durante questo tempo? Sono andata in giro per la citta, ho visitato alcune chiese e ho fatto un po' di shopping.

A: Bene. E quali sono le tue impressioni sull citta? E' molto bella pero mi sembra che non. Marco, ti presento mia cugina Carla. Lei e americana. Molto lieto di conosceriea, signorina. Il piacere e mio. Pero diamoci del tu.

Q: Ti dispiace? Niente affaftto. Da quanto tempo sei a Roma? Sono qui gia da una settimana. Gia da una settimana? Allora, che cosa hai fatto di bello durante questo tempo?

A: Sono andata in giro per la citta, ho visitato alcune chiese e ho fatto un po' di shopping/ Bene. E quali sono le tue impressioni sull citta? E' molto bella pero mi sembra che non. Marco, ti presento mia cugina Carla. Lei e americana. Molto lieto di conosceriea, signorina. I

Act Today! Mail Order Card!

Bullets on Benefit Dramatization   Call to Action   Testimonials

Cost per order (CPO) can be figured in much the same way. If you paid $300M going into the mail, and you received 20 orders per thousand (or 2 percent response) coming back, you would have paid $15.00 to get each of your customers. If you spent $400M on your mailing and received the same number of customers, you would have spent $20.00 to get each of your customers.

All other things being equal, imagine the cost differential between these two packages if you were mailing 3,000,000 pieces at 2 percent return! With the first package, you'd have 60,000 customers at $15.00 each; with the other, 60,000 customers at $20.00 each—only a 10¢ difference in the cost of the individual mailings (30¢ versus 40¢), but overall a $300,000 cost difference!

You can see that if the present control costs only $300M in the mail, you can't very well design a test package that costs $400M in the mail unless you're awfully certain it will outpull the control enough to more than offset the higher cost. Otherwise, why change the control?

You need to know about CPM and CPO in direct response advertising. *We are measured,* so somewhere along the line we all have to deal with accounting-controlled creativity because full evaluation is possible. Those in general advertising do not have such strict accountability.

When you're told you can't use odd-sized envelopes or big brochures, or order cards with paste and patch and peel-off, it takes a lot of fuel out of your imagination. And when you're constantly saddled with #10 and 6" × 9" envelopes, 11" × 17" two-color brochures and simple two-color order cards with a BRC back, it can take all the creative challenge out of the job. It also ensures that everything will soon start to look the same.

But numbers must have their due; after all, the increased costs of creative formats can be big. If you're going to be a smart creative type today, you'll have to fight the numbers people with their own numbers, learn to understand costs, and argue effectively. When you run over budget in one area of your planning, know it, and compensate by cutting back in another.

For example: You don't have to live with #10 or a 6'" × 9" outer envelope. There are seven other standard sizes with windows, like a Monarch or a 6" × 11 1/2" (a #14). An 11" × 17" brochure may be economical, but so are 25" × 8 1/2", 12 1/2" × 8 1/2", 8 1/2" × 7". Take a look at some of your low-budget alternatives. They can be absolutely inspiring!

You can't do this kind of creative juggling without the help of a good artist or art director with some grounding in production. Although you should be aware of certain basics yourself, any good direct mail production person should be able to give you input on the following. Digest it. In addition, try to arrange trips to a printer and to lettershops, and visits with computer printing representatives.

You may feel now that one such visit will be more than enough for you, but you'll find once is really barely beginning.

Here are the minimum production basics you should digest for creative planning in a CPO-oriented business.

- United States Postal Service specifications and charges for first and third class mail (to include weight and size limitations, return addresses, and outer envelope requirements such as window placement, barcodes and "white space").

- Lettershop inserting capabilities and limitations (number of pieces, envelope sizes, and how papers must be folded or nested for inserting).

- Economical brochure formats (what makes them economical, how do special sizes and folds increase costs?).

- Cost differentials between a #10 envelope, a 6 × 9 envelope and a jumbo (9 × 12) envelope.

- The difference between 100 pound stock, 90, 80, 70, 60, and 50. Why are some papers *too heavy* for brochures? When will some lack opacity? What is a matte finish?

- How to quickly guesstimate the increased cost of four-color over two-color printing. What do you need to know?

- The cost of an average two-color order card (BRC) for a #10 or a 6 × 9 envelope. (25M, 50M, and 100M quantity).

- The lightest reply card stock to make it safely through the return mail (smallest permissible size, largest size).

- The average cost of a four-page folded letter, two-colors on 60 pound offset (25M, 50M, and 100M quantity).

- Computer printing—ink jet and laser: Which is best for what? What minimum quantities are required? What new things are being introduced? (There's always something new in this field.)

The Golden Age of Direct Mail is past. You can no longer totally separate creativity from cost. But once you've established your rules of thumb, move on to create and dream and imagine. If you go too far, somewhere in your mind a little warning bell will sound—and back on track you will go!

Guideline 7: The Basic Law and Direct Mail

Remember the customer. The final guideline for everything you do is a reminder to question. Don't get too close. Step back. Think first, second, and finally about the customer. *Be* the customer. Does it make sense to you? Will it make sense to the customer? Could it make *more* sense to the customer?

THE TECHNICALLY CORRECT LETTER OR "IS THAT ALL THERE IS?"

Now that you've learned some technique, you'll be able to spot the technique in every direct mail package. You'll also spot a lot of packages that are 99 percent technique.

We've all seen them. They are direct mail packages that are patently uncreative, a boring, stringing together of "Here," "Now," "Act today," all lined up with an equally unsophisticated offer presentation and a letter that sounds strangely familiar—totally impersonal—and embarrassing to those of us who care about bad images and lingering accusations of junk mail. And yet, most of these packages incorporate all the rules and formulas!

Look closely at these uninspired offerings. The products or services may vary, but the mailings persistently go on and on in the same way with the same tone, or lack of it. Two or three of the products could even be interchanged and one might never notice. Flat, humdrum sales spiels.

This bad image is being perpetrated by new practitioners who have come upon the rules and formulas and are applying them in megadoses. They have technique down pat; if you dissect and analyze their promotions you'll find there's nothing specifically wrong with them. They follow the rules. They represent the formulas. They are technically correct.

There's nothing creatively *right* with them either. They are totally lacking in individuality of expression and any hint of creative excellence. Their authors have copied "success" and applied all the do's and don'ts you've learned in this chapter. Period. Not a thing more. Even more distressing, this technically correct, mediocre direct response works! Yes, you'll find that such advertising can indeed pay off—but only under optimum conditions.

It works with an exclusive market or an unusual new product or an unbeatable offer. Given these optimum situations, the promotion supplies only what is required in a form that is technically acceptable. And as long as it has a hold on an exclusive product, the prime market, and the best possible offer, it will continue to work.

But once the competition gets in, once the price is no longer competitive, once the market erodes or becomes marginal, these mailings cease to work, because these writers don't know how to *sell*. Direct marketers know that selling starts the minute the prospect says no. Once the mailbox is full of offers, these technically correct packages can't even get through, much less hold their own with strong selling appeals.

Here you are at least 50 percent on your way to direct response marketing success; you've got technique down and are ready to go. But there's *another* 50 percent. Sure, you can go out and be a technician right now, today. But you'll never make creative director or promotion manager, or leader or teacher or top banana *without the creative part.*

Creativity adds style and tone. Creativity uses its tools to grab the prospect and carry the prospect through a direct mail package or print or broadcast until the prospect gets to a point where it makes more sense to say yes than no. Creativity sells!

We'll be doing some important creative work in the chapters ahead to give you the other 50 percent—creativity as it relates to concept development, creativity in determining the benefits and copy strategy, your approach, and your layout—creativity in pulling together the big ideas and writing them down.

Before you move on, however, be sure to try out the guidelines in the Exercise at the end of this chapter. Then we shall devote the rest of this book to helping make sure you never are guilty of technical mediocrity.

Guidelines for the 21st Century

THE CHANGES IN DIRECT MAIL

Only a few years ago, direct mail was a "set" medium, with its own rules that you broke at your peril. A direct mail package had—at the minimum—an outer envelope, a reply envelope, a letter (at least two pages and probably more), a brochure, and an order form.

But change is coming. In fact, it's here, according to Don Kanter, who has been doing direct reponse creative work for 20 years. The changes, he says, are focused on one objective: faster, stronger, more telegraphic communications with the prospect.

Why? Two reasons, Mr. Kanter says. First, "mailbox clutter" is becoming real, just as TV clutter did some years ago. Only a direct mailing that grabs and holds the prospect's attention—from the envelope though every component—has a chance of working. Second, we are now talking to the TV generation, which grew up with visual symbols. Unlike us older folks who grew up reading books, the TV generation is less inclined to stay with you if you don't get your message across very quickly.

Basically, the specific changes are in two areas:

1. *Shorter Copy and Better Copy*. Kanter believes that direct mail historically has been overwritten, because direct mail does not impose the discipline for tight, concise writing that space or broadcast does. Now that discipline is being imposed by outside factors, it means that the direct mail writer must edit and polish copy, making every word justify its existence. A four-page letter (or longer) may still be the best way to go, but it must be a beautifully written, meticulously polished, and lovingly edited four-page letter.

2. *Quicker Communication through Graphics*. At long last, the designer is becoming an equal partner in the direct mail creative process, as we learn what our brethren in general advertising have

always known: Graphics communicate more quickly and more forcefully than words.

An added benefit of the designer's involvement is that we are improving the appearance of direct mail, as well as the level of taste. The old "direct mail look" that was distinguished by type piled up on virtually every component, is slowly disappearing.[2]

This is good perspective from two stalwart pillars of direct marketing, Don Kanter and Bob Stone. The points are important and you will see changes in all aspects of direct mail as you go along today. For example, many of us have taken the letter and set down our messages in compelling one-sentence paragraphs—a format that allows the "restless" as well as the "lazy" eye to enter and leave easily, returning each time for instant reinvolvment (see the examples in Figures 4–9 through 4–11). Some letters are being combined with computerized reply forms (across the bottom) for production efficiencies.

But while we're slimming some things down, other formats with 5 to 10 times *more* information are gaining favor. *Infomercials*, the half-hour televison commercials, are one example, and *magalogs* (magazine catalogs) are another. Interestingly enough, the lazy eye seems to like these and, if they are easy on the eye, they work like crazy despite their increased costs. Good magalogs are truly entertaining and involving and motivating and filled with all the things a good direct mail package has, in abundance! (See Chapter 8 for a fine example of a magalog.)

Although many new formats and techniques are being tried without careful testing, you can be sure that magalogs, because of their cost, are carefully tested against the more modest direct mail package. You'll find formats and techniques that save money are far less likely to be tested than those that require increased budgets, for the obvious reason. I say, test everything!

Anatomy of a Successful Letter

Here are some of the elements that make up a successful direct mail letter. (You may be able to come up with still more points; if so, just add them in. The rules are always expanding and changing. See Chapter 7.)

Try to combine many of the following rules and guidelines and elements to make up a promotion that's almost pure technique. (In the next chapter you will learn how to add creativity to your technique.)

- Use a salutation.
- Use a logical spokesperson.
- Use "you" throughout.
- State offer on page one—or—
- Use a Johnson box to introduce the offer and emphasize it.
- Begin with a strong opener, then go back to it at the end just before the close to "frame" your letter.
- Use Charter or Membership in a Club when you can (exclusivity).
- Test a premium (use the word "Free").
- State major benefits up front.
- List all features.
- Personalize the appeal.
- Involve your reader with dramatizations.
- Include testimonials to build credibility.
- Emphasize dollar savings; use price comparisons.
- Test an offer deadline.
- Use odd numbers, 9s and 7s in particular, with prices under $100 ($9.97 is not perceived as $10, $14.99 is not perceived as $15).
- Indent the first line of each paragraph.
- Use wide margins and short paragraphs (no more than two sentences).
- Use a broken sentence structure at the end of each page to carry over to next page.
- Use specifics; don't generalize.
- Use takeouts or margin notes to emphasize points in the letter.
- Promise fast delivery—immediate gratification.
- Use a strong guarantee to build credibility.
- Use a call to action near the end.
- Offer charge convenience or installment purchases.

- Offer cash payment incentives.

- "Limit" supplies—set a tone of urgency.

- Use an 800 number to facilitate ordering.

- Use a stamp or token for involvement.

- Use "P.S." to restate a major selling point, pull the prospect back into your sales message.

Practice in combining pure techniques is useful, but don't stop here! On to the next chapter on how to nurture creative concepts.

Notes

1. *Direct Marketing Association's Statistical Fact Book, 1994-95 Edition.* (New York: Direct Marketing Association, Inc., Publication Division, 1995). To order, inquire at the DMA, 1120 Avenue of the Americas, New York, NY 10036-6700.

2. Bob Stone, *Successful Direct Marketing Methods, 5th ed.* (Lincolnwood, IL: NTC Business Books, 1994).

CHAPTER FIVE

Nuturing Creative Concepts: How to Sharpen Your Creative Judgment and Grow a Concept

This chapter can make the difference in whether you become a mere technician or a creative leader. It will help you identify the essence of what sells in every product or service that comes your way, play an important role in creative teamwork, and take the lead in deciding what direction the creative appeal should take, what aspects of the creative should be tested, what benefits will be promised, and what moral imperatives will be used. Learn these methods well, and you'll be equipped to rise through the ranks to top advertising and marketing positions. Pass them by, and risk stagnating in the cubicles.

To help you through, I promise to be clear, concise, and not take the easy outs of ambiguity. Stick with it, and you'll gain valuable creative skills.

First, you need to know some definitions. What *is* a creative concept anyway? And what does it have to do with creative strategies?

According to *The American Heritage Dictionary of the English Language*, a concept is simply "a general idea or understanding, especially one derived from specific instances or occurrences. A thought or notion."

Although it's somewhat redundant, a *creative concept* is a creative idea, thought, or notion. A *strategy*, on the other hand, is a plan of action, with military connotations. In marketing, a strategy is an aggressive plan. *Creative strategy* is the part of the marketing strategy that applies to creative development. *Tactics* (according to *American Heritage*) is "the technique or science of securing the objectives designated by strategy."

Once you understand these concepts, you're already ahead, because many direct marketers do not acknowledge that they *need* a creative strategy or plan as such. I say, you most certainly *do* need a strategy, and it's going to be immensely important to you, whether the strategy development is a group effort or you go it alone.

A well-known rule for all direct marketers is "sell the benefits!" But few people stop to wonder

- How do you decide *what* the benefits are?
- How do you know how many benefits to use?
- How do you determine *which* benefits to use?
- Are all benefits equal, or are some benefits more important than others?
- Once you know the benefits, exactly how do you present them?
- Does the benefit always go in the headline?
- Is the offer the most important benefit?

Answering such questions is hard work every time, and without a clear creative strategy the answers can be disastrously misleading. (Frankly, I don't even advise you go it alone, but more about that in a minute.)

As part of the marketing plan, your creative strategy must incorporate the input from research and marketing with logical step-by-step creative planning and tactics, culminating in a definite creative direction. Before you can begin to develop your strategy, however, several preliminary steps are necessary.

The Creative Team—Some Friends You Can Count On

In creating winning direct advertising, two heads really are better than one, three could be even better, and five or so might be best. Take one good writer, add a designer, then a creative director, toss in a marketing specialist and/or a product manager, maybe even a production person and you've got a creative team.

I'm not suggesting that the team help with your writing, but a team approach is ideal in formulating your copy strategy. You're going to need the team's talents to do this thoroughly. Each person brings something to the table. One person alone in a room *cannot* come up with as many ideas as three or four or five people brainstorming around a table. The easy stuff will come fast; you'll need the team when you dry up on ideas—you'll need them as a sounding board, both to suggest new approaches and to reinforce your own thinking.

The Selling Proposition

Let's review, for a minute, those first steps you picked up in Chapter 2.

We'll assume you've done your research thoroughly. This means that you understand the product positioning, its branding statement; you know what the product or service is, how it works, how it looks, and what it does; you are familiar with the competition as well as the company that produces your product and why that company is particularly qualified to do so; you know the market or customer; and you know the offer.

You have also tested your selling proposition. As we discussed in Chapter 2, proposition testing is your first critical go, no-go step in the creative process—your last chance to say "No Thanks" to a promotion that doesn't make sense to the customer. You will turn down, for example, a 60-day cruise for busy executives, or a 30 percent price cut for good customers, because your motto is, "Take no dogs. Have no failures."

Now you're going to learn how to develop a creative selling proposition with winning features. Take, for example, a brand new monthly magazine called *Vital Woman*. It's the first comprehensive magazine devoted to women's health and fitness, designed to appeal to active, busy women between the ages of 18 and 34. It will be priced competitively (one year, 12 issues, $19 by subscription) and published by a company with considerable experience in health and fitness publishing (credibility).

Check out your product's positioning and the offer in relation to the market. Does the product make sense to the market? Do you feel comfortable with the market and the offer? Sound O.K.? Then let's accept the project, and take it with us to serve as one example of how you'll go about developing your own creative strategies, starting with benefits and features.

How to Extract Your Benefits from Your Product Features

The word "extracting" sounds painful, and it should. "Pulling" the benefits is not easy, and in many cases, you may feel you have to pry them out. If your selling proposition makes sense, however, you've already avoided a major problem. If you had been uncomfortable with the basic proposition, but took it on anyway, here's where you'd start to get into trouble.

For example, the wrong selling proposition could have led to a benefit that didn't fit the market, like promising a group of young women that your product would make them look younger. In the case of the one-third price cut offer mentioned earlier, you might have ended up discovering that the benefit was in fact a creative person's curse, because it would indicate to the customer that the product had been overpriced all along.

Let's assume that our *Vital Woman* proposition holds. Before we do any real extracting, we need definitions for features and benefits.

Features are the physical characteristics of your product or service—the facts about the product: It is 10" high; it comes in three colors; it is bound in leather; it has dozens of gourmet recipes; it has an unconditional guarantee.

Benefits are the promises of your product or service for the prospect—the involving "you" is ever present: It is easy for you to use; it will color-coordinate with your room; its fine quality is a reflection of your good taste; people will admire your cooking; it offers you security because it is a safe, sound investment.

To help you catch on to benefit extraction, here is a slightly different illustration:

- *Feature:* The copier mechanism moves 10 copies through per second.

  Benefit: This saves time for you (the customer).

- *Feature:* The computer weighs 10 pounds and measures 18" × 12" × 3".

  Benefit: This allows you to move it easily and store it conveniently in a small space.

- *Feature:* The course has four workbooks and eight audio-tapes.

  Benefit: This material will enable you to move ahead in your profession.

- *Feature:* The insurance policy pays its holder $70 a day for every day he or she is in the hospital.

  Benefit: You can use the money to relieve worry and anxiety.

- *Feature:* The book club offers a selection of six books a month at 30 percent off the publisher's price.

  Benefit: You can be up-to-date and well-read, plus save money.

OFFER AS BENEFIT

Wait a minute, you may be thinking; isn't the feature really a benefit in the last two examples here? (Get $70 a Day . . . Save 30% off.) Good point—and the answer is tricky. Certainly, price or savings and money gained are benefits. When you have a product or service that's similar to others but offers a clear financial advantage, or when you have a group of products with an established price and you offer them to customers at a significant savings, price or savings can clearly be the primary benefit.

But when you introduce a new product or service to your market or a known product or service to a *new* market—and your price is merely competitive with that of similar products and services—it is not a benefit. (Even if it is *lower*, remember that "Nothing is a bargain if you don't want it!") And, of course, if your product itself can't be compared, because there is no other product quite like it, price can hardly be considered a benefit.

In any situation where you have a big price advantage, where the saving is significant or where money itself is the focus, then the money or the offer does become the big benefit—and how the product or service will enhance your life becomes secondary to this. For example:

> Primary: "Save $1,000 with this sensational offer."

> Secondary: "And enjoy all the advantages of having a deluxe what-cha-call-it in your home."

These differences will become clearer as we move forward, but let's go back now to the project we've just accepted and see how *Vital Woman* figures its features and benefits.

Vital Woman is a new monthly magazine devoted to women's health and fitness. Because it is the first (only) magazine to do this, the price or offer will not be the major benefit.

> It has 96 pages, many illustrated articles in color, two major features in each issue concerning major health topics and women, nine regular departments covering the art of self-care, fitness and exercise, nutrition, natural healing, reader questions and answers, preventive medicine, family assistance, advice on healthy relationships, and controversial topics.

> The magazine has ten editorial advisors, all prominent woman physicians, who will contribute from time to time as well as advise.

> Subscribers will be invited to send in questions and to share their experiences with other subscribers. The editorial board will digest current information, give both sides, then offer its point of view.

> As a new publication, it will be priced at $19 for the first year.

You've just read a long list of features. How many benefits can you extract?

This sounds easy enough, but once you actually try it, a lot of questions can come up, like "Is this *really* a benefit?" "Isn't this benefit too small?" "Isn't this benefit too large—too amorphous?" Let's work it through together.

First, go back to your selling proposition. Who is the market? (Active, busy women between the ages of 18 and 34.) All right. Be 25 and female for a while. Now look at the features again and make a pass, using raw data. For example:

- *Vital Woman* can help you take better care of your health and *overall* well-being because of its information.

- *Vital Woman* will help you be *well informed* on medical topics that pertain to women. Then, when you go to your doctor, you will be able to *communicate better* regarding your own personal health problems.

- *Vital Woman* will give you *current medical and health advice that you can count on* because it comes from (or is reviewed by) a board of prominent physicians.

- *Vital Woman* will help you understand and deal with many common health problems, saving you time, money, and worry.

- *Vital Woman* is qualified to cover important medical and *health topics* for women because it is directed by a board of prominent woman physicians.

- *Vital Woman* is *involving and easy to read* because it has many illustrations in color.

- If you sign on now, you will be able to take advantage of a *special offer that saves you money.*

Not bad—for a first pass. (You may even have more than I've shown here. Good!)

You'll be able to pull a variety of nice specific benefits from the departments, too.

- *Vital Woman* enables you to talk about your health problems and get answers from top physicians (with Q and A sections).

- *Vital Woman* shows you how to diet and exercise for a healthy, well-tuned body.

- *Vital Woman* gives you guidance on a healthy outlook and positive relations with others.

- *Vital Woman* enables you to apply the principles of natural healing so you can keep medicines and drugs to a minimum.

- *Vital Woman* affords you an open information exchange so you'll be informed on controversial health topics.

If the editors are generous with their information, you can expand considerably in all of these areas with specifics. But how do you select the *major* benefits. Are these all true benefits? Which are more important? Which should be subordinated? How might they be strengthened? Enlarged?

Growing and Pruning Benefits

On your first pass, your benefits may seem pretty obvious—even mundane. For example, look at the first benefit, "*Vital Woman* can help you take better care of your health and overall well-being because of its information." So what? I don't know about you, but this leaves me ho-hum. How can you turn a broad, blah statement like this into a big benefit—even a moral imperative?

Here's where you'll have to start employing your imagination (and your salesmanship). Some benefits are blah because they are too broad or too big. Others need dramatization. Most can gain by honing in on basic human desires or aspirations.

To help you start thinking, here are some examples of how easily blah benefits can be reworked.

> *Blah benefit*:
> It will make your hair curly.
> *Rah benefit*:
> Have the beautiful soft curls you've always dreamed about!—or—Save time and money and always look good!
> *Blah benefit*:
> You'll be able to make more money.
> *Rah benefit*:
> Never worry about money again!—or—Make $100,000 a year—even more!
> *Blah benefit*:
> You'll feel better with this vitamin compound.
> *Rah benefit*:
> Regain the vitality of youth!
> *Blah benefit*:
> This course will help you in business.
> *Rah benefit*:
> How to make it to the top in a rough job market!—or
> If only one person is promoted—make sure it's you!
> *Blah benefit*:
> Win a new car.
> *Rah benefit*:
> Win the car of your dreams!
> *Blah benefit*:
> Improve your complexion.
> *Rah benefit*:
> Youth market: Banish ugly blackheads and pimples forever!
> Mature market: Enjoy the soft smooth skin of youth!

Two things should become apparent as you play around with benefits and the many ways they can be stated. First, you can expand or contract your benefits throughout your promotion, rephrasing them and regrouping them to tell your story from several different angles. Second, your basic benefit development and the hierarchy of benefits (or relationship of one benefit to another) depend heavily on the specific values and aspirations *of your target market*.

For example, in the above example regarding the "vitamin compound," an easy assumption might be that this is for an aging citizen who wants to feel peppy again. However, say it's for an eight-year-old boy whose mother is concerned about his growth. She wants to make sure he has all the vitamins and nutrients he needs, but the *last* thing she wants him to have is *more* vitality!

In looking to further enhance a group of benefits, you'll find this next step is essential. You cannot determine your big benefit or major benefit without it, nor can you build your promotion and put your benefits in a reasonable order until you have it.

Determining Your Hypothesis

The word *hypothesis* may put you off a little at first, but just like *concept*, it's easy when it's defined. A hypothesis is merely an assumption or a proposition. (Tom Collins, former creative head of Rapp & Collins, first used this term in creative concept development. He applied the term in developing a group of testable space ads, each embodying a different assumption, or hypothesis.) For our purpose, a hypothesis is an assumption regarding the market and what it wants or desires, and how this ties in to your product and its benefits.

When copy or concept testing is conducted in direct response advertising, it is, in truth, hypothesis or assumption testing.

A hypothesis is determined by overlaying your product's big benefits on your market profile (demographics, geographics, and psychographics) and the corresponding values of that market. From this you nurture the one assumption that is based on the broadest and strongest appeal to your defined market.

Once you have determined your hypothesis, you will be able to sort and order all your benefits in a proper hierarchical or descending/ascending order, and you will be able to theme your promotion and develop your "hooks," headlines, and leads.

You'll notice I've introduced a new element here: *corresponding values*. Let's back up for a minute and do a checklist:

Benefits? O.K.

Hypothesis? O.K.

Market profile? O.K.

Corresponding values? Tilt

I owe you an explanation of *corresponding values*. Big benefits are big because they hit certain deep-seated human needs or drives. Basic drives, desires, and aspirations rule every one of us to a degree. They're not just the big drives such as sex, greed, and fear (as some oversimplifiers may think they are), but a whole range of desires and concerns that change and shuffle around inside people depending on 1) how old they are, 2) how much income they have, 3) where they live (geographically), 4) their education, 5) the socio-economic structure they come from, 6) their life style, 7) whether they're single or married, parent or childless, and 8) the tempo of the times.

There are dozens of research groups that segment and target markets and offer studies that categorize people by a combination of geographics, values, and lifestyles. These groups have different purchase patterns: they buy different things for different reasons.

Then there are "cohort groups" made up of people who have all gone through the same major world experiences at roughly the same ages: the "Depression" babies, the "World War II" generation, the "Silent" generation, and so on. For example, the Depression group's attitudes regarding saving, debt, and credit in no way resemble those of the Baby Boomer cohorts. These cohort groups also represent major differences in age with all the changes that maturation and old age produce.

Such intricate segmentation has become extremely important in direct marketing today. Thanks to the computer and the availability of vast data banks, we are able to analyze our own customers and apply what we learn to target our prospects with far more efficient techniques than ever before; lifestyles and other selectors figure heavily in this targeting.

In the future, as such targeting becomes even more sophisticated, we will truly reach out to prospects in actual one on one relationships. According to Peter Francese, president and founder of American Demographics, Inc., "The end game of this process will come when businesses market to individuals rather than to consumer segments." [1]

If you're lucky, you'll have access to all such new research. Use it. You will learn a lot about your prospect market, what is important to it, what it aspires to, what motivates it, how it spends its time and money.

Understanding these things is crucial to developing your hypothesis, for it gives you the key to your emotional appeals. It shows you how to couch your benefits and mold them to your market. Your ability to choose and develop those approaches with the greatest potential appeal will determine the success or failure of your promotion.

If you don't have access to scientific segmentation, take the clearest profile you can get of your market from your research and from media selection and media profiles (demographics from the lists that work, and readership studies from publications whose subscribers respond well). Also, get a subscription to *American Demographics*,[2] one of the finest profile sources for marketing and media people, and for smart copywriters.

In determining the drives and needs and aspirations of your market, be wary of the business market and the split appeals mentioned in Chapter 2. The basic drive in many of these cases should be corporate recognition or advancement, whether one person or several people (or several levels of decision makers) are involved. (For obvious reasons this will seldom apply to professionals and entrepreneurs.) At the same time, business and industrial direct response advertising today is targeted to incorporate the different needs and desires of decision makers at various levels in any one company, personalized to each level's specific requirements. (More about this strategy at the end of the chapter.)

Here are several fine examples of the appeals and promises that have been used by direct response specialists. This first group, by Vic Schwab, cofounder of Schwab/Beatty direct response advertising agency and a true pioneer of direct response, is as valid today as it was in 1942.

Advantages People Want to Gain[3]

Better Health
Greater strength, vigor, endurance. The possibility of longer life.

More Money
For spending, saving, or giving to others.

Greater Popularity
Through a more attractive personality. Through personal
   accomplishments.

Improved Appearance
Beauty. Style. Better physical build. Cleanliness.

Security in Old Age
Independence. Provision for age or adversity.

Praise from Others
For one's intelligence, knowledge, appearance, or other evidences of
   superiority.

More Comfort
Ease. Luxury. Self-indugences. Convenience.

More Leisure
For travel, hobbies, rest, play, self-development.

Pride of Accomplishment
Overcoming obstacles and competition. Desire to "do things well."

Business Advancement
Better Job. Success. "Be your own boss." Reward for merit.

Social Advancement
Moving in better circles. Social acceptance.

Increased Enjoyment
From entertainment, food, drink, and other physical contacts.

People also want to:

Be good parents   Be creative

Have influence over others   Resist domination by others

Be sociable, hospitable   Satisfy their curiosity

Be gregarious   Emulate the admirable

Express their personalities   Appreciate beauty

Win others' affection   Be proud of their possessions

Be "first" in things   Be efficient

Improve themselves mentally   Acquire or collect things

Be recognized as authorities

And they want to save:

Money, time, work, discomfort, worry, doubts, risks, embarrassment,
    offense to others, boredom, personal self-respect, and prestige.

Vic Schwab warned, however, that trends and times themselves
change our aspirations and desires; appeals and values come and go
in popularity, and this, too, must be taken into account. (When you
consider the youth of the fifties, sixties, seventies, eighties, and
nineties, it's clear that there can indeed be extreme value swings
every decade.) This second list comes from Bob Stone: [4]

Basic Human Wants

The desire to gain: *The desire to avoid loss:*

To make money   To attract the   Avoid criticsm

To save time   opposite sex   Loss of possessions

To avoid effort   To be an individual   Physical pain

To have health   To emulate others   Reputation

To be popular   To take advantage   Danger in buying

Enjoyment   of opportunities   Loss of money

Cleanliness   Trouble

Praise

To be in style

To gratify curiousity

To satisfy appetite

To have beautiful
    possessions

Andi Emerson, President of the Emerson Marketing Agency, also lists human needs.[5]

Eight Basic Human Needs

1. *Making Money*

   Improve job skills, increase pay

   Learn new job skills, get better-paying jobs

   Outside spare-time income

2. *Saving Money*

   Sales, close-outs, discount operations, factory-direct, introductory offers, pre-pub offers, charter member offers

   Longer-wearing, less replacement cost

   Elimination of expense (do-it-yourself, reduce overhead, cut down consumption)

3. *Winning Praise*

   Improve homemaking, gardening, etc., skills

   Awards, citations, certificates for generous or meritorious actions

   Get better grades in high school or college

4. *Helping Children and/or Family*

   Health appeals (food, vitamins, medicines, exercise)

   Education

   Recreation

5. *Saving Time and Effort*

   Physical drudgery

   Instant results, overnight benefits

   Carefree maintenance

6. *Impressing Others*

   Specific status symbols (possessions)

   Indirect status symbols (memberships, certificates, awards, speeches, chairmanships, etc.)

   Education and knowledge (traveling, speech, courses, degrees, books, art, music)

7. *Having Fun*

   Traveling

   Family outings, picnics, etc.

   Nightclubs, race tracks, movies, bowling, dancing, etc.

8. *Self-Improvement*

   Physical (weight, muscles, hair, clothes, makeup, sex appeal)

Mental (education, philosophy, psychology, controlling others, influencing others)

Spiritual (religion, helping others, self-control)

Andi cautions that the strongest motivations are unconscious motivations that must be indirectly tapped if they are to work most effectively. For example, you can't come right out and say that this is how your prospect can impress others!

Richard Shaver, President, Response Imperatives, Ltd., has added six basic drives to the eight basic human needs from Andi Emerson.[6]

Six Basic Drives

1. Self-preservation
2. Love
3. Gain
4. Duty
5. Pride
6. Self-indulgence

Dick Shaver stresses the importance of distinguishing between the needs and the wants that your product or service will satisfy, considering both needs and wants as they apply to your market.

Enough! You have your benefits, you know your market, you're able to extract the market's corresponding values (desires, needs, aspirations), and you can now formulate your hypothesis, based on strong, emotional appeals that will reach the greatest possible number of people in your market.

All you need now is a diagram showing this, but how about a sandwich instead? Follow this recipe:

- Take one slice of market, clearly segmented and defined.
- Spread it liberally with a thick mixture of values, aspirations, and desires or drives.
- Take one fine slice of appropriate prime benefit and place it carefully on top.
- Sprinkle with creative thinking and heat well.
- Serve up garnished with secondary benefits.

What you get is one hot hypothesis, the quality of which may vary depending largely on the big benefit you use and the contents of your value mixture.

This process can work in reverse as well. When marketers have a product and are trying to define the prime market for that product, they use a similar process to determine first the needs or desires that can be served by the product or service. Then the marketers find the market that best embodies these established needs and desires. For example:

> This product produces more attractive skin because it softens dry skin and removes wrinkles. Everyone wants to look better, have a better complexion. But only older people (and most particularly older women) are concerned with dry skin and wrinkles. This leads you to the prime market—(you guessed it) older women.

Easy as the hypothesis recipe sounds backward and forward, I hope you'll agree that this is something you should practice before moving along, because in application, it is hard work. You'll have an opportunity to try it in the exercises at the end of this chapter.

Figure 5–1 is a perfect example of a strong hypothesis (in reverse). The product is a book on build-it-yourself home and yard projects. The market, very briefly stated, is young families in the middle to upper-middle income category. The prime benefit is pure wish fulfillment based on a hypothesis that goes something like this: Many young families need loads of home improvements that they cannot afford to buy. Now you can provide all these things for your family, save money, and proudly say "I did it myself."

Applying What You've Learned

Now let's apply what you've learned about benefit selection and hypothesis development to *Vital Woman*. Let's make a second pass at *Vital Woman*'s primary benefits.

As you'll remember, our market is active, busy women between 18 and 34. If you follow the recipe and spread the values or aspirations on here, using Vic Schwab's listings, you'll opt for "better health" and "improved appearance" first off. But you might also consider 1) increased enjoyment, 2) pride of accomplishment, 3) resisting domination by others (i.e., the medical profession), 4) being up-to-date, and 5) saving yourself from worry, doubts, and risks. Then add helping children and/or family, self-improvement, pride, and self-preservation from the other lists.

In choosing values and aspirations, it is particularly important for you to understand your market in relation to the times and current lifestyles. While Vic Schwab was looking at homemakers, you're dealing with a market of greater variety—probably women who work outside the home. They will also be representative of the times by having interests in health and fitness and self-improvement that are typical of young and middle-aged people today.

FIGURE 5–1   Rodale Press: A Strong Hypothesis at Work

Courtesy of Rodale Press, Inc.

Let's go back to the first benefit again: "*Vital Woman* can help you take better care of your health and overall well-being because of its information."

Although good health and well-being are primary benefits, this benefit is too vague and all-encompassing. You can state it more succinctly by tailoring it to its prime market. For example, if the market were older women 55 to 60, you might say that *Vital Woman* would help restore vitality and a new enthusiasm for living and doing (under Schwab's listings). As we're talking to women 18 to 34, however, we have to consider what's more important to *them*.

Here is one theory or potential hypothesis: Young, active women today want to be in charge (pride or self-preservation?). Taking control or resisting domination by others is important to today's women, particularly in the areas of health and medicine. They question doctors and expect explanations. Less and less do they accept medical instructions on blind faith.

They are most comfortable when they can obtain qualified medical and fitness input so they can decide (at least in part) what is best for them.

Let's take another of the benefits for a moment: "*Vital Woman* will help you be well informed on medical topics that pertain to women. Then, when you go to your doctor, you will be able to communicate better regarding your own personal health problems."

Here is another hypothesis that might apply: Many women are uncomfortable talking to male doctors about their female-related problems. Many of them feel doctors are unsympathetic, do not listen carefully or answer questions fully. If these women were better informed, they could have a better relationship with their doctors. Vic Schwab might have said they want to be recognized as authorities, or Bob Stone might say they want to be recognized as individuals.

There is still another possible hypothesis, and it has to do with confidence and medicine. Today there are so many changes, new treatments, and new drugs, that doctors are deluged with information. Many of them fail to keep up. To prevent doubts or fears about good health and good treatment, many women take it upon themselves to keep up with medical developments (self-preservation). This is all right, but in fact it seems to take us right back to the first benefit: "*Vital Woman* can help you take better care of your health and overall fitness because of its information."

The hypothesis that we set up first applies here as well, and this hypothesis can be enlarged and strengthened.

Earlier hypothesis: Young, active women today want to take charge. Being in control, or resisting domination by others, is important to today's women, particularly in the areas of health and medicine. They question doctors and expect explanations. Less and less do they accept medical instructions on blind faith.

Revised hypothesis: Today's women want to be informed on important health and fitness issues so that they can take control of their lives and improve their relationships with their doctors.

However, we still have *other benefits* that come into play.

"*Vital Woman* will give you current fitness and health advice that you can count on because it comes from (or is reviewed by) a board of prominent woman physicians."

"*Vital Woman* is qualified to cover important medical and health topics for women because it is directed by a board of prominent woman physicians."

Under the need for competent information to avoid risk, worry, or fears about lack of health data, you now have another hypothesis: Women feel more confident when they know their health and medical information is screened by a group of prominent physicians—and preferably woman physicians (the implication here being that woman physicians will empathize well with other women because they understand their problems).

Obtaining the information comes before who gives it. So now we're beginning to build a pyramid—to establish a hierarchy of benefits and hypotheses. And obtaining information is the base.

At this point, everything seems to flow from the statement, "When women are better informed they can take control, make decisions wisely, ask good questions, evaluate answers." . . . This enables them to avoid risk and worry because they can understand and solve or prevent many health problems and live a more healthy life. (And, of course, save time and money.) . . . This allows them to better communicate with their doctors (be recognized as individuals, not dominated).

Let's stick with this for now and see where it takes us on the next leg.

Constructing Your Copy Platform

Surprise! You have just laid the base for a copy platform.

If you've been following closely up to here, you've already accumulated enough material to start playing with your major headlines and subheads (and, no doubt, if you have a strong creative bent you've already been doing just that).

Up to this point, by the way, this may all be part of a team effort and you may be part of the group. There is no reason why creative meetings, or brainstorming sessions, synectics, or creative planning groups consisting of writers, artists, creative directors, product managers, marketers, and production people can't get together to hammer out a hypothesis and benefit hierarchy. I recommend it, in fact.

Although there is also no reason that you can't go it alone, this is where two heads can be better than one. If you are working with a publication, its editors may have already worked out some benefits and a hypothesis in structuring their editorial plan.

Authors, inventors, and manufacturers all have strong ideas about their products or services and what they'll do for people. Marketers, managers, and well-wishers of all kinds will add their two cents as well. You'd be smart to listen carefully. You might pick up valuable ideas; then again, maybe not. You must be the judge. From here on, your role in the group becomes more and more important. You're approaching the place where one head (*your* head) may be better than two. The copy platform ultimately *belongs to you.*

Again, we'll start with a definition. Your *copy platform* is simply a restatement of your hypothesis and your sub or secondary assumptions in direct response advertising prose, or deathless promotional terms that incorporate the "you."

Let's line up the hypothesis and benefits on the left and extract the copy platform on the right.

1. *Main hypothesis:*

Women want to be better informed about their health and fitness so that they can take control, make wiser decisions. This enables them to avoid risk and worry because they can understand and solve or prevent many health problems and live a more healthy life.

2. *Secondary (or alternative) hypothesis:*

Good information allows women to better communicate with their doctors (be recognized as individuals, not be dominated), ask good questions, evaluate answers.

3. *Major benefits:*

Vital Woman gives women current medical and health information that they can count on because it comes from (or is reviewed by) a board of prominent physicians.

Vital Woman is qualified to cover important medical and health topics for women because it is directed by a board of prominent women physicians.

4. *Secondary benefits:*

- *Vital Woman* is enjoyable and easy to read because it has many color illustrations.

- *Vital Woman* has top physicians to answer reader questions (Q & A sections).

- *Vital Woman* has diet and exercise information.

- *Vital Woman* offers guidance on a healthy outlook and positive relations with others.

- *Vital Woman* presents principles of natural healing that keep medicines and drugs to a minimum.

- *Vital Woman* provides an open information exchange on controversial health topics.

1. *Main platform statement:*

You are the primary diagnostician. Let *Vital Woman* help ensure that the one person who can take care of you best does a good job.

- Take charge of your own health with *Vital Woman*.

- Put your health in the best hands—your own.

- Save the time and cost of unnecessary doctor visits.

2. *Secondary platform statement:*

You can make sure your doctor takes you seriously. (Why should you feel neurotic every time you feel sick?)

- Your doctor will listen when you ask, explain when you question.

3. *Major copy points:*

Every month you are invited to sit in on your own private physician's council on health and fitness.

or

Join a round table of foremost women physicians. Sit down every month and listen. Ask questions. Women doctors understand.

4. *Secondary copy points:*

- Over 10 pages of color illustrations, dozens of charts, drawings, and graphs make every issue of *Vital Woman* an enjoyable and informative experience.

- Let's talk about your health problems. When you have questions, ask *Vital Woman*'s board of physicians.

- Keep in shape the right way with *Vital Woman*'s medically approved diet methods and exercises.

- Let *Vital Woman* help keep your head and heart in balance.

- Get sound information on natural healing. Keep medicines and drugs to a minimum. Save money.

- Understand the pros and cons of important issues like abortion, your legal rights in the hospital, a birth plan. Contribute your opinions.

Under your secondary benefits (and copy points) will come all the specifics (the "as ifs," "likes," and "for examples") that strengthen your copy.

You'll find there's more than enough material for your basic copy platform here. You also have two possible hypotheses. So you'll want to decide beforehand which one you'll be featuring or how you might combine them. Or, because you have two hypotheses, you can also suggest a *concept test* here, one hypothsis against the other.

Some Things to Settle before the Final Strategy Statement

If you're on your toes, you may be wondering at this point why I've neglected to mention one major benefit: "If you sign on now, you will be able to take advantage of a special offer."

I've saved it for last because this is the offer and, as your offer, it's too important to go in with the other benefits. It is a benefit, but not the big benefit; that comes from the product itself. (Think about it—this is a new product; the offer is not a benefit until the product is a benefit!)

Because *offer* is important, whether or not you are in charge of its formulation, it is critical that you know how to judge a good offer, and how to recognize a weak one. And since you've been through Chapter 3, you can do just that.

Take the *Vital Woman* offer of $19 for the first year, for example. How might you strengthen it? Thanks to Chapter 3, you know this is a perfect place to use the initial "Charter Invitation," enabling your prospect to be "first on" and a "privileged" subscriber with the lowest going rates.

How else can you strengthen this offer? A guarantee? Of course. The product is untried and virtually unknown. This is a natural place for a one-hundred percent money-back guarantee. (If this sounds daringly generous to you, relax. Your prospects will appreciate it and few will ever take advantage of the guarantee.)

Something else? A response incentive? Sure. If you can convince the powers-that-be that this will justify the added expense, you might suggest testing a highly related, qualifying premium—something that's inexpensive and particularly appealing to your prospect market. How about a low-budget booklet: *Answers to 24 of Women's Most Serious Medical Questions?* It has good copy potential for you.

So you have 1) charter invitation, 2) special charter subscription price (you might want to suggest a price test here), 3) premium incentive, and 4) full guarantee. You might also want to apply another response motivator to your offer—a deadline.

Now you have a strong offer. Your promotion has a good chance of success. What else might you consider before you lock up your creative strategy?

MISCELLANEOUS
RECOMMENDATIONS

This is the time for miscellaneous recommendations or ideas that in some cases may need consensus, or the approval of others.

Remember *voice* (who's talking) and *credibility* (why this person is qualified)? Well now's the time to decide who should sign the letter. In this case, since your market is women and your subject is women's health, recommend that your spokesperson be a credible, logical woman. (A woman doctor? Publisher? Editor?) I suggest you consider a woman publisher in this case. Publishers can speak logically and glowingly about *Vital Woman*'s editorial merits. And because *Vital Woman* is a medically oriented publication, how about adding your medical advisory board—right up front on the letterhead?

Go back to Chapters 3 and 4 and make sure you've thought through all the major techniques and guidelines that apply here. Although more may come out as you write, it's good to try to pin down as many aspects of the package as you can at this point.

If you're working with a team, now's the time for "legal" considerations to come up; also, some companies have their own "rules" and customs. Sometimes it's as simple as who signs the letter. You may think the publisher's the best choice, but your executive vice president may change your mind because she's decided she wants to sign your letter. (So let's be gracious and keep our jobs!)

Don't go overboard on motivators and involvement devices either. They're expensive and require testing. And remember—credibility *and* the Basic Law!

KEEP YOUR FORMAT
OPTIONS LOOSE

In the case of *Vital Woman*, you'll want to recommend a standard direct mail consumer package with brochure (because your specs indicate that *Vital Woman* will be heavily illustrated). Also, a brochure can give additional credibility to a new, as yet unpublished product.

You may not need all four pages to tell your story in the letter; you may not want a lift letter, but it's good to know it's in the budget if you do. So plan for both.

Before creativity carries you too far, however, get a clear feeling for budget—is it "sky's the limit" or "standard and small"? Pin it down *before* you move beyond this stage. But don't let *them* pin *you* down on format yet. Hold out! Hedge! You're not ready to finalize any format decisions yet, whether you have a $15,000 budget or a $500,000 budget.

CONSIDER THE COMPUTER

Speaking of budget, at this stage you should also think about computer personalization. Good personalization can change the way you plan your package or packages. It will affect copy, design, and format, as well as costs.

Computer letters have considerable appeal if they're done properly. Sweepstakes, for example, often use dramatic computerized components because everyone likes to see his or her name in print (up in lights, with dramatic headlines and value certificates that claim the prospect may have won a million dollars or more). On the other hand, people also respond well to the more intimate, personal feeling of a dignified computerized letter. (This does not mean simply computer-printing a name on the front page of a letter four or five times. That is a dull and tacky use of computerization and it impresses no one.)

Certain kinds of situations lend themselves to good computer personalization, however. Here's how to determine your course. Use computer formats only

1. If you have a package in which several components, in addition to your outer envelope, should carry the prospect's name and address for dramatization and credibility.

    *   Membership cards or personal invitations
    *   Sweepstakes components
    *   Financial applications, insurance certificates, and plastic cards
    *   Business letters that require personal salutations
    *   Warranties and service contracts

2. If you have customer data in your computer that can be used for a very personalized selling story.

    *   Last purchase date
    *   Product or category of product purchased
    *   Specific deadlines
    *   Serial or warranty numbers
    *   Appropriate personal information—birthday, anniversary, number of children

3. If your quantities and/or budget will be large enough on your test rollouts to make computerization cost-effective.

4. If you have up-to-date, accurate computer data. For example: you may not want to computerize your mailing if the computer can't give you gender or first names.

Remember this: always computerize your reply form. Period.

Consider this: Don't always computerize your letter salutation (even when you have gender). Instead of "Dear Mr. Jones" or "Dear Ms. Smith" try establishing a good relationship right up front with a warm, friendly "Dear Fellow-Gardener" or "Dear Book Lover" or "Dear Colleague" or "Dear Concerned Parent," and so on.

Figure 5–2 shows an example of artist and designer working together to create a very unusual mailing. This tabloid-style front

FIGURE 5–2   TCI Cable Television: An Unusual Personalized Tabloid Mailing

Entertainment Herald
PARK RIDGE METRO EVENING EDITION

NUMBER 19   APRIL 1993

EXTRA!! EXTRA!! EXTRA!!
GREGORY IMM SEIZES CONTROL OF ENTERTAINMENT INDUSTRY IN PARK RIDGE, IL!!!

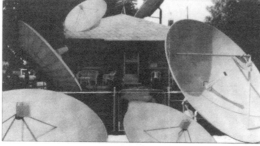

Imm **strikes multi-billion dollar deal, puts several movie chains, concert halls, coliseums and live theaters under one roof in Park Ridge, IL** (See related story on Page 2)

PARK RIDGE, AP—
Earlier this week, Gregory Timm announced plans to leverage a multi-billion dollar deal with the entertainment industry.

Timm said "I've struck a deal with TCI Cable TV to get offerings of every nearly every major entertainment facility installed in my home for only $19.95, saving forty dollars!"

"Our home is becoming a high-tech entertainment facility for stage plays and musicals, sporting events, blockbuster movies, superstar comedy, concerts and

virtually any other form of commercial entertainment available on the market."

"We'll also have educational programs & good stuff for the kids," Gregory reported. "Not to mention, great reception!" "Simply brilliant!" TCI said of Timm's unprecedented transaction. "Such negotiating prowess is amazing."

Basically, Gregory is paying pennies for a product that costs millions upon millions of dollars to produce.

This transaction gives

Timm even more control over home entertainment than cable kingpin Ted Turner. Never before has anyone seized more control of the entertainment industry.

"With this deal, I'll have the world at my fingertips," said Gregory with a huge smile. "President Roosevelt's legendary 'New Deal' pales in comparison with this...and I think he'd be a little jealous." A spokesperson for TCI Cable Television, the intermediary, confirmed that this unprecedented deal is, in fact, legitimate.

Timm home is now a communication center with sports, news, movies and music.

Famous Stars Visit Imm Home
Gregory and family enjoy time with favorite actors and musicians

PARK RIDGE, AP—
Several well-known actors, actresses, musicians and sports heroes dropped by the Timm home at 1023 Vernon Ave.

"I've always enjoyed seeing them," Gregory Timm said, "but to actually invite them into my home truly is a dream come true." Everyone in Gregory's family agreed.

"The whole thing just snowballed! First, Neil Diamond came by and sang a few of our favorite songs, then Mel Gibson and Danny Glover dropped in three times! It was great to have them all in here in Park Ridge."

Well-known performers enjoying the company of the Timms.

"Harrison Ford brought by a few adventure stories, then we had sing-a-long with Elton John and Eric Clapton, and Tom Cruise charmed everyone with his tales of how he got the girl," Gregory said. "Michael Jordan floated through the air and gave us a good look at his knees, and with a grand slam, all-star baseball player Dave Winfield drove himself and three others home."

Timm also reported that Chevy Chase, Goldie Hawn, Eddie Murphy, Whoopi Goldberg, Robin Williams and George Burns all swapped jokes while the family gathered around to laugh.

"Arnold Schwarzenegger, Bruce Willis and Sylvester Stallone muscled in to bring real action to the party, and we all enjoyed great peace of mind knowing MacCauley Culkin was watching the house," Gregory said, excitedly.

When it was all over, the Timms had hosted more than a hundred famous guests. "This is most fun we've had in a long time. It was wonderful to have them in Park Ridge. We're looking forward to their next visit." Gregory said. "They want to meet our friends, so we're going to have a great big party."

New Park Ridge Sports Arena Opens Today

PARK RIDGE, UPI—
The most versatile and comprehensive sports arena in the world opened today at 1023 Vernon Ave. Owner and general manager of the arena, Gregory Timm, said "This arena is truly unique because it will become home to over one hundred different sports."

Timm said there will be a lot of big-ticket sports like NBA and college basketball as well as NFL and college football, but there will also be plenty of other great sports like auto and horse racing, golf, tennis, skiing, bowling, billiards-even hunting and fishing.

"Perhaps the best part about the arena," says Gregory, "is that there is never a waiting line for the restroom and the refrigerator is always only a few feet away."

Sold-out concert held specially for Gregory Imm

PARK RIDGE, UPI—The biggest concert event of the year was held recently at 1023 Vernon Ave in honor of Gregory Timm of Park Ridge. The all-star musician said "Although millions of people saw my performance, I wanted to make it extra special for Gregory, my No. 1 fan."

Reportedly, other fans would have paid a hundreds of dollars for Timm's seats. "Had I known, I would have gladly scalped a few spots on my sofa to the highest bidders," Gregory said. "It was nice not to have crazed fans pushing at me from all sides during the concert, even though it was a jam-packed sell-out. And the acoustics were amazing thanks to TCI's DMX Digital Music Express."

"There was only one disappointment," said Gregory. "When the concert ended, I jumped up to get a pen and paper for an autograph, and when I returned, the musician was gone."

Huge fight breaks out in home at 1023 Vernon Ave

PARK RIDGE, AP—
"I don't really know how it all got started," said Gregory Timm. "I turned on cable TV and suddenly there were two giant men dancing around and swinging at each other right there in my home."

Gregory reported that after about three minutes, they stopped fighting and sat down to rest. Then after a bell rang, the men got up and started fighting again. This occurred several times until one of the men fell,

beaten and exhausted.

When asked why the police weren't called, Timm's reply was, "And miss the fight of the century? No way! The whole thing was far too entertaining."

INSIDE:
• Gregory Timm's journey aboard the Space Shuttle has some to remember. See TRAVEL, B-1.
• Timm's influence expected to affect current news in the economic industry. Story, C-3.
• Can Stadium Theater house Gregory Timm's baseball game? See page D-2.

FIGURE 5–2   (Continued)

page was folded down and mailed to an entire town. But each family or resident had his or her *own personalized version*. The tabloid dramatizes the family's total involvement in exciting entertainment happenings. "You, John Sample, are the star of every event . . . you are in the picture!" You could say, it brings the message "home." The back states exactly what it is: "The Deal Behind the Cover Story" with offer, response device, motivators, message, and call to order cable TV from TCI Cablevision.

Figure 5–3 shows a friendly software mailing to Parsons Technology customers. This mailing actually demonstrates the software's abilities to produce personalized greeting cards, announcements, and invitations through the examples shown on the cover and inside the first spread. The address, showing through the window, appears on the folder cover. The first spread also includes a personalized letter and personalized instructions. Inside are the full details with a call to action.

WHEN IS A DIRECT MAIL FORMAT MORE THAN A DIRECT MAIL PACKAGE?

We've been breezing along under the assumption that we want a direct mail package. That may not be the best strategy at all! A direct mail package may be just fine for *Vital Woman*, but you may want more than this for your next assignment. You may be thinking, "How about a second mailing as a follow-up? Or a telephone call? How about an advance postcard to alert the prospect to expect my mailing?"

Interpreted broadly, format can cover the shape of the entire promotion. In a few customer direct response programs, this can mean an additional effort. In almost all business-to-business programs, format includes more than one mailing or promotion.

Major format planning, a series of mailings, two-part promotions, and so on, are generally part of the big picture or the main marketing plan and therefore precede the creative strategy planning. It's important that you understand these formats nonetheless, because each embodies a promotional strategy. They will also affect your creative strategy development, particularly in business-to-business creative planning.

If the budget allows, testing a follow-up or announcement postcard is perfectly legitimate if you have good reason. ("An announcement of importance is coming—watch for it!" "Since we cannot repeat this offer, we're extending our deadline to make sure you don't miss this one last chance.") A good and logical announcement preceding your direct mail can increase response some 25 percent. A good follow-up should produce as much as 50 percent of the original response.

Such components should go into your creative strategy as extra steps to test with clear statements of objective. You should spell out

FIGURE 5–3   Parsons Technology: A Personalized Mailing That Demonstrates the Product

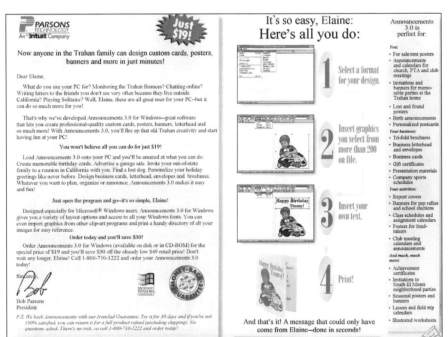

their role in relation to your main package, name your spokesperson, set down your timing (justify it), and justify your reasons for the medium. For example:

- Use the telephone as a follow-up so that we can find out *why* people don't respond.

- Use local billboards to announce the coming mailing since we're saturating a defined geographical area.

- Use a postcard to remind prospects of the deadline and what they'll lose if they miss it!

WHEN TO USE A TWO-STEP FORMAT

Follow-up reminders and advance announcements are used to draw attention to your original or primary package. Their job is to help you get the most response from your prospect lists in a well-targeted market.

In markets that are diffuse or difficult to target, a different kind of two-step process is often used. This is a very popular form of direct response for business-to-business mail and for large-ticket consumer products. It is generally known as *inquiry generation*. Step one is prospect qualification. Step two is inquiry fulfillment.

You see dozens of ads in magazines and newspapers, on the radio, even on TV, that end with, "Call this 800 number for more information." Sometimes it's a simple direct mail package or a postcard with an invitation to write or call. These are all lead getters, to be used

- When you have an expensive product and expensive promotion package that you don't want to waste on unqualified prospects (people who are very likely to throw it away).

- When you do not have a good, reliable list of prospects (by name, title, and address) and you want to build one.

The two-step's job is to produce *qualified* leads. There's no room for teasers here. You want to turn away unqualified prospects. At the same time, you may want to encourage prime prospects by offering a highly qualified premium—something (information, perhaps) that only a *good* prospect would want. ("For the discerning individual who is prepared to invest in the finest automobile ever made . . . " "Examine our free book and see if this is the kind of office equipment that can help your company increase productivity . . . .")

Step two is the information that fulfills the inquiry: "Enclosed is the information you requested." (This is a mandatory copy line, by the way—a rule that helps make sure your fulfillment package gets opened!)

This step represents a second component in your format planning and it must also fulfill the requirements of your creative strategy whether its objective is to make a sale, open the door for a sales call, or initiate a request for more information.

Your fulfillment package or information kit can now be considerably personalized if you wish and if your budget allows. You and the art director can do wonderful things with envelopes, brochures or booklets, letters, reply devices, and motivators with the knowledge that you will be speaking to prime prospects.

Also (budget permitting), you can add a third step to the two-step—a step for nonrespondents or a follow-up for "more information" requests—and on and on, for that matter. *Strategy* must work hand in hand with *timing* here. Any further steps should become part of your overall format plan as well. Without this, you can't create. (Just try to do a credible follow-up or an inquiry fulfillment letter when you have only a vague idea of the last time the prospect heard from you.)

Figure 5–4 shows one in a colorful series of prospect postcards. They're travel postcards from a fictitious "Dan" who always encounters problems on his varied vacations, but rises above them and has a great time, thanks to his travel insurance.

FIGURE 5–4   One of a Series of Reminder Postcards

Rather than mail out expensive insurance documents to prospects who were not actually planning travel, American Express Canada's Global Assist Travel Protection Plan sent out a regular series of these postcards to entertain and remind the prospects that when the time came, they were ready to serve them. (Naturally, an 800 number was included.)

In planning a two-step format, walk through your procedures carefully. Overlay your timing scheme. What do you want your prospect to *do?* What do *you* do next a) if the prospect responds, or b) if the prospect fails to respond? Is your timing realistic? Don't keep your inquiry waiting more than a few days. Hot inquiries cool off quickly.

Bear two things in mind at all times while you are plotting your strategy: the budget (stay within it) and the Basic Law—is all this going to make sense to the prospect? Stop. Let the idea cool. Then step back and reexamine it with a fresh eye.

Beyond the two-step formula lies pure business-to-business creative strategy development, where in many cases your format planning can go on and on and your creative strategy can become a little more complex. Not a lot more complex—remember, you'll still have just one basic objective, to acquire and cultivate (sell) customers.

Budgets are generally pretty liberal in the business-to-business area, as many businesses are playing for some very large stakes. (What's a $500,000 direct mail investment played off against a $10,000,000 contract?)

You may end up strategizing a whole series of informational mailings. Some may not even require immediate response. All will require creative strategy statements. (Remember the comparison of business and consumer objectives in Chapter 2?)

Some mailings may be *real* packages or dimensional mailings instead of standard direct mail packages. Dimensional mailings are usually gifts or premiums in tubes, envelopes, or boxes that dramatize a promotional theme. These premiums can run in a series of three, four, five, six, or more, and can go on for a year. They raise awareness and generally work to pave the way for the salesperson's call.

For example, a coffee cake, sent to customers to highlight a new sunrise pick-up service, a firefighter's hat to dramatize new solutions for the manager who's always "putting out fires," or a miniature paperweight, pencil cup, or pen holder to remind the prospect of your company. Good dimensional mailings should carry a letter and the gift should be closely related to the product or service and its sales story or theme.

This pretty well outlines your format possibilities in both business and consumer direct mail. Before you draw up your strategy (or strategies), however, there is one more consideration: how to set up testing strategies against an established control.

STRATEGIZING TO "BEAT THE CONTROL"

If you're developing your creative strategies to test against an established control, be very sure of your objectives and hypotheses.

Analyze the hypothesis underlying the control as well as the basic selling concepts so you don't unconsciously repeat it in another format or a new copy presentation. (You can, of course, always capitalize on what works by improving on it!)

Make sure you are testing a *specific creative idea* that you can explain in the context of every single component in your package.

New offers, premiums, involvement devices (tokens, stamps), and motivators (deadlines) should all be tested separately *in the control package*, not in a new, untested package. *An untested package should carry the same offer and motivators as those of the control.*

Remember the cardinal rule for testing: No test can incorporate and measure more than one variable. For example: Let's say you're testing a concept based on a new hypothesis and you also add a token, which has not been used before. The mailing works wonders. You win the test. But what won? Your execution of the new concept? Or the token? Or both? Worse still—if it lost, what was responsible for the loss? Perhaps the loss would have been far worse without the token. Perhaps not. This is no way to learn.

A smart creative person sets testing sights clearly and specifically and defines objectives and how these can be realized with the test package. The test then is a pure test of yes or no. Yes, the creative concept worked; no, the creative concept did not work. You learn either way. A gray test (in which you learn nothing) is the only bad or poorly executed test.

When to break the testing rule: Many professional free-lancers, when challenged to beat the control, execute mailings that pull out all stops: new creative concepts for new hypotheses, new involvement devices and motivators, new graphics, new formats—all in one package.

Their goal is to win, not to learn. Besides, they've already learned what makes winners and if they go up against a control by someone who doesn't know better, anything goes. If they do win, this is good for the free-lancers' business; their clients will call on them again. If they don't outdistance the control, however, their clients lose doubly: no new, stronger control, and no clear, usable testing data as to why something failed.

It's safe and scientific to go for a yes or no, "let's find out" test. It's heroic (and maybe foolish) to go for broke unless the testing history and/or the present control has blatantly ignored good direct response technique and, particularly, the use of proven motivators and response devices. Here's some sound guidance from two top pros, Jim Kobs and Sol Blumenfeld:

AN ORGANIZED APPROACH
FOR BEATING THE
CONTROL [7]

Top creative people are not always able to verbalize their approach
to creativity. An exception is Sol Blumenfeld of Sol Blumenfeld &
Associates. Here is his organized method for idea generation, which
he calls a five-track approach to beating the control:

1. *The subtractive approach.* This seeks to improve the effectiveness of a given mailing by reducing costs, thereby reducing the cost
per inquiry or sale. One way to do this is by using a "stripped down"
version of a winning package such as going from a 6 × 9 size to a
10 size, using a smaller circular, eliminating one element from the
package, and so on. Another way to accomplish the same thing is to
develop a new mailing that's more economical such as a self-mailer.
These approaches usually won't outpull the control in percent
response, but they can often produce a lower cost per order.

2. *The additive technique.* This means adding something to a control package that may increase its efficiency in excess of any
increased costs. Usually it involves inserts. A classic example is the
so-called publisher's letter, which was originated by Paul Michaels
when he was with Greystone Press. At other times the mere addition
of a token, stamp, or other involvement device can provide a substantial boost in results.

3. *The extractive approach.* This technique entails drawing on the
contents of an established ad or mailing and extracting a thought or
idea that can be built up as the main appeal. Blumenfeld cites an
example for a publication's subscription campaign in which he
picked up a very human appeal that was buried in the body copy of
their control ad. He developed it into a new headline, which substan-
tially beat the control.

4. *The segmentive technique.* As you might guess, this one entails
segmenting your market and developing one or more special promotions aimed at those different segments. Blumenfeld points out that
correspondence schools often use a special women's package,
because they have found that their normal packages simply don't
work as well with the female market. Likewise, record clubs often
use separate packages for country music, teen, and classical market
segments. Understandably, this technique requires that the copywriter
be familiar with the list universe to which he or she is writing and its
customer profile.

5. *The innovative approach.* This category is characterized by
Blumenfeld as being highly original, even wild. He believes that
every test series should contain at least one or two ideas that fall into
this category, because they can often produce more dramatic
improvements in results than the other approaches.

The Creative Strategy

Creative strategies often exist under different names, such as *creative plan, creative work plan, copy strategy*. Sometimes it's just a yellow pad with a free-lancer's notes. And sometimes it's a structured presentation by the creative director or the copywriter for a group of peers.

Some forms are shorter than the creative strategy outline I'm giving you here. But the considerable detail of your creative strategy is your assurance that you've covered your bases, thought through all the points, cleared the concepts, and pinned down important details before you start to execute your promotion.

Let's go over the elements of a good creative strategy again.

From the original selling proposition you should have 1) your product and its positioning or branding statement, 2) the market (its demographics and psychographics), and 3) the offer, 4) your hypothesis, then 5) your copy platform, starting with your major benefit, working down through your secondary benefits, and ending with a list of features.

It's also good to include a brief statement regarding the competition (which in the case of *Vital Woman* is nonexistent). You'll also want to set down your recommendations regarding motivators, spokesperson, and credibility.

Finally, you'll want to have some idea of format and, in the case of direct mail, postage, then testing considerations, if they apply. And that's it! "Format" should also take into consideration the entire program or promotion format. In our case this means only one direct mail package and its components, but as you've seen, in some business-to-business promotions and some high-ticket consumer programs, you'll want more than one effort or package. You may also need to develop substrategies or separate plans for the details of the longer, more complicated programs. This may also be necessary if you use more than one medium or have more than one level of decision makers in business-to-business promotions. We'll cover this in a minute.

These strategies may seem like a lot of work, but take heart. Once you've gone through all the steps, you can be comfortable with your creative direction and confident that you have the creative tools to execute a successful direct response promotion.

Let's pick up where we left off with *Vital Woman*.

A CREATIVE STRATEGY OUTLINE

Title of Job: Vital Woman magazine, the first comprehensive magazine devoted to women's health and fitness.

Competition:	None. This is the first such publication.
Market:	Active, busy women between the ages of 18 and 34. (Working women who

have shown an interest in health and fitness publications, exercise book buyers, etc.)

Offer:

Charter Offer, 1 year for $19; full money-back guarantee. Premium (*Answers to Women's Most Troublesome Health Questions*). Charter privileges.

Hypothesis:

Women want to be better informed about their health and general well-being so they can take control of their lives, make wiser decisions. This enables them to take better care of themselves and solve or prevent many problems.

Copy Platform/Benefits:

Vital Woman, the first magazine devoted to women's health and fitness, will enable you to take more responsibility for your own health

- Via expert medical advice on health and fitness.

- Via a better understanding of women's health and fitness problems.

- Via a natural approach to health.

The result will be

- A better relationship with your doctor.

- A healthier, happier life.

First Copy Statement:

You are the primary diagnostician. Let *Vital Woman* help make sure that *the one person* who can take care of you best does a good job.

- Take charge of your own health with *Vital Woman.*

- Put your health in the best hands—your own.

Don't waste time and money on unnecessary doctor visits.

Second Copy Statement:

Make sure your doctor takes you seriously. (Why should you feel neutrotic every time you feel sick?)

Third Copy Statement:	Join a round table of foremost women's physicians every month. Sit down and listen. Ask questions.
Secondary Benefits/ Features:	• Sound information on natural healing (keep medicine and drugs to a minimum) • Pros and cons of major women's health issues • Reader Q's and A's • Medically approved diets and exercise • Emotional and interpersonal advice • 10 pages of color, many illustrations throughout every issue
Recommendations:	• Use a deadline for the offer. • List full advisory board on first page of the letter. • Make the spokesperson a credible woman (female publisher or executive vp).
Format and Postage:	Direct Mail Package, Third Class Indicia • Outer envelope • 4-page letter • Brochure • 1-page lift letter • Reply card (BRC)

The Creative Strategy for Business-to-Business Marketing

Use the same creative methodology and strategy outline for the business market as for the consumer market, with one major difference.

In Chapter 2, I mentioned that businesspeople are human and that your appeals to them should take this into consideration. However (and here's the big "however"), some of them (those who are employees) are not buying for themselves. They are purchasing for a business, one that is owned by someone else, and their needs and desires are tricky, as you'll see in the next chapter.

In a sense, you have a relatively easy hypothesis that, in one form or another, will apply to all business promotions. It is based on the appeal to do a better job for the company and help the company make more money, with the hope that personal gain and/or recognition will follow.

This can be accepted as your hypothesis in many cases, but it must be carefully couched in terms that are not self-serving, and your benefits must represent primarily benefits *to the business* or to the people whom the business serves. You must honestly convince your decision maker that his or her action will indeed help the company, and thereby draw positive recognition. Then you must provide (through a careful presentation of benefits and features) the tools that your decision maker can use to present the case to a superior or to peers for consensus or for approval.

If you have several levels of decision maker, you'll need separate creative strategies for each level. For example: You have major research equipment for sale. Engineers in the research department must be convinced of the need for such equipment. Top management must understand that your company makes the best in the world. The purchasing agents must feel that your company is a good, price-competitive company with which to do business. Here you might consider a three-level program.

1. An ongoing corporate image-building campaign for top management that runs every month for a year

2. A two-step program (qualification and fulfillment kit) for delivering extensive information to a research engineer

3. A two- or three-step program with an incentive to request a sales call on the third level, the purchasing agent

You'll need three strategy outlines because you have three markets, three slightly different hypotheses, three different formats, and three different spokespersons (CEO to CEO, Inventor to Engineer, Sales Rep to Purchasing Agent).

Benefits, hypotheses, copy platforms, multiple formats, and test situations—with all these converging possibilities, you can see how important it is to execute your creative strategies with your heart beating on the inspirational level and your feet firmly grounded in budget, timing and pacing, and the Basic Law.

You will have to bring together harmoniously (and creatively) a group of separate elements. At all points as you develop your copy, you'll have to remember these elements and know when to pull them in or push them into the background. Some elements, of course, will always be up front, others will come and go, a few just come on once. It's a little like an orchestra—and you're the conductor. Maintain harmony!

These exercises will give you practice in benefit extraction, hypothesis recognition, and package development. Work them out carefully and don't peek at the solutions until you've given them your best try. When you feel comfortable with them move on to the next chapter— and the w-r-i-t-i-n-g! Please don't skip the exercises in this chapter. They are hard, but they are also very important for your understanding and growth. Mastering them (even a little) frees you to devote your creative energies to good writing, as you'll see in the chapters ahead.

Benefit Extraction

See how many benefits you can pull from the following list of product features. The product is a collection of art sculptures of American songbirds from the Smith Mint.

Features

- There are 6 songbirds in the collection; it is limited to 7,500 sets.
- They are designed by Arnold Fox, a well-known bird artist.
- They are all 10" high, life-size.
- The birds are Bluebird, Tufted Titmouse, Chickadee, Finch, Goldfinch, and Tree Swallow.
- They are handpainted.
- They cost $100 each. You may pay in installments.
- They will be shipped at the rate of 1 every 3 months.

Before reading further, translate these features into customer benefits. When you are finished, compare your list to the following possible results from a first try:

Features	Benefits
• There are 6 songbirds in the collection; it is limited to 7,500 sets.	• You'll belong to an exclusive group of collectors.
	• You'll own a unique collection that increases in value with time.
• They are designed by Arnold Fox, a well-known bird artist.	• You can enjoy the artistic excellence of the collection in your own home.
• They are 10" high, life-size.	• The natural beauty of the collection will enhance your home and give you personal pleasure and joy.

- The birds are Bluebird, Tufted Titmouse, Chickadee, Finch, Goldfinch, Tree Swallow.

- They are handpainted.

- They cost $100 each. You may pay in installments.

- They will be shipped at the rate of one every three months.

- Your friends will be impressed.

- No one else will have another set exactly like yours.

- You can pay for the collection easily.

How did you fare? Did you miss any of the benefits above? Have any additional ones of your own? (Note: "Teams" regularly can extract more benefits than individuals working alone.)

Hypothesis Recognition

Each of the five ads shown in Figures 5–5 through 5–9 has a strong hypothesis. Write down the hypothesis for each ad. Remember, the hypothesis is not a promotional statement, but an assumption about the prospect, based on recognized human needs, drives, and desires. Try starting your hypothesis with a statement about the assumed market. For example, "Many people feel . . . " or "A lot of women think . . . ." (You'll find the answers at the end of the exercises.)

Case Studies

Consider the two cases that follow. Like *Vital Woman,* their basic promotion format is a single direct mail package. One is to a consumer market, the other to a business market. Review the cases, then complete the following steps.

1. Draw up a list of your product's features; extract the benefits. What is the primary or big benefit(s)?

2. What appeals, desires, or aspirations does your market have that can apply to the big benefits?

3. Based on your answers to Questions 1 and 2, what is the hypothesis or creative concept underlying your overall promotion?

4. How will you establish credibility?

5. State your offer. How can you make it stronger?

6. What kind of outer envelope do you recommend? Describe your outer.

7. Paraphrase the outer envelope copy line.

8. What is your postage?

9. Who is speaking?

FIGURE 5–5   What Is the Hypothesis for This Ad?

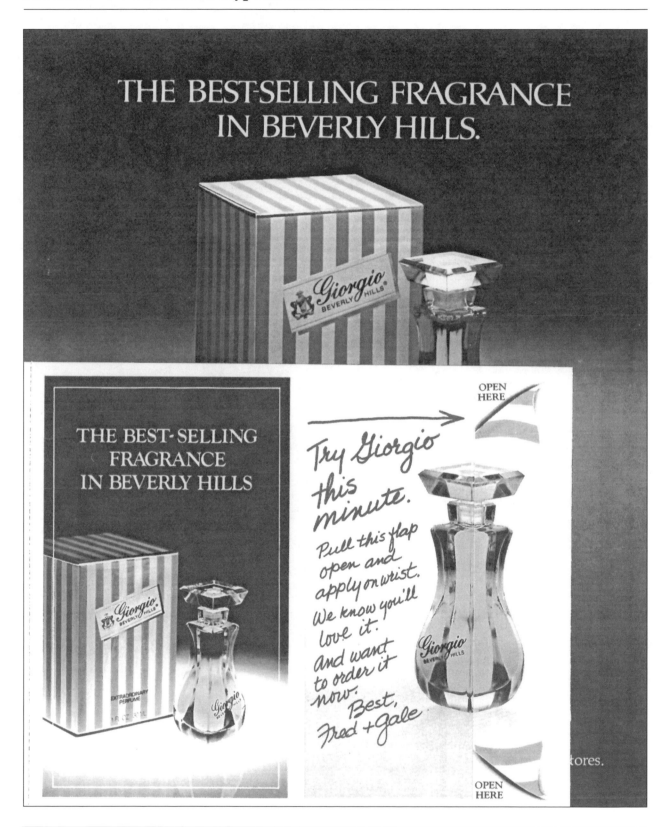

Courtesy of Giorgio, Inc.

FIGURE 5–6   What Is the Hypothesis for This Ad?

SMALL
MEDIUM
LARGE
EXTRA
LARGE

If you're not sure what size sweater to order, ask your operator.
She'll make sure you get the one that fits.

Sharon, or Judy, or Marion, or Janice—yes, even Ed or Bob or Mike—any of our more than 300 operators who man (or woman) our Lands' End phones on any one shift, can reassure you as to size, or even color, or fit, or availability. We encourage all of our more than 1,000 operators to be well-informed about the clothing and soft luggage in our catalog. And they are.

The fact is, they enjoy being helpful, so they stay abreast of most of our products and procedures. Including our unconditional, two-word guarantee: GUARANTEED. PERIOD.*

If you already have one of our catalogs, you'll find it convenient to have it at hand when you call. If not, why not ask for one? Or, if you prefer, mail back the coupon below. It's free—the catalog, that is.

Remember, you can call us toll-free any hour of the day or night, at 1-800-356-4444. One of us will answer. We certainly don't want you to talk to a machine. Never have, never will. Furthermore, we impose no time limit on calls. They last as long as it takes to satisfy you.

Repeating: 1-800-356-4444. It's even an easy number to dial!

LANDS' END
DIRECT MERCHANTS

© 1989, Lands' End, Inc.

Please send free catalog.
Lands' End, Inc.   Dept. D-23
Dodgeville, WI 53595

Name _____
Address _____
City _____
State _____ Zip _____

Or call toll-free: **1-800-356-4444**

THE NEW YORK TIMES MAGAZINE / JUNE 11, 1989   123

FIGURE 5–7   What Is the Hypothesis for This Ad?

Source: The Teaching Company™

FIGURE 5–8   What Is the Hypothesis for This Ad?

You've improved product quality, invested in new technology, even lowered your prices...

So why is the competition gaining on you?

A critical element may be missing from your competitive strategy—a focus on your relationships with your customers.

In a world of parity products and services, the quality of your customer relationships may be the only thing that can set you apart.

The key question: How do you ensure that your sales and service people have the skills they need to build and maintain lasting partnerships with your customers?

The very survival of your company depends on the answer to that question. And we can help you.

We're Learning International, the world's leading training company dedicated to strengthening clients' sales and service performance. For more than 30 years, we've been helping the world's most successful organizations to outdistance the competition.

We provide market-tested training programs for both sales and service professionals. Training that will help you leverage every point of customer contact to your advantage.

Training that will help your people develop the skills needed to win new business — and build customer loyalty.

Training that will help you not only achieve a competitive advantage, but sustain it. In a word, training that gets results.

If you'd like to know more about what Learning International can do for you, or to obtain a copy of our white paper on the new buyer-seller relationships, *Profiles in Customer Loyalty*, call or write today.

Learning International
225 High Ridge Road
Stamford, CT 06905
1-800-456-9390,
extension 79

Learning INTERNATIONAL

6E 9

Courtesy of Learning International.

FIGURE 5–9 What Is the Hypothesis for This Ad?

BARRON'S

THE DOW JONES BUSINESS AND FINANCIAL WEEKLY

Dear Investor,

Somewhere in the financial pages of your newspaper you'll probably find a sentence very much like...

"Shares of XYZ Corp. continue their meteoric rise, making almost daily appearances on the list of stocks reaching new highs..."

Have you ever read something like that and wondered why these meteors always leave without you?

Or why dividends always seem to grow faster on other people's stocks? Or how other people spot these stocks in the first place?

Anyone who invests can be forgiven for feeling at times that the markets traffic in closely guarded secrets -- and that the flow of traffic never passes your door.

But the truth is that no one -- not even the largest brokerages and institutions -- can keep tabs on more than a fraction of the thousands of investments offered.

The best stockpickers aren't prophets. They use published information, just as you do. They've just learned how to gather and interpret it better.

If you've read this far, you're presumably interested in finding a way to do the same. We suspect you'd be even more interested in finding twelve ways to do the same.

That's what a BARRON'S subscription brings you. And now, BARRON'S has a new look, so its wealth of information is easier to access and use.

1. To begin with, there's BARRON'S Market Week which one celebrated stockpicker called "the primary source of data that any intelligent investor requires." All the markets' statistics, plus our famous "Market Lab" covering earnings updates and comparisons, volume figures, investor sentiment readings -- everything you need to make better-informed decisions. These 80-plus pages of statistics give you the

(inside, please)

10. Paraphrase at least the first paragraph of the letter.

11. If you decide you need a brochure, explain why and paraphrase your main headline. What illustrations will you use, if any? How will you use them?

12. Should you have a lift letter? Who is the speaker? What is the proposition or new point of view?

13. Consider the order card: How does it present the offer? What motivates response? Does it have an involvement device?

Use the following Creative Strategy Statement outline to help you with your strategy.

1. Title and product positioning

2. Competition

3. Market

4. Offer (price and terms)

5. Rationale or hypothesis

6. Major benefit(s)

7. Secondary benefits and features

8. Copy platform

9. Recommendations (for credibility, motivation, involvement)

10. Direct mail format/postage, outer envelope, letter, brochure, lift letter, order form, other

CASE STUDY 1:
A CONSUMER PUBLICATION

Situation: A large, well-known mail order company, the Homemakers Corporation, wants to test launch a new magazine called *America's Cooking*.

They will send direct mail to 300,000 names.

From the test, they hope to learn which are the best lists and offers and whether the overall magazine concept can grow at an affordable cost per order (CPO).

You have been invited to participate in the test by developing a package to run against the control. The control is straightforward and basic direct mail package.

Product Data: *America's Cooking* will be the first magazine to represent the many American groups with ethnic cooking traditions all across the United States. It will focus on indigenous American cooking and family traditions, ethnic cooking passed on to us by our mothers and grandmothers. There will be particular emphasis on "easy" and "quick" meals throughout, and on inexpensive ideas for meals as well.

Each monthly issue will contain a lead story about an American town, its people, how they eat, their favorite local dishes, their traditions, their "community cookbook." There will be features on money-saving seasonal specials, quick and easy meals for modern American families on the go, fancy cooking for special entertaining.

Each issue will carry lots of four-color pictures and over fifty recipes. The recipes are bound in a center section (to cut out and save).

One of the mainstays of the magazine will be its executive editor, the woman who founded the Homemakers Corporation, and who is well known to the catalog customers because of her cookbooks and recipes. She is affectionately known to the catalog customers as Mrs. Annie Morris. (Every time a catalog order is filled, a free recipe card from "Mrs. Annie" is included.)

Market Description: Homemakers Corporation's own catalog customers are the inspiration for the magazine. They are almost 100 percent female, aged 25 to 50. Well over 70 percent are married. More than two-thirds of the market work—generally in clerical or factory jobs (some do part-time work). Their families are all in the middle-income category.

Some 250,000 of these customers will be tested along with 50,000 former catalog customers.

Frequency and Price: *America's Cooking* will be published 12 times a year for $15 a year when it starts. After a year, the price will go up.

CASE STUDY 2:
A BUSINESS PUBLICATION

Situation: A nationally known bank publishes a weekly economic forecast newsletter, *The Finance Bulletin.* Eight black-and-white pages of type, it is distributed exclusively to bank officers and their clients. The bank now wishes to test mail a promotion soliciting paid subscribers outside its immediate banking circle. You have been invited to design one of the test packages for this mailing.

Product Data: The newsletter goes to press Friday night so that it reaches its subscribers on Monday via first-class mail. Its board of senior economists sits down on Friday and reviews the week with the editor, who then finalizes all items and closes out the issue at the printer. These senior economists are all well known in finance and banking; one of them has written a book on a new economic theory.

The newsletter itself covers the stock market, bond market, commodities markets, interest rates and the "Fed," international banking and money movement, GNP, wage and employment statistics—all data (everywhere in the world) that can affect investments and monetary affairs. It does this with the help and contributions of six senior bank economists, forty staff economists, and an editor and research staff of three.

The Finance Bulletin works not only to spot major economic trends first (and to call them to its readers' attention), but also to reveal the stories behind much of the economic news today. *The Finance Bulletin* gives hard-to-find data on which financial officers can make sound business decisions. It tells *why* things happen, not *what* has happened. This kind of information is not readily available in newspapers and magazines.

Market Description: *The Finance Bulletin* will be test mailed to 100,000 top business executives, largely CEOs and chairmen of small to medium companies, chief financial officers at larger companies, treasurers, division heads, brokerage firm executives, financial consultants, and money managers of all kinds.

Frequency and Price: *The Finance Bulletin* will be published weekly, 52 times a year. It costs $1,200 for 52 issues.

Answers to Hypothesis Recognition

1. Giorgio: This is identification, not imitation. Many people desire to emulate the wealthy. But they can't afford the trappings of the Beverly Hills life. Now, they can be one of the "Beverly Hills Crowd" because they'll *smell* like them with Giorgio. (P.S. The ad and Giorgio were a smashing success!)

2. The Lands' End ad assumes that many people don't try mail order soft goods because they are afraid the products won't fit. This, in turn, means they'll have to bother with returns. The ad assures them that their sales representatives won't let this happen.

3. This ad reminds us that no matter how much education we have, no matter how much we read now or used to read, many of us still feel inadequate and just plain dumb about most of Western literature due to the immense body of work from every century. Now we can solve this problem, gain understanding and confidence, and never feel dumb again—without ever leaving our car (or home).

4. When things go wrong in a company, the one in charge often puts the department heads through a review process that seldom holds the secret. Learning International can bring management new perspectives, strategies that can correct the problem for your company in a competitive world.

5. This letter "lead in" from Barron's is a classic hypothesis for investors. Most investors feel that they are missing out on the good deals because they lack insider knowledge or personal insights that tell them when to buy stocks. Now you can uncover the truth and understand how the big money-makers "do it."

Notes

1. Peter Francese, "Managing Market Information," *American Demographics*, September 1995, p. 63.

2. *American Demographics* (American Demographics, Inc., Box 68, Ithaca, New York 14851).

3. Vic Schwab, *How to Write a Good Advertisement* (New York: Marsteller Inc., 1976), pp. 20–21.

4. Bob Stone, *Successful Direct Marketing Methods* (Lincolnwood, IL: NTC Business Books, 1994).

5. Andi Emerson, "8 Basic Human Needs to Increase Mailing Response," *DMA Manual,* Release #6102 (New York: Direct Marketing Association, Inc., January 1978).

6. Richard W. Shaver, "The Planning Process," *The Direct Marketing Handbook*, ed. Edward L. Nash (New York: McGraw-Hill, Inc., 1984), pp. 29 and 30.

7. Jim Kobs, *Profitable Direct Marketing* (Lincolnwood, IL: Crain Books, an imprint of National Textbook Company, 1981), p. 92.

CREATING THE DIRECT MAIL PACKAGE

The moment of truth has arrived. It's been a long journey, but now it's inspiration time.

You've done your research—thoroughly. You know the rules. You have a handle on your market and a list of customer benefits. You've pulled your big benefit, created a hypothesis, and squared off the proposition with a good offer. You've locked in your creative strategy (except for format requirements) and you're nurturing a concept. Good. But now things change.

Up to this point you may have been working as a team with your product managers, marketing directors, creative supervisors, production managers, art directors, artists. From here on, you're on your own. Well—not entirely. If *you* are a writer, you still need your designer or artist.

This chapter is for you, the writer. If the rest of the team reads along, however, they will certainly develop a respect for the work you do and the effort you put into your creation. They'll be more understanding—and less likely to nit pick. Perhaps. It's worth a try.

What Will Be Expected of You, the Writer

Up to now, you've been asking a lot of questions, making a lot of assumptions. Listening. Thinking. Planning your strategies. (And taking notes, I hope.) Now it's your turn to create.

Just what is expected? First, that you will write, and that you will do so along the lines set down in your strategy, employing the direct response technique you have learned.

You are to develop creative ideas and full copy for a direct mail package that can be visually executed. (Or a print ad or broadcast.) This means you must work with the chosen artist or designer in the creative process.

Terms You Must Know

The following terms are the language of creative production, and you need to be familiar with them to communicate with the artists and production specialists with whom you work.

Artist/designer: Free-lance artists often refer to themselves as *designers.* In many agencies and companies artists working under an art director do the layouts while *art directors* supervise the design. For clarity, I will use the term *artist* or *designer* to signify the person who designs the package and executes the layouts.

Finished copy: Even though it may yet have to move through layers of approval, and you may ultimately have to make some changes, the *finished copy* is your initial completed copy for all parts or components of the direct mail package (or for any creative work) as you first present it. (*Final copy* usually refers to this same copy after you've put in the "client's" alterations or changes.)

Layouts or comprehensive art: The design of the direct mail package is executed by the artist or designer. "Rough" layouts used to be a first pass or a graphic "roughing out" of the promotion. Today this step has been almost totally eliminated by the Macintosh computer. *Comprehensive art (comps)* or *layouts* are practically indistinguishable from the final printed piece, thanks to computer technology.

Once your ideas start to jell, start talking with your designer. He or she will want to start conferring with you well before comps are begun. Prior to presenting copy and comps to the client, the two of you will want to have several work sessions together at the Mac.

Layouts for direct mail are full size and cut and folded into a dummy package that closely resembles the proposed real thing. Headlines are set, as are subheads and, in most cases, even the body copy is set. Illustrations can also be included; die cuts, tokens, stamps, and seals are all simulated. The objective of the layout is to show precisely how the finished direct mail package will look, how the parts of the package will interrelate, and how colors, special designs, and visual effects will be employed in conjunction with your finished copy. Once layouts and copy are approved and all changes or modifications are incorporated, the artist outputs the computer images onto film.

Copywriter's roughs: A *copywriter's rough* is a very rough, hand-drawn layout of the package, done by a *writer.* (See Figure 6–1.) It is customary for you as the writer, when presenting finished copy executed without an artist's collaboration, to accompany the copy with

FIGURE 6–1   A Copywriter's Rough for a Three-Panel Brochure

your own miniature layouts, or a folded paper dummy of the direct mail package, as you envision it. This is also a good way to work with artists, to show them what's in your head. No one expects you to draw well, but your roughs should indicate your thoughts about format, illustrations you'd like to use in your brochure, where your headlines go, the general feeling and layout of the promotion, suggestions for tokens on the order form, layouts for the letterhead, envelope size, die cuts, and copy positioning.

You may not have realized that copywriting also entails designing packages and visualizing formats. I encourage you—as a writer—to visualize your entire package and set down these ideas along with your copy. Chances are you won't be able to keep yourself from doing so anyway. You'll find your words create a picture in your mind. These ideas are starting points that a good artist will bend and rework in creating his or her designs—designs that please you both.

How to Work with the Artist

Your final creative product depends a lot on how you prefer to work with the artist, or how your company or client wants you to work. There are two extremes, and there are degrees in between.

At one extreme, you may go it alone, without a team (or without an artist on your team), and you may be expected to produce only finished copy with copywriter's roughs. In this case, try to make arrangements, at some point, to discuss these roughs with an artist or art director. Even more important, request an opportunity to see and discuss the *artist's own comps* and final treatment of your ideas and suggestions.

At the other extreme, you may work closely with an artist from the start. In this case, you may not need your copywriter's roughs. It depends on how you're most comfortable and how well you and the artist communicate.

Here are some possible working scenarios for artists and writers:

- You amble off to your lair like a grizzly bear preparing for hibernation, only to return some days later with creative direction and solid copy ideas to discuss with the artist.

- You immediately sit down with the artist and start comparing ideas, trying out copy approaches and formats together.

- You and the artist meet (circling each other carefully) to discuss ground rules and procedures. You set goals and plan a meeting for the next steps.

My advice to you is, open up! Don't hold back when working with an artist. Explain your concepts, your reasons, your concerns, your fears, your problem areas, your precious big idea. Let the artist know exactly how you attack the problem. Let the artist join you in the creative process.

Keep an open mind! You may already have an idea, but the artist may give you something far better. Don't push the artist into your visuals. (Artists are visual experts, remember?) Give the artist the input and the opportunity to create. If the artist has followed your creative process closely, it's likely that he or she will be excited and eager to jump in with ideas.

Kick the ideas around together. Ask participatory questions: Can we show the theme on the outer? How can we tie the offer into the letterhead visually? Should we budget for a standard #10 package, or do you feel the need for something bigger? Given this kind of headline and the picture requirements, should we go to a really big brochure or stick with a miniature treatment?

Listen carefully. Of course you already see your package in your head. But you may learn something here. The artist may see it better and if you click, the two of you can go off into the sunset building beautiful direct mail castles, each of you inspiring the other, and spurring each other on to even greater heights. This can and does happen often, and yields a reward of good creative work for both of you.

However, this collaboration can happen *only* if you open your creative doors and let the artist in. Whether you're just starting a project, or meeting with copywriter roughs after you've finished writing, you must allow the artist to join your team. Otherwise, you'll be a solitary player, looking for a mundane, lazy artist who will take directions from you without question, who will try to develop the visuals in your head to suit you. What a loss.

You and your ideas lose good graphic input, the artist loses the inspiring challenge and opportunity to contribute, and the client (or your boss) loses a shot at a strong, graphically compelling package.

No one can really tell you much more about working with an artist. A lot of it is chemistry, but your relationship at least will get off on the right foot if you can pull together most of the following for the artist as soon as possible:

- Your outer envelope copy ideas
- Your order card copy
- Your letter leads
- Your brochure heads
- Your visual requirements (pictures, graphs, charts)
- Any sketches you may have made; other packages, ads or pictures that demonstrate your ideas
- Your research—particularly samples of past control packages and tests that worked and/or failed for this specific product or service

In the course of your meetings, the artist should be able to come up with as many rough layouts as you both feel are necessary before proceeding into final layouts. Some, if not all, of these can be done on the computer. The Mac is extremely flexible and accomodating.

How long should this writing and artist collaboration take? No one can tell you how long inspiration takes, but there certainly are reasonable guidelines for plotting your time to get a package out.

How to Budget Your Time

There are two considerations in planning a project timetable: 1) how much time you need, and 2) how much time you are given.

Although you and the artist may be working together, before the two of you can start to work out illustrations and ideas for rough layouts, you may want to come up with some kind of creative noodling on your own.

Assuming you are given proper research materials, and that you and your creative strategy planning team can bone up and meet at least twice *before* you begin writing (whether the team is you—solo, you and your boss or client, or five to six well-intentioned coworkers from the art, marketing, research, and production departments), it is not unreasonable for you and the artist to produce final copy and layouts (or comprehensive art) for a full direct mail package in four weeks from your *fully-prepped* start time.

If you include research and planning, however, you'll need a total of at least five to six weeks to complete a package. It's nice if you can get a little more than six weeks, say a week or two more. In most cases, however, you may be given a little less—a lot less in a few instances.

When do you cry "Uncle"? Some free-lance copywriters never say "Uncle." They take on jobs that most writers do in four weeks and whip them out in two weeks or even one week—and they do competent work. How? Why? First, they're very experienced. Next, most free-lancers don't have the luxury of controlling work flow. They must work when they can get work and store up the dollars for a dry period. (And direct response advertising *can* have dry periods.) These free-lancers must be willing to work nights and weekends when the work is there, and yes, they do get exhausted. And yes, it can ultimately affect their work. And no, it's no great fun either.

As for you—you first need to know what is unreasonable as well as what is reasonable before you even consider attempting the absurd. Here are some guidelines to apply for starters, whether you're working on your own or within a company or agency.

1.   In making all of these decisions you have to estimate how much time is open. What else is on your schedule? Do you have two or three other assignments? Are you taking the kids to school, or gardening, or having a house guest or going to the opera? Are you willing (or expected) to work late? Every night? Weekends?

2.   When you are approached with a totally new package for a new product and asked to do full copy and comps, you should be given five to seven weeks from the start. (You'll need at least a week of this for the research and strategizing.)

3.   You may not get your grand total of five or more weeks from the client or your boss; you may get only four weeks, including all your prework. This is not *madly* unreasonable, if you have quick access to all the background material and get your creative planning down within a week. But it's tight, particularly for a beginner.

4.   Now let's say you're asked to do the job in two to three weeks. Feel free to do it, if you know your product and you are comfortable about the schedule. On the other hand, be aware that this is bordering on the madly unreasonable.

Whatever your work load or personal lifestyle, at this point you have every right to express concern regarding your ability to do your best work on such a tight schedule. (Even if you do take it on, you should make this point.)

Make sure you have everything you need to move into the job. Every single day counts. You can't afford to wait even 24 hours to get a full look at the product line or testing history. (All of us need a respite—a day or two or three at some point in our work when we can step back for clearer vision and perspective. This schedule won't give you any.)

A word of caution: Clients will promise *anything* to get you to accept an unreasonably tight schedule, including 24-hour approvals. Don't believe it. Their hearts may be in the right place, but I have yet to find a client (or company) that can come through with full data in 24 hours *or* overnight approvals.

Let me draw up an optimum time frame for you, showing places you can scrimp a little while keeping a small safety margin. A game plan like this can also help you deal with several jobs at once, each in different stages of development. And bear in mind that your creative development needn't wait until the client says "Go!" It can start at any time—even in your first meeting. So take notes from day one!

Time Frame for Copy and Layout Development of a Direct Mail Package

	Best Case	**Options**
Week 1	a. Assignment is given. b. Research is received and studied (creative juices start).	These three weeks can be combined into one week, especially if you are working alone and if background material is readily available.
Week 2	First creative strategy meeting. (Start notes.)	
Week 3	Final creative strategy meeting.	
Week 4	a. You start writing. b. Have first meeting with the artist. (Start comps.)	
Week 5	a. You continue to write, revise, rework. b. Meet with art director visual ideas, heads, leads, all thoughts for or artist (Present your visual ideas, heads, leads, all thoughts for format and involvement devices. Here the outer envelope should be firmed up in your mind. So should the brochure concept and order card. The letter can be finalized later, as it requires little work from the artist.) Artist should start work on comps for initial ideas.	Weeks four and five can be condensed by a few days, but use caution here or your work may suffer!

Best Case	**Options**
Weeks 6–7 Now you and the artist hammer out all the details and finalize the visuals and copy. Major changes can still be made but you need this time for reworking and polishing your copy and for your final comp lockup.	Crucial time. Don't cut it more than a day or two even if you are working alone and doing a copywriter's rough.
Totals: *6–7 weeks to presentation of copy and comps*	*4+ weeks to presentation of copy and comps*

Now, to get you started writing! This should come as no surprise, dear writer, but you *have* started. If you've done all the prework, sat through the meetings and made notes, your head should be bursting with ideas. So how about putting a few deathless words on paper?

Getting Off on the "Write" Foot

Your computer is humming, your pen is poised or pencil sharpened, and your artist is already starting to visualize. So . . . write! There's no longer any excuse to put it off. Or is there?

Most writers can give you a dozen good excuses at this point. The garbage has to go out. Someone (any living creature) should be fed (the writer, most likely). A magazine or newspaper must be read . . . a letter answered . . . a friend called . . . a bill paid . . . a file drawer cleaned. No task is too onerous or too small, as long as it keeps you from getting started.

This is normal behavior, no matter how much (or little) you enjoy writing. Don't let this discourage you, but don't let it deter you, either. After all, you have your copy strategy and copy platform. And you have all that research behind you. You have a schedule—and the artist is waiting (not to mention the client)!

If the storehouse of experience has fueled your imagination properly it should be humming along with your computer. And your subconscious should be mulling over the creative opportunities before you—ready to telegraph a great idea while you are in the shower, shaving, eating, trying to sleep, or even talking with your mother-in-law.

I personally have never been able to drum up anything inspiring by staring at a roaring fire or looking out to sea. Maybe you can. But whenever and however you get your inspiration (and it may come at the strangest times and in the strangest places), *write down* your ideas. Many writers carry paper and pencil (or a pocket recorder) with them or keep a pad by the bed for just this reason.

Some Pointers to Get You Started

You're moving into an area that requires great discipline and determination. Don't feel guilty if you hold back or procrastinate. Every writer does, but every writer also develops little rituals or disciplines that start the creative juices flowing. Let me pass a few on to you

1. Bill Jayme, indisputedly one of our best writers, says, "A writer should be in a cold room because chill quickens the brain, should be hungry as an incentive to earn, and should dress only in underwear so as to place an obstacle in the way of chucking the job at hand in favor of heading for the neighborhood bar."

2. If you're not in the writing mood, good exercise such as jogging or calisthenics—or even a long walk—can put you there. After a half hour's workout, you'll be relaxed but wide awake. (Then again, just the threat of exercise is enough to get some writers going.) Suit yourself.

3. Learn to recognize your most productive hours. Understand your mind and your body. Every good writer can tell you his or her best hours for writing. Some are morning people, some are evening. Find out when you work best, then save those hours for the hard stuff.

4. Discipline yourself. If you don't have a deadline, set one. Then do not put off until the last minute or claim "I write best under pressure." No one writes best under pressure. You will write best when you have enough time to let your original work cool off a bit. Then come back to it cold. You'll be amazed at what a little time and a new perspective will do.

5. Start a dialogue in your head. You've decided who you'll be. You know to whom you're talking. Imagine one person representing this market. Be an actor, sit down and talk to this person. You can do it anywhere. Every time you like what you hear, write it down, wherever you are.

6. Do an outline for your brochure *and* for your letter. Be sure to check your notes.

7. Start collecting headline ideas in your imaginary conversation. Think of ways to attract the attention of your one-person market with the benefits, ways to hold this market's attention. (What would stop *you* and draw you in if you were this market?)

8. With every idea, every bit of dialogue that leads to your headlines, ask yourself "Will this make sense to the customer?" "What is my justification for saying this?" "Can I carry through on it?"

9. What if ideas don't come—nothing seems to jell? How can you jar the creative process and tickle the imagination? Two good ways: using the testing history, or using a swipe file.

The Testing History. If your product or service has a good testing history, and you're lucky enough to have a collection of former direct mail packages and ratings on how well they pulled (your response index—see Chapter 2), see if you can figure out why one did well, why another didn't.

For example: Let's say a women's service magazine calls on you to create a new subscription solicitation package. Among the research materials provided is a full direct mail testing history that goes back several years. You are given fourteen different packages, each one indexed against the others, and marked to show the original control and those that subsequently replaced the control. All of the packages were professionally executed. Let us assume that all the offers were the same. Why did some succeed and others fail? What a delightful mystery!

First, look for similarities among the winners—similarities in format, design, copy approach. Check for long copy versus short, drawings versus photography. Look closely at the ways in which the offer is stated, compare the "bells and whistles" and the benefit emphasis.

What is promised on the outer envelope? How does each letter start? What is different about the losers? Compare, compare, compare, and gradually you'll be able to draw up your points, a list of the things the winners have in common. Once you're satisfied, you must decide how to capitalize on those points—the similarities—without copying the winners or doing a thinly modified version of the control.

Your job here is not to reinvent the wheel, but *to take what works one step further.* Think of all the things you're learning about your market! What a great way to get started when you have the history to help you!

Swipe Files. All good creative free-lancers or creative departments in direct marketing operations have what we call *swipe files.* These are extensive collections of other people's work. No one actually or consciously steals from them. Rather, swipe files are used to generate ideas. If you don't have a swipe file, start one! If you need access to one now, the Direct Marketing Association in New York City has one of the finest in the world. It's an extensive collection of hundreds of direct response campaigns submitted to the annual DMA Echo Awards competition. These awards cover all kinds of direct marketing and all media. You can view this collection of DMA winners in their library, even if you are not a bona fide member of the association.[1]

What Do You Write First?

If you're holding back simply because you're not sure what to write first, let me dispose of the problem for you right now.

A few top professionals suggest you write your order card first. Ed Nash, formerly executive vice president for direct marketing at Bozell, Jacobs, Kenyon and Eckhardt, advises writers to do the ad coupon or the order card first because it is the one element of the promotion that is most often saved. He says "Later, when the time comes to write out the envelope and perhaps a check, the coupon itself is the only reminder of the reasons behind why they tore it out in the first place. The headline is gone. The pictures are gone. All that remains is the reply card or coupon."[2]

There's a lot to be said for coupon writers, but three of the best direct response writers I know start with the outer envelope! As all your prospects and customers will start there, too, surely it deserves your finest efforts and early attention. After all, success depends upon getting the envelope opened.

The majority of the writers I've questioned claim they generally start with the letter itself, and that has much to recommend it. In your letter you address the customer one-on-one. It can help you feel closer to your prospect and it enables you to develop your sales dialogue. As you'll see in the next section, it facilitates your selection of an approach.

Once you've started your letter, you may go right to the outer envelope with ideas for a copy promise that ties in to your letter.

You can also start moving from the letter to the brochure as insights for headlines and illustrations that work best outside the restraints of the letter come popping into your head.

Frankly, talk about where to start can be misleading. Neither you nor I nor anyone else can control the creative imagination once it gets going. It's entirely possible to come up with a great envelope line as you start your letter, or a headline for the brochure. It's equally possible for you—fired with inspiration—to charge through a first draft of the letter in an hour or so. The fact is wherever you start, before you know it, you'll be working all your components along together, moving back and forth from one format to the other.

Choosing an Approach

As you, the spokesperson, sit down to write your letter—ready to start a dialogue with one person who embodies your prime market's characteristics—how do you plan to break the ice? What's your approach?

Think of your prospect as someone you'd like to know better. You want to start a relationship. You want to arrange a date. How you approach this prospect will determine the success of the relationship.

Ask yourself: How well do I know this person? (Is this a new prospect or a regular customer?) What's my proposition? How do I intend to get my prospect interested? What's my first sentence, my lead-in? What's the "hook" that will capture my prospect's attention on the envelope? And carry her/him into the letter?

First, review your copy strategy for a minute:

What's the hypothesis?

What's your big benefit?

Is the offer *the* big benefit?

Do you have a premium? Something FREE?

Is this a totally *new* product or service?

Who *are* you as actor?

Whom are you addressing? And what moves him or her?

Now you need a good *approach* to break the ice. Otherwise you'll stutter and stammer and drag your feet, and your prospect will go dancing off with someone else! Actually, you and your artist could have picked an approach when you had your first meeting; if you didn't, now's the time.

First, an explanation of what "approach" means and how it came to be. Twenty-some years ago, professional copywriters gave labels to different approaches to their direct mail packages. In a test, the creative director or copy chief making the assignment would make sure that each writer took a different approach—that is, each writer led into the creative product from a different point of view or different angle, or with a different hook.

Writers don't seem to talk much about approaches these days. It's possible that they are not fully aware of the process or analytical enough about their own work to know how and where to employ each approach. Maybe they call it something else. But these approaches are there nonetheless—in every direct mail package ever produced. And, these approaches can be analyzed, just as offers and structuring can be (see Chapter 3); they can be modified and combined, one with another.

Your approach starts on the outer envelope, then moves right to the first paragraph of your letter. Your approach helps you decide whether to use a Johnson box or a headline at the top of your letter. It sets the tone for your package. You want your approach to grab your prospect by the eyelashes and lead him or her through your letter to the point where it makes more sense to say "yes" than "no."

If you understand approaches, how and why you use one approach as opposed to another, you'll be in an excellent position to explain your finished copy, the graphics, and the direction or style of your package as a whole when you make your presentation.

If you move up to creative director (soon, I hope), the approach concept can offer you a useful tool for critiquing work. For example, suppose the artist and writer follow the creative strategy, but their package somehow just doesn't "come off." It is not very helpful to comment, "it just doesn't come off," or "it's not quite on target." As a creative manager you can instead use the approach concept and suggest they switch approaches or try combining a couple.

Twelve possible approaches are discussed in this chapter. No doubt there are others, but with these (and combinations thereof), you're in a good position to get started. They are

1. The Generic Approach
2. The Invitational Approach
3. The Secret Approach
4. The Testimonial Approach
5. The Identification Approach
6. The Assumptive Approach
7. The Question Approach
8. The Negative and Problem/Solution Approach
9. The Fantasy Approach
10. The Analogy Approach
11. The Story Approach
12. The Be-a-Hero Approach

Many of the approaches are illustrated with examples taken from actual direct mail packages. These examples are representative of the finest direct mail I've encountered over the last 5 to 10 years; all winners. Some products and services seem to call for a specific approach (like an Invitational Approach for a new product introduction). Others are a question of pure creative choice—your choice. But first, review your hypothesis and make sure your selected approach enables you to move into the hypothesis quickly and easily and appealingly.

Twelve Approaches to Direct Response Copy

THE GENERIC APPROACH

The most widely used approach is the *Generic Approach,* a basic and straightforward approach that starts right in with the major benefit and the offer. The Generic Approach is best (safest) when you're writing business-to-business mail, when you're testing a brand-new product and have no control package, or when you have a very exciting premium or unusually strong offer (offer-as-big-benefit). But don't play it safe too often. All the other approaches can also be applied to both business and consumer mail and generally are a lot more fun for you. The following are simple illustrations of the Generic Approach:

Offer/premium as lead:

Dear Customer:

Here is a once-in-a-lifetime opportunity to purchase the Forbush Slip-Shod at 50% off its regular price. And—with every purchase, we'll send you absolutely FREE . . .

The big benefit as lead:

> Dear Friend:
>
> Let me tell you about a remarkable new way to finance your children's education painlessly and risk free!

New product/first mailing lead

> Dear Reader:
>
> Now, for the first time—study the intimate life of the black snail—follow his daily patterns, his cycle changes and eating preferences—every month in a new magazine from the publishers of Zilch Havas:
>
> *Black Snail Review*
>
> Just $13 for 12 Monthly Issues

You'll find that a lot of direct mail packages are generic. It's a popular approach both for creative professionals and, unfortunately, for tacky technicians.

Figure 6–2 shows a delightful Generic Approach from Nightingale-Conant for an executive self-improvement program, Lead the Field. The outer was a 9" × 12" brown kraft envelope with a simple "Management Reports" (and address) as the corner card and an overprint in red, saying "Update."

The clever "pencil" drawings along with the highly involving questions on the folder/cover inside catch the prospect's interest immediately. The cover itself serves as a business folder/brochure, enclosing a six-page letter filled with excellent copy and more engaging drawings that deal with the problems/solutions and benefits as they relate to "you," the prospect. The reply card, the only four-color element, carries a big benefit and strong offer. Lots of benefits, strong copy, and delightful drawings have made this a winner for Nightingale-Conant for over eight years and still going. (The copy was written by direct response pro Bob Matheo; the drawings are by Chuck Dickinson.)

THE INVITATIONAL APPROACH

An approach well-suited to a new product or service, or to a product that you're introducing to a totally new market. It is based on the assumption that everyone likes to be invited to things and that an invitation is always welcome mail even when the recipient realizes that it is tainted with commercialism.

At its best, the *Invitational Approach* is elegant in appearance—an announcement of importance (trumpets blare). The outer envelope states "The Favor of Your Reply Is Requested." Inside is an exclusive, "limited" invitation (offer) with a few-are-chosen tone, "so please R.S.V.P." (reply) now.

FIGURE 6–2   The Generic Approach

Courtesy of Nightingale-Conant.

The most effective Invitational Approaches have the style, tone, and design of a call to the royal court:

Her Royal Highness and all the knights and ladies of the court, extend to you, John Sample, an exclusive invitation . . . .

FIGURE 6–3   The Invitational Approach

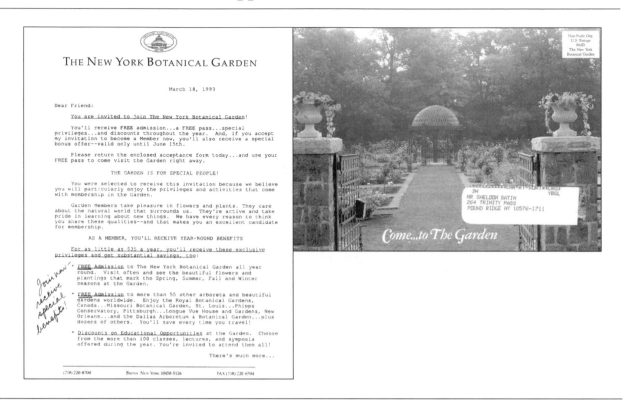

FIGURE 6–4   "Invitations" Work

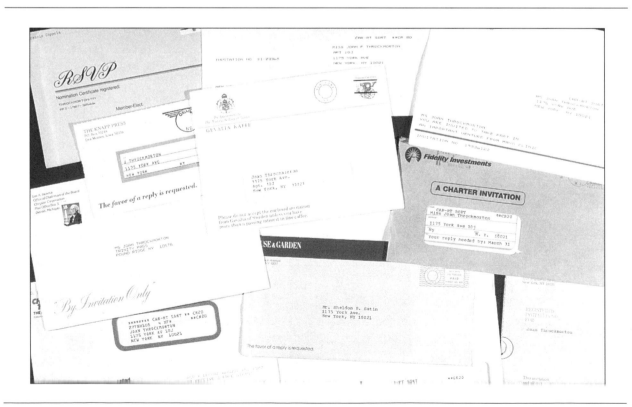

If you choose the Invitational Approach, make sure the graphics reflect the elegant invitational feeling from the outer envelope to the reply card.

Not all invitations have to be stark and formal, however. Check out the truly inviting outer envelope in Figure 6–3. The letter begins simply, "You are invited to join the New York Botanical Garden!" If you need convincing that invitations work, look at Figure 6–4, a montage of a few invitations I received one spring week!

THE SECRET APPROACH

The *Secret Approach* is a close friend of the Invitational Approach, but it is carried one step further. Not only have *"you"* been selected and invited, but you are also being made privy to classified, beneficial data that's certainly "not for everyone." Because everyone likes to "get in on a secret" this approach has wide appeal and can be a lot of fun for you to execute.

Figure 6–5 shows one of the finest examples of the Secret Approach that I've come across—a truly superior direct mail package, done by one of our top creative writers, Ken Scheck, for *Fortune* magazine. Because Fortune's big appeal is answering that age-old success question, "How did those guys do it?" you can believe this envelope got read and opened. The "secret" theme is carried out in the brochure and the lift note. The letter lead-in is pure great writing. The reply card is important and dramatic because of its basic simplicity.

Figure 6–6 promises all sorts of fascinating knowledge, surprises, and mystery for the traveler with Special Expeditions, a travel/tour company that provides unusual outdoor adventures to exotic places.

"Fascinations," as some call them, are a form of secret because they hold the promise of secrets revealed on "how-to do something." Fascinations are fascinating half-facts backed by the credibility of a page number that implies you'll get the rest of the story later. In a word, they are terrific teasers.

Although great writers like Jim Punkre and Gene Schwartz perfected fascinations, Mel Martin was their inventor and master. (Before his death in 1994, he did most of his fascinations for newsletter publications from Boardroom Inc.)

Figure 6–7 shows a remarkable group of fascinations on a jumbo outer envelope for Rodale Books' "Yankee Home Hints" written by Gene Schwartz. The fascinations continue throughout the letter inside.

THE TESTIMONIAL APPROACH

Another powerful tool is the *Testimonial Approach*. Apply it at the right time and for the right reasons, and you'll walk away with a winner. Give the Testimonial Approach your serious consideration when you have a product or service that requires the kind of credibility that only customers can provide.

FIGURE 6–5   The Secret Approach: *Fortune*

1271 Avenue of the Americas
New York, NY 10020

Bulk Rate
U.S. Postage
Paid
FORTUNE
Magazine

Shhh...

...The secrets on the back
of this envelope are not
for everyone!

FREE GIFT INVITATION
(see details inside)

FOA4DW5
JOAN THROCKMORTON
JOAN THROCKMORTON INC
PO BOX 452
POUND RIDGE NY 10576-0452

Outer Envelope—Front

WE TELL SECRETS!

The Ikea Secret that has customers storming stores and causing 10-mile back-ups on the highway. It starts with ...

(continued inside)

The Donald Bren Secret for becoming a billionaire. Buy a remote, water-poor, tax-distressed scrub patch that happens to lie directly in the path of ...

(continued inside)

The Clayton Homes Secret for building a $260,000,000 business. Find yourself a 30-year-old named Bubba. Listen carefully to everything he says. Then ...

(continued inside)

The PepsiCo Secret that's winning the fast-food wars. They discovered that their biggest competitor—McDonald's—was making a *huge* mistake. The guys at the golden arches goofed when they...

(continued inside)

The H. Wayne Huizenga Secret that rocketed Waste Management, Inc. to the top. Then made Blockbuster Video an industry legend. Both times, he ingeniously used ...

(continued inside)

500-2

Outer Envelope—Back

RETAIN FOR YOUR
PERSONAL RECORDS:
▼

FORTUNE'S COVER PRICE
$79⁰⁰

YOUR COST
$29⁰⁰

YOU SAVE
$50⁰⁰

RISK-FREE VERIFICATION

You risk nothing when you send for FORTUNE now. If not completely satisfied, simply cancel. We'll refund *every* penny you paid. And you may keep your free gift. No questions asked.

PLEASE RESPOND BY: **APRIL 24, 1992**

YES!

☐ **I accept your private offer of FORTUNE for 20 issues for just $29.00.** I understand that this price is OVER 63% off the newsstand price. Please start sending my biweekly issues right away. And please send me my extra two free issues as well as my free copy of Fortune's Guide to Successful Investing.

FOA1PX6
JOAN THROCKMORTON
BOX 452 BOX 155
TRINITY PASS
POUND RIDGE NY 10576-0452

FORTUNE

SEND NO MONEY

Reply Card

Courtesy of *Fortune* Magazine.

FIGURE 6–5 (Continued)

FORTUNE

Come listen to a new voice in your mind,
whispering the secrets of greatness ...

Just say "YES, I'LL LISTEN!"
and you may try it at a savings that's
just like getting 12 big issues free
-- PLUS, get an impressive FREE GIFT that's
yours with our compliments!

Dear Colleague:

The best ideas come in a whisper, not a shout.

A moment. A voice. Then an idea that changes your life
and career. One idea. Bright. Sharp. Like a diamond
in your mind.

You know how it feels. You know because you've been
there -- you've heard the voice.

But what you may not know is that every other week the
world's most successful business achievers (one of every
3.4 is a CEO, Chairman or President) literally STOP WHAT
THEY ARE DOING just to "listen" ...

    ... they stop and listen to a voice that
    ignites their creativity like no other
    business publication ever has or ever will.
    Its name is ... FORTUNE.

Now you are invited to try FORTUNE yourself, without
risking a single penny!

FORTUNE. There is nothing else like it. Nothing. It
is the ONE source that is passionately devoted to the
adventure of business ideas ... the secrets of greatness.

FORTUNE. It's the idea magazine. We treasure great
ideas. We love to find them. Turn them over and over
like precious jewels. And then present them to you!

FORTUNE is where you'll find out why mighty McDonald's is
running scared because PepsiCo's Chief Executive simply
had a new idea ...

    How a car salesman down in Tennessee built a
    brand-new $260,000,000 business. All because he
    listened to "Bubba" and simply had a new idea ...

Why Americans are causing traffic jams and near riots as

(over, please)

FORTUNE

Dear Friend:

When your first issue of FORTUNE arrives, sit back
contentedly and smile.

Now you've got a secret all your own -- a fantastic
deal on FORTUNE!

* You save $80 off the cover price for 30
  issues. That's just like getting twenty
  big issues free!

* You get a free gift copy of FORTUNE'S GUIDE
  TO SUCCESSFUL INVESTING ... packed with over
  90 pages of mouthwatering personal investment
  recommendations!

* You get two extra free issues of FORTUNE ...
  just for saying YES to this invitation!

* You get our 100% guarantee of satisfaction:
  if you are ever less than totally satisfied,
  you may cancel and receive a full refund on
  every penny of your entire subscription.
  That's every penny!

Remember, your colleagues who buy FORTUNE at the
newsstand will pay $80 more for the same number
of issues! This really IS a great deal. But you
must hurry. This offer ends September 21, 1992!

                Best regards,

                Brian Wolfe

                Brian Wolfe
                Consumer Marketing Director

P.S. You read that correctly. It's no mistake. You
      really DO save $80 off the cover price. But
      only with this invitation. Don't let it slip
      away. Mail the card today!

Lift Letter

they flock to one particular store. It seems that a man
back in Sweden simply had a new idea...

FORTUNE. It's where you unlock the secrets of
greatness. You'll learn Walt Mitchell's secret. One
day he went to work and quit. Just quit. At forty-one.
Today he runs his own $25,000,000 business...

You'll learn Wayne Huizenga's secret. He used it to
take Waste Management to the top. Now he's using it
again at phenomenally successful Blockbuster Video...

That's FORTUNE. We dig inside success. We tell you the
real story. After all, we don't want you to simply read
about success -- we want you to actually experience the
moment when great ideas are born.

    Nothing gets you closer to that moment, I
    promise. No other publication brings
    you as near to the flame of pure creativity
    as FORTUNE!

Every page crackles with the energy of fresh ideas.
Breakthrough strategies. Ingenious designs.
Revolutionary products. Companies to watch. Managers
on the march. Entrepreneurs to keep your eye on.
Investments to pounce on.

One caveat. Don't read FORTUNE as soon as it arrives.
Save it for when you're alone. Quietly close the door.
Unplug the phone. Settle into your most comfortable
chair. Open your crisp, new copy. Then, listen to the
voice...and the whisper of your dreams.

Your satisfaction is 100% guaranteed. You must be
thrilled and inspired by the compelling stories in
FORTUNE. If not, we will refund every cent you paid for
your entire subscription. That's every cent.

That's a promise!

                Best regards,

                James B. Hayes

                James B. Hayes
                Publisher

P.S. It will also be my pleasure to send you a
      gift copy of Fortune's Guide to Successful
      Investing...plus two extra free issues of
      FORTUNE. That's my way of saying thanks
      ...and welcome to FORTUNE!

Courtesy of *Fortune* Magazine

FIGURE 6–6   Another Secret Approach

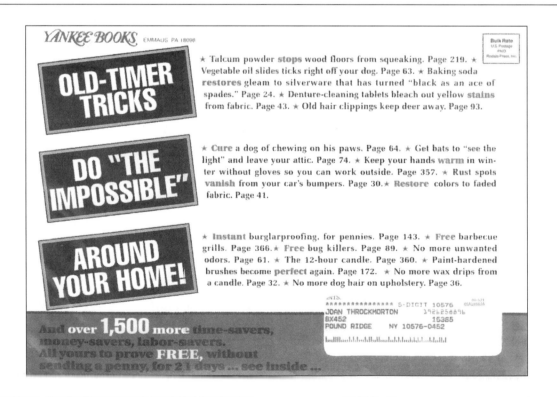

FIGURE 6–7   Fascinations on an Outer Envelope

For example: Products that imply they can improve health or fitness or personal appearance, products or services that promise to give the prospect new or improved skills, financial services such as insurance, investment opportunities—any products or services with intangible benefits (promises that can't be proved by product examination or demonstration and therefore create skepticism on the part of your prospects).

You'll also want to consider the Testimonial Approach when you have a product that generates a lot of unsolicited praise.

Caveat: Too many raving testimonials may create just the opposite of the desired effect. If your company is well known, you can dispel this problem with a modest disclaimer. If your company is unknown, temper your choice of testimonials and give as much data as possible about the contributors. A testimonial signed with only initials ("J.T.") or by "A Satisfied Customer" is worth nothing. A testimonial with full name, town or city, and state *and* a photo is worth pure gold.

You can use testimonials on the outer envelope, in the letter, and/or in the brochure. You can even use an entire letter of praise as a testimonial lift letter. You can also combine the Testimonial Approach with just about every other approach. Figure 6–8 shows testimonials used only on the outer. But what testimonials—Henry Kissinger, former Governor Bruce Babbitt, Alvin and Heidi Toffler. You can bet this outer got opened.

FIGURE 6–8   The Testimonial Approach

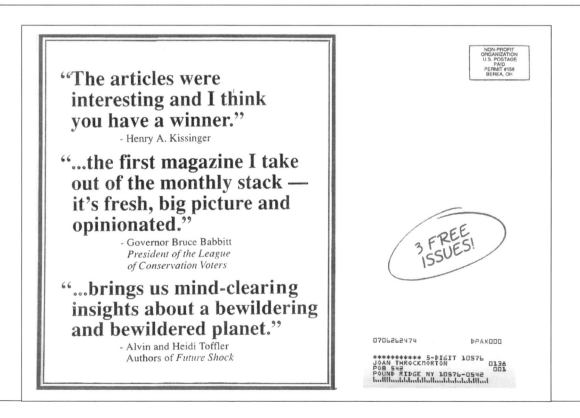

When you examine the *Identification Approach,* you're liable to
think of it as flattery. But it's really a lot more than that. In some
cases, it does indeed work to appeal to the perceived self image.
This was most effectively demonstrated over fifteen years ago by a
fine creative free-lance writer, Ed McLean. He found a new hook
(and a new way to make his letter more personal) by examining all
the mail order and magazine subscriber lists that were being used
(rented) for his mailing.

He began a famous letter "If the list upon which I found your
name is any indication, this is not the first—nor will it be the last—
subscription letter you receive. Quite frankly, your education and
income set you apart from the general population and make you a
highly-rated prospect for everything from magazines to mutual
funds."

His prospects were undoubtedly complimented and, because of
this, listened to his message (and responded to it). But this approach
can also be used to quickly establish an affinity between the writer
and the prospect by implying the writer knows the prospect's interests and shares them. It says "I know who you are. You're someone
special who shares some important interests with us. That's why we
know you're going to like our offer."

Some of these uses are as simple as "Dear Fellow Book-Lover" or
"Dear Fellow Romantic" or "Gardeners like you and me . . ." or "Why
Texans like us just seem to have more fun!"

Some of the best Identification Approaches start to qualify and
involve the prospect right on the outer envelope, then carry them
into the letter by building on the outer envelope copy. Take the
envelope for a business letter from Apple Computer, shown in Figure
6–9, that immediately identifies me (based on "the list on which I
found your name"). Since nothing is more important to me than my
name, I'm immediately drawn in and curious. Although the personal
titles may not be totally accurate, they're close enough to tell me that
this company understands me and my problems. The letter reinforces
this beautifully:

> Dear Ms. Throckmorton:
>
> If you're managing a small advertising firm, you may have to be an
> art director one moment, and a media planner the next. Then you
> might take on the role of research director. Then it's back to
> being an art director. It's enough to make you question your own
> identity.

Here's another winner! Unlike so many letters that fail to involve,
this letter (written by Emily Soell and originally sent out to sell subscriptions for *Vanity Fair* magazine), *did* get read, thanks to its first
paragraph:

FIGURE 6–9   The Identification Approach: Apple Computer

Dear Ms. Throckmorton:

You may just be the solution.

Here is the problem: How do you find the right subscribers for an extraordinary magazine—BUT, a magazine that isn't for everyone? A magazine that is, in fact, for only a handful of bright, literate people who still, in this world of instant communication, love to sit down with a good book.

The letter for Condé Nast *Traveler* shown in Figure 6–10 was used to launch the publication and remained the control for over four years. (This was also written by Emily Soell, vice chairman, chief creative officer, DraftDirect Worldwide and a master at perceived self-image selling.) It is a wonderful example of how people *want* to see themselves and how they dream of traveling. It makes the prospect feel very special, and it promises special experiences to go with a sophisticated outlook. Whether readers take the trips or just use the magazine to dream about travel is unimportant.

If your market is fairly clear-cut, the straightforward Identification Approach can work for you, too. (Bikers, Gardeners, Investors, Educators, Colleagues, Busy Executives, Texans, Chefs—if you can name it, you can use it!)

FIGURE 6–10   The Identification Approach: *Condé Nast Traveler*

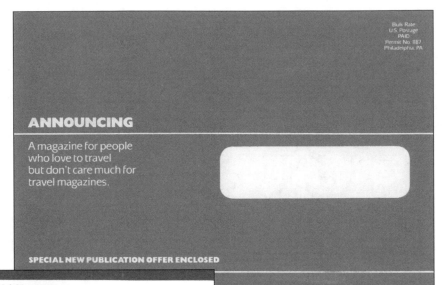

Bulk Rate
U.S. Postage
PAID
Permit No. 1187
Philadelphia, PA

ANNOUNCING

A magazine for people
who love to travel
but don't care much for
travel magazines.

SPECIAL NEW PUBLICATION OFFER ENCLOSED

Condé Nast Traveler

From the publishers of *Vogue, Gourmet, House & Garden,*
GQ and *Vanity Fair*...

...something new and completely different in travel magazines,
for people who demand the unique—both when they travel
and when they read magazines.

NOW ONLY $1 AN ISSUE

Dear Friend:

We know you...

...You find a few extra dollars in your pocket--a crack in your
impossibly busy schedule--and what do you do?

Take off, that's what! For a Greek Island, a Caribbean beach, a
Colorado ski slope...for a French pension, a Spanish posada, a New
England inn...for carnival in Rio or Venice or New Orleans...to see
the beautiful people in today's new hot spots or find a spot where
you'll see almost no one at all.

In many ways we <u>are</u> you...

...<u>Not satisfied</u> only with guided tours and main attractions, but
always poking around in the nooks and crannies of the places you go.

...<u>Endlessly curious</u> about the culture, the history, the people--how
they live, how they make their living, where they make their homes.
Wondering what it would be like to live there yourself.

...<u>Wanting to know</u> how to get around easily, independently, to see
the <u>real</u> place, interact with the people, be welcomed, be able to
take home--not just photographs--personal experiences.

You don't get much help from conventional travel magazines.

BUT...now there is a new magazine that leads you to the back roads,
down side streets and cobblestone lanes...to colorful shops, pubs,
local restaurants...food, flower, antique markets...docks and
pocket parks and small churches you love to explore. Tells you how
much it costs to buy a cottage there, rent a condo, own a chalet
in the mountains or a villa on the sea.

A magazine that makes the history of a place come alive in its

(over, please)

You can also use the "negative" identification ploy as a lead in. It comes out something like "Only dedicated photographers need apply" or "published only for a select group of people who are seriously interested in . . ."

If you know the demographics of your present customer market, you can do a playback identification for prospects. A sort of "Our McFarland customers are affluent, talented, well-traveled. We think you should be among them." This is similar to the identification/flattery of the original McLean lead.

Caveat: Don't go too far afield or your approach may indeed dissolve into meaningless, soupy flattery.

THE "IF" OR ASSUMPTIVE APPROACH

The *Assumptive Approach,* instead of identifying a gardener or a Texan or an upper middle-class affluent, uses "if/then." It identifies product or service benefits in terms of the identified market and its goals and desires.

The "if" might be one of the following phrases: "If you'd like your garden to flourish . . . If you'd like the inside story of what's going on in Texas . . . If you'd like to shop in one of the world's most stylish stores . . . If you'd like to have a beautifully-decorated home . . . ."

This "if" is followed by a "then": "then surely you'll want to take this action (buy this gardening book . . . subscribe to this local magazine . . . order from this catalog) and realize your dreams and desires."

The letter in its most popular form is front-loaded with one benefit after another, ("If you . . . if you . . ."), culminating in a clash of cymbals as the offer is presented with the logical conclusion: "then have we got something for you . . ."

The If/Assumptive Approach enables a writer to fire off all benefits quickly and efficiently at the start of the letter, then move right in to the selling proposition on page one. It is often used in conjunction with the identification approach, which acts as qualifier on the outer envelope.

Figures 6–11 and 6–12 show examples of the Assumptive Approach done for a business service from National Demographics & Lifestyles, Inc. in conjunction with Standard Rate & Data Service, Inc. (Figure 6–11) and for *Family Life* magazine (Figure 6–12) in a letter written by Ken Schneider, another of our top writers.

THE QUESTION APPROACH

A well-formulated *Question Approach* can be one of the most powerful ways to involve your prospects, as these all-time great advertising headlines attest:

Do you make these mistakes in English?

Does your child ever embarrass you?

FIGURE 6–11   The Assumptive Approach for a Business Service

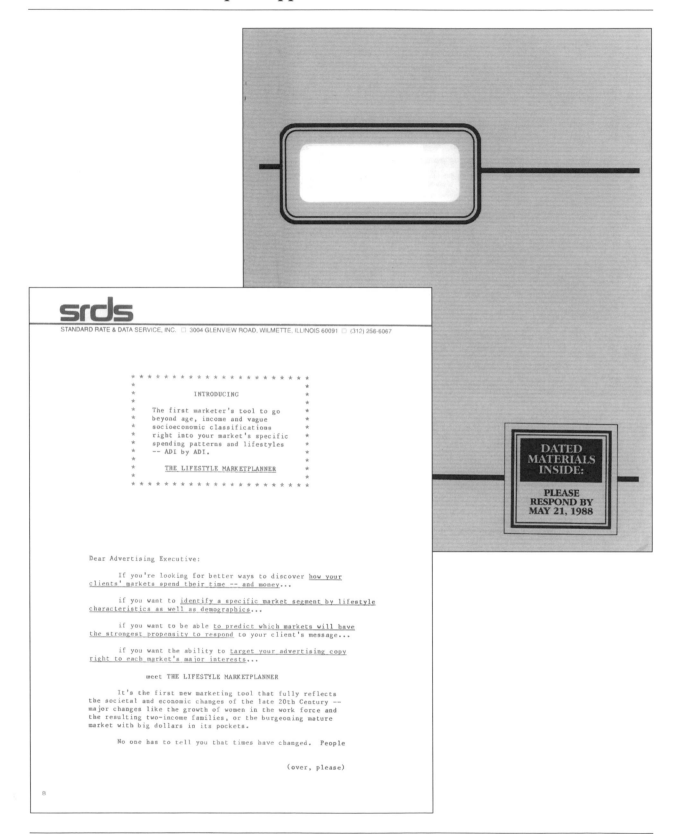

From National Demographics & Lifestyles, Inc. in conjunction with Standard Rate & Data Service, Inc.

FIGURE 6–12   The Assumptive Approach for a Consumer Magazine

Finally, there's a fresh, new magazine for parents that celebrates the joys, the wonder, and the magic of living with—not just raising—children. The magazine for a new generation of moms and dads, that takes up where the "baby magazines" leave off. The new magazine for you and your child…

Introducing *family life*

You're invited to try our next issue free, with no risk…

Dear Fellow Parent:

    If you're tired of magazines that dwell on the problems of bringing up children and overlook the pleasures...

    If you've outgrown the "drool and diaper" stage. and could use a magazine geared to the 3 to 12 age group...

    If you've been disappointed with magazines that just don't speak your language when it comes to dealing with children's issues and family growth...

    Then I've got exciting. happy news for you!

    Because now there's FAMILY LIFE! The fresh. new magazine for parents and children that respects your intelligence. rewards your creative nature. and fuels your imagination.

    A magazine so unlike the rest. you'll wonder why it took so long for somebody to get it right!

    To prove it to you. I want to send you the next issue FREE!
If you like it. continue as a Charter Subscriber -- and enjoy our low discount price. If you don't like FAMILY LIFE. there's no obligation to subscribe. But you can keep the free issue no matter what.

                                        over please...

Self-evaluation, quizzes, and seeking the prospect's opinion are also good examples of the Question Approach. ("Can you score over 90 on this Personality Test?")

When do you use it? Look at your hypothesis and your major benefits. Can you come up with strong involvement questions that allow you to move right into your main benefits?

Figure 6–13 illustrates a beautiful example of the Question Approach in action, directed tastefully to mature market prospects by Blue Cross/Blue Shield of Florida. The outer envelope copy gets the prospect's attention with a strong question. The hypothesis: The mature market is a skeptical market that insists on quality and value (and "hype" turns it off). The big benefit: You'll save money without sacrificing quality.

Notice the friendly letter approach and the brochure cover reinforcing value and quality benefits. Notice, too, that these people seem mature and real *and* interesting. They are not models from a thirty-something agency nor escapees from a nursing home for the decrepit.

Figure 6–14 is a well-known 9" × 12" jumbo outer envelope that was the control for The Hume Group, Inc., "Successful Investing & Money Management" program for some ten years. Inside was an eight-page letter with a four-page insert and a lift letter. But no brochure. Naturally, most all of us can answer "yes" to the first three questions. The fourth question is inside, however. The back of the outer also carries a strong teaser. (This is one of my own samples.)

Caveat: The Question Approach can also be tricky. When you plan your question, make sure it involves your prospect by capitalizing on those human needs and desires reflected in your hypothesis and fulfilled in your benefits; otherwise a question can have negative effects. Just as we're all unconsciously compelled to finish the unfinished sentence, so we are also ornery enough to unconsciously say "no" when someone is trying too hard to make us say "yes":

"Wouldn't you rather have a Buick?"

"Aren't you sorry you're missing out on all the exciting things that are happening in . . .?"

"Are you ready to share one of the best kept secrets in the world of antiques?"

THE PROBLEM/SOLUTION AND THE NEGATIVE APPROACH

No matter how bad things may be, advertisers always try to ignore the negative and latch onto the affirmative. And well they should. Negative selling can be very difficult—and dangerous. At least it can be here in the U.S.A.

FIGURE 6–13   The Question Approach

Blue Cross
Blue Shield
of Florida
P.O. Box 1798
Jacksonville, FL 32231-0014

BULK RATE
U.S. POSTAGE
PAID
Blue Cross and
Blue Shield of
Florida

Have you made this
common mistake with
your Medicare
supplement insurance?

Inside: How to be sure that
you're NOT *wasting money*
with your current coverage

3302A0510319
John Q Sample
Mega Direct
2100 Palmetto St.
Clearwater FL 34624

SEOSE-1.292B

Blue Cross
Blue Shield
of Florida

P.O. Box 1798
Jacksonville, Florida 32231-0014
1-800-876-2227

> To be smart about how you manage your money, take
> a second look at your Medicare supplement insurance
> coverage. You may be making a common mistake!

Dear Florida neighbor,

Are you paying for Medicare supplement insurance coverage
that you really <u>don't</u> <u>need</u>?

I know it's a question that you wouldn't expect to hear from
a company that sells Medicare supplement insurance -- but
there's a good reason for asking it.

It's quite possible that you're making a common mistake by
paying for <u>more</u> coverage than necessary. And at the same
time, you could be <u>missing</u> out on some of the valuable
<u>quality-first</u> extras that we offer at Blue Cross and Blue
Shield of Florida.

> In a recent issue of <u>Kiplinger's</u> <u>Personal</u> <u>Finance</u>
> <u>Magazine</u>, the executive director of the Medicare
> Advocacy Project warns that "some seniors try to
> cover themselves for <u>everything</u> and end up paying
> <u>far</u> <u>more</u> in premiums than they will ever get back
> in benefits."[1]

Other financial planners agree. It just <u>doesn't</u> make sense to
pay <u>hundreds</u> <u>of</u> <u>extra</u> <u>dollars</u> <u>a</u> <u>year</u> to insure yourself
against an <u>occasional</u> expense that you could readily afford.

That's why you'll want to know about CompCoverage Plan A.

It's small on price, yet big on the quality, dependability
and financial security that's important to you.

Compared with the coverage that you have now, CompCoverage

FIGURE 6–13   (Continued)

Be smart.
Spend less.
And enjoy
real quality...

"Paying for more Medicare supplement insurance than you really need...is a common mistake—and it's like throwing money out the window."

*Matthew Smith
Financial planner*

With CompCoverage Plan A
Medicare Supplement Insurance from
Blue Cross and Blue Shield of Florida

**Blue Cross
Blue Shield**
of Florida

SB-1292

Take a
second look
at your current
insurance...

I f you take pride in being smart about how you manage your money, we urge you to think again about your present Medicare supplement insurance plan...and to consider, in its place, Blue Cross and Blue Shield of Florida's CompCoverage Plan A.

CompCoverage Plan A could be a very smart financial move for you. This plan fully meets all state and federal regulations for Medicare Supplement Insurance. As you'll see on the next page, it features *very low rates.* When you compare these rates to what you're currently paying, you could be enjoying real savings. And while CompCoverage Plan A features *moneysaving rates,* it's designed for Floridians who truly want the best!

With our commitment to outstanding quality and excellent service, you'll see for yourself why Blue Cross and Blue Shield of Florida is the health insurance company chosen by *more* Florida residents than any other!'

"[Plan A] also can be a good choice if your aim is to cover catastrophic costs," says Geraldine Dallek, executive director of the Medicare Advocacy Project in Los Angeles. She warns that in opting for broader, more expensive policies, some seniors try to cover themselves for everything and end up paying far more in premiums than they will ever get back in benefits.

**Kiplinger's Personal
Finance Magazine,
July 1992**

You could
be spending
less while
you enjoy the
quality and
peace of mind
of Blue Cross
and Blue Shield
of Florida
coverage!

**How much
could you save?
Please see inside...**

COMPARE THE BENEFITS. COMPARE THE SAVINGS.

Our CompCoverage Plan A could
be a very smart financial move for you!

Why is our CompCoverage Plan A so much less expensive than other Medicare supplement insurance plans?

It's simple. CompCoverage Plan A is designed for people who don't need insurance to cover every little cost and deductible. In other words, if you can afford to pay Medicare's Part A deductible you can pay a lower monthly rate for your insurance.

For example, CompCoverage Plan A doesn't cover Medicare's hospital deductible of $676. If you were to be

Save up to hundreds of dollars each year, starting right now!

Compare your current insurance rates with the economical rates of CompCoverage Plan A. With CompCoverage Plan A, you could save on your insurance premiums every month. Add it all up and you could save thousands of dollars during your retirement years.

Deduct an additional 2-1/2% off the cost—for life!

After you enroll in Blue Cross and Blue Shield of Florida's CompCoverage Plan A, you'll be eligible to enroll in our convenient Automatic Payment Option...which will give you additional savings of 2-1/2% on your premiums, each and every month. And you'll be free of the fuss and bother of dealing with premium bills...a real plus when you're traveling!

hospitalized, you'd need to pay that deductible yourself. However, for month after month, you'll be saving money on your insurance costs—up to hundreds of dollars each year, depending on the plan you now have. When you look at the big picture, it's likely that you'd come out ahead.

And, if you ever decide that you want more coverage, Blue Cross and Blue Shield of Florida offers other Medicare Supplement Insurance plans with more benefits. You can easily switch from CompCoverage Plan A to another Blue Cross and Blue Shield of Florida plan at any time...with no lapse in coverage.

Qualify for our "Same Age Forever" promise for lower rates for life!

Here's another advantage of enrolling with Blue Cross and Blue Shield of Florida at this time. The younger you are when you enroll, the lower your rates will be—no kidding!—for as long as you're enrolled with us.

Your rates in the years to come will be based solely on the age at which you first enroll with us. (We call it our "Same Age Forever" promise.) This will be true, even if you switch from one Blue Cross and Blue Shield of Florida plan to another. While we may have occasional across-the-board rate increases that affect all of our subscribers, we guarantee that your rates will never go up just because you are another year older, or because of the condition of your health, or based on the number of claims that you file.

COMPCOVERAGE PLAN A							
Age at enrollment	65	66-67	68-69	70-71	72-74	75-79	80+
Monthly Rate	$49.30	$52.10	$57.00	$65.10	$69.20	$73.20	$77.20

(If your zip code begins with 339, 321, 322, 323, 334, 335, 336, 337, 328, 329, 335, 336, 33*, 338, 339, 342, 344, 346 or 347, the above rates apply.)

See how CompCoverage Plan A helps cover
the expenses that aren't paid by Medicare

Medicare does NOT PAY	PLAN A COVERS	YOU PAY
Part A Hospital Services:		
$676 hospital deductible each benefit period		$676
$169 a day co-payment for days 61-90 in a hospital	✓	Nothing
$338 a day co-payment for days 91-150	✓	Nothing
100% of Medicare-allowable expenses for additional 365 days after Medicare hospital benefits stop completely	✓	Nothing
Calendar year blood deductible (first 3 pints of blood) if the deductible is not met by the replacement of blood	✓	Nothing
Part B Physician Care and Medical Services		
20% of Medicare-approved amount (Part B co-insurance) and 20% of Medicare-approved charges for durable medical equipment	✓	Medicare's $100 Part B deductible

The Outline of Coverage that you'll receive when you enroll includes complete details and limitations of the benefits shown above.

Not connected with or endorsed by the U.S. Government or the Federal Medicare program.

If you'd like your Part A Hospital Deductible covered as well, consider our CompCoverage Plan B.

As you can see, our moneysaving Plan A does not cover Medicare's $676 Part A in-hospital deductible. If you'd prefer a plan that does cover your hospital deductible, you should consider our moneysaving Plan B. It provides all of the coverage of Plan A, plus coverage of this $676 deductible.

To enroll in CompCoverage Plan B, complete the Enrollment Form and check the appropriate box on the form, indicating that you want Plan B coverage. You'll find the monthly rates for both Plan A and Plan B listed on the back of the Enrollment Form.

For more information about Plan B or other plans that we have available, please call toll-free 1-800-876-2227.

It's easy to make the switch...

Your acceptance is guaranteed as long as you're at least 65, a Florida resident and enrolled in Medicare Parts A and B. All of your pre-existing conditions will be covered from the minute you're enrolled. And, we'll help you make the switch with no lapse in coverage.

Simply fill out the enclosed Enrollment Form and send it to us. If you have any questions, just call our toll-free number for help. Be sure to enroll today—so you can start saving on your rates right away.

Need advice on the right coverage for you?
Call us toll-free 1-800-876-2227

FIGURE 6–14   An Envelope Using the Question Approach

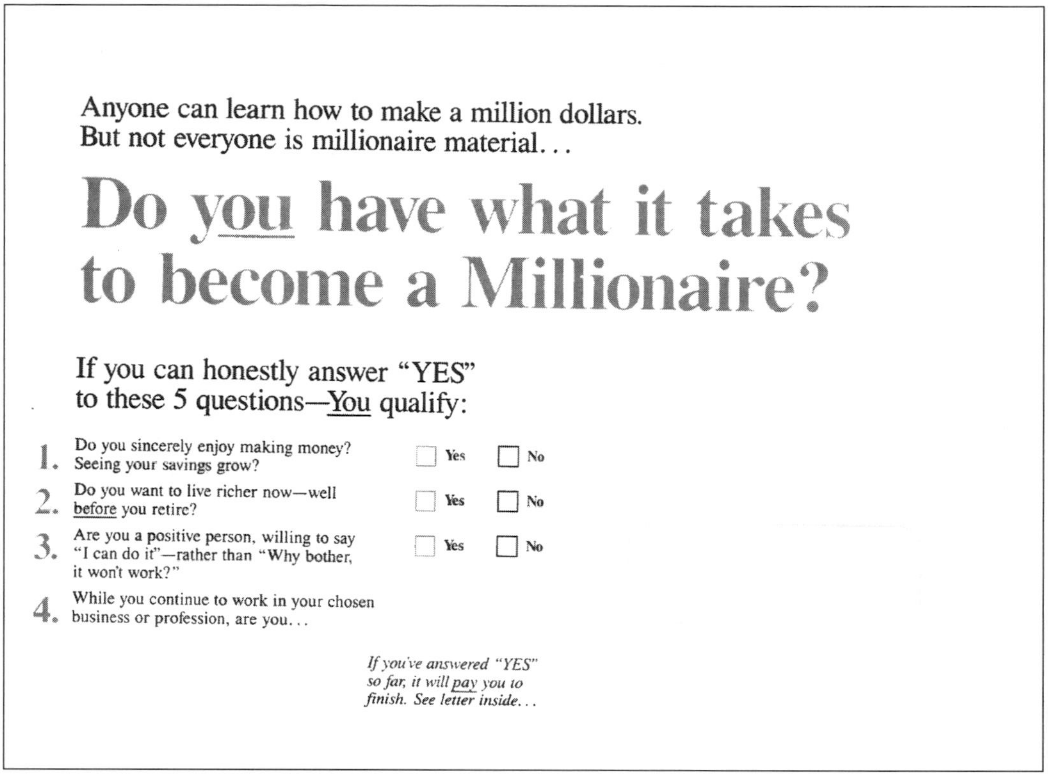

Anyone can learn how to make a million dollars.
But not everyone is millionaire material...

Do you have what it takes to become a Millionaire?

If you can honestly answer "YES"
to these 5 questions—You qualify:

1. Do you sincerely enjoy making money?
   Seeing your savings grow?   ☐ Yes   ☐ No

2. Do you want to live richer now—well
   before you retire?   ☐ Yes   ☐ No

3. Are you a positive person, willing to say
   "I can do it"—rather than "Why bother,
   it won't work?"   ☐ Yes   ☐ No

4. While you continue to work in your chosen
   business or profession, are you...

*If you've answered "YES"
so far, it will pay you to
finish. See letter inside...*

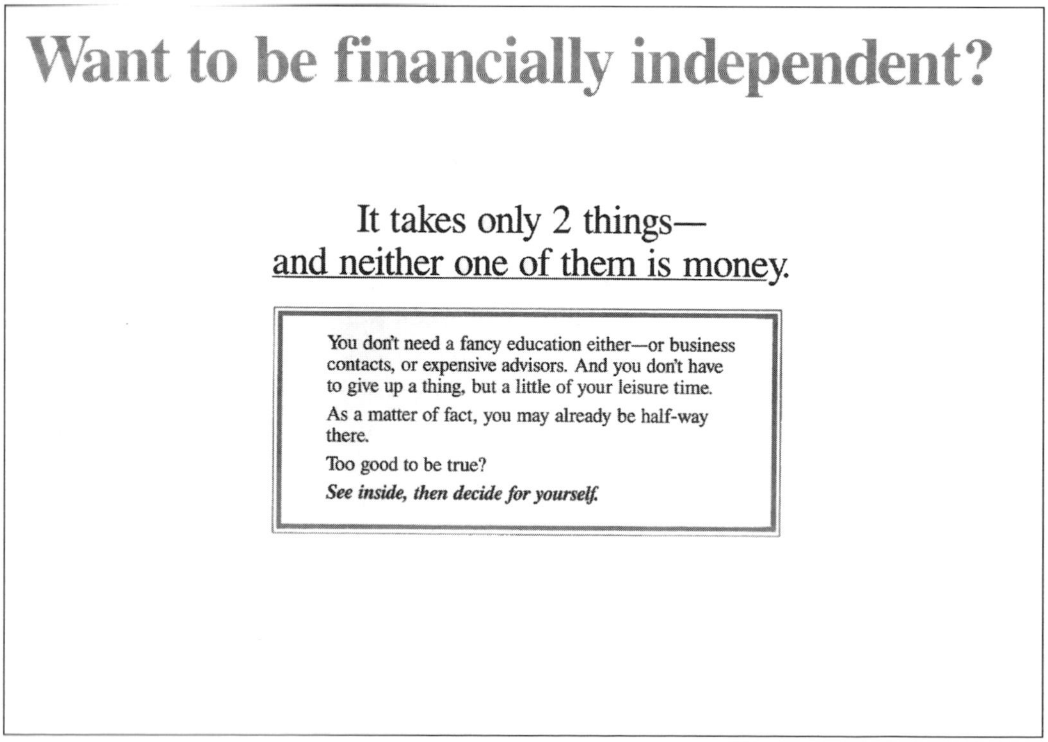

Want to be financially independent?

It takes only 2 things—
and neither one of them is money.

You don't need a fancy education either—or business
contacts, or expensive advisors. And you don't have
to give up a thing, but a little of your leisure time.

As a matter of fact, you may already be half-way
there.

Too good to be true?

See inside, then decide for yourself.

This doesn't mean you can't use involving curiosity arousers like

Warning—this material is not for everyone.

Open this only if . . .

Only the dedicated need apply . . .

This may not be for you . . .

The *Negative Approach* or *Problem/Solution* in all its glory implies "you" (the prospect) are having a problem (whether you know it or not) because you are missing out on something, then it offers you the solution. It warns of gloom and disaster and it asks the prospect to participate and help alleviate the problem.

This approach is often used in fund raising. And it's not dangerous there, it's smart. Here are some examples:

Contribute to my campaign. If the opponent wins, up go your taxes.

Help this one child and you'll be helping all mankind—and feel the better for it.

Help conserve our forests and make sure your children enjoy these trees. Your contribution of $X can maintain one acre for a year.

Other examples are: "A clear and present danger." (A heart-tugging situation at most.) "Specific action needed." Often intangible, but strong, altruistic benefits for the reader. (For examples of top-notch fund raising packages, see Chapter 8.)

The Problem/Solution Approach can be used in consumer products and services and in business-to-business as well, as long as "you" and benefits predominate. Poorly executed, it may offend your prospects. Properly executed, it can be the strongest of direct response approaches, particularly in print advertising. The method here is: Set up the problem, then knock it down.

Figure 6–15 pictures a wonderful, fun example of this. The problem, from the looks of the 12" × 6" outer, seems to be "people." Interesting people, sure—now who are they and what are they doing that "costs me millions?" Since the prospect is supposed to identify with the problem, the people are all fictionalized in drawings—just "employees." However, once inside, they receive real personalities; they are "type cast." And it becomes clear how these employee *types* steal valuable time. Of course, the solution is offered in a CRM training video that can solve the prospect's problem. A free preview and premiums motivate response.

Here's how you use the Problem/Solution Approach combined with the Question Approach:

"Do you make these mistakes in English?"

"Will you be able to support your family if you get ill?"

"Is your job boring and unrewarding?"

Strong stuff.

FIGURE 6–15   A Problem/Solution Approach

Courtesy of CRM Films, L.P., Peter T. Noble Associates (design); Elizabeth Miller, Miller Direct (copy).

THE FANTASY APPROACH

An approach used primarily by sweepstakes writers and by top professionals when the hypothesis and benefits lend themselves to building dreams or building appealing imaginary situations is the *Fantasy Approach*.

There will be times—many, I hope, for your sake—when your product or service and its hypothesis cry out for the Fantasy Approach. It says, in effect, "Imagine this . . . imagine that . . . then imagine that you can . . . ." Just as you get the reader, dreaming or fantasizing right along with you, you pop up with the answer or solution: "Well, now you can . . ." or "No need to worry, here's your solution." There are some things you have to watch out for as you build the fantasy, however.

Most important: Don't cut the reader out by building *your* fantasy. This is a common mistake. At every step, you have to make sure your prospect can move into the fantasy easily and identify totally with the description you provide. Too much description and detail may lose you some prospects, who will say, "Wait a minute. That's not *my* fantasy." Give your readers room to move and to imagine within the fantasy framework you provide.

Figure 6–16 is an excellent example of the Fantasy Approach, written by the late Linda Wells and designed by David Gordon for *Martha Stewart Living* magazine. It talks about dreams and having dreams realized. The brochure itself is clean and relatively simple, showing the essence of the homemaker's dream in entertaining, decorating, creating. The letter does the rest.

The following pure fantasy creates a framework that brings every reader into it. This was written some time ago by the late Henry (Hank) Burnett. He began his fantasy for *Islands* magazine above the Johnson Box offer and before the salutation. Notice that Hank described the island conceptually, not physically. He offers you the "essence" of island. This allows you all the freedom in the world to visualize your own particular sort of island paradise, not the stereotypical one that may or may not appeal to you:

> Somewhere out there, beyond the blue horizon,
> lies the island of your dreams . . . isolated by
> oceans from trouble and strife, from concrete
> and plastic, from politics and pollution . . .
> a place where geography grants immunity from
> the impositions and incivilities of day-to-day
> life in an over-civilized world. Now you can
> find it, explore it, experience it and enjoy it . . .
> through the pages of a magnificent new
> magazine for the escapists in us all:
>
>   I S L A N D S
>
> This is your invitation to run away with us to
> the most intriguing islands on earth . . . to
> become a Charter Subscriber at a special low rate
> . . . and to get your copy of the Premier Issue.
>
> Dear Fellow Romantic: . . .

FIGURE 6–16   The Fantasy Approach

BULK RATE
U.S. POSTAGE
PAID
MARTHA STEWART
LIVING

Dream & Do
with **Martha Stewart**

*I
Accept*

SHAKE BEFORE OPENING — FREE BURPEE BAS

P.O. Box 53098, Boulder, CO 80321-3098

It's more than a
magazine of pretty pictures.

It's a magazine of possibilities.

A magazine of opportunities.

A magazine of useful, practical
ways you can make your dreams of
gracious living come true.

And the next issue of
MARTHA STEWART LIVING
is yours to try with
my compliments.

Dear Reader:

First you have to have a dream.

When I started setting the dinner table for my mother,
I was three years old. The napkins were paper. The dishes,
glasses and cutlery were -- well, utilitarian. But even as
long ago as that, I had a vision of something better.

As I grew up, my dream picture came into focus. I saw
a table draped in damask, with old roses in an antique vase
and candles flickering over an elegant array of sparkling
silver, crystal goblets and glimmering china.

Soon, my dream extended to a whole house and garden, to
a whole way of life. I took up modeling as a teenager, worked
my way through college, became a stockbroker, switched to
catering -- and finally faced the fact that money couldn't

Courtesy of *Martha Stewart Living.*

Fantasy-come-true can also be used (in addition to the Negative Approach) in fund raising. "Imagine what you could do to help realize this dream" is an excellent approach to fund raising as long as the dream is realizable.

Some advice on sweepstakes: The entire sweepstakes concept is based on fantasy—the popular fantasy of "striking it rich"—and the sweepstakes popularity fluctuates. It goes *up* in difficult economic periods, *down* in stable or improved economic times.

If you have a hand in working with sweepstakes professionals, keep in mind that you'll draw a better class of customer if the sweepstakes and its prizes are themed to complement or emphasize the product or service offered, rather than overshadow it. If you're called upon to do the sweepstakes writing, there are several basics to remember.

- Go heavy on the hype. This is one place where it's clearly permissible. ("Imagine!" "Imagine!!" "Imagine!!!")

- Emphasize the Grand Prize and the smallest prize (the one that offers the best odds because so many are awarded). These are the two upon which most response is based—the fantasy of winning the grand prize; the reality that you just might win the smallest prize.

- When the main prize is money (research shows that money is the most popular prize) fantasize about all the things that "you can do with it." Build dreams.

- Use words like "imagine," "life of luxury," "dreams come true," "time of your life," "beyond belief," "high life."

- Add involvement devices—peels, tucks, scratches, pastes, check-offs, initials. *As opposed to all other direct mail, clutter and confusion make sweepstakes more appealing.* Don't frown—this is tested and proven.

- Don't restrain the artist either. He or she should want a lot of illustrations, big seals, sunbursts, official-looking borders, and computerized forms.

- As with strong premium offers, fight to maintain a position of prominence for your product or service—lest your prospect forget that an order is still the objective.

- Learn from the real pros. Study sweepstakes mailings from the magazine business—*Reader's Digest*, Publisher's Clearing House, American Express, and American Family Publishers. They've been at it for years.

THE ANALOGY APPROACH

An approach that's recommended only if it comes to you in a blinding flash of inspiration is the *Analogy Approach*. It can happen—the perfect analogy—something so close and so much a part of the prospect's experience that he or she moves through it with you right into the product or service benefits saying "yes, yes, yes" all along the way.

Even the perfect analogy is tough to execute effectively, however, so you won't find many of these. Figures 6–17 and 6–18 show the first pages of two letters that were tested for a magazine on staying healthy or on the concept of "wellness."

The first one (Figure 6–17) is a straight generic approach with a cold, pragmatic tone; the other (Figure 6–18) is warm and friendly with a touch of humor along with a perfect analogy—one of the best I've ever come across. It's a combo analogy-cum-question approach, and it's loaded with involvement! (You'd be safe to guess that the hypothesis here is "Most people know less about their bodies than they do about their homes. Once they realize the absurdity of this situation, they'll want to change it.") And you can safely guess the winner while you're at it.

FIGURE 6–17   A Cold Generic Approach   **FIGURE 6–18   A Warm Analogy Approach**

Read the first pages of these two letters and see why the Analogy Approach is stronger.

THE STORY APPROACH

People enjoy a good story, and if you have a short, relevant one that pulls your prospect right into your benefits, don't be afraid to use it. If the story is *very* good (and very pertinent) and your writing is especially keen, you might even consider starting on the envelope.

Stories seem to do quite well for their copywriters—not necessarily true stories, you understand, but stories that really drive home the benefit.

Figure 6–19 shows the first of several excellent stories by "Bill" (William North) Jayme. It was the Control for *Science 79, Science 80, Science 81, Science 82, Science 83, Science 84, Science 85,* and *Science 86* (when the magazine was folded into another publication). Notice that it starts on the outer with "Was it an accident? Or deliberate? Introducing Science 84."

Caveat: Although the *Story Approach* allows you to use drama and all your descriptive talents—*beware of humor.* Humorous writing is very hard to pull off. What tickles your funny bone may leave some of your market cold. Most of us do well to play it safe and not try humor or attempt to be clever. (Clever usually ends up "cute," something we all must avoid at any cost.)

THE BE-A-HERO APPROACH

The *Be-a-Hero Approach,* attributed to the late Paul Bringe, a well-known direct mail consultant, is the most popular and logical approach for business-to-business mail, or for any situation where your prospect is not buying directly for himself or herself.

Ostensibly, your business approach has an end goal of increasing corporate profits—doing something that will save the company time or money—but, altruistic motives asides, you are still talking to a weak human being. So what might motivate your business prospect? One answer, said in different ways is, "You will be a hero," which means personal corporate recognition, rising success in the company, and possibly a promotion or a raise.

Your prospect, who may very well have to persuade the boss (and others) to agree to your desired action, needs your support and assurance that the action will be positive and innovative for the company. And you must provide this prospect with the tools to get the message across.

You started into this chapter expecting to come out of it with your creation firmly in hand, but look what's happened—you still haven't written a headline! You are, however, a lot further along than you think, and this will become clear as you pull it all together in the chapter. Chapter 7, as a matter of fact, is really a continuation of this chapter. I'm breaking it up just to give you a breather and a chance to have a light snack, as well as to try your hand at selecting an approach in the following exercises.

FIGURE 6–19   The Story Approach

THE SUN DAGGER
WAS IT AN ACCIDENT? ■ OR DELIBERATE? ■ INTRODUCING SCIENCE 84.

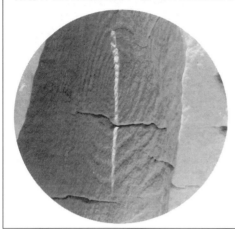

NON-PROFIT
ORGANIZATION
U.S. POSTAGE PAID
AMERICAN
ASSOCIATION
FOR THE
ADVANCEMENT
OF SCIENCE

```
                                CAP-RT SORT** CP 20
        1205661018                           DP552
        MR. JOAN THROCKMORTON
        1175 YORK AV
        NEW YORK, NY 10021
```

SCIENCE84
IT'S THE EXCITING
NEW MAGAZINE FROM
THE AMERICAN ASSOCIATION FOR
THE ADVANCEMENT OF SCIENCE.
MAIL THE ENCLOSED CARD PROMPTLY
AND GET A FREE COPY OF THE
NEXT EXCITING ISSUE.

Dear Reader:

She hoisted herself up noiselessly so as not to disturb the rattle-snakes snoozing there in the sun.

To her left, the high desert of New Mexico. Indian country. To her right, the rock carvings she had photographed the day before. Stick people. Primitive animals.

Up ahead, three sandstone slabs stood stacked against the face of the cliff. In their shadow, another carving. A spiral consisting of rings. Curious, the young woman drew closer. Instinctively, she glanced at her watch. It was almost noon. Then just at that moment, a most unusual thing happened.

    Suddenly, as if out of nowhere, an eerie dagger of light appeared to stab at the topmost ring of the spiral. It next began to plunge downwards -- shimmering, laser-like.

    It pierced the eighth ring. The seventh. The sixth. It punctured the innermost and last. Then just as suddenly as it had appeared, the dagger of light was gone. The young woman glanced at her watch again. Exactly twelve minutes had elapsed.

Coincidence? Accident? Fluke? No. What she may have stumbled across that midsummer morning three years ago is an ancient solar calendar. And in scientific circles, it's hotly debated as <u>one of the most intriguing archeological discoveries of recent years</u>.

    It may change forever history's perceptions of America's early Indian peoples. And as an astronomical and geometrical marvel, it may rival Stonehenge.

<u>If science whodunnits like this set your intellect a-jogging</u> . . . If you take pleasure and pride in keeping up with everything significant that's being discovered, explored, invented, postulated, verified . . .

Choosing an Approach

As a direct response professional, your keen, analytical eye is going to look at every piece of direct mail a little differently in the future; especially now that you know the writer is employing an "approach." It's good practice to keep an eye out for the approach in your direct mail. See how effective each approach is in pulling you in. Could you have improved on them? Chosen a better approach?

Some products and services cry for certain approaches, others almost seem to adapt to any approach. Match each of the approaches below with the right product/benefit/hypothesis in the list that follows. The hypothesis (in parentheses) often points the way to the right approach.

Approaches

Generic/Offer Approach

Story Approach

Fantasy Approach

Testimonial Approach

Question Approach

Invitational Approach

Product/Benefit/Hypothesis

1. A travel magazine that brings you picture stories of cities and countries around the world. When you subscribe you are also entered in a big travel sweepstakes. (The pleasure and cultural enrichment of reading about—and possibly visiting—faraway places.)

2. A new limited editions club. Membership in this select collectors' group ensures that you will be offered quality objects with sound value that others cannot purchase. (Desire to belong to an exclusive group.)

3. Correspondence course on conversational Spanish for business people. In Spain, without a working knowledge of the language, you cannot hold your own and maintain the respect of the native Spanish executives. (Desire to be successful.)

4. A new camcorder that every family can use and enjoy. Now's the time to buy because the price is at an all-time low. (It enhances the quality of life. And increases enjoyment.)

5. An amazing new book that can change your life. The Smith book tells how John Smith amassed a fortune. Now you can do the same. (It offers security, freedom from money worries.)

6. A request for a clothing catalog. Order this catalog and enjoy fine clothing. And we will treat you royally. Our customers are fussy, tasteful people. And they stay with us. (People who are nervous

about buying through the mail will look for assurance that they are using a quality company that doesn't make mistakes and readily accepts exchanges and returns.)

Do your answers agree with these? Don't worry, you don't have to agree. You may have come up with good creative solutions of your own, and that's what it's all about. Shall we test?

Answers

1. *Fantasy Approach*
2. *Invitational Approach*
3. *Question Approach*
4. *Generic/Offer Approach*
5. *Story Approach*
6. *Testimonial Approach*

Notes

1. Direct Marketing Association, Inc., 1120 Avenue of the Americas, New York, NY 10036-6700, or 1111 19th Street NW, Washington, DC 20036-3603.

2. Edward L. Nash, *Direct Marketing Strategy/Planning/Execution* (New York, NY: McGrawHill, Inc., 1982), p. 231 and 258.

CHAPTER SEVEN

DEATHLESS PROSE

You have just arrived at the portals of creativity with five suitcases, one large trunk, a pair of binoculars, and your Nikon camera around your neck, a tennis racquet under your arm, and golf clubs at your feet. (Oops, you dropped your raincoat!) What's this about creativity and inspiration? Think you can't get off the ground with the creative equipment I've been hanging on you—approaches, time frames, artist relationships, laws, and guidelines? Are you possibly suspecting that actual writing could become nothing more than a simple mathematical formula that you put into a computer—and out pops your copy, incorporating everything you've learned? That you'll never actually arrive at a point where you have to create? Doubt no more. You are there. Now is the time to go off and GET IT DOWN! No more procrastination. Ready or not—write! Now. Don't come back until it's down. Check your baggage at the hotel, strip to your bathing suit or whatever, throw caution to the winds, and dive in. You'll never know where you are until you do. No excuses. Get going.

Stage One: Get It Down

The command "Get it down!" is not my idea of fun nor is it something I've invented just to torture you. GET IT DOWN is your first logical step to writing and whether or not you want to accept it— now is your hour! At the self-imposed command "Get it down"—and you must impose this command on yourself with every job, large or small—several things may happen.

217

1. You start right in, raring to go, full of ideas. You write for an hour or so—then you fizzle out.

2. You sit there struggling with your copy lead. You have ideas— even a possible approach—but you can't seem to eke out the first sentence.

3. You go back to Chapter 6 to see about getting started again—on the write foot.

4. You write on (and on for hours) despite your doubts. Then you read it back and you hate it. (In extreme cases writers can even hate themselves and doubt their abilities at this stage.)

Question: Why am I telling you all this?

Answer: Because it's terribly important that you do not become discouraged. You must understand that *all* writers have these problems (although some don't like to admit it). Not even William Shakespeare, T. S. Eliot, or Gabriel Garcia Marquez could roll off one deathless phrase after another.

Writing is hard work. It is a tough craft. No one would bother with this nasty business if there weren't some big emotional rewards. What's more, writers don't communicate constructively about their writing, as Barbara Goldsmith attests in this excerpt from an article in the *New York Times Book Review:*

> Ultimately, although millions of words have been written on the subject, the public has been given little help in understanding the writing process. Few writers are adept at explaining exactly what they do, and, indeed, many do not seem to understand it themselves. William Faulkner thought of himself as a man "running along behind [his characters] with a pencil trying to put down what they say and do." Somerset Maugham wrote, "There are three rules for writing the novel. Unfortunately, no one knows what they are." And Marianne Moore warned the writer, "Be there when the writing is going on." The late Tommy Thompson, in urging writers to get over feelings of inferiority, offered only two words of advice on how to feel professional, "Get dressed."

> It is a truism that the more skillful the writing, the more invisible the act of creation. If the writer has done a competent job, his insights become so lucid and universal that they seem to belong to the reader himself. What follows, then, is the assumption that the reader could have produced them. This is, no doubt, in spite of all evidence to the contrary, why the fantasy endures that the writer merely extracts one's story as a dentist would pull out a loose tooth. One is reminded of how Michelangelo informed a man who admired one of his angel carvings that his job was not difficult, because the angel had been inside the stone all along. Michelangelo had simply set it free.[1]

A WORD ABOUT YOUR
REWARDS

As a direct response writer you can take comfort in the techniques. You have formats and sequences to follow, rules that protect you, structures such as AIDA to help you organize. In short, a lot is already done for you, but a direct response writer cannot thrive and prosper on technique alone.

If you don't already have a hundred ideas jumping around in your head, this is inspiration time—the time to visit the storehouse of your imagination. If your curiosity has done its job, you'll have lots to work with. Start associating familiar experiences with your prospect and your product. Let your mind go. This is where "creative people" enjoy themselves!

Imagine you are the prospect. Imagine your needs and desires as the prospect. Considering the major benefit, the hypothesis, and the offer, try to come up with the most appealing, compelling approach. Imagine letter starters, outer envelope copy, brochure heads. Wander around and *imagine*. Review your notes. Have fun! Get involved! Be excited! Start your dialogue!

Caveat: You are not writing a novel or a story or an article of your choice here. Your product is selected for you; your market is established. How flexible is your mind? How elastic *is* your imagination? Can you empathize with people who are totally different from you? Can you get excited about a product or service that may not appeal to you? If you cannot (and indeed there may be times when you can't), you're not going to be very creative. You're even liable to be boring. And miserable. And hate the whole process.

You may not be able to write glowingly for the Republicans when you are a Democrat at heart, or vice versa. Or you may pull back from praising a product or service when you have serious reservations about its quality. These are moral issues and my advice is to steer clear. Don't tackle things you can't believe in.

However, if you plan to make a living as a direct response creative person, you must be prolific and you must *enjoy* being prolific. You must be able to imagine how it feels to be a young college student or a middle-aged business executive or an elderly citizen. As Bill Jayme puts it, "I can become a pregnant woman in nothing flat. A broke pregnant woman." You must empathize. You must identify your prospect's needs and desires, and link them to your product's benefits with flair and imagination and enthusiasm. You must enjoy doing this! Because (aside from the attendant satisfaction and the money) that is all there is.

Give yourself a fair chance. Test and try yourself on a variety of assignments. If this process continues to make you uncomfortable or miserable—or if you really believe you can't pull it off, try as you will—you should not be writing copy for direct response advertising. Even if you manage to get by, you will be unhappy, and that's no way to live.

BITTERSWEET—BUT
WORTH IT

Writing is a bittersweet experience to be sure. The hard work of simply GETTING IT DOWN (followed by a lot more hard work) is balanced or offset primarily by the fun, the joy, the pure exhilaration of crafting words and spelling out ideas that will reach (and deeply affect) your prospect.

Creative expressions and bright promotional ideas seldom come easily. You must gather insights and inspirations quickly as they come, then work hard to enlarge on the best of them. Cull and discard as you go, replacing your first good idea with a bright new flash as it comes shooting out of the blue. Rework your words. Listen to them. Change them around. Imagine. Talk to your prospect. Then *be* your prospect. Now try it again.

If you can do this, if you can pick up this challenge and enjoy it, you will be special. You will be a craftsman, a dreamer, a magician, an actor, a salesperson! You will be a writer who moves and affects others. You will be proud of yourself. And well you should be.

Enough of the rewards. On with the hard work.

I've divided your writing into three distinct stages or steps, and GET IT DOWN is Stage One. This is not to say that everyone works carefully in three clear-cut stages like this, nor even that you have to do it this way. But consciously or unconsciously, professional direct response copywriters *all* go through an approximate version of this and it should be helpful to you to know you are not alone, and to have a little trail of crumbs to start you through the woods.

Once you're into Stage One, you may be wondering, once you begin to GET IT DOWN, just when you can stop. If you're going nicely, don't—for heaven's sake—stop simply because it's 5:00 P.M. or because the fire bell rings or you hear the phone or it's getting dark.

Stop when you can do no more. When your resources are exhausted. When you're left without an idea in your head. When you're sick of the whole thing and are convinced you're writing drivel. (Actually, drivel's not so bad at this stage, so don't let that stop you either!)

When you finally stop, you're likely to have

1. A half-finished letter
2. Two-and-a-half finished letters
3. Two headlines and one full brochure segment
4. An unacceptable copy line for your outer envelope (and a good visual concept)
5. Reams of copy that ramble on and on without clear component definition or structure
6. All of the above or some of the above in different combinations

Good show! Now leave it alone—but in a safe place; go out and take a shower, see a movie, have a drink, go to dinner. Do anything *but* think about your writing. If new inspiration forces itself through, of course take notes, then set them aside quickly.

Give yourself at least twelve hours of peace—more if you can. You have just emerged from the GET IT DOWN stage and you deserve a rest.

Stage Two: Start Over

If Stage One is GET IT DOWN, why should Stage Two be START OVER? You won't ask this question after several years in the business, but it's a fair question for now. Let me explain it this way (and I hope the analogy holds):

> You are given $500,000 in a quiz show and told to furnish your house. If you fail to use up the funds in 24 hours, you will lose them. Thanks to speed and perseverance, you succeed. Now the mad rush is over and you have a little time, so you start to look at your house and what you've accomplished. It is a strange mixture of wonderful things and pure garbage. What a mess, but one worthy of careful salvage.

> As you walk through it, you automatically discard some things (for the tag sale). How could you possibly have picked them up? Other things are inappropriately placed, so you move them around. Some articles have to change locations from one room to another, but they're worth keeping. Still other things are on the borderline, so you set them aside in a separate area in the basement for future consideration.

> You also find that you have two sofas and three coffee tables. You judge them carefully and keep only the best. Actually, with a little modification one of the coffee tables can be moved into the media room. There's a problem with the bedrooms, however. You don't have nearly enough bedroom furniture to go around. You will need more.

> The living room rug was the first thing you purchased—an Oriental, something you've always wanted, your prized possession. Your living room is decorated around it. Unfortunately, this means one of the easy chairs just doesn't work out. You can give it to the Salvation Army—or save it for later.

And so it goes. But need I go on? You can see where I'm heading, and where you'll be heading once you return to your copy. You may be lucky, of course. Everything may fall into place. You may not throw out one thing or rearrange even one paragraph (although nothing like that has ever happened to me or any writers I know).

Chances are, you'll feel like most good writers—somewhat discouraged, somewhat elated as you meander through the maze of words and phrases. You'll want to set things right first off. Look, here's a great headline for your brochure lying uselessly in the letter copy! (What a find!) And here—down here near the bottom of this page of letter copy—look at this gem! Why not *start* your letter with it? Try. See.

The next three paragraphs have all the right data, but yuk—need a rewrite. Let's set them aside. By the way, if you're changing your outer envelope, how about this headline from the brochure? Try. See. And while you're at it—need a Johnson box?

Does your spokesperson have clear and logical expressions—*in character?* Hold tight to your spokesperson and direct every word that goes through his or her head so it comes out naturally, credibly. And how about another character's point of view? Maybe in a lift letter?

Now you're into the heavy stuff. You should be cutting, copying, pasting, adding copy, killing copy, changing initial perceptions—even searching for a new approach.

Stage Two is your real, hard-core, make-or-break creative time. Here's where you can cop out and do it the easy, technician's way, or hang in and craft something beautiful—something that gives you a warm feeling of satisfaction (your reward).

Unfortunately, there's no way to begin Stage Two until you've done Stage One, and Stage Two generally takes off by blasting Stage One off the page—or literally picking it apart. Stage Two can take a long time, by the way. You may have to leave your work, then come back to it many times before you're finished. Even a simple double postcard takes time—if you care.

Everyone has a tendency to get discouraged at this stage, including the most experienced professionals. The secret to keeping it fresh and good is your determination, coupled with a schedule that allows you time to back out of the trees and look at your forest with perspective.

Before we move on to Stage Three, here are some pointers to help pull you through Stage Two.

YOU AND THE WRITTEN WORD

To begin with, you must understand the language in which you are communicating. A basic grounding in elementary grammar, spelling, and punctuation may prove more important to you at this stage than a college degree in English literature. You need a knowledge of what's correct, combined with an understanding of (and an ear for) what's popular or common.

As a writer—and especially as a copywriter—you have an obligation and a position of power. Your obligation is to move people to action *by communication.* This is the power of the salesperson. But you must go one step further; you must communicate by bending words and phrases to your purpose.

This is another power—the power of persuasion that enables you to have an effect on the way average people use words. You can alter the rules of proper English for dramatic effect and get away with it. You can adapt punctuation to serve your purposes. You can introduce new words (word or terms from another language) or new ways of using old words and phrases. You can even start new idioms and expressions. ("Where's the beef?") And in so doing, you can begin to change usage. ("Winston Tastes Good Like a Cigarette Should" is a classic example.)

This is heady stuff. But you will have no power to change words and phrases and punctuation if you do not understand what has gone before. You cannot break the rules of our idiom to move your market to action if you do not know what those rules are. You must know, for example

- How a sentence is structured (can you parse a sentence?)
- When to use commas, dashes, hyphens, quotations, apostrophes, exclamations, colons, semicolons, ellipses, and so on
- The that/which quandary and all the who/whom/whose answers
- Spelling and capitalization and split infinitives

I will not offer a basic grammar course here, but if you are going to be a direct response writer, here are six books that are indispensable equipment:

- Fowler's *Modern English Usage* (Second Edition), Oxford University Press, 1965. Paperback edition, reprinted 1983.
- *The Chicago Manual of Style* (Fourteenth Edition), The University of Chicago Press, 1993.
- *The Elements of Style* (Third Edition), William Strunk, Jr. and E. B. White, Macmillan Publishing Co. Inc., 1979.
- *Roget's Thesaurus in Dictionary Form*, Berkeley Publishers, 1983.
- *The American Heritage Dictionary of the English Language*, Houghton Mifflin Company, 1976.
- *Webster's Third New International Dictionary–Unabridged*, Merriam-Webster, Inc., 1981.

WHAT TO CONCENTRATE ON

Concentrate on the following aspects of your package as you begin writing:

a. Your letter's tone (who are you?). Set it and stick with it.

b. Your letter's lead (Johnson box or no Johnson box).

c. Your envelope copy (if you decide to have copy).

d. Your brochure headlines (then the subheads).

e. A clean, clear statement of your offer for the order card.

f. Decision to lift or not to lift (letter).

STARTING TO VISUALIZE

Begin to develop the following visual aspects of your package:

a. Envelope—white or kraft, large or small, black and white or lots of art and photography? Justify it!

b. Brochure—list exactly what you feel requires illustration. Justify it!

c. Your involvement devices and motivators—can you incorporate them easily? Do they make sense with your copy? With your visuals as you are planning them?

DEVELOPING STRONGER COPY

Once you have your leads and headlines in place, gather your specifics for stronger copy. For example:

Weak	Strong
• It's big.	• It's big—a full 12" × 60"
• It does all your chores for you.	• It washes your dishes, takes out the garbage, waxes the floor, and turns off the light.
• You'll have a truly enjoyable trip throughout the area . . .	• You'll see mountains 12,000 feet high, visit an old-fashioned country store, ride in a cable car with breath-taking views.

WORKING TOWARD CREATIVE UNITY

Work toward creative unity in all parts of your direct mail package. For example, if you're using the invitational approach, keep your tone elegant and use words like "invite," "preview," "exclusive," "invitation," "please reply" in all parts of the mailing, and make sure your graphics reinforce this with every component.

MAKING SURE EACH MAJOR COMPONENT CAN STAND ALONE

Since you can't be sure which piece will be read first, give your full story in the letter, your complete offer on the order card, and everything possible in the brochure. If it can't carry your offer, make sure the brochure at least refers to the offer on the enclosed order card and urges the reader to look there.

GIVING YOUR PACKAGE MORE CREDIBILITY AND INVOLVEMENT

To give your package more credibility and involvement, you might want to consider the following:

- A picture of the company plant, grounds, or offices
- A picture of "your customer service rep"
- A stronger guarantee
- Testimonials with names, and pictures if possible
- A list of specialists, directors, or advisors on the letterhead
- Incentives and motivators (tokens, stamps, deadlines, limits, and all kinds of premiums)

REMEMBERING YOUR OBJECTIVES—ALWAYS

Review your hypothesis, copy strategy, and testing research. Precisely what will your package prove in its testing?

- That a new product or service itself will have appeal to a specific market?
- That an old product or service will have appeal to a specific new market?
- That X hypothesis is stronger than Y (or the control) hypothesis?
- That you can beat the existing control—all stops out—and the devil be damned! Remember the inherent dangers in this last option. A laurel wreath if you win, the lions if you lose (see Chapter 5).

Stage Three: Polish It Up and Lay It Out

Everyone likes to skimp at the polishing. If you're working with an eager artist, he or she will jump from rough layouts to finished comps. If you're close to the final deadline, you may be tempted to give your work a read-through or two then commit it to a disk or hard copy.

Stop! Don't let it happen this way—not if you care for your copy!

First, don't leave your rewrites and copy polishing until the last minute. Start the minute you GET IT DOWN and *don't stop polishing* until it's snatched from your hands at presentation time. But also leave time *between* rewrites to reestablish your objectivity. (If you don't give yourself at least 12 hours—preferably twice that—you won't be able to distinguish between the smooth and the rough.) And remember, without polishing time, even your best copy concepts will fall under the curse of mediocre work.

Second, make sure you see comps well before your deadline. No artist should keep you in the dark or present layouts that you haven't gone over together. When you do go over them, see that you and the artist have plenty of time for last-minute changes.

Review Chapters 3 and 4. How do your components stack up? Does the outer envelope attract attention, qualify your prospect, and make a promise? Does your brochure track? Does the order form look important? *It's not too late.* You can still change a headline or a word or even a concept and a layout if you've left enough time for polishing and revising comprehensive art work.

You'll find there is almost nothing worse than doing a good job but realizing at the last minute that the copy line on the outer envelope is all wrong or your letter's lead can be vastly improved by reversing one sentence. If this happens to you—and it can happen to the best writers—be sure you have the time to change it.

PROCEDURES FOR POLISHING AND FINE-TUNING YOUR COPY

As I said before, no good copy is ever really finished. You can always add a comma (or take one out), break up a long paragraph, or cut a word.

1. *Stick to the short of it.* If you are like most good writers, you have overwritten. Don't apologize. This is common practice in Stages One and Two. It's healthy and it's helpful to you. Now—improve by cutting.

You'll have a lot to work with when you go in to clean up and reorganize your house. Here's where you start trimming and culling, and you shouldn't stop until your copy's due.

- Look for places where one word can replace a phrase.

- Test a paragraph by leaving out a weak sentence or phrase. See if the idea comes through *without* the sentence. (Some entire paragraphs may prove dispensable.)

- Check to be sure you have no useless repetition.

- Test your adjectives and adverbs. Cut them out if they don't strengthen the copy.

- Bring in an outsider. Get a fresh, second opinion.

Be merciless. Wise cutting never fails to improve your copy. After a few passes even you, the author, will find you can do without some of your favorite flowery phrases. While you're cutting, remember the basic admonition to all direct response copywriters: Keep it simple. Use words of few syllables, short sentences, and short paragraphs. Remember, this is a communication that must motivate!

By Stage Three you want to produce what is called *tight copy*—where every word has at least one job to do, sometimes more. Tight copy is "fiddle-proof," too. Outsiders can't move in to change things around. The minute they try, it becomes clear that you've been there before, and anticipated, and chosen the best route.

2. *What else do you look for as you review your copy?* Each time you go back to your copy, read it to yourself. Then read it aloud.

Does your eye have trouble moving through it, does your tongue stumble? How is it on the ear? Does it move smoothly or is it awkward?

Have you bridged? Good copy moves easily because someone has worked hard to help it along with bridges or transitions that carry the reader from one paragraph to another. Look at these bridges in lead sentences here: "The construction wasn't always that simple. In 1962, the government built . . . " or "And that's just part of your gift. You'll also receive, absolutely free, this . . . "

Break up large bodies of copy. Four or five sentences can make two paragraphs, not one. (As a matter of fact, some of the tightest, most exciting letter copy uses *one sentence* paragraphs! No matter how lazy the reader's eye, it's constantly drawn back in with these one-sentence zingers. But beware—to do this well, you must have perfect command of the art of outlining.)

Don't run details together or data of equal importance; break it out and line it up. Use sidebars or columns with bullets. Use frequent subheads or "window" subheads in the middle of heavy brochure copy to pull the reader back into the text.

Emphasize your important words with underlines, italics, and ALL CAPS.

In your letter use margin notes to call attention to strong selling points or use a second color, or emphasize the entire paragraph by indenting or boxing it.

Break punctuation rules for dramatic emphasis and style! Jump ahead with a dash in your letter copy—like that! Or run your thoughts together with ellipses . . . many writers do . . . and it's very effective *if* you don't overuse it!

Kill pet words. Edit your copy for repetition. Some words can pop up two or three times in the same paragraph. Unless you've planned it that way for emphasis, weed them out and substitute. For example: *Planned repetition:* "Go out and check the prices at your local market; go to the shopping malls; go to convenience stores. Go and see for yourself!" *Pet word syndrome:* "It's a special chance to go over the summer stock. Next time you go to your local market, go to the special summer widget counter. You'll go crazy!"

Eschew slang, jargon, lingo, dialect, or colloquialism unless it is in the character of your spokesperson and you are very, very sure that it is current (and widely understood) and that your market will identify positively with it. If you must use it, do so carefully.

Don't be clever or cute. Somehow, most of us deep down inside are dying to be comedians, to make others laugh. Unfortunately, 99 and 44/100 percent of us are not funny. I must assume that you (and I) fall into this majority. I *could* be wrong about you.

3. *Read the additional guidelines.* At the end of this chapter, you'll find these helpful suggestions: "A Creative Checklist for Your Components" and advice from Pat Farley on direct mail copy.

Judging Comps

You're into your fifth (or fifteenth) copy revision, major changes are made, things have come together nicely, and you've reviewed roughs and met with the artist on several occasions.

Now it's time to look over the completed comps in conjunction with your final copy. (If you've been working closely with the artist, there will be no surprises at this stage.)

By the way, the word "judging" is used advisedly here as it's still not clear *who's* doing the judging and how. These are the choices:

1. The artist and the writer have met, but worked independently up to this point. Both feel strongly about the direction of the package and their own creative ideas. They judge each other.

2. The copywriter (a free-lancer) brought the assignment to the artist (a free-lancer) in the first place. In all meetings the copywriter directs and judges and the artist merely follows.

3. The reverse of 2.

4. The copywriter and the art director have worked closely together all down the line. They respect each other. They both contribute to each other's work. The client or their immediate supervisor will be the judge.

Obviously you'd do well to work for the fourth option. It is certainly the optimum way to achieve the best work from two talented people. Let us assume that is where you are. Now it's time for your final evaluation.

First, make sure all the visual concepts have been executed as you agreed, and that the readable copy is correct. (Some of the best artists can't spell or reproduce copy correctly on the comps despite the fact that everything was delivered "electronically.") Check to see that every one of the components is there, life-size, in full color (or exact colors to be used), folded properly, and inserted correctly in the full-size envelope.

Here are some final checkpoints for you:

- Has the artist given enough specific graphic representation (particularly with the photos) for nonvisual people?

- Has the artist provided a sample of envelope, brochure, or letter stock if it's something a little out of the ordinary?

- Has the artist shown how to nest and insert the components so that the client understands the order of insertion? (Where possible, reply card on one side, letter on the other.)

- Has the artist shown how to nest and insert the components so that the process can be handled by automatic inserters? (Most lettershop equipment cannot insert open edges into the envelope mouth.)

- Is the letter folded with the first page on the outside, not on the inside like ordinary correspondence? (This lets the prospect see the salutation as the letter is withdrawn from the outer.)

- Are the layouts neat, clean, professional? (Computer comps should look like "the real thing.")

- Do the art and format of the outer envelope contribute to its excitement? Do they imply value, help convey "open me" or "I'm important"?

- Is there art and copy on both sides? (If it's a strictly promotional outer envelope, many professionals use both sides. After all, who knows which side your prospect sees first?)

- Does the letterhead design work with your copy to convey the feeling or impression you're seeking to convey from the speaker or letter writer?

- Has the artist carried out your letter configuration as you blocked it out?

- Does the order card look important? Valuable? Clean and uncluttered? Worthy of carrying back the dictates of your customer?

- Does it fit the tone of the offer (and the tone of the overall package)? A loud multifaceted sweepstakes offer deserves all the pizazz it can get: a business-to-business inquiry reply card (should you even decide to use a reply card) should be dignified and include an 800 telephone number; a fundraising or joining offer might include a membership card. (See Chapter 3.)

- Can it be easily filled in—is there enough space? If the card is to be computer addressed or labeled, is it the proper size so that the address will show through the outer envelope's window without shifting around in the mail? And—oh yes, make sure it's not going out on glossy stock that resists ink or smears! (It happens.)

- If there's a BRE, is it large enough to carry your order form without folding it?

- Does the brochure give an exciting dramatization of your hypothesis? Does it show the benefits and features clearly (using charts, graphs, lists, photographs and illustrations, questions and answers)?

- Is there visual unity among the various components of the package? (Not *too* much unity and coordination or the components will all blend together and look blah.)

- Is the material easy to read? Does its layout guide the eye gently from point to point?

- Has the artist maintained style throughout? This means unity in the treatment of headlines, subheads, and captions. It means unity in selection of typefaces, the amounts of white space, and the general feeling. (A little diversity in type styles is fine, but some designers go too far with three, four, or five styles on a single spread.)

- Although san-serif type is just fine for headlines, make sure the artist does not—ever—use it in the body copy. It is too hard to read.

- Body copy in reverse type is a no-no. So is printing body copy over a busy background (like a sky with lots of clouds).

You and the artist will no doubt cover any or all such points as they arise. If you have any questions or doubts, now is the time to discuss them. Remember, the whole objective here is to make the package compelling, involving, and easy to look at *and read*. Anything that does less than this must be reexamined. As the artist retires to make some final revisions, you'll want to prepare *your* work for presentation as well.

Preparing Your Copy for Presentation

There are lots of ways to prepare your copy for persentation, but here's what you're shooting for: Ultimately you want to present copy and comps together, so that your audience (client, boss, whoever) perceives the unified, finished whole, but at the same time you want to keep the two separate so that they can be examined and evaluated on their own.

This used to be easy with rough, hand-drawn layouts and typed copy. They *were* separate and sometimes the client had trouble envisioning them combined as a finished product.

No more. Nowadays, copy and comps are combined in a finished product that actually looks printed, four-color photos and all. There's not much left to the client's imagination. And this can be good. Or bad.

Often a client confuses the design with the words. A good design, for example, can be rejected because one line of copy is "off." Or vice versa.

To give both copy and design the best show, I suggest you present one or the other first. I'd like to see you present the copy first, but usually the clients are too itchy to get their hands on the comps. Don't fight it. Either way, present your copy separately in a booklet or folder, the old way. (Some copywriters include a copy of the layouts in the back of the copy presentation, but this is awkward unless you are presenting mini copywriter layouts instead of full comps.)

Some free-lance writers present only one set of copy, some two. One writer presents the original pages on extra-heavy quality stock, and nothing else.

If you're working for an agency or a large company, the number of copies will depend on the number of people in the presentation.

No one likes to present to a committee, but in many cases it will be necessary. It should *not* be necessary for any committee or group or single person to read your copy on the spot. (More about this in a moment.)

HOW SHOULD THE COPY BE ORGANIZED?

Quite simply, your copy should be set up for presentation in the exact same way that you sent it (on diskette) to the artist/designer, complete with graphic instructions. Here are some guidelines:

1. Have a cover sheet with date and title.

2. Put the copy in the same order as the comp package: outer envelope, letter, folder/brochure, order card, other components. (BRE copy is optional; this is not a creative function except for suggested overprint copy such as "Urgent, Process Immediately.")

3. Present each component separately, on 8 1/2" × 11" plain bond paper, one side (unless, like many agencies and writers, you have special paper for copy presentations). Label each component clearly at the top and include a date. (Headers will do.) You can also give general production specifications at the top. This is particularly important if you are using only copywriter's rough layouts.

4. Put your graphic instructions at the side in parentheses. Figures 7–1 through 7–4 are typical examples of *copy setups*.

5. The letter copy should be set up *exactly* as you want it to print. (See Figure 7–2.) Although the artist can certainly contribute good ideas, *you* are primarily in charge of the layout for your letter. Your objective is to help the reader through . . . to offer the eye an irresistibly absorbing pattern of words and phrases. If the eye escapes for just a moment, there is always something new to catch it and bring it back. Here are some suggestions to help you:

a. Put your instructions for the letterhead, lead-in headline, and/or the Johnson box (if you have one) at the top of the first page.

b. Use Courier (typewriter type) or a similar strong serif type emphasize that *this* component *is* the letter.

c. Keep ample margins (at least 1 1/2" on each side). Your job here is to help the eye move easily from one thought to another back and forth, up and down. (Don't make it fight its way across a wide copy line.)

d. Check your big (read "hot") break at the end of page 1. Will everything fit comfortably between the salutation and the first break—with lots of air? (You may have to cut, shuffle or rewrite or change your page 1 break.)

e. Remember to keep all paragraphs short—especially your lead paragraph.

FIGURE 7–1   Copy Setup for an Outer Envelope

```
Outer Envelope: 6" x 11 1/2" -- 4/c


Front of Envelope:


(Illustration: black and white photo of headquarters,bleed
shot at 50% tint with window die cut. Run copy above and to
the left of window):

URGENT; Dated Material Enclosed




Back of Envelope:


(Bleed repeat of photo on front. Run copy only on envelope
flap)

P.O. Box 564 · Smithtown, Nebraska 70001
```

    f.   Indent each paragraph five spaces to lead the eye into the copy.

    g.   For emphasis and pacing, indent or center an entire paragraph or space off and center an important copy line. (See examples.)

    h.   If you have a row of examples or a list of features and benefits, stack them and set off each one with a bullet or a box or a dash. You can also indent these and double space between them.

    i.   Don't be shy about margin notes either. People repond to them, so if they fit with the feeling of your letter (the President of the United States probably wouldn't have margin notes when writing the Queen of England), use your pen to call attention to important points in your copy.

    j.   Don't forget your ellipses, dashes, underlines, italics, ALL CAPS, and exclamations! But don't overuse them.

    6.   Lift letter copy, as your main letter, should be set up exactly as you want it to print. If you have copy for the outside (or back) of the lift, you can include this on a separate sheet with instructions.

    7.   Brochure, flyer, folder, or buck slip. These should be set up to follow the artist's comps. Your copy can be single-spaced or double spaced (no one agrees on this) with double-spacing between paragraphs and at least four to five spaces to separate large blocks of

FIGURE 7–2   Copy Setup for a Letter

EW New Program   2   November 9, 1995

<u>Letter: 4 pages, 8″ x 10″ folder to run on corporate</u>
<u>letterhead, 2/c, blue and black with blue sig, cut on page</u> 4

> Let's whip up some spirit here -- some teamwork.
> No one seems to care about this project."

> "enough talk. Here's what we're going to do!"

> "I never know what he's thinking. What's your
> guess today? Is he in a good or bad mood?"

> "She's criticised my reports for the last time.
> I'm asking for a transfer."

> "What do you mean I said I'd have the figures by
> Friday? How could I promise something like that?"

Dear Concerned Executive:

Sound familiar? They should, because these comments result from management situations that most of us executives
face every day.

The way you handle or avert such situations is the
difference beween managing and leading. And it makes the
difference in how you move ahead in your company.

> Managers <u>run</u> things. They are more concerned with
> people's roles than with their needs. Managers"
> authority stems from their position. Conflict is
> often the outcome.

> Leaders build and grow companies through people.
> They replace conflict with productive, harmonious
> dialogue, teamwork and long-term loyalty. They in-
> spire respect and admiration. Their authority
> comes from personal relationships.

If you are not already actively working to enhance and
develop your valuable leadership skills, may I make a simple
suggestion:

> Spend one hour a day for a week with the <u>Executive</u>
> <u>Leadership Program</u> (ELP is our Education Warehouse self-
> administered program for executives like you). Spend
> it in the quiet of your home, before work or after --
> wherever it's most convenient. But after each hour's
> reading, listening and practicing, you <u>must</u> promise

FIGURE 7–2 (Continued)

to go to your office and apply what you have just
learned in three business situations.

If within a few weeks you don't agree that your newly
gained insights and abilities are already positively affecting the way you relate to the people around you, return the
program to me, and I will personally see to it that your
money is refunded in full.

Making this promise doesn't worry me one bit, by the
way. You see, I believe you will accept. If you do, I know it
will work for you.

<u>Why I'm betting you will elect to take EL</u>P

We all have the basic qualities of leadership within us.
Sometimes it comes out more strongly in sports, social life,
college, the armed services. These qualities need only to be
developed and applied in business.

It it's that easy, you may wonder, why doesn't everyone
become a leader? Doesn't everyone want to be a leader?

Not necessarily. Many managers would like security,
recognition, and the rewards that go with it. Unfortunately,
they don't have the tools -- or know where to find them -- or
bother to apply them. <u>They are not willing to work at it</u>.

<u>I have a theory about yo</u>u. If the results of leadership
are what you want -- you will automatically self-select yourself and take advantage of this opportunity because

  • you will be eager to learn the tested Education
    Warehouse steps to enhancing your skills, and will-
    ing to work at perfecting them ...

  • you will welcome the freedom and flexibility to
    teach yourself at your own speed, imposing your
    own disciplines ...

  • you will want to start seeing results immediately
    -- right away -- in your office.

And because you have both the ability and the determination, you will live a self-fulfilling prophecy. You will
indeed increase your leadership performance.

As a result, I could promise you riches and power, but
the rewards of applied leadship skills go far beyond advance-

FIGURE 7–2   (Continued)

EW New Program   4   November 9, 1995

ment. While you work to develop your skills, you will find
that there are valuable intangible rewards, like the inner

satisfaction of knowing you're doing more for your company --
and making good business friends at all levels.

> You may find that your fellow workers begin to treat
> you with greater respect, that they listen more keenly
> to your ideas and opinions; that your people will be
> more enthusiastic and eager to tackle new projects for
> you; that top management will take more notice of your
> achievements.

This doesn't mean that you change your personality or
your style. Developing leaadershop abilities is primarily
recognizing and understanding four crucial aspects of leadership, then learning to incorporate these into your daily management pattern.

If you're as informed as I think you are, you may be
wondering what makes ELP different -- or better -- or more
effective than other leadership programs.

> We do. Education Warehouse Systems. Our business
> is helping business people become more effective.
> And we've been at it for 20 years. We have ten pro-
> grams presently in use by thousands of top execu-
> tives from major corporations around the country.
> Scientifically developed, allof our self-administer
> ed programs have been field tested over and over
> again.

As a matter of fact, I've taken the <u>Executive Leadership
Program</u> myself. And I had some immediate, exciting changes
when I started applying the skills.

You may find right off, as I did, that you hadn't <u>really</u>
listened to some of your people in the past. I mean listened
<u>hard</u>. I do now. And it's made a difference.

I don't act implusively anymore, regardless of business
pressures. I'm more sensitive to my fellow workers and their
problems. These are the kind of changes you can expect.

I think you'll appreciate the way the program's set up,
too. All it requires from you is a standard cassette player
and your full attention. There are two books that you'll
use along with the tapes. One's a workbook and the other's
your confidential business diary.

The diary leads to the most important part. Right off it
asks you to identify three problems you are presently facing
on the job. Then it works with you to solve these problems

FIGURE 7–2   (Continued)

while you are actually self-administering the course.

     This alone can be worth many times the price of the program. And, you get the benefits from day one!

     I also found playback and review helpful in several areas. It was reassuring to have the ability right there at hand to practice, relearn, to strengthen by repetition.

     It doesn't take much time to digest it. The daily applications will be rewarding and long lasting:

     how you conduct more productive meetings that give
     you the loyalty of the people around you ... how you
     get others to support your ideas ... how you improve
     individual performance without criticism ... how you
     delegate to create enthusiasm ...

     how you prevent common misunderstandings that could
     lead to conflict ... how you enlist the friendship and
     cooperation of your peers ... how you make sure you
     are heard and recognized by top management.

     You can take ELP in as little as six to eight hours, but you will use what you learn for the rest of your life.

     So spend a week -- or longer -- with the course. Apply your new skills to those major on-the-job problems that you identified. Practice in every business situation. Slowly at first. Then increase, as you gain confidence.

     But by all means get started now, if you agree that leadership skills are indispensible to attaining your management goals. Simply complete the enclosed reply card and return it to me today.

                    Sincerely,

                    James P. Forbusher
                    President
                    Education Warehouse Systems

P.S. The cost of ELP is $119.95. Hardly a consideration
     when you think about the benefits. (In fact, your
     company might willingly pay for the course, as it
     certainly will improve your effectiveness and over-
     all contribution.)

copy or headlines. You should have two spaces between all secondary heads and subheads and your body copy. Set a style for headlines, subheads, and lead-ins throughout to make your order of importance clear to the artist and the client. Title them in the margins. *Be consistent.* For example:

Main heads: all caps

Secondary heads: upper and lower case, underlined

Subheads: upper and lower case

Lead-ins: Underlined

Put your indications for art and photography in parenthesis in the margins so that it is easy to see where your copy fits in the artist's layout. Figure 7–3 gives you a good idea of how all this works together.

8. Your order card (see Figure 7–4) may present a layout problem as it often has a right and left side as well as a front and back. Keep your instructions clear and set up your copy so that it makes sense to a naive reader coming upon it for the first time.

In all cases, your objective is to make a professional presentation that gives your copy the best possible reception. Now let's talk about that reception.

Preparing for the Presentation

To begin, all work *must be presented by its creators.* Your baby should not be allowed out into the callous world without you the first time around. Whether it's one-on-one with your boss or a client, or a full-court press with the marketing team, you can turn your baby's introduction into another rewarding aspect of your work.

In the process you've just been through, note that nothing has been left to chance. You've had rules and guidelines, research findings, creative strategy development, hypothesis development, approach strategies, and clear objectives. To present (or "sell") your creative solution, you simply retrace your steps to explain why you've done what you've done—*before you show copy or comps or hand out anything.*

Start with a restatement of the objectives. Then review your creative strategy. (If you worked totally alone at this stage, of course, you'll have to go through it step by step, including the research findings.)

Once your client or team starts moving along with you through these points (and assuming that there is consensus in reviewing the basic strategies and assumptions), you are ready to discuss your creative decisions.

FIGURE 7–3   Setup for a Brochure

```
Health Book                1              November 9, 1995


Premium Flyer for enclosure in Health Book: 5" x 7", 2/c, red
and black


Front of flyer: (Large Red Cross at the top)


Head:           EMERGENCY FIRST AID

                A Guide to 11 Critical Areas


                (Sunburst)

                FREE! This 50-page booklet, filled
                     with diagrams, charts, drawings
(Body copy)

        Do you know

        -- the primary sign of internal bleeding
        -- where to look for a child's pulse
        -- how to recognize a third degree burn
        -- how to help a choking pregnant woman
        -- what CPR means and how to use it
        -- when to ignore advice in pamphlets,
              brochures and even first aid manuals
        -- how to allow fluids to drain from the mouth
        -- how to put an unconscious person in the
              recovery position

        If so, you might save a life. If not, you'll just
        stand there ...

Emergency First Aid

        Every adult should master these emergency aid
techniques. You owe it to yourself, your family and your
friends to familiarize yourself with each page of this
valuable book.

        It brings you full guidance, diagrams and drawings on
handling 11 of the most common emergencies plus a national
list of poison control centers, a Home Safety Checklist and a
section to help you start a Family Health Diary.

        We'll rush you a FREE copy of Emergency First Aid as
soon as you request your free examination copy of THE HEALTH
BOOK.

        Keep it in a safe place. Be prepared. It could be the
most valuable book you own!
```

```
Health Book                2              November 9, 1995


Back of Flyer

        (Copy next to head, boxed)  Yours -- FREE --
                                    When You Order
                                    THE HEALTH BOOK

Head:   Emergency First Aid,
        A Guide to 11 Critical Areas

        Sometimes, no matter how careful we are, things go
        wrong -- very wrong. When this happens, don't be
        a distraught, frustrated bystander. Act quickly,
        cooly and with confidence. You could be the
        difference between life and death.

Lead:       Learn to administer first aid effectively in 11
            situations

        (Illustrate 3-4 spreads from booklet)

            Bleeding...Bone and Muscle Injuries...Breathing
            Crises...Burns...Choking...Electric Shock...Foreign
            Objects...Heart Attacks...Poisoning...Seizures...
            Unconsciousness

(Body copy)

        Identify the crises, execute treatment procedures, apply
        preventative measures, learn how to improvise, how to
        help yourself, what not to do (complete with diagrams
        and drawings).

        • Safety-Proof Your Home -- A checklist of over 40 ways
          to prevent home accidents.

        • Set Up a Family Health Diary -- a quick reference in
          case of illness at home or when you travel. Good
          records are the first step in preventative self-care.

        • Emergency First Aid -- to make sure you can think
          fast, keep a cool head and a hopeful attitude.

Bottom head:

        Yours FREE when you send for THE HEALTH BOOK! Act NOW!
```

FIGURE 7–4   Copy Setup for an Order Card

```
Health Book                3              November 9, 1995


Order Card--HEALTH BOOK 4/c, one perf, BRC back


Front of card:

Head to run across top, both sides:

FREE BOOK -- FREE LOOK   Two FREE Offers for You


Left-hand side:

(Illustration of THE HEALTH BOOK in color with Emergency
First Aid)

        FREE BOOK   (Illus. Emergency First Aid token)

        Move this token to your
        Free Examination Card
We'll send you a FREE copy of Emergency First Aid
  at the right

-- just for looking at THE HEALTH BOOK
Return your request card today ...

(To run along perf)  Detach here and mail today


Right-hand side:

FREE LOOK -- No strings, no obligation (TOKEN goes here)

☐ YES -- I'll take a free look at THE HEALTH BOOK. If I like
what I see, I'll pay $7.95 for each of three easy monthly
installments (plus postage and handling). If I'm not
absolutely satisfied, I may return the book in 15 days and
own absolutely nothing. In any case, Emergency First Aid is
mine to keep, free of charge.


                  (addressing goes here)


SEND NO MONEY     SMITH MEDICAL BOOKS • JONES, IOWA 92300
-----------------------------------------------------------
Back of reply card:


Left-hand side: BRC

Right-hand side: DETACH HERE AND MAIL TODAY!!
```

GLAD YOU ASKED THAT
QUESTION . . .

In each case you will have a reason for your choices and decisions. Nothing you've done was "intuitive" or "instinctive." In the same way, you can explain every component of your package.

There is a reason for your approach. There is a reason for your outer envelope copy line. There is a reason for your choice of spokesperson. There is a reason for your lead-in paragraph. There is a reason for the Johnson box. And so on. You should welcome questions, as they allow you to reinforce your creative position.

As you field all questions intelligently, you carry your listeners along with your own story of creative development that can convey to them some of the enthusiasm you felt in doing your package. If you are doing a formal presentation of a major new package, I suggest you consider doing a brief written rationale to leave behind with your copy. People don't always listen and they most certainly do forget.

The same reasoning approach applies to the artist's presentation if he or she joins you. Everything in the layouts is done for a reason—the format, colors, artwork for each component—all have a rationale. If you are presenting with the artist, by the way, it's a good idea to have an informal run-through or rehearsal.

YOU'RE ON

There you stand with the artist, "booked" copy, rationale, and comps in hand.

What's the best or most productive agenda? How do you proceed? If you can pull it off, here's the optimum sequence.

1. First, don't let *anyone* see your copy or layouts before you're ready. It will be distracting and raise many unnecessary questions.

2. Get everyone's attention. Be dramatic. And enthusiastic. On your feet if it's a group meeting.

3. Review the objectives, go over your conclusions from the test history and other research. Make sure everyone is following your reasoning; make sure they are with you.

4. Review the creative strategy development, the hypothesis and big benefit. Make sure they are following; make sure they are with you.

5. Pause for questions. Wait. Listen.

6. Discuss your approach.

7. Bring out the comps. Show how these reflect the approach. (The artist, if you have one, will probably want to do this part of the presentation.) In some cases, although it's not necessary, you may want to read your outer copy and also your letter's lead-in as you present the comps.

8. Go over tokens, deadlines, other motivators, and incentives. Discuss the envelope. (Again, your artist may be contributing here.)

9. Let the artist describe the brochure. (You may want to head off a discussion of copy here until the graphic presentation is over.)

10. Once it's over, pause for questions.

11. Now for a serious look at the copy.

12. Pass out your copy books (and rationale, if you have one), deliver the layout to the proper person, and

13. *Break for the door!*

The best creative presentation ends *before* any one person starts reading copy. Copy must be read in peace and quiet, thoughtfully. Comments on the copy should be presented at your next meeting, after all those concerned have discussed and coordinated their thoughts on changes. You cannot do creative writing and designing by committee.

For your sake, I hope all presentations turn out as easy as 1 through 13. Chances are, few of your presentations will go according to the list above. We've all gotten trapped by the client who insists on reading the copy *right now.* As the client reads, he or she starts to ask questions. The next person then picks it up—and so on around the group. You want to kill. To die. To do anything to get out.

Take heart. All writers have been there. More than once. At least you will have a reason for everything you've written. If someone wants you to change copy, you can defend your points logically. In many cases, you can even explain how and why the promotion will be weakened if it's changed, as long as they agree with your rationale.

A professional enjoys presenting his or her baby to the public as much as does any proud parent. The professional also wants to protect that baby from mistreatment. You will, too. Wait and see.

Revisions: Getting Your Creation Ready for Its Next Big Public Appearance

Once your initial presentation is over, take a well-deserved bow. Ideally, your presentation was well received because you were well prepared.

Now, however, you're in for some copy revisions. Don't let this bother you. I've never met a writer—good, mediocre, or superlative—who hasn't had to put up with a moderate number of revisions. Often these are purely technical; sometimes new product or pricing data have been introduced while you've been working away. Occasionally, there will be questions of phrasing or clarity or emphasis

HOW TO GET THROUGH
THIS WITH YOUR SPIRITS
UP AND YOUR CREATION
INTACT

Even the most experienced creative people can get burned or wounded or just plain angry at this stage. If you've worked hard and honestly and had a successful presentation (no misunderstandings, no major misconceptions from the start, no lag in communications) then you deserve to have your rights read and I'm going to read them here.

First, get yourself a mouthpiece. You'll need one central contact who represents the client, or one who speaks for your company (usually your boss), or—if you are a free-lancer—get the individual who signed you on for the project. All suggestions (or dictates) for copy changes must flow through this one individual. You cannot—*must not*—deal with a committee on copy revisions, or you may certainly be driven to distraction.

Your mouthpiece should mull and consider changes thoughtfully and pass them to you with clear explanation, constructively—and not one at a time, but all together, at a designated time.

Next, evaluate the criticism, slowly and carefully and with a cool head. There are several types of criticism.

1. *Legal criticism:* This really isn't criticism at all, of course. This is what happens to your copy when (and if) your mouthpiece has to submit it to the corporate lawyers. There's just one point for you to remember here. Lawyers are out to make doubly sure that nothing rocks the boat. For this reason, they are extremely cautious and conservative. (Total stasis suits them fine.)

When you are told of legal changes, if some of these present enormous problems (such as, "We don't want to use the word *free*"), try to fight back. Or ask your mouthpiece to reason with them. Remember, their decisions are not cast in stone (well, not always). In many cases, you can persuade them to compromise or come up with reasonable alternatives. Give it a try before you give up.

2. *Constructive criticism:* Come on, now—you *know* some suggested changes will be good for your baby. You're not the only one who knows how to care for it. Be honest. Compliment the giver and show him or her how smart you are in recognizing good thinking. After all, everyone has an interest in seeing your baby become a healthy adult!

3. *Destructive criticism:* Here's where you get "I don't know. This just doesn't sound right . . . " or "It's not what I expected . . . " or "Maybe we shouldn't push so hard here . . . " or "Why does the envelope look so promotional?"

If this sort of thing gets past your mouthpiece you have two choices: reason it out; draw the line.

Most of us humans, working with others and striving to get along, will opt first for reasoning it out. But it's also important to know when it's right and proper to draw the line.

Often, all you have to do is refer back to the strategy statement and show how the copy reinforces the points. Sometimes people forget or lose sight of what you'd agreed to in the first place. Then again, you'll find many people just can't express themselves clearly. A little calm probing on your part can turn a threatening mountain into a molehill. Here's an example of this in action. It happens all the time in one form or another to all creative people:

Client:	"I dunno. I just don't like this."
Writer:	"The letter you mean?"
Client:	"Well, no—but look here on the first page. This is all wrong."
Writer:	"What exactly bothers you?"
Client:	"Well, the positioning . . . the approach . . . the feeling, I guess."
Writer:	"O.K. But I thought we'd all agreed on this in the beginning. What exactly is wrong?"
Client:	"Ah—first off, the widget isn't 'attractive.' It's 'beautiful.' And then, you call it 'strong,' here. That's no good."
Writer:	"What would you rather call it?"
Client:	"Ah, sturdy. That's the word. Sturdy."
Writer:	"Now let me read it to you. You'll find the widget is beautiful and surprisingly sturdy. How's that?"
Client:	"That's good. Nice. Nice letter, too."

Unfortunately, it's not always this easy. At some point you may have to cut or shoot. Here's a guideline that can help you: Listen carefully for little changes—a favorite word here or there. A personal preference. Be honest with yourself. Does this little change hurt the big concept? Jar the rhythm? Ruin the feeling? Create pet word syndrome through overuse? *Will it hurt response?*

If none of the above, be gracious. Give in here and pick up your points in a more important area.

Sad to say, nonprofessionals can't tell the difference between a harmless little change and one that absolutely pulls the keystone out of good tight writing ("Can't you just move this paragraph down to here?"). Or one that blasts a basic concept right out of the water.

But *you* know the difference because *you're* the master builder. And here, you have to hold the line. If you have your strategy statement, blasting a concept (or destroying a hypothesis) is easier to fend off than destroying smooth-flowing, well-paced copy construction.

If someone is set on destroying the concept, however, you must defend yourself and make it clear that the copy can no longer do the job it set out to do. Go on record. Be firm. Try to come up with a satisfactory alternative.

Although this really should not happen to you if you've moved through your presentation with a mutually agreed-to creative strategy, cruel reality forces me to admit that some copy changes that seem blatantly unfair (and unprofessional) may be foisted upon you from time to time. And you will have to make these changes, or lose the job.

If you can't hold the line, try to explain how and why you believe the copy has been seriously weakened. Then try to make the best of it. At some point in your career, you may even have a few samples of your work that you're ashamed to show. Join the group. It's happened to all good creative people.

There is an emotionally satisfying alternative that some have tried. But it doesn't make any friends. Or help get more work or a better position. You can snatch your copy away, stride from the room, slam the door and refuse to capitulate. I suggest you file this under "soothing fantasies" instead.

How Long Should You Hang around with Your Creation?

I'm always surprised at the number of free-lancers who abandon their creations at the door of the art department. Once final copy is approved, they turn and run without a backward look at their work.

On the other hand, many ad agencies and in-house promotion departments insist that the writer stick with the package right to the printer and through the proofing. If you have a choice, opt for the latter, whoever your client may be.

- It proves that you care. And if that's not directly important to you at the time, you'll find it is important to your client or your boss, and to your future.

- It enables you to take part in the many small, and often significant changes and decisions that arise as the original comp is transformed into final proofs.

- It allows you to participate in actual picture selections or changes and/or photography sessions—so that the illustrations will be as you envisioned them.

- It lets you participate in solving unforeseen crises should such arise.

- And—let us hope it never happens, but—it assures that if copy needs cutting at the last minute, you are the one to cut it.

There are too many writers who dropped their project and ran, and couldn't even recognize the final package when they saw it.

Enough said.

Evaluating Your Work

Once your package is in the mail and your job is truly done two things are owed you (aside from a pat on the head, a big fat check, a raise or a promotion): 1) samples, and 2) test results. This sounds like a simple, obvious assumption. It's common courtesy to give you three to five (or more) finished samples, and a report on the relative success of your brainchild once the test results are in. Everyone who's worked with you on the job will agree with this, but you may—just may—have to work hard to get either.

Free-lance writer, agency, or in-house, samples are usually mysteriously hard to come by. Often "the overruns are short" (they didn't print enough). Sometimes there are so many people on the distribution list that it's hard to scrape up enough for the writer; more often, people just forget. Keep at them. Don't give up. *Samples are owed you.* You need them for your sample book if nothing else.

As for test results—that's a different story. If you are working in-house or as an agency, results shouldn't be hard to obtain. Free-lancers may have a tougher time. Believe it or not, some clients don't tell free-lancers when they have a winner; maybe they forget(?). Some clients even hesitate to come clean and tell them if they have a big loser. The best clients, of course, are as open as they can be about the details.

This is important, because the more you can learn about the test results (overall response, backend response, specific response from various lists, comparative response to control/other tests) the better for you and the client. Remember, a good test is one in which you *learn.* The best test, of course, is one in which you win *and* learn. (And when a package goes into your sample book, it's always nice to be able to dub it a winner.)

You may also be able to participate in a debriefing session on the test, its objectives and achievements and next steps. This is good procedure for agencies and in-house operations, but if you're a free-lancer, don't count on it.

Too many good writers lose interest once they've finished creating their packages. They forget to push for samples or ask about test results, or they aren't aware that they are entitled to these things. Time goes by. Then all of a sudden, it's too late. They end up without samples or a clear knowledge of what happened. After all that work. Can you believe it?

Believe it. But don't let it happen to you!

A Creative Checklist for Your Components

1. Outer envelope: Everything begins—or ends—here. Review Chapter 4. Then ask

    • Does my envelope copy make a strong promise?

- Does it offer my prospect an irresistible tease?

  If I use copy, does the copy tie in to the letter lead?

- Will the envelope look important enough to get through the mailroom and/or past the secretary?

- Will it stand out in the mailbox?

2. Letter

- Is my lead strong and compelling (instant involvement plus big benefit)?

- Does it reflect the hypothesis?

- Is my approach the most effective approach, considering the hypothesis?

- Have I framed my letter with the lead, returning to it at the close, using logical references to it where possible in the body copy?

- Is my offer properly set off on page one (using a Johnson box if appropriate)?

- Do I carry sentences over from one page to the next and try to make the sentence break on page one irresistible?

- Am I putting the P.S. to the best possible use?

- Does my nuts 'n' bolts sum up the full offer with clarity and a pace or tone that implies action?

- Do I give my prospect a reason to act now?

3. Order Card (or Form)

- Do I state *what* is being ordered, what the form itself represents (to order the Deluxe Widget Holder . . . , to subscribe to *Black Snail* magazine)?

- Do I start with a prospect commitment (Yes, please send me . . . Enter my subscription . . . I accept the invitation . . . O.K., I'll give it a try . . .)?

- Do I clearly restate all terms of the offer?

- Has the guarantee been spelled out dramatically?

- If there's an 800 number, is it a prominent choice?

- Have I limited the decisions to prevent inertia?

- Will a near-illiterate, or a well-trained dog, find the form equally clear and easy to use?

4. Brochure (or Flyer or Folder)

- Does your copy track, drawing your prospect in with a strong benefit headline, leading your prospect through your word and picture story with good subheads and lead-in lines?

- Are all the features and benefits of your product or service clearly set down and, where possible, dramatized visually?

- Does your brochure story flow in an orderly pattern and build or develop as your prospect moves along?

- Have you added a brochure coupon (or order form) if you're not price testing?

5. Other Components

- If you've decided to include a lift letter, does it offer a clear, new point of view that underlines a major benefit?

- Have you taken advantage of the "buck slip"? If you have an unusual product feature, a brand-new feature or benefit or "hot" news, an important deadline, a premium in your offer— all of these can be emphasized with a buck slip (a small, 5" × 7", 3" × 4", or 3" × 8" miniflyer).

Some Tips from a Pro

The following tips on direct mail copywriting are from a fine copywriter, Pat Farley, and represent some of the best I've come across. Apply them at all stages of your copy development.[2]

1. Begin writing by defining the product and what you're selling in one concise sentence. Until you can do this, you won't create anything good.

2. Even if you're selling something that the best in the business have sold 10,000 times before, never automatically adopt their copy points and the sequencing of those points. Identify features and benefits on your own before you agree to follow the historical approach.

3. Listen to your client. Often, clients unknowingly provide great examples; wonderful descriptive phrases, even themes and leads can come from the client's conversation.

4. Good copy "sings," which means it has rhythm. To achieve this, combine short, staccato-like sentences, even partial sentences, longer sentences, deliberate repetition, occasional alliteration.

5. Starting sentences with "and" or "but," and piling one example on top of another, separated by ellipses can create a breathless sense of rushing along that literally pulls readers forward.

6. Not ending where people expect you to end (perhaps by changing the end of a cliché or using different words to conclude a well-known phrase) and occasional abrupt transitions can jolt a reader into paying closer attention.

7. Keep words, sentences, and grammar at a reading level slightly below your market's to make it easy. Emphasize short,

"Hemingway-like" sentences and break long sentences apart with ellipses and dashes. Never use semicolons—they stop readers. Avoid hyphenating words at the ends of lines as it makes reading more difficult.

8. When you're done, look at your paragraph lengths. The first paragraph of a letter should be no more than one or two lines, three at most, to make it easy to begin reading. Make all pages look easy and interesting by varying lengths. Break up long paragraphs. Be especially careful with narrow columns that can turn any short paragraph into an unending monster.

9. Stay in either the active voice or future tense—"you'll see" . . . "you'll find" . . . "order now." Past tense is passive, complex verb structures are boring and hard to follow. Contractions make the copy warmer and more personal.

10. Don't become a slave to reading copy aloud. While it's valuable, copy is READ, not heard. There are times when structures that are hard to say read perfectly well.

11. Whenever someone has to reread a sentence or ask for clarification, change the copy—it will bother a substantial portion of the audience as well.

12. Suit imagery and vocabulary to the market and the product. If you're selling a magazine, for instance, the copy should reflect the style of the magazine.

13. Never ask a reader a question in a key headline or on the outer envelope that can be answered, "No, I don't want this" or "I don't care."

14. The letters in a package should be personal and look like letters, with "typewriter type," a salutation and a signature. Be careful with fancy type subheads—while they can be effective, they also dilute the personal impact of the letter.

15. Use "I" and "you" with more of the latter. Flatter the reader but be careful of revealing too much personal knowledge in this privacy-sensitive era. Never reveal anything you wouldn't want strangers to know and don't reveal any information that isn't important to the sale.

16. Follow the "rule of three"—a series of three has more rhythm and balance than two or four examples or adjectives. But break the rule once in a while to create some pacing.

17. Odd numbers ("seven reasons why," "21 basic rules") are more effective than even numbers.

18. Tell the full story to skimmers and browsers with your brochure's headlines, subheads, boxes, photograph captions, bullets, callouts, and bursts. Use sidebars and insets to call attention to subsidiary but important benefits. In letters, tell the story with

subheads, indented paragraphs, itemizations, or starred lists and the use of your second color. *Never* let the artist break a letter for color because he or she will merely emphasize what already stands out.

19. Mention the product on page one of the letter; include price and offer if either is a key selling point. If the letter has a "story" opening, consider a "preface" above the salutation to state the offer. The writer should be the one to decide upon the style of the preface—big, fancy type, a classic Johnson box, centered lines or an indented paragraph.

20. Finish your letter by returning to the theme you began with to re-evoke the dream in closing the sale. If you can tie your theme into your selling points throughout the presentation, the package will be much stronger. But it isn't necessary to "theme" every element—sometimes a brochure that takes a slightly different angle or presentation strengthens the entire package.

21. If available, include testimonials. They are unbeatable assurance. Names are better than initials; specific comments on specific aspects of the product are better than general praise; results are more powerful than opinions.

Test Yourself on Editing and Polishing

Improve each of the following excerpts by cutting, "pet" word weeding, bridging and breaking out ideas, dramatic punctuation, and graphic emphasis (indents, caps, underlines). Each excerpt is followed by a number in parenthesis, representing a minimal number of potential improvements. See how well you can do. See if you can do even better than the minimum. It's not easy.

1. Dear Stove-Watcher, Batter Mixer, Sauce-Stirrer,

If you're like most homemakers you probably spend a lot of time in the kitchen. For example, if you don't eat out at all over the next 12 months, you will have to cook 1,095 meals.

With that many meals—plus all the other things you're busy with—who has time to fuss at every meal? (7 possibilities)

2. So, after having spoken these cold, hard truths, what do I have that I can offer you? Simply this. I can offer a monthly source of plans and strategies to help you make your work work for you, instead of the other way around. The name of this source is MOVING UP! and it talks about the working life like no other magazine ever has. (6 possibilities)

3. In these superb figurines I have something from my most loved dances to look at and to remember, to hold on to, to cherish, to make those living moments come alive over and over again. It is extremely gratifying to see the classic moment from each ballet captured in perfect elegance, plucked out of time by a true artist's sensitive touch. (6 possibilities)

4. Dear Reader:

If you don't mind being trampled and having your money taken, read no further. But, on the other hand, if you're sick to death of being short-changed on every dollar you spend, if you are mad at the prices you pay for phony quality and rip-off repairs, and if you are wary of what you're told and wary of the advertising that supports it and want to know how to fight back and protect yourself then welcome to Publication X, the first and only publication that tells you where you're getting short-changed, how your family's well-being may be endangered, and how to spot it and what to do about it. (12 possibilities)

Notes

1. Copyright © 1984 by The New York Times Company. Reprinted by permission.
2. Pat Farley, President/Creative Director, Farley Creative, Lynn, MA.

A GALLERY OF THE GOOD STUFF

> The best letters seem to me the most delightful of all written things, and those that are not the best the most negligible. If a correspondence, in other words, has not the real charm, I wouldn't have it published even privately; if it has, on the other hand, I would give it all the glory of the greatest literature.
>
> —*Henry James to Charles Eliot Norton in 1899*[1]

W e are about to spread a little glory over some outstanding examples of fine letter writing. Sit back and relax while I treat you to some top armchair entertainment. First, however, let me explain the objectives of this tour.

In a world of sterile, technique-laden letters—a place where it's even possible to purchase computer software to generate "customized" personal letters—we all need a little inspirational reinforcement. Something to remind us that direct mail can—and indeed frequently does—soar above the commonplace mailbox stuffing.

I also want to surround you with quality here and throughout this book in the hope that you'll come to expect that same quality from yourself and from others. A home that's filled with beautiful music or works of art, whether or not it puts forth musicians and artists, does certainly develop individuals with a keen appreciation and sensitivity to music and art. Perhaps this book can provide you with quality experience in direct marketing. Surround yourself with excellence, learn to recognize the good stuff, and it will be easier for you to appreciate it and work toward it in everything you do.

As you move through the good stuff—examining it critically, learning, understanding why it's good—you might wonder why so many examples throughout this book come from publications. There's an answer for this. As Aaron Montgomery Ward was a pioneer in mail order, so book clubs and particularly magazines have been pioneers in the use of direct mail to acquire members and subscribers. Many of them have been at it for half a century, even longer.

They generally test a good bit (and learn more than the non-testers, certainly) and they use top creative people to execute their direct mail. Some of the best free-lancers in America vie for the control position with certain publications. Those publications afford them a true creative showcase for their best work and a place to measure themselves against their peers.

I've often been challenged for not including more work from groups such as banks and insurance companies. When they do exemplary work, they, too, will be included. What's the point in showing you mediocre examples of direct marketing?

Learn from the Best

Now, sit back and relax with a snack while I treat you to some top armchair entertainment. We'll start off at the top with a great classic—a Direct Marketing Association Gold Mailbox winner. (The Gold Mailbox is one of the highest awards given to direct mail by the DMA.)

This particular Gold Mailbox classic is commonly referred to as the "Admiral Byrd" package. Written by the late Henry Burnett in 1968, the letter was sent to 13,600 top U.S. business executives to enlist their participation in a $10,000, 26-day round-the-world trip. (A difficult offer at best for busy executives.) The objective was to get only 50 participants. Seven hundred responded. Against a budget of $5,230, some $600,000 income was generated.

The inspiration for the lead in the letter came from a famous ad by polar explorer Ernest Shackleton in a London paper in 1902:

> Men wanted for hazardous journey. Small wages, bitter cold, long months of complete darkness, constant danger, safe return doubtful, honor and recognition in case of success.

This package broke two major rules. (Remember, you can break the rules after you've been playing around with them for a while—*if* you're an accomplished creative type!)

1. It did not use a color brochure to dramatize the benefits.
2. It did not carry a reply card. (Nor did it enclose a telephone number.) Prospects were "qualified" by writing a letter, using their letterhead or personalized stationery, accompanied by their deposit of $2,500!

The outer envelope, although computer-personalized like the letter, carries only this simple corner card:

Edward C. Bursk
Admiral Richard E. Byrd Polar Center
18 Tremont Street
Boston, Massachusetts 02108

Now read through the letter (Figure 8–1), then we'll talk some more.

What a promise. Immortality! Adventure! Danger! All for a greater good. Talk about moral imperatives!

I hope it's absolutely clear to you by now why no brochure was included. How much better for the good writer to use prose and let the reader use imagination! Sure, one picture is often worth a thousand words, but one stimulated imagination is often worth 10,000 pictures!

And how about the P.S.? It's delivered like a throwaway line—but what impact and persuasion! A video record for your children and grandchildren. You couldn't have a stronger clincher.

The style and tone in the letter was tremendously effective. Credible. Involving. Motivating. Burnett's approach was "generic," but generic of heroic proportions.

The next three packages have all been controls (continuing winners) for *over* ten years. The letter in Figure 8–2 has been the control for the *Wall Street Journal* for *22 years*. The approach here is strong story—the lure of the Horatio Alger American-dream-recognized. And in a business-oriented mailing this has proven unbeatable. The package has been "tested down" frequently, as have many unbeatable controls. That is to say, it has been carefully tested component by component to see if certain production efficiencies would leave it unaffected in its pull and therefore allow it to prosper at an even lower CPO than before. The letter has been reduced in size over the years from three pages to one sheet, two sides, the reply form has been reformatted and a few buck slips have been added now and then. It has survived and prospered, thanks to its crafty writer, Martin Conroy. The least we can say about Martin is that he's the best story teller direct marketers have ever known. Now pour yourself a glass of wine. Then read. And appreciate.

The letter shown in Figure 8–3 is by another top writer whom you've also met in Chapter 6, Ken Scheck. This is his great *Economist* letter, now nearly 15 years old and holding its own (except in Canada, but more about that in a minute).

Ken takes an identification approach that makes the reader feel very special—privileged, actually. The letter itself is beautifully laid out so that the reader can move easily from page to page; the inside

Text continued on page 270

FIGURE 8–1   A Classic Gold Mailbox Letter

KIRKLAND 7-9800

EDWARD C. BURSK
SOLDIERS FIELD
BOSTON, MASSACHUSETTS 02163

EDITOR ·
HARVARD BUSINESS REVIEW

Please reply to me in care of:
Transpolar Expedition
Admiral Richard E. Byrd Polar Center
18 Tremont Street
Boston, Massachusetts 02108

September 3, 1968

Dear Mr.

As Chairman of the Admiral Richard E. Byrd Polar Center, it is my privilege to invite you to become a member of an expedition which is destined to
make both news and history.

It will cost you $10,000 and about 26 days of your time. Frankly, you
will endure some discomfort, and may even face some danger.

On the other hand, you will have the rare privilege of taking part in
a mission of great significance for the United States and the entire world.
A mission, incidentally, which has never before been attempted by man.

You will personally have the chance to help enrich mankind's fund of
knowledge about two of the last earthly frontiers, the polar regions.

I am inviting you to join a distinguished group of 50 people who will
fly around the world longitudinally, over both poles, on an expedition which
will commemorate Admiral Richard E. Byrd's first Antarctic flight in 1929.

Among the highlights of this transpolar flight - the first commercial
flight ever to cross both poles and touch down on all continents - will be
stopovers at the American military/scientific bases at Thule, Greenland, and
McMurdo Sound, Antarctica.

Because this expedition has the interest and support of much of the Free
World, you and your fellow members will be honored guests (in many cases,
even celebrities) at state and diplomatic receptions throughout the itinerary.
You will have the opportunity to meet and talk with some of the world's important national leaders and public figures, such as Pope Paul VI, the Emperor
of Japan, General Carlos Romulo, and many others who are already a part of
history.

By agreeing to join this expedition, you will, in a sense, establish
yourself in history too. For you will become a Founding Trustee of the new
Admiral Richard E. Byrd Polar Center, sponsor of the expedition.

Your biography will be recorded in the Center's archives, available to
future historians. The log, photographs and memorabilia of the expedition
will be permanently displayed in the Center. And your name will be inscribed,
with those of the other expedition members, on a bronze memorial tablet.

FIGURE 8–1   (Continued)

- 2 -

Before I continue with the details of the expedition, let me tell you more about the Byrd Polar Center and the reasoning which led to its establishment this summer.

Located in Boston, home of the late Admiral and point of origin for each of his seven expeditions, this nonprofit institution will house, catalog and preserve the papers and records of both Admiral Byrd and other Arctic and Antarctic explorers.

But the Center will have a more dynamic function than merely to enshrine the past. It will be a vital, viable organization devoted to furthering peaceful development of the polar regions, particularly Antarctica.

It will become, in effect, this country's headquarters for investigation and research into the scientific and commercial development of the poles. The Center will sponsor, support, initiate and conduct studies and expeditions. It will furnish comprehensive data or technical assistance to the United States, or to any university, institution, foundation, business organization or private individual legitimately interested in polar development.

In other words, the Center has set for itself a course which the Admiral before his death endorsed wholeheartedly. He foresaw that mankind would one day benefit enormously from development of Antarctica's vast potential. And he perceived that Antarctica's unique and diverse advantages and resources might best be developed by private capital in a free enterprise context.

The Byrd Polar Center is dedicated to these objectives. And the essential purpose of this commemorative expedition is to dramatize the role that private enterprise - and private citizens - can play in the opening of these last frontiers.

At the same time, the expedition should help prove a few other important points. It should demonstrate the feasibility of shrinking the world through longitudinal navigation. It should also help blaze a trail for commercial air travel over the South Pole. Presently, to fly from Chile to Australia, you must go by way of Los Angeles, even though a straight line trans-Antarctic route would be far shorter.

There is another factor I should mention, one which I think lends a certain urgency to the work of the Center. Development of the polar regions enjoys a high official priority in the Soviet Union - higher, some believe, than in the United States.

The Center's activities can provide a tangible, effective complement to those of our own government, and over the long term, contribute meaningfully to preservation of the Arctic and Antarctic regions for peaceful purposes.

These objectives, I think you will agree, are entirely valid. And important, for the future of humanity. It is for this reason that the inaugural activity of the Byrd Polar Center will be an expedition of such scope and magnitude.

The expedition will be led by Commander Fred G. Dustin, veteran of six polar expeditions, advisor to Admiral Byrd and one of the intrepid group which

FIGURE 8–1   (Continued)

- 3 -

spent the winter of 1934 in Little America on Byrd's Antarctic Expedition II. Commander Dustin is a member of the U.S. Antarctica Committee and President of the Byrd Polar Center.

Considered the ranking American authority on the polar regions, Fred Dustin is probably better qualified to lead this expedition - and brief members on virtually every aspect of the polar regions - than any man on earth. The Center and the expedition are fortunate to have Commander Dustin, as you will discover should you decide to participate.

The flight will be made in a specially outfitted, four-engine commercial jet with lounge-chair-and-table cabin configuration. A full flight crew of six will be headed by Captain Hal Neff, former pilot of Air Force One, the Presidential plane. Special clothing and equipment, such as Arctic survival gear, will be provided by the expedition and carried aboard the plane.

The expedition members will meet in Boston on the evening of November 7, 1968, for briefing and a reception and send-off party with the Governor of Massachusetts, Mayor of Boston, local officials and directors of the Byrd Polar Center. Next day, we will take off, head due north from Boston's Logan International Airport and follow this itinerary (as I have not yet visited all these places myself, I have drawn on the descriptions submitted to me by Commander Dustin and the other experienced people who have planned the expedition):

Thule, Greenland

Far above the Arctic Circle, past the chill reaches of Baffin Bay, lies desolate Thule, the northernmost U.S. air base. Almost 400 miles further north than the northern tip of Alaska, Thule was originally surveyed as a possible military site by Admiral Byrd and Commander Dustin. Here, in the deepening Arctic winter, you will get your first taste of the rigors of polar existence. You will have the chance to inspect the installations and meet the men for whom Arctic survival is a way of life.

North Pole

According to those who have crossed the North Pole, you will completely lose your day-night orientation. Sunrise and sunset can occur within minutes of each other, a strange and unforgettable phenomenon. After Thule, you will cross the geographic North Pole, just as Admiral Byrd did in his pioneering trans-Arctic flight with Floyd Bennett in 1926. A memorial flag will be dropped.

Anchorage, Alaska

After crossing the pole, the plane will bank into a 90° left turn and head south, over the Arctic Ocean and Beaufort Sea, past Mt. McKinley, North America's highest peak, and on to Anchorage. There, you will meet the Governor and key officials.

Tokyo, Japan

The highlight of your stopover in Japan will be an opportunity to meet the Emperor and Premier. (Fishing; excursion to Hakone and Atami by bullet train; tea ceremony at private homes.)

FIGURE 8–1   (Continued)

- 4 -

<u>Manila, Philippines</u>

General Carlos Romulo, the legendary patriot and statesman, an old friend of Admiral Byrd, will give the expedition a warm welcome in Manila. (Folklore performance; hunting for duck, deer, wild boar and a special species of water buffalo; fishing for tuna and marlin.)

You will note that here and elsewhere we have prearranged a considerable amount of hunting, fishing, and so on. These activities are optional. (Members of the expedition will be asked to indicate their preferences 30 days before the flight.) For those who do not want to participate in any of these events, there will be sight-seeing, golf and many other things to do.

<u>Darwin, Australia</u>

Hard by the Timor Sea, tropical Darwin offers some of the world's most superb beaches. You will have time not only to sample the sand and water sports, but to see Australia's great outback. With its spectacular chasms, canyons and gorges, the rarely visited outback is a scenic match for our own West.

<u>Sydney, Australia</u>

You can look forward to an enthusiastic reception in Sydney by the Prime Minister and government officials. For one thing, Australia is on particularly good terms with the United States. For another, Australia has traditionally been in the vanguard of nations involved in Antarctic exploration and development. (Hunting for kangaroo, crocodile, buffalo, wild boar, duck, and geese; or off-shore fishing for rifle fish, salmon, and giant grouper.)

<u>Christchurch, New Zealand</u>

This is our staging point for the flight to Antarctica, and it couldn't be more appropriate. Most of the early expeditions departed from New Zealand, and Admiral Byrd is still considered a national hero there. New Zealand is Antarctic-conscious and its people take almost a proprietary interest in the frozen continent. You will be something of a celebrity in New Zealand, and can expect a thoroughly enjoyable visit while the expedition awaits favorable weather reports from McMurdo Sound. (Deer hunting - where deer are so plentiful that they pay a bounty; fishing for all of the great species of marlin - in an area known for the greatest marlin fishing in the world - also Mako shark.)

<u>McMurdo Sound, Antarctica</u>

I am told that only a total eclipse of the sun is comparable, in emotional impact, to the first sight of Antarctica. Once experienced, neither can be forgotten. If you prove to be like most who have seen Antarctica, you will need somehow, someday, to return. And when you do, the emotional impact will be just as profound. That is what the Antarctic veterans say.

For Antarctica exists well beyond the boundaries of the world you know. You will see there a sun you have never before seen, breathe air you have never before breathed. You will see menacing white mountains towering for thousands

FIGURE 8–1   (Continued)

- 5 -

of feet over a black ocean in which, with luck, you might survive for 45 seconds. You will see the awesome Ross Ice Shelf, as large as France, with its 50 to 200 foot ice cliffs cleaving the sea for 400 miles. You will see the active volcano, Mt. Erebus, 13,000 feet of fire and ice.

And you will see the huts, so well preserved they seem to have been inhabited only yesterday, which Shackleton used in 1908 and the ill-fated Scott in 1911. Antarctica, apparently, is not subject to the passage of time as we know it.

At McMurdo Base, you will meet the military men and scientists who inhabit this strange, alien territory. And you will inhabit it for a while too - long enough to feel its bone-chilling cold, to hear its timeless silence, to perceive, at the very edge of your composure, the terror of its mindless hostility to human beings.

While you are there, you will learn, as few men have ever had the opportunity to learn, about Antarctica. You will learn about survival, but more important, about what men must accomplish to truly open this formidable frontier.

South Pole

Admiral Byrd was the first man to fly over the South Pole. In all of history, probably fewer than 200 men have crossed the pole, by air or otherwise. As a member of this expedition, you will join that select group.

Punta Arenas, Chile

From the South Pole, you will fly to Punta Arenas, on the tortuous Strait of Magellan which separates continental South America from bleak Tierra del Fuego. The visit here will be brief, but you should get some idea of the flavor of this nearly forgotten outpost.

Rio de Janeiro, Brazil

This memorable stopover will include a diplomatic reception You will also have a chance to relax and sample the sights and sounds of fabulous Rio. (Special plane to Belo Horizonte for hunting boar, duck, jaguar, panther, water buffalo, crocodile and deer.)

Dakar, Senegal

You may never have expected to see Dakar, but you will on this expedition. (Tribal dancing; safari.)

Rome, Italy

No trip would be complete without a stop in Rome, where we will be received enthusiastically. During our stay there we will have a private audience with the Pope.

FIGURE 8–1   (Continued)

- 6 -

<u>London, England</u>

From London, the expedition will fly back across the Atlantic and terminate with a debriefing, critique and farewell dinner in Boston, on December 3.

As mementos of the expedition, you will receive a leather-bound, personalized copy of the log book and a piece of the fabric from Admiral Byrd's original plane mounted in crystal.

You will also be presented with a framed certificate from the Admiral Richard E. Byrd Polar Center, affirming your appointment as a Founding Trustee and expressing appreciation for your interest in, contributions to and efforts on behalf of the Center and its objectives. In the future, you will be kept fully advised of the plans and activities of the Center, and be invited to participate to whatever extent you wish. And of course, you will have life-long access to the Center's archives and services.

Most important, you will take back with you a once-in-a-lifetime experience. The day may come when journeys to and over the poles are commonplace. But today, the privilege is available to very few.

It is true, I think, that this privilege does carry responsibility with it. By the time you return, you will have received a comprehensive indoctrination course in the polar regions by the world's leading authorities. Your responsibility will be to make the most of the knowledge you will gain, to become an active advocate - perhaps even a disciple - of polar research and development.

It is a responsibility which, I trust, will weigh easily upon you. For once the polar air has been absorbed into your bloodstream, there is no cure. Like others who have been stricken, you will probably find yourself reading every word you can find on the North and South Poles. And, most likely, thinking about your next trip.

But first of all, you must decide about this trip. If you have a sense of adventure, a certain pioneering spirit, and if the prospect of taking part in a mission of worldwide significance and historical importance appeals to you, perhaps you should consider joining the expedition. It is doubtful that you will ever have another chance like this.

Obviously, you can't make a decision of this magnitude instantly. But a word of caution: reservations will be accepted in the order received - a total of only 60, including ten standbys. The departure date, remember, is November 8, 1968, so there is little time to waste.

The price of $10,000 includes food and beverages, all accommodations (the best available under all circumstances), transportation, special clothing, insurance, side excursions - virtually everything except your travel to and from Boston.

Money received will go into escrow at the United States Trust Company in Boston until the time of the flight. To the extent that revenues from the

FIGURE 8–1   (Continued)

- 7 -

trip will exceed costs, the activities of the Polar Center will be accelerated.

To reserve your place in the expedition, just drop me a note on your letterhead or personal stationery, with your deposit check for $2,500, made out to the United States Trust Company. Incidentally, if anything prevents your leaving as planned, you can send another in your place; otherwise, cancellations cannot be accepted later than 30 days before departure.

If you have further questions, please write to me in care of the Transpolar Expedition, Admiral Richard E. Byrd Polar Center, 18 Tremont Street, Boston, Massachusetts 02108.

I hope we may hear from you soon - and that we will welcome you to the expedition.

Sincerely yours,

Edward C. Bursk

Edward C. Bursk

ECB:EHK

P.S.: We have just made arrangements for a professional camera crew to accompany the flight, and as a result we will be able to provide you with a short film clip and sound tape of your experiences.

FIGURE 8–2 The 22-Year Control for the *Wall Street Journal*

THE WALL STREET JOURNAL.

World Financial Center, 200 Liberty Street, New York, NY 10281

Dear Reader:

On a beautiful late spring afternoon, twenty-five years ago, two young men graduated from the same college. They were very much alike, these two young men. Both had been better than average students, both were personable and both -- as young college graduates are -- were filled with ambitious dreams for the future.

Recently, these men returned to their college for their 25th reunion.

They were still very much alike. Both were happily married. Both had three children. And both, it turned out, had gone to work for the same Midwestern manufacturing company after graduation, and were still there.

But there was a difference. One of the men was manager of a small department of that company. The other was its president.

What Made The Difference

Have you ever wondered, as I have, what makes this kind of difference in people's lives? It isn't a native intelligence or talent or dedication. It isn't that one person wants success and the other doesn't.

The difference lies in what each person knows and how he or she makes use of that knowledge.

And that is why I am writing to you and to people like you about The Wall Street Journal. For that is the whole purpose of The Journal: to give its readers knowledge -- knowledge that they can use in business.

A Publication Unlike Any Other

You see, The Wall Street Journal is a unique publication. It's the country's only national business

(inside, please)

FIGURE 8–2   (Continued)

daily. Each business day, it is put together by the
world's largest staff of business-news experts.

Each business day, The Journal's pages include
a broad range of information of interest and significance to business-minded people, no matter where it
comes from. <u>Not just stocks and finance</u>, but anything
and everything in the whole, fast-moving world of
business ... The Wall Street Journal gives you all
the business news you need -- when you need it.

<u>Knowledge Is Power</u>

Right now, I am reading page one of The Journal.
It combines all the important news of the day with
in-depth feature reporting. Every phase of business
news is covered, from articles on inflation, wholesale
prices, car prices, tax incentives for industries
to major developments in Washington, and elsewhere.

And there is page after page inside The Journal,
filled with fascinating and significant information
that's useful to you. For example, we have introduced
a new section called <u>Marketplace</u> to give you insights
into how consumers are thinking and spending. We
reveal how companies, products and services are
competing for market share. There is coverage of the
latest technological innovations. Plus, daily features
on the challenges of managing smaller companies and
workplace issues ranging from health to law.

In our third section -- <u>Money & Investing</u> --
The Journal's coverage of investments has been re-
organized to make reading even easier, faster, more
useful. You'll find improved graphics, easy-to-scan
stock quotations and a front page that summarizes all
the day's market news. Even a daily column on personal
money management.

If you have never read The Wall Street Journal
-- or if you haven't picked it up in some time -- you
cannot imagine how useful it can be to you. Or how
convenient it is to find the news you need.

Much of the information that appears in The
Journal appears nowhere else. The Journal is printed
in numerous plants across the United States, so that
you get it early each business day.

<u>A 13 Week Subscription</u>

Put our statements to the proof by subscribing

FIGURE 8–2   (Continued)

for the next 13 weeks for <u>just</u> $34. This is the
shortest subscription term we offer -- and a perfect
way to get acquainted with The Journal. Or you may
prefer to take advantage of our <u>better buy</u> -- one
year for $129.

Simply fill out the enclosed order card and
mail it in the postage-paid envelope provided.
And here's The Journal's guarantee: should The
Journal not measure up to your expectations, you
may cancel this arrangement at any point and
receive a refund for the undelivered portion of
your subscription.

If you feel as we do that this is a fair and
reasonable proposition, then you will want to find
out without delay if The Wall Street Journal can
do for you what it is doing for millions of readers.
So please mail the enclosed order card now, and we
will start serving you immediately.

About those two college classmates I mention
at the beginning of this letter: they were graduated
from college together and together got started in
the business world. So what made their <u>lives</u> in
business different?

Knowledge. Useful knowledge. And its application.

<u>An Investment In Success</u>

I cannot promise you that success will be
instantly yours if you start reading The Wall Street
Journal. But I can guarantee that you will find
The Journal always interesting, always reliable,
and always useful.

Sincerely,

Peter R. Kann
Publisher

PRK:db
Encs.

P.S. It's important to note that The Journal's
      subscription price may be tax deductible.
      Ask your tax advisor.

FIGURE 8–3 A 15-Year Control Using the Identification Approach

The Economist

May I send you

3 FREE ISSUES

of what may be the most influential

(as well as selectively distributed)

newsweekly in the world?

Dear Colleague,

Every Monday morning, a rather unusual publication arrives at the desks of a select circle of individuals in positions of power and influence.

The readers of this discreetly (one is almost tempted to say reluctantly) publicized newsweekly include presidents (of countries, banks, universities and Fortune 500 companies), ranking executives (in business, government and industry) and prominent thinkers (in law, science, economics and military strategy).

Now, it may not surprise you to learn that the average personal income of North American subscribers to this singular periodical exceeds $144,800 per annum. However, it may surprise you to discover that despite the enormous clout and affluence of its world renowned readers...

> only a relative handful of Americans are aware of the existence of this exclusive publication, much less the intelligence it provides.

But now, with this letter, you are cordially invited to join the extremely select circle of men and women who wouldn't think of beginning each business week without the incomparable insight and reporting of... The Economist.

> Enclosed you will find a non-transferable order card. Return it to me and I will send you three absorbing issues of The Economist to read at my expense. These three issues will be yours to keep free whether or not you decide to become a subscriber.
>
> However, should you wish to join our distinguished roster of American subscribers, I will then reduce the $3.50 cover price to just $1.66 for each of your 30 issues. This will save you 52% on newsstand costs.

But why The Economist? Why you?

Courtesy of *The Economist*, The Economist Newspaper Group.

FIGURE 8–3   (Continued)

- 2 -

First, let me make it plain that I am not writing to you today because I think you may not be earning $144,800-a-year, or at least not <u>yet</u>. (Of course, many of our most distinguished subscribers earn considerably less than our reader-average -- this makes them no less distinguished in our eyes.)

However, allow me to assume that <u>The</u> <u>Economist</u> is not exactly a "household name" with you. Perhaps you've never even heard of us at all! It <u>is</u> possible, of course, that you have heard vague references to us as an erudite publication read only by an elite cadre of professional economists and other exotic abstractionists.

Well, <u>nothing</u> could be further from the truth!

> <u>The</u> <u>Economist</u> is much more than just a magazine of
> economics and finance -- it is, in fact, the <u>only</u>
> true world-class newsweekly expressly compiled to
> increase your understanding of the critical inter-
> relationships between global affairs and the tough
> realities of today's marketplace.

Indeed, as the events of the past decade underscore, the "global village" has become reality. To put it another way, when the Mideast shudders... the world shivers. And so on. But that's just part of it.

Relatively a short time ago, it was universally assumed that U.S. management techniques were decades ahead of the rest of the world. It was, after all, just under 30 years ago that French author Servan-Schreiber touched off an international bombshell with his sweeping indictment of Europe's antiquated approach to business. Since then, there have been changes, to say the least.

> Today, many of the most revolutionary management
> and productivity innovations are being put to the
> test in Western Europe, Japan and elsewhere.
> Smart American businessmen -- those with a global
> perspective -- are gaining an extra edge by
> keeping close tabs on developments in world
> business. <u>The</u> <u>Economist</u> is their potent "secret
> weapon".

But it's not an ironclad secret. In the often cut-throat world of news-gathering <u>The</u> <u>Economist</u> is that rarest of all media species -- a universally admired and astonishingly respected publication -- as is remarkably demonstrated by these comments from the press:

<u>The</u> <u>Wall</u> <u>Street</u> <u>Journal</u>: "It (<u>The</u> <u>Economist</u>) should be bound in leather and made required reading..."

FIGURE 8–3 (Continued)

- 3 -

Time Magazine: "...exerting an influence far beyond its circulation... its calm authoritativeness has made it a favorite of political and business leaders in the U.S. as well as Britain."

The New York Times: "May be the most sensible publication in the English language."

International Herald Tribune: "This unique journal... in which sheer intellect, backed by integrity and a bold welcoming of new ideas has held such sway over statesmen and governments."

Newsweek: "Abroad it is required reading at the pinnacles of power. In the U.S. The Economist is a week-end habit on Wall Street and in the White House."

Very well. We're pleased to know The Economist is considered required reading at 1600 Pennsylvania Avenue. But how does our publication relate to you?

Perhaps I can answer this best by pointing out that most men and women in business will never receive the letter you have in your hands right now. They will, of course, receive solicitations galore to subscribe to run-of-the-mill business newspapers, magazines and newsletters. But not The Economist. Why not?

The reason is simply that most managers, throughout their careers, will never be called upon to handle the critical information or make decisions of the scope and magnitude of those who require The Economist. I believe you have already made or will soon be called upon to make such critical decisions. I can't put it more bluntly than that.

> But what, exactly, can you
> expect to find in the pages
> of The Economist?

For starters, do not expect to find a rehash of what's already been covered by The Wall Street Journal, The New York Times, Fortune, Forbes or Business Week. Unlike these otherwise splendid periodicals, The Economist's reporting is in a class by itself -- world-class.

Instead, count on discovering a clear and penetrating picture of how the forces at work today are shaping the world in which you will work tomorrow. For example...

Feel jittery about the effects of continuing world turmoil? Who in his right mind doesn't? Terrorism. Revolutions and threatened invasions. Nuclear sabre-rattling. It's a wonder the world is able to absorb and survive as many shocks as it does!

FIGURE 8–3 (Continued)

- 4 -

The Economist can sort it all out for you. Each week we
bring you six to eight indepth articles that clearly
define and analyze the week's critical developments.
It's tough minded, clear-headed observation that brings
the world down to size.

Wonder what's going on in other business capitals? You should.
Exciting things are happening in virtually every corner of the world.
Never before has it been so important to stay abreast of so many
business developments in so many different places!

Here, again, The Economist is your key. Whether it's
the prospect of another bumpy ride for the auto
industry, trade restrictions and protectionism
affecting the U.S. market, the problems of investing
in gold, the potential for factories in space, or the
promise of superconductors.

Afraid of missing out on new ideas, new breakthroughs? Welcome
to the club. After all, who among us hasn't dreaded the possibility
of being rendered obsolete by a microchip!

Rest easy. The Economist, in its widely-acclaimed
"Science and Technology" section, keeps you up-to-the-
minute on what's being discovered, invented or just
plain dreamed about! Computers that think. Drugs that
boost brain power. Microchips (never turn your back on
one!) which pack nearly 100 million components on a
sliver of silicon. Telecommunications that are bringing
the whole world into the office and living room.

But be forewarned. You'll see a
very different America when you
look at your country through the
"eyes" of The Economist.

Maybe it's a kind of "hothouse" effect. Or maybe it's simply a
case of being too close to the action to see it clearly. Whatever
the reason, it is our opinion that domestic news media often
present a somewhat feverish overwrought picture of what's really
going on in the United States. Pity, really.

You see, someone once said that when America sneezes the world
catches pneumonia. We tend to (cough) agree. And so, every week,
The Economist devotes six full pages to a close look at America...
but from a distance, of course. We call it our "American Survey"
and, believe me, you'll find the perspective positively refreshing!

268

Chapter Eight

FIGURE 8–3 (Continued)

- 5 -

In recent issues, for example, we've discussed which
Bill Clinton will be the president of the United States.
Will it be Mr. Clinton the free trader, or the trade
warrior? The public spending prodigal, or the deficit
cutter? The scourge of Congress, or the back-slapping
legislators' friend? In his efforts to win election, he
hinted at being all things.

We've warned about protectionism; defined the need for
long term economic cure; questioned the boundary
between affirmative action and reverse discrimination;
and explained how far down inflation should be pushed
for economic growth.

Whether you agree with our conclusions or not, I think you'll come
to agree with the experts -- that our weekly "American Survey" is
simply the most cool and level-headed appraisal of the U.S. political
and business scene in print today!

The final judgement, however, is best left to you. And in the
paragraphs that follow I intend to make it as enticing as possible
for you to agree to sample several issues of The Economist.

<u>Why I must insist that you read your
first three issues of The Economist
absolutely free</u>!

It has nothing, I assure you, to do with spending too much time
"in the mid-day sun" or any of those alleged Anglo-Saxon quirks! You
may, if you like, chalk it up to my sense of fair play.

You see, it's simply that I'm very conscious of the fact that in
all likelihood, you've never seen anything remotely resembling The
Economist. And so it just wouldn't be reasonable to ask you to
subscribe to our publication sight unseen.

Of course, you may look over your free issues as you wish but,
frankly, I rather hope you'll read The Economist with a decidedly
jaundiced eye. In other words, be as skeptical as you like! Doubt
our every word! Make us prove to you that our predictions and surveys
give you an extraordinarily accurate look at where our confusing
world is headed.

Then, if the first three issues leave you unimpressed,
if you decide for any reason at all that The Economist
is <u>not</u> the remarkable source of invaluable intelligence
I promised it would be, simply write "cancel" across
your bill and owe not a cent.

FIGURE 8–3   (Continued)

– 6 –

Should you decide, on the other hand, that our
magazine <u>is</u> a truly unique addition to your regular
reading, just remit by check. You'll then receive a
total of 30 weekly issues of <u>The Economist</u> at our
special introductory rate of only $49.90 -- a savings
of $55.10 on newsstand costs.

But, putting savings aside for the moment, I sincerely hope
you'll take this opportunity to experience one of the world's most
distinguished and respected weekly publications.

Find out how stimulating it can be to read a <u>world-class</u>
newsweekly that gives you a perspective you simply can't get anywhere
else.

Yes, <u>try</u> <u>The</u> <u>Economist</u>.

Try <u>The</u> <u>Economist</u> now while this special invitation to read three
absorbing issues at our monetary risk is still in effect. All it
takes is a checkmark on the enclosed card!

Cordially,

M. M. Scardino
President

MMS: lcu

P.S. As mentioned earlier, this invitation is non-transferable.
      It is valid in your name <u>only</u>. If you decide not to accept
      my offer, please <u>do</u> <u>not</u> pass it along to anyone else. I would
      prefer you simply discard it. Thank you.

leaf is nested in a folder consisting of the two outer leaves. (This is a tested technique that works because the pages stay together; it makes easier reading than single pages that fall *and* fall out of order.)

Oh yes, Canada. Figure 8–4 shows a very interesting letter, in an identical format, that was tested against the Scheck letter about four years ago. And it's still testing quite well *outside* the United States, particularly in Canada. This letter, by Richard Riccelli, uses the question approach. Look the two letters over carefully and tell me why Riccelli's letter wins in Canada.

This last oldtimer, called the Sandhill Crane in Figure 8–5, is a delightful story approach fund raiser for the Nature Conservancy by Frank Johnson. It has created a crush of fan mail over the years and has only recently been beaten by the package in Figure 8–6 (the one with the "younger" bird on the outer).

The sandhill crane package has gentle, effective humor. Who could resist this indignant fellow on the envelope? Or the teaser copy? Or that fantastic salutation that immediately flatters as it positions the reader.

Frank is a pure wordsmith of the old school; his turn of phrase and choice description, his considerate commands and candid exposition can serve well as a lesson for all aspiring writers. Study every sentence. Understand and appreciate the craftsmanship until you come to the point where you can say, "I wish I had written that."

Caveat: although the story approach allows you to use drama and all your descriptive talent, remember that humor—humorous writing—is very hard to pull off. What tickles your funny bone may leave some of your market cold. Most of us do well to play it safe and not try humor or attempt to be clever.

Now to that young night heron on the envelope in Figure 8–6. This was Donna Baier Stein's successful effort to take those elements that worked well for Frank and use them with a totally different tone. Her letter takes the straight generic approach and doesn't fool around with humor or history. She sticks to the facts. And her facts make a strong case.

What will happen? Will the sandhill crane regain its leadership again in a year or so? Or will the night heron hold its lead? Or will something still stronger come along (like an owl)?

I'm not going to tell you the answer because I don't know. But I do know that comparing top packages and their competitors is a good exercise, as it encourages you to be analytical while you appreciate. Say, for example, you were asked to do a package to beat *The Economist's* current control (Figure 8–4) or Martin Conroy's Two Young Men (Figure 8–2). Make a list of all the things you'd include and the elements you'd avoid. See what you can learn from these superlative letters.

Another truly great writer, who handles humor as well as Frank Johnson, is Bill Jayme (whose story approach you saw in Chapter 6).

FIGURE 8–4   The Letter That Beat the Control Outside the U.S.

YOURS FREE

A THREE-ISSUE SAMPLE SUBSCRIPTION TO THE ECONOMIST.

YOURS TO TRY WITHOUT COST OR OBLIGATION TO CONTINUE.

Dear Colleague,

   Did you know? -

- The top five nations for long-life expectancy are Japan, Holland,
  Spain, Canada and France.

- The five highest cost-of living cities are Tehran, Tokyo,
  Abidjan, Stockholm, and Zurich.

- When it comes to foreign aid, Canada is twice as generous as
  the United States.

   Read only the U.S. press and you might end up with a wholly
one-sided - dangerously inaccurate - view of the entire world.

   Which is why THE ECONOMIST is so popular among the ranks of
Canadians in the know.

   It's unAmerican.

                     The International Weekly

   THE ECONOMIST is the news and business weekly whose beat is the
whole world - including America's prominent place in it.

   As both a news magazine and a business magazine combined, THE
ECONOMIST is keenly aware and quite quotable on how those two vital
interests mix and combust.

   In Politics -

- "Russia's economic problems are the result of reforms that have
  gone too slowly - not as the government argues, too fast...."

   In Industry -

- "High-definition television's main selling point — cinema-quality
  images — is fairly trivial. Will viewers pay big sums for sharper pictures? The jury is out. But the only person better at
  killing off a technology than a well-intentioned regulator is a
  commonsense consumer."

                                              (over, please...)

Courtesy of *The Economist,* The Economist Newspaper Group.

FIGURE 8–4 (Continued)

-2-

In <u>Finance</u> -

- "Fund managers are switching their money from South-East Asia to
  Latin America. Although the two regions are expected by most
  economists to be the fastest growing in the world, shares are
  cheaper in Latin America. Following last year's extended bout
  of China euphoria, the 'Pacific-rim century' as an investment
  concept has become rather too well discounted."

In <u>Science</u> and <u>Technology</u> -

- "There is no practical reason to create machine intelligences
  indistinguishable from human ones. People are in plentiful
  supply. Should a shortage arise, there are proven and popular
  methods for making more. The point of using machines ought to be
  they perform differently than people, and preferably better."

In the <u>Arts</u>, <u>Books</u> and <u>Sport</u> -

- "A reassessment is taking place of work produced under the Nazis.
  Half a century after the second world war, people are gingerly
  coming to grip with the uncomfortable idea that good stuff can be
  produced by bad people...."

Just like that THE ECONOMIST brings you a fascinating and coherent
collection of fast-breaking, first-hand reports every week. As you can
see, it's hardly the stuff of academia - unless, of course, you make
the world your school and its events your lessons.

Chrétien, Clinton, Major, and...You

THE ECONOMIST is written with style and verve and wit. It's
breezily skeptical and impressively knowing. A vibrant and stimulating
read whose authority and influence is felt worldwide.

In fact, should you decide to accept this free offer, you'll join
readers like Prime Ministers Chrétien and Major, Presidents Clinton and
Yeltsin.

You'll join top international executives who so closely monitor
THE ECONOMIST, the magazine's coverage often leads the very markets it
follows.

You'll be part of an unbroken, <u>150-year-old</u> tradition that links
you to successes in business, finance, politics, science, education,
technology, the arts.

And whether it's Russia's struggle to dampen the fires of author-
itarian nationalism or China's struggle to embrace capitalism in a
communist society, you'll find exactly what you need to know in easy-
to-find, easy-to-scan and easy-to-understand sections of the magazine
titled <u>Asia</u>, <u>Europe</u>, <u>Britain</u>, <u>International</u> or in the world-renowned
<u>American Survey</u>.

FIGURE 8–4   (Continued)

-3-

America Revealed

Free of local bias, free of narrow national interests, THE
ECONOMIST is free to reveal America like you've never seen it before:

On American politics: "The younger Republicans are not merely
more conservative. With their hearty suspicion of government and
championing of states' rights, they also herald the rebirth of the
New Federalism."

On women in business: "Firms are scrambling to make themselves
more sensitive to their female employees: that is, less likely to be
sued by them. Several companies now have special programs dealing with
sexual harassment...ranging from rewriting employee handbooks to
educating workers not to make dumb-blonde jokes."

On the American way of death: "Cigarettes have been so closely
and definitely associated with death that their use is falling steeply.
Cars are subject to rigorous safety standards, licensing, registration
and codes for safe use. Not so with guns. Every year 38,000 Americans
die of gunshot wounds. If any other common household objects were
found to be so dangerous to health and safety, they would be banned....'

Ah-ha!

At first, it can be a bit startling how dead-on, how utterly
revealing, THE ECONOMIST can be...

"Why didn't I see that!"..."But of course!"...
"Just as I suspected!"...

...are typical comments from Canadian readers happily writing in
with their latest "ah-ha" experiences.

After even just a few issues of THE ECONOMIST you, too, will
start to see things with a new clarity, a sharper focus, a deeper
understanding.

Charting the World

Helping you at every turn are THE ECONOMIST's charts. Illumi-
nating and instructive, THE ECONOMIST is noted for its charts.

  - Business confidence in 21 countries. It's up in the U.S.
    Down in the "new Europe."

  - Bankruptcies by nation. Soaring in the U.S. Sinking in
    Germany.

  - Book-buying per head. Swedish and German readers lead.
    The Japanese and Russians lag.

THE ECONOMIST even charts the cost of a "Big Mac" at McDonald's
restaurants around the world. It's an amazingly accurate comparative

(over, please...)

FIGURE 8–4   (Continued)

-4-

of international currency!

Use these charts to bury conventional wisdom. To spot where things are headed before the crowd catches on. To connect seemingly random events in business and finance - and turn them to your advantage.

See For Yourself FREE

The world-class coverage...the international range...the uniquely unAmerican perspective...why not see for yourself everything that makes THE ECONOMIST, well, THE ECONOMIST?

- If until now you've only heard of THE ECONOMIST, but have never seen it first-hand, here's a perfect chance to do so free.

Mail in the enclosed voucher and THE ECONOMIST will start a trial subscription for you.

The first three issues are yours free. You'll receive three weeks of THE ECONOMIST to evaluate and enjoy at no cost.

After that, you agree to either end your free trial or continue.

- If you decide to stop, just write "cancel" when the bill comes, return it and that will end that. The three issues are yours.

- If you decide to continue your trial subscription, good news: pay just C$65.00 + GST and you'll receive 27 additional weeks of THE ECONOMIST - 30 issues in all - at an incredible C$70.00 off the newsstand price.

Your satisfaction is guaranteed. You can cancel any time during your subscription and THE ECONOMIST will immediately refund your money for all unmailed issues.

"Oh what power...
to see ourselves as others see us!"
- Robert Burns [1786]

That's the idea behind THE ECONOMIST - and the promise behind this invitation to subscribe. Exercise the power THE ECONOMIST will give you. Mail in your voucher good for your three FREE issues today.

Sincerely,

M. M. Scardino
Chief Executive Officer

MMS:rrc

P.S. The New York Times called THE ECONOMIST "remarkably complete, tightly edited...one of the most respected magazines in the world." The Wall Street Journal said, "It should be required reading." While Newsweek noted, "It is required reading at the pinnacles of power."

Send for your free sample subscription and see if you agree.

FIGURE 8–5   A Delightful Story Approach Fund Raiser

Dear Investor:

   The bug-eyed bird on our envelope who's ogling you with such dis-
temper has a point. He's a native American sandhill crane and you may be
sitting on top of one of his nesting sites.

   As he sees it, every time our human species has drained a marsh,
and plowed it or built a city on it, since 1492 or so -- there went the
neighborhood. It's enough to make you both edgy.

   So give us $10 for his nest egg and we'll see that a nice, soggy
spot -- just the kind he and his mate need to fashion a nest and put an
egg in it -- is reserved for the two of them, undisturbed, for keeps.
Only $10. (Watch those cranes come in to land, just once, and you're
paid back. Catches at your throat.) Then the cranes can relax, and so
can you. A bit.

        How will we reserve that incubator with your $10?
        Not by campaigning or picketing or suing.

        We'll just BUY the nesting ground.

   That's the unique and expensive and effective way The Nature Conservancy goes about its non-profit business. We're as dead serious about
hanging on to nature's precarious balance as the more visible and vocal
conservation groups. But our thing is to let money do our talking.

        And we buy a whopping lot of land: starting with
        60 acres of New York's Mianus River Gorge in 1951
        (now 395 acres), we have protected 2,000,000 acres
        -- about the area of Rhode Island and Delaware.
        The plots are spotted coast to coast and from
        Canada deep into the Caribbean, 3,157 of them
        sized from a quarter of an acre to hundreds of
        square miles.

   All of it is prime real estate, if you're a crane or a bass or a
sweet pepperbush or a redwood. Or a toad or a turtle. And a lot of

FIGURE 8–5 (Continued)

-2-

it's nice for people, too -- lovely deserts, mountainsides, prairies, islands. (Islands! We own huge Santa Cruz, off the California shore, and tiny Dome Island in Lake George, and most of the Virginia Barrier Islands, and dozens more.)

So besides being after your $10, we invite you to see a sample of our lands. We have 38 chapters in 32 states. Check your phone book. If we're not there yet, call me at (703) 841-5388. We'll guide you and yours to a nearby preserve where you're most welcome to walk along one of our paths, sit on one of our log benches, look about, and say to the youngster we hope will be with you, "This will be here, as is, for your grandchildren." Nice feeling.

We do ask that you don't bother the natives. E.g., there's a sign in one preserve that says "Rattlesnakes, Scorpions, Black Bear, Poison Oak/ARE PROTECTED/DO NOT HARM OR DISTURB." For $10, you're privileged not to disturb a bear or stroke a poison oak. Bargain.

> Bargains in diverse real estate are what we look for and find. Not just any real estate. We've been working for years to make and keep a huge ongoing inventory of the "natural elements" in each of the United States (so far, 30 are done). These "State Natural Heritage Programs" identify what's unique, what's threatened, what's rare or a rare natural sight to see in each state: animals, birds, plants, bugs, lakes, river systems, swamps, waterfalls, woods ... and cranes' nests.

Then we try to acquire those places that desperately need protection and preservation. We think big. Early last year, the Richard King Mellon Foundation gave us the largest single grant ever for private conservation: $25,000,000 to launch the National Wetlands Conservation Project.

We expect to match that grant over the next five years and create a $50 million revolving fund to protect outstanding examples of threatened aquatic and wetland systems from the Atlantic coast to Alaska. The work has already begun, copying successful projects like the protection of Elder Creek in Northern California, the preservation of the endangered manatees' wintering habitat in Crystal River, Florida, and the acquisition of the whole Canelo Hills cienega (desert spring marsh) in Arizona.

But we don't just shovel cash at these projects. We buy some lands, trade for others, get leases and easements, ask to be mentioned in wills. Then we give or, preferably, sell up to 40 per cent of what we buy to states, cities, universities, other conservation groups -- any responsible organization which wants and loves the land so much that it doesn't

FIGURE 8–5   (Continued)

-3-

mind our clever lawyers making it very difficult for anyone to "improve" any part of it, ever. Unless the someone can build nests or eat acorns.

That cash flow replenishes our revolving fund, every dime of which is plowed into the unpaved and as yet unplowed. All this activity generates a lot of fascinating true stories, and lovely photos. These we put into a small (32 pages) but elegant, sprightly and adless magazine, our report to our 200,000 members every other month: The Nature Conservancy News.

Here you may find that the land you and the rest of us have just bought is harboring a four-lined skink, or a spicebush, or boreal chickadees, or kame and kettle topography. You've a lot to learn and see that's most intriguing, as you'll discover.

The Nature Conservancy News also describes well-led tours of our various properties, tells you what we're doing in your state, and shows you how you can help and have some healthy fun at the same time.

You see, the millions of acres we own are mostly watched over by volunteer stewards -- wonderful men and women who are proud to show off their lovely charges. These likely include bats, salamanders, toadstools and such. Or cranes. You'll be invited to Nature Conservancy chapter meetings nearest you.

And if you paste the complimentary white-oak leaf sticker we've enclosed with this letter on your bumper, back pack, boat, hang glider, pool, bicycle, wheelchair ... wherever, you'll attract grateful grins from your fellow cognoscenti.

Now, you may think it's disproportionate to brag about how we're raising millions for our projects and then ask you for only $10. Who needs you?

We need you, very much! Those hard-headed foundations and corporations and ranch owners and such who give us money or property must be convinced that our ranks include a lot of intelligent, concerned, articulate citizens: people who know we ought to let nature alone to tend to much of this finite earth and all its creatures ... if we're to be among the creatures.

Yes, we need you and your ear and your voice -- and your $10 ($10 times 200,000 members buys a lot of acres). Please join us today, like so: Get a pen. Check and initial the "membership application" form that your hand is touching. Tear off the Interim Membership stub, sign and pocket it, and wait six weeks or so for your first magazine and permanent

FIGURE 8–5 (Continued)

-4-

card. Enclose a check for $10 in the return envelope (more, if you can spare it). NOTE that it's tax-deductible. Mail the form. Go.

Thank you, and welcome!, dear wise fellow investor in nest eggs. For your fanfare, listen for the wondrous stentorian call of that sandhill crane*.

Sincerely,

Nancy C. Mackinnon
Membership Director

* We borrowed his picture from Country Journal magazine where he illustrated an article about the International Crane Foundation of Baraboo, Wisconsin. The photo is by brave Cary Wolinsky. And we don't actually know if the crane is as upset as he looks. Maybe he's smiling? Certainly he will if, when he leaves the Foundation, his first motel stop has been reserved with your $10.

NCM/km

The most recent Nature Conservancy financial report filed with the Department of State may be obtained by writing to: New York State, Department of State, Office of Charities Registration, Albany, New York 12231, or The Nature Conservancy, 1800 North Kent Street, Arlington, Virginia 22209

If you like to read financial statements, this one is a beauty. We're rather vain about it. Do ask

FIGURE 8–6   A New Nature Conservancy Factual Generic Approach

Dear Friend of the Family,

It goes (almost) without saying that the baby black-crowned night heron on our envelope depends on you for her survival.

But you have dependents, concerns of your own. So why should you help this short-legged, short-necked bird who's usually awake only at night?

Because her future is your future. The wetlands our baby calls home are vanishing -- under the plow, bulldozer, cement truck. And the streams, bogs, ponds and marshes that are <u>basic</u> to both your lives are being destroyed as never before.

Saving them is imperative . . . and worth the cost.
Just $10 from you and we can do it.
The Nature Conservancy can <u>buy</u> the land this heron
-- all of us -- need to breed, roost, survive.

Home for our heron chick is the Virginia Coast Reserve, the last intact fully functioning, barrier island ecosystem on the Atlantic coast of the United States. We are rescuing this, one of America's Last Great Places, through a coordinated plan of purchases and agreements.

And we'd like to let <u>you</u> in on the deal.

Since 1951, The Nature Conservancy has been protecting wetlands, rain forests, prairies and beaches. To date, we've helped protect more than 8.0 million acres in the U.S. and millions more through our Latin American, Caribbean and Pacific programs. Our work has already rescued numerous species from extinction.

Not a bad record. And it explains why in a recent poll by <u>The Chronicle of Philanthropy</u>,

The Nature Conservancy was rated
America's #1 environmental organization,
with regard to accountability
and expenditure of funds.

Our night heron chick and I are inviting you to join this most influential, effective and prestigious environmental organization at <u>a price that's less than half what others might</u>

(over, please)

FIGURE 8–6   (Continued)

-2-

pay.* More on this bargain in a moment.

Only a few lucky souls ever hear the nocturnal heron's flat and eerie "quawk." And only a few informed and intelligent folks -- like you -- ever get a chance to join such an auspicious real estate deal. One that's advantageous to us all.

The Nature Conservancy works with special partners throughout America to safeguard the shrinking natural areas of our country. We're not out to save the world, just the most important parts of it.

Our strategy is simple. And amazingly effective. We find natural habitats that are in danger and we buy them. It's the best of America, combining good ethics, sound business and visionary outlook.

Right now, we have more than 825,000 members who each contribute $10 (or often more!) a year. With their support, we're able to exercise some muscle on behalf of those animals, plants and natural places that need it.

So in addition to black-crowned night herons in Virginia, we help provide homes for free-ranging bison in Tallgrass Prairie. Black spectacled bear in Ecuador. Chinook salmon in California. Uakari monkeys in the Amazon basin. Sandhill cranes in Florida. Margays in Central America. And many, many more than I can list here.

Some of our protected wildlife are noble. Some are cute. Many, like the night heron chick, have faces only a mother could love.

But we don't save species because they're cute or appealing. We save them because, given the interdependence of life on this planet, a threat to any of them is a threat to us all.

Each year, the U.S. loses 290,000 acres of wetlands -- an area larger than half of our national parks. Over a quarter million acres, gone forever. Those wetlands absorb contaminants and sediments from the water we drink, make a buffer against coastal flooding, and give safe haven to 600 wildlife species and 5,000 plant species.

So just as our baby heron needs her mother to bring her fish
parts to eat, she needs you to invest
just $10 to protect what's left of her -- our -- home.

Last year, with contributions of $10 or more from people just like you, we completed

FIGURE 8–6 (Continued)

-3-

744 projects and brought under our protection a total land area over one-third the size of Connecticut.

In that state alone, we oversee 55 preserves. And with 62 Nature Conservancy chapters in all 50 states, we currently own and manage more than 1,500 preserves throughout the U.S., the largest private system of nature sanctuaries in the world.

If we're doing so well, why do I ask you to join?

<u>Because you're exactly the kind of person we need right now.</u>

And while we've been extremely successful, the problem we face is extremely large. Also, we've discovered it's not enough just to protect acreage.

We must protect ecosystems. Set up buffers between protected habitats and "civilization." Engineer cooperation among government, business and people. And discover ways that allow human beings to live more wisely on the land.

Now, in this new era of new environmentalism, a top priority is saving America's Last Great Places: like Adirondak Park in northern New York state; Nipomo Dunes, California; the embattled Florida Keys; and the Virginia Coast Reserve, where our heron chick lives.

In many parts of the world, we're saving land. Using creative techniques like debt-for-nature swaps and Adopt-an-Acre programs. Trading know-how with partners in the tropics through staff exchange projects. And investing, each and every day, in an additional 600 acres of critical habitat for the survival of rare and endangered species.

<u>By saving just a fraction of our country's undeveloped land, we can save our natural heritage</u>.

I know it's fashionable these days to talk about making a choice between environmental protection and prosperity. Between birds and jobs.

But you can't ask people to choose between protecting the environment and feeding their families. And you don't have to. Instead, <u>join The Nature Conservancy</u>.

When you do, you'll save thousands of broken homes and keep your own planetary habitat from shattering as well. You'll join a savvy partnership of real estate and business experts, lawyers, ecologists, biologists, foresters and more.

(over, please)

FIGURE 8–6   (Continued)

-4-

And you'll receive:

A full year's subscription to the full-color magazine, <u>Nature Conservancy</u>, filled with engrossing articles and gorgeous photographs of the animals and places you're helping to save.

A 10% discount on most purchases from The Nature Company catalog and stores.

A newsletter from your state chapter regularly detailing how your support is protecting natural habitats right where you live.

Exclusive invitations to special social events and field trips at Nature Conservancy preserves near you.

An official membership card.

Of course, the most important benefit is a little harder to quantify -- the advantage of living on a planet that still provides a home for black-crowned night herons. The intangible, immeasurable value of keeping our earthly family intact.

Think how much we stand to gain. Then remember how little this costs.

Just $10 for 12 months. Less than 20 cents a week.

That's an amount you can't afford <u>not</u> to spend.

<u>So join us, America's leading conservation group, today</u>. Send your check now for just $10 in the return envelope. Or send more if your bank account and commitment allow.

But do it <u>now</u>. If you don't do it for yourself, do it for the younger generation. On whose behalf your membership will protect our Earth.

Sincerely,

Donna Cherel

Donna Cherel
Director of Membership

P.S.   Although the black-crowned night heron on our envelope is not yet a threatened species, the wetlands she calls home are still in danger. With your help, we can save America's wetlands and their species before it is too late.

P.P.S.   If you join right away I'll mail you a brand new tote bag featuring our feathered friend, the black-crowned night heron. She'll remind you to stay away from plastic bags and conserve resources!

NH-LT-NHT-5   *Dues are normally $25. You can join for $10 through this special invitation only.

Figure 8–7 shows a package done for *Worth*, a magazine on personal investing and money management, written by Bill and designed by Heikki Ratalahti.

Bill at first declined to take on this job, feeling that all financial publications pushed the same income-enrichment promises. Then he and Heikki started lining up all the funny things that might happen when people acquired "real wealth," the advantages and disadvantages. And before they knew it, they had a fun, new approach and an early mailing for *Worth* that became a big winner.

Tongue in cheek, Bill offers a great involvement device by asking the reader to find out if he/she really wants to be "filthy rich" by taking a test "inside." Who could resist?

The test inside is delightful and makes the point—most of us indeed do want to be "filthy rich." The brochure does a clean, but dramatic reinforcement of the letter's message.

Our next example of great direct mail, shown in Figure 8–8, carries an entirely different tone. Its message is equally strong—in fact, the package practically shouts. This is a compelling, totally involving, hard-sell masterpiece by the master of strong, staccato copy, the late Gene Schwartz.

Its hypothesis or basic, underlying assumption is a killer: People feel helpless and out of control when dealing with business and government in our world today. This product promises to give them control. It promises to show ordinary people how to be treated like VIPs. And, incredible as this promise may sound, Gene puts forth a foolproof, can't-lose offer to back up his promises.

Check out the envelope (it measures 11 1/2" × 6 1/8"), note the headlines, read the letter. Count the benefits! Gene was one of our best salesmen.

Stop and stretch a minute, then back to the show! And what better star to start you off on the last leg than Ken Schneider. Ken's work is clean, crisp, fresh, invigorating and terribly, terribly good. Figure 8–9 shows one of my favorites (for *Walking Magazine*) that seems perfect for a magazine edited not necessarily for readers, but for "doers."

Every piece is linked to every other by "the foot," "steps," and walking, of course. And it's loaded with concise, sparkling copy that says it all. Notice the short paragraphs in the letter. The benefits in the brochure lead you in *without one single feature until the inside spread*. All in all, it's as good as a direct mail can get.

Our final package isn't a package at all—it's a magalog. Figure 8–10 shows one of the best, most successful magalogs I've seen to date. Created by Jim Punkre, who's been writing winners for Rodale Press for decades, it demonstrates this fine writer's versatility. For the magalog is really part magazine, part advertising spreads, one after another for a full 20 pages, *nine* colorful 10 3/4" × 17" spreads—each as involving as the one before it.

FIGURE 8–7 A Tongue-in-Cheek Involvement Device

Find out if you really want to be

FILTHY RICH

Take this test.

BULK RATE
U.S. POSTAGE
PAID
WORTH
MAGAZINE

JOAN THROCKMORTON
PO BOX 452
POUND RIDGE NY 10576-0452

CHARTER INVITATION

worth

It's the sophisticated new magazine about
... money—making it, investing it,
... it.

...vited to reserve Charter Perks &
... and to preview our next issue
... cost or obligation.

FREE

Dear Reader:

It was Scott Fitzgerald who observed, "The rich are different from us."

It was Ernest Hemingway who then shot back, "Yes. They have more money."

But money isn't all that the rich have more of. They also have more worries...

...so before you accept this invitation to move up higher financially, you may want to consider some of the pros and cons:

DISADVANTAGES of being rich	ADVANTAGES of being rich
You'll start hearing from long-lost cousins looking for loans.	
You won't be able to get away with sending the Red Cross just $10.	
Total strangers will corner you to ask which stocks to buy.	
You'll be expected to use the Full Service pumps, to buy Super, and to tip.	

(over, please)

Courtesy of Jayme, Ratalahti, Inc.

FIGURE 8–7 (Continued)

```
          DISADVANTAGES              │              ADVANTAGES

You'll have to dress for the opera. │

Whenever you throw a dinner party,  │
you'll be expected to provide       │
valet parking.                      │

No guest will ever again show up    │
bearing a bottle of wine.           │

Political candidates will want to   │
be introduced to you.               │

None will want voters to see you    │
together.                           │

You'll feel obliged to buy the      │
Forbes 400 issue each year to see   │
if you've made the list of          │
America's richest.                  │     You'll have tons more money.
```

So, now then. Do you really still want to be rich? You do? Great! And
I think you're going to feel right at home immediately with WORTH, the
sophisticated new personal finance magazine that encourages you to think
rich, live rich, and be rich.

                    FREE EXAMINATION ISSUE

The next issue of WORTH will be out momentarily, with our exclusive
investment information, strategies and insights. Where can you find the
best values, the best service, the fewest risks? WORTH will tell you.

        Additional goodies. If you like the first issue, you can then
        enjoy other Charter freebies and perks including a special
        survival guide to help protect and enhance your lifestyle,
        plus a unique report on mutual funds to make your investment
        choices easier. Read on!

WORTH is backed by the publishing subsidiary of Fidelity Investments, one
of the nation's most prestigious financial institutions. The magazine
operates totally independently. It's totally unfettered. Totally
unbiased. And I think you'll find that it's also totally unique.

Unlike other personal finance publications, WORTH is written and edited

FIGURE 8–7 (Continued)

for a very special kind of individual. The assumptions we've made about you are these:

> If you're not already living on Easy Street, you're by now only a block or two away.

> Your day-to-day investing decisions are being handled quite capably by various professionals in your employ — a money manager, stock broker, banker, et al.

> You enjoy being a part of the investing decisions made on your behalf — reading about them, discussing them, often making recommendations of your own.

> And ... being human, you can't help wondering at times if you couldn't be doing even better.

Helping you to do better is precisely where WORTH comes in. The magazine is written for lay persons in easy-to-grasp, conversational English — not industry jargon. But it brings you information, ideas and advice that are normally reserved for professionals. And it takes the long-term view, not the short.

For example:

    o when the nation finally rebounds from recession, which market sectors will be first to reward investment?

    o what opportunities lie waiting in international markets as European markets integrate, and as Hong Kong reverts to China?

    o which products and services stand to make the most money from the greying of America — the elderly and retired?

    o where might you invest to help meet the needs of America's newest immigrants — housing, education, day care centers?

    o which U.S. companies stand to profit most from the rebuilding of Russia and Eastern Europe?

    o what's ahead for technology issues — genetics, communications, transportation, space?

    o how might you turn a penny or two when the government finally decides to overhaul the nation's health care system?

    o as the environmental movement gathers force, what investments should you maybe think about dumping?

We live in exciting times! And from the standpoint of making money,

(over, please)

FIGURE 8–7   (Continued)

nowhere will you get better answers to questions like these than from the
stories and columns in WORTH.

> Features like The Advisor — financial management tips,
> investment opportunities, money myths. Intrigue — the inside
> scoop on the movers and shakers, the deals they're putting
> together.
>
> ROI (Return on Investment) about getting the most value for
> your money — vacation hideaways, high-tech toys, lifestyle
> gear, food and wine. And our private sage and seer,
> Contrarious, written under a nom-de-plume with the knowing
> outlook of a 30-year investing veteran. . .

. . .but come experience WORTH for yourself on us — compliments of the
house.

The magazine is published ten times a year, so as to give you plenty of
time for absorbing each issue fully before going on to the next. . .for
gaining in-depth perspective on strategies. . .for mulling over new
opportunities, ideas, avenues and options. I think you'll find it
enormously stimulating. . .and quite a bit of fun.

> SEND NO MONEY. When you mail the enclosed card promptly,
> you'll receive a copy of our very next issue for your
> examination. No cost. No obligation.
>
> OWE NOTHING. If for any reason you feel that the magazine is
> not for you, just return the subscription bill marked "cancel,"
> and that's that. You've spent nothing. You owe nothing.
>
> LOW CHARTER RATE. But if, on the other hand, you find WORTH
> to be pertinent — interesting, informative, relative to your
> interests and goals — your price as a Charter Subscriber is
> just $9.97 for a full year.

PLUS OTHER FREEBIES & PERKS. By reserving now, you save from the very
start. You save in perpetuity. You have a full refund guarantee at all
times on all copies still to go. And in the special flyer I'm enclosing,
you'll read about other valuable Charter benefits that include a free
survival guide, and a special mutual fund handbook.

EARLY POSTMARK. Only so many copies of the next issue are being printed
— no more. In fairness, first come, first served. Avoid disappointment.
Mail the card at your earliest convenience. Why not be rich just as soon
as you can? Or at least a bit richer?

                              Yours cordially,

                              W. Randall Jones

                              W. Randall Jones
                              Chief Executive Officer

RJ:aa

worth
The net result of intelligent investing

FIGURE 8–7   (Continued)

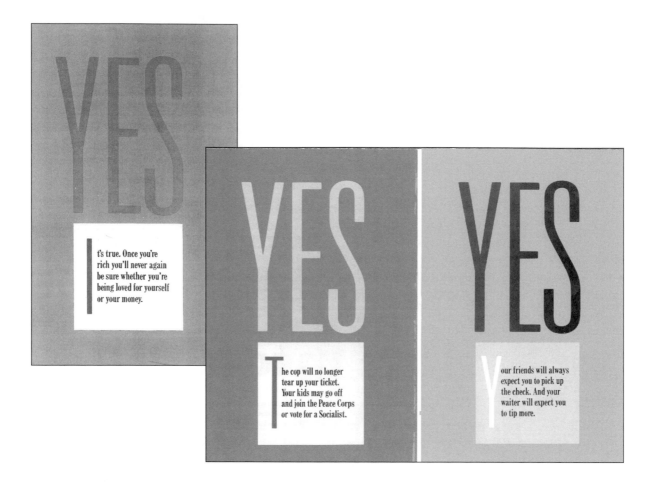

FIGURE 8–7   (Continued)

FIGURE 8–8   A Hard-Sell Masterpiece

Yours FREE Inside.

These 3 Trigger Words instantly get the lowest price on anything you buy.

an IRS
y that
ax return.

**This Trigger Sentence
instantly clears up
problems with your credit report**

**This 6-word Trigger Letter
instantly starts a bidding war
among car dealers, by return mail.**

✔ These 4 trigger words get you instant attention in a hospital emergency room.
✔ This trigger question instantly tells you at once if a used car is a lemon.
✔ This trigger sentence instantly makes sure you're never disturbed at home again by unwanted sales calls!
✔ This trigger question instantly saves you thousands on the price of a new home!

Prove it yourself, on page 1 inside, instantly!
No cost! No risk! No commitment!

k-
t
he's going to churn your account.

```
     Why? Because they tell them that you're in the know!
            That you have powerful friends!
        That the only sane way to handle you is to
               give you exactly what you want!
```

```
That's why they're called Trigger Words, Dear Friend,

     Because they trigger instant action!  Instant compliance!
Instant servitude!

     Every organization has these Trigger Words.  They're how that
organization separates out the people who must be obeyed from the
people who can be exploited.

     How they tell, in seconds, whether you're a VIP, or a patsy.
Even by letter, or on the phone.

     Take the IRS.  The majority of the time, the IRS either
terrorizes or bleeds you.  But the IRS doesn't like trouble, any
more than you do.  So they have Trigger Phrases every agent looks
for, that tell them instantly when to give favors instead.

     The most powerful of these Trigger Phrases is "Form 8275."  You
simply take those two words, and request that form from the IRS
headquarters in Washington by calling 1-800-829-3676.  Don't ask
them about it, or they'll simply deny it exists — just tell them
they must send it to you.

     Once you get it, fill it out, and send it with your return.
That's all there is to it.

     From that moment on, no agent in his right mind is going to
audit your return.  You've just told him that you know his boss,
```

```
                                              (over, please)
```

FIGURE 8–8   (Continued)

---

and his boss will attack him if he tries to attack you.

What's he going to do? He's going to toss your form aside and go on to the pile of patsies where he can build his career. Goodbye, agent! Goodbye audit! All because you know two tiny words!

3 Trigger Phrases that make your stockbroker cut you in, rather than cut you up.

1) To slash every mutual fund commission you pay him: *"Where are the Break Points on this trade?"*

2) To make sure that you always get the best price on every transaction. *"Let me see a record of the trade in Fitch's Time and Sales."*

3) The one question you must always ask when being presented with a hot stock tip! *"Is it an Initial Public Offering (IPO)?"* If it is, you must tell him to get lost; you're not interested in something so speculative.

Have you heard of Break Points before? Or Fitch's Time & Sales?

They're VIP tools. Obsessively guarded. Like you are being dealt a royal flush rather than a pair of deuces.

But you have to know enough to put them to work. You have to show that you're on the inside. You have to trigger respect, and then servitude.

That's why we give you Triggers like these every month in *Straight Talk.*

Dave Ellis learned that his shares of worthless stock could be sold for $85,000.

Just look at the incredible new power these Trigger Words give you every day!

If you've got a problem with your credit report, just call them and say, *"I want you to comply with the Fair Credit Reporting Act."* Instantly, that error vanishes from your report.

If you're looking at a dazzling late-model used car, and they're willing to negotiate, just ask, *"I want to see a copy of this car's title history from Carfax."* Watch their faces turn purple if the car's a lemon.

If someone offers you a Rolex for less than full price, and you

2

FIGURE 8–8   (Continued)

Overnight, Arthur Sjoquist cut his credit card interest by 10 percent.

want to be sure it's not a fake, just ask yourself, *"Does the second hand stop at each second?"* If it does, it's a fake.

So easy, because now you speak with a Millionaire's Voice!

The simple sentence that gets any household appliance fixed for free, even if the warranty expired!   *Call the manufacturer and say, "I'm a dedicated customer, and my warranty expired x days ago.   I know you stand behind your products, and I know you'll fix my toaster oven without charge."*

✔ The simple sentence that starts a bidding war among car dealers, without your even setting foot in their showroom! *"Please fax me your best price on (make and model of car)."*   Send this letter, or fax, to the three largest dealers in your area. The bidding should give you your car for an incredibly low 1 or 2 percent over their net cost.

✔ 7 words that cut your telephone bill by hundreds each year, plus give you crystal-clear calls! Call the phone company and tell them to, *"Please analyze my bill for cost savings."* The rest is automatic, and the phone company pays every cent of the cost.

Gwyneth Feely is $5,600 richer because she read one paragraph.

✔ The simple sentence that makes sure you're never disturbed at home again by unwanted sales calls! *Call the Direct Marketing Association and tell them, "Put my name on your national Do Not Call List."*

✔ The simple sentence that keeps a hospital from robbing you blind! *"I am calling the People's Medical Society to have your bill audited."*

In a hospital emergency room, they will pass over other patients, to give you immediate care!

Call the hospital. Get their emergency line. Say, *"I need an ambulance."*   When you get there, every hospital's iron rule is that you must be attended to that very same instant. Nurses, doctors, emergency units will scurry to your side, even if they have to run past a line of waiting patients that stretches out two full city blocks.

✔ The 9 words to make sure your passport isn't taken when you're traveling overseas are, *"Let me give you a photocopy of my*

(over, please)

3

FIGURE 8–8   (Continued)

Patricia McGehee doubled her husband's life insurance coverage, and saved $1,000 a year doing it.

passport."   Give that photocopy to every hotel clerk and shopkeeper who asks you for your passport. That way, a confederate of theirs can't walk off with your valuable original.

✔ There are 3 Trigger Numbers that get your phone calls through when everyone else gets a busy signal — even on Christmas, or when there's been an earthquake. They are: 10288 for AT&T, 10222 for MCI or 10333 for Sprint (just dial one of these 5-digit numbers prior to dialing the area code and number you are trying to reach).

✔ This question makes sure every cent of your charitable donations go where you want! *"What percent of my donation goes to administrative costs, and what percent ends up helping your charitable cause?"*

✔ This question keeps you from being robbed when you hire household workers! *"Are you bonded?"*

Did you know that reputable household workers need to be bonded?

That administrative costs — which otherwise can eat up to 95% of your charitable donation — are required by law to be revealed to you? *You do now.*

And this is only the beginning! There are hundreds more of these Trigger Words that make them break the rules for you. That make them drop everything else to please you. *For example:*

✔ 3 words to get the best price on any purchase, without an instant's haggling! Page 7 of your Free book.

✔ 7 words you can say tomorrow to increase your take-home pay! Page 18 of your Free book.

✔ 10 words that save you thousands on the price of a new home! Page 12 of your Free book.

✔ The phone number that could easily save you half the price on your next hotel room. Page 11 of your Free book.

✔ 5 words that stop a family member who wants to borrow money, without hard feelings. Page 6 of your Free book.

✔ 4 words that keep your employer from robbing your pension fund. Page 2 of your Free book.

✔ 6 words that get you free prescription drugs.

4

FIGURE 8–8   (Continued)

✔ 2 words that get you more college financial aid than you ever thought possible, no matter how high your income!

**Unless you're given these Trigger Words,
you're going to support
all the rip-off artists in the universe!**

✔ This question screams out that a sweepstakes promotion is going to take you for a ride!

✔ These 3 words in a job ad warn you to stay far away!

✔ These 4 words in a business opportunity ad tell you it will scam you out of every cent of your money.

Ken Fargo followed our advice and saved $2,500 on his brand new car.

✔ These 3 words on a credit card application tell you it will cost you hundreds of dollars a year in excess interest.

✔ These 3 words on a mutual fund prospectus tell you to take your money elsewhere...if you ever want to see it again!

New Trigger Words are invented every month. But no one tells you about them...except us! Every month, we give you the keys that unlock the doors that, all your life, have been sealed shut!

And they now swing open to you automatically! Without hassle, without question, without hesitation!

**Our *Straight Talk* Newsletter
Must Make a Hassle-free $100 a Month
For You,**

Or it Doesn't Cost You One Red Cent!

Our guarantee is that simple. After a combined 30 years of guiding people like you into negotiation-free, embarrassment-free fortune building, we unconditionally promise you this:

Send for your free trial issue of **Straight Talk** today. Read it through. But, above all, BEGIN PUTTING IT TO WORK TO TRANSFORM YOUR FINANCIAL WELL-BEING. BEGIN TRACKING ITS IMMEDIATE RESULTS.

Jane Conway saved $800 a year on her credit card alone.

Do the same for the second issue, and the third, and the fourth. . . all the way up to the twelfth. Track those results for every one of those 12 months. And if the results haven't astounded you,

(over, please)

5

FIGURE 8–8   (Continued)

---

just drop us a line one full year from now, and we'll refund every cent of your money, at once!

Yes, Even if You Cancel
On the Very Last Day
Of Your Subscription, You Get
Every Cent of Your Money Back!

In that case, ALL 12 months of *Straight Talk* that you've received are yours free. Plus all the Bonus Reports that you've received when you subscribed, are also yours free.

Plus, as a New Trial Subscriber,
You Receive Almost Half Off
The Regular Yearly Rate!

Where that yearly rate is now $75 a year, you save $35.50 and get it for only $39.50 a year.

Just think for a moment how trivial the cost of this subscription is. It comes to less than one dollar a week. Less than the cost of a movie for the two of you every month.

PLUS, AS a New Trial Subscriber
You Receive Five Free Reports!

These reports sell, at this very moment, for $10 or more each.

But every one of them is yours free, as our gift. . . even if you cancel on the very last day of your subscription.

We're ready to rush them to you, tomorrow. Just call 800/777-5005 right now.

Ken and Daria
Ken and Daria

P.S. Uncle Sam wants to repay your generosity! That's why he could very well guarantee the purchase of your next home! So you move in with little, or even no money down! Page 31.

That's why he could very well pay for your M.B.A., or the retraining you need to get a far better job. Page 55.

That's why he'll let you make the interest on your car loan deductible from your taxes. . . if you know the right way to ask him. Page 39. And that's why he'll pay for the gas for your car. Page 61.

6

DNGE

FIGURE 8–8   (Continued)

FIGURE 8–8 (Continued)

AT LAST...
Tells You in Seconds That You're Being Scammed!

Every one of the secrets described below is given to you as our Gift with your Free Trial Subscription!

✔ Tells you in seconds that your *mutual fund* is sneaking in a hidden charge for their marketing and advertising fees. Page 71.

✔ Tells you in seconds that you're paying $50 too much on every $1,000 bond. Page 30.

✔ Save $65 in bank fees every year, by having the bank drop the $1.25 charge every time you use an ATM machine! Page 71.

✔ How to outwit the Nursing Home Racket! Now, the Nursing Home can't seize your folks' house — or ever force them out of that Nursing Home, even if they can't pay a penny more! Page 36.

✔ Travel brochure tip-offs: If it says "view" the sights, you'll stop at them just long enough to take a snapshot. If you read "why not enjoy," you know that every one of them will cost you extra! Page 24.

✔ Did you know that rogue IRS agents send out thousands of letters every year that start: "Dear Taxpayer, You owe. . ." These letters are totally bogus. These agents know that, rather than question them, most taxpayers would rather pay through the nose — as long as it's less than $589! Instant protection is on page 15.

✔ Never pay a *car repair bill* when it's first given to you. What you do instead is (see page 5).

✔ If you have trouble with a car repair, never call the mechanic. You don't have to. Call this number instead, and let the person who answers get you exactly what you want. Page 5.

✔ Why the tires of a used car tell you in seconds if the owner of the lot is a crook. Page 12.

✔ When you go to rent a car, look for "Extra Mileage Charge." Or "Fees for Extra Drivers." Or "Drivers Under the Age of 25." If you find them, go somewhere else. Page 12.

Tells You in Seconds That Hidden Credit Card Costs Are Boosting Your Interest Rates to 30 Percent or More!

✔ Tells you in seconds that the *repairman* put back the old parts in your car, and charged you for new ones. Slashes hundreds off your bill. Page 11.

✔ No-friction way to *shave interest off your car loan.* Why is everybody so happy about it? Because everybody wins. Page 12.

✔ One-third of all *adjustable mortgages* are "miscalculated" in favor of the bank. One call tells you whether they owe you thousands, and exactly how to get it back. Page 30.

✔ Why let *the IRS* withhold 20% of your pension. Cure is on page 16.

✔ Tells you in seconds that you're paying *double commissions to your broker on* every trade. Instant cure: page 51.

✔ Tells you in seconds that you're paying your broker commission on *twice* the number of shares that you wanted to buy. Page 50.

✔ *How solvent is your brokerage firm?* One phone call tells you. Page 30.

✔ *Credit card due dates* are a scam! They cost you an 18 percent finance charge for every day after you receive the bill until that due date arrives. Instant solution on page 40.

✔ You think you're paying a finance charge on $50, but *the credit card company charges you* a finance charge on $1,000. Who's right? They are, unless you read page 52.

✔ *How much interest do you really pay the credit card company for a cash advance.* 32.93 percent! Get it for one-fifth as much where we show you! Page 12.

✔ *Skipping a month on credit card payments* costs you higher interest, and scams you into giving up your grace period for that month. What to do instead: page 12.

✔ For just a $5 bucks, you can get a complete report on every FDIC-insured bank in your state, along with a "decoder kit" for understanding what the Feds think about YOUR bank. Send a check for $5 to. . . (See page 14.)

✔ Why the strongest possible way to *clean up a bad credit report* costs you nothing! Page 4.

✔ Quick-fix solution to any *lawyer problem* you have. Page 74.

✔ When past performance in a *mutual fund* means absolutely nothing! (They'll hate us for letting you in on this one.) Page 6.

✔ How never to be cheated out of *your Social Security payment.* (Millions of people just like you are every year.) Page 14.

✔ HIDDEN TRAP: If you're sucked into it, your spouse collects only 35 percent of *your Social Security benefits.* Page 14.

✔ Any *retail dealer's warranty* is going to be good for them, and bad for you. That's why we give you your own fill-in-the-blanks iron-clad warranty. Page 4.

We give you the Trigger Words!
The Instant Bonanzas!
The $1,000 Freebies!
The Big-Money-Fast Breakthroughs!
And we guarantee every one of them!

Our names are Ken and Daria Dolan. You may have heard us on our daily radio show on the WOR Radio Network. We're proud that it's heard in over a hundred cities, and it's one of the most popular programs in every one of those cities.

I (this is Ken talking) graduated from Boston College. I served as a naval officer in Vietnam. Joined a major New York Stock Exchange firm as an account executive and then founded and served as Vice Chairman of a prominent investment banking firm. All those years of experience are at your service now!

I (this is Daria talking) graduated from Webster College. I served as a vice president of a major New York Stock Exchange firm and have advised major financial firms from coast to coast. All those years of experience are at your service now!

We have the background to know when new Trigger Words are being coined! We have the daily contacts to know where the Instant Bonanzas and Big-Money Freebies are springing up! And every month, we pass them on — at once — to you!

We know the people who run America — the smartest and the richest — and they know us well enough to tell us nothing but the truth!

With these Trigger Words, hassles are a thing of the past. Confrontations are as out-of-date as the horse and buggy. You tell them, in Trigger Word Code, what you want, and they immediately scurry to get it for you!

Please don't take our word for this! We want you to prove it to yourself, a hundred times over, before you risk a penny!

Every inside secret described in this mailing piece is given to you in your five Free premiums. And you prove them all, before you risk a single penny.

Why not let us take all the risk for you — today!

Ken and Daria
Ken and Daria

DNGG

FIGURE 8–8 (Continued)

Just a few extra gifts from the Dolans:

INSTANT WAY
to collect stock profits, without the slightest tax penalty.

INSTANT WAY to know that a buyer for your home will pay any price you ask. Page 32.

INSTANT WAY to never have a Social Security check lost in the mail or stolen. Page 19.

INSTANT WAY to get a refund for the full amount you paid for a product, even if it's now on sale. See page 24.

INSTANT WAY to create your own private grace period with the credit card company. No finance charge

for two months. Page 45.

INSTANT WAY to slice $300 a month off your mortgage. Page 5.

INSTANT WAY to walk away from taxes on your high-turnover mutual funds. Details on page 62.

✔ How much in estate taxes will your kids owe on your home? Hundreds of thousands of dollars? Or absolutely nothing? Page 70 makes the difference.

✔ There are at least 20 million unsafe cars on the road today. One phone call makes sure that you won't buy one of them. Page 36.

✔ How to never pay a commission when you buy a mutual fund. See page 46.

✔ When you do NOT need life insurance. When life insurance is sheer waste for you. (Keep your yearly

premiums, and go for a cruise around the world.) Page 17.

✔ Low-commission life insurance. Why buy any other kind? Page 47.

✔ Never file your taxes before August 15. Why bother? Why hurry? Page 16.

✔ Official IRS rules says you don't have to pay the entire sum due on taxes — but don't expect them to tell you! Form 9465 allows you to exercise your constitutional right to be given installment payments. Page 11.

✔ 9 ways to avoid IRS penalties if you owe back taxes. Page 12.

✔ Flight canceled? No problem. Get on a new one in five minutes, even when the other passengers are waiting at the reservation desk for an hour. Page 52.

Prove every one of these secrets, FREE without the slightest bit of risk!

One Phone Call Gets Them All FREE

FREE tax preparation advice. Page 8.

FREE consultations with top lawyers. Page 17.

FREE luxury vacations — for you, and your spouse, and your kids, and your cousins. Page 50.

FREE surgery. FREE Christmas tree. (You just have to know how to ask Uncle Sam for them.) Page 47.

FREE upgrades when you rent a car. One little question gets them for you. FREE credit check. Plus FREE credit information for other members of your family.

FREE credit counselor who gets your creditors to waive interest charges, and cancel late payment charges. Page 31.

FREE credit counselor who gets you up to four years to pay your bills. See page 32.

FREE energy-saving audit from your utility company. Page 37 gets it for you.

FREE maid and FREE use of a car overseas. Page 55.

FREE college scholarship search service! Lists more than 150,000 loans, grants and scholarships. Page 62.

FREE government funding for your kids' college tuition. Doesn't require your paying back one cent. See page 61.

✔ How to to turn $16,000 into $115,000 without the slightest risk. (The same strategy and the same percentage increase works if it's $160, or $1,600.) Page 51.

✔ The single sheet of paper that could add $10,000 to the price you get for your home. Page 21.

✔ How to deduct 100 percent of your gambling losses from your taxes. Little-known IRS form 529 does it for you. Page 42.

✔ How to buy Treasury bills below face value, and without a cent of commission. Page 74.

✔ Take your kids to DisneyWorld for $14 each a day! That includes airfare, first-class motel, and rental

car with unlimited mileage. Page 74.

✔ How to start an IRA with as little as $250. Page 12.

✔ Two-sentence letter that helps you cancel any contract. (We've already written it for you.) So completely legal, they won't even put up a fight. Page 7.

✔ The smart way to loan money to your kids to buy a home. Your money's protected if they get in trouble, and they have a lifetime tax deduction if they don't. Page 84.

✔ Cuts 25% off your property tax bill. Page 19.

✔ How to make your second home as tax-deductible as your first. Page 21.

✔ Income the IRS asks you please NOT to report. Not to pay taxes on. Not to bother them with. Page 16.

Prove every one of these secrets, FREE without the slightest bit of risk!

Big Money Fast!

✔ Billions of dollars in unclaimed money! One phone call tells you how much is yours. Page 5.

✔ Expensive-tasting wines for under $10. An $8 bottle tastes like it costs at least $25. Page 41.

✔ Why pay $100-$250 an hour for a lawyer, when you can get one for exactly $8 to $10 a month? Page 44.

✔ How to get back the money your lawyer has lost for you. You only have to know one phone number. Page 8.

✔ How to make garage sale income tax-free, without cheating! Page 13.

✔ Up to $1,000 for expenses if you get into an accident 100 or more miles from home. Page 64. This way, they pay not only to have your car repaired, plus now you get money to finish your trip by air.

✔ An extra $10,000 to invest, tax-free. Page 31.

✔ Is this the most overlooked $5,000 tax-free deduction? Page 12.

✔ Suddenly your bank fees come down from a $9 monthly service charge to $0. From $15 for check printing to $5. From bounced-check charges of $20 to $7. From stopped-check charges of $25 of $10. Page 6.

✔ How you can earn up to $70,000 a year tax-free. Page 44.

✔ How to start your own travel agency. Just call one number. Start-up costs can be as low as $3,000. And many home travel agencies make $25,000 or more the first year alone. Page 15.

✔ Posh weekend suites for the price of a single hotel room! A single phone call gets one for you. Page 81.

✔ How to cut out the agent's yearly commission from your insurance policy. (The savings could run into the thousands.) Page 16.

✔ 35 little-known tax deductions. Wigs, swimming

pool, air conditioning, Christmas gifts at the office, hair removal, hair transplants, mobile car phone. résumé preparation costs, special diet foods. Page 13.

✔ How to get a 36 percent "rebate" on medical expenses or dependent-care costs. Guaranteed! Page 14.

✔ Save up to 40% on long distance phone bills. Page 12.

✔ Earn 24 percent on your money with zero risk. Guaranteed! Page 9.

✔ How to buy the house of your dreams with no down payment! Not one penny! Page 14.

✔ Cut your car rental costs in half. Page 12.

✔ The fine art of taking a fully tax-deductible vacation. Here's what you can deduct: airfare, car mileage, car rental, meals and even passport fees. Page 14.

✔ How to transform your moving expenses into tax deductions. Page 14.

Prove every one of these secrets, FREE without the slightest bit of risk!

(See other side) ▶

FIGURE 8–9   A Package That Appeals to "Doers"

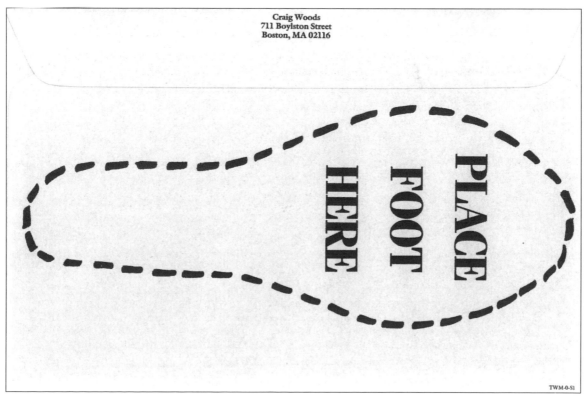

FIGURE 8–9 (Continued)

Congratulations! You've just taken your first step toward viewing life a whole new way—at walking eye level. Where awareness is heightened. Senses are piqued. And body and soul are renewed, refreshed, and reborn.

Introducing The Walking Magazine. Your opportunity to try a free issue without obligation is enclosed.

CHARTER INVITATION

Dear Friend:

Centuries ago, a very astute young Chinese man proclaimed, "A journey of a thousand miles starts with a single step."

And you've just taken yours! Now things will just get better and more exciting from here. Because this journey can lead you to better health, a better attitude, a brighter outlook, that exuberant feeling of accomplishment.

Walking makes it happen. Walking for exercise. Walking for relaxation. Walking for discovery. Walking for companionship. Walking for inspiration.

Fact of the matter is, once you start walking, you never know where it might lead!

> And that's the why and wherefore of THE WALKING MAGAZINE.
> America's one and only magazine designed exclusively for
> walkers and people who want to start. (100 million
> people across the country already have!) If you haven't
> started yet, you should. If you have, we can help you
> get even more out of it!

Now I realize your immediate question is, "Gee, how hard can it be? I've been doing it since I was 10 months old." Of course you have. But it's important to understand that there's a big difference between walking to get from one room to the other, and walking to get from feeling "down" to feeling "up." And that's what THE WALKING MAGAZINE is all about.

> Getting up. Getting out. Getting going. To feel better.
> Look better. See new things. Meet new people. Share
> new experiences. Be alone if you like. Enjoy yourself.

Whether you've been walking for years or you're just taking your first invigorating steps, you'll discover a wealth of fascinating new ideas and exciting possibilities in every issue of THE WALKING MAGAZINE.

You'll see how walking strengthens the heart and lungs. Helps you control or even lose weight. Fights osteoporosis. Increases stamina, giving you more energy. Helps you sleep better. Strengthens and loosens joints, ligaments, and tendons. Tones and strengthens muscles. Firms the upper body, calves, buttocks, hips, abdomen, and thighs.

over please...

FIGURE 8–9   (Continued)

<u>Relieves stress</u>. Improves your mood and mental outlook. Helps lower blood pressure and may help lower cholesterol levels in your blood. And gives you a feeling of self-reliance, of doing something for yourself.

<u>Sound too good to be true</u>? It's medical fact. Is it any wonder that so many people are putting away their running shoes and turning on to walking? Walking is practically injury-free exercise. And you can do it at practically any age. (However a good physical examination by a doctor is recommended before you begin <u>any</u> exercise program.)

<u>Step-by-step instructions</u>? Well, yes, to a point. You'll learn the right and wrong way to walk to maximum benefit. You'll find out how long you should walk, how often, and at what pace. You'll find suggestions on where to walk. How to walk there. And what you're likely to see along the way.

> <u>City walks. Mountain walks. Country walks. Mall walks.
> Neighborhood walks. Seaside walks. Lake walks. Not just
> in this country. But around the world. England. France.
> Sweden. Germany. Italy. Japan. China. You'll walk
> the globe with THE WALKING MAGAZINE.</u>

<u>You'll learn what to wear</u>. What to take. What to do when you get there. A picnic perhaps? We'll suggest a few "walking recipes." A beautiful sunset? We'll point you in the right direction. A soft, isolated spot on a sandy beach? We'll show you the "X" that marks the spot. It's all in THE WALKING MAGAZINE.

Take the next step

<u>Try a free issue</u>. Take a good look at THE WALKING MAGAZINE with a free issue. If you like what you see, you can continue your subscription, receive 5 more issues (a total of 6) at the low Charter Subscriber rate of just $9.95, a savings of 44% off the cover price.

<u>No obligation</u>. If, on the other hand, THE WALKING MAGAZINE isn't all I've said it is, simply return the invoice marked "cancel." You'll owe nothing, have spent nothing, and be under no further obligation whatsoever. But the free issue is yours to keep.

<u>Guarantee</u>. Once you do decide to subscribe, your satisfaction continues to be guaranteed, or we'll refund your money on all the issues you've yet to receive.

<u>Act now</u>. Return the reply portion of the order card in the postage-paid envelope provided today. But SEND NO MONEY. Try your FREE ISSUE first. Then decide...

<u>Decide if THE WALKING MAGAZINE</u> isn't just what you've been looking for to help you feel better, look better, and live a happier, more satisfying life. I think it is, and I hope you'll agree.

Sincerely,

Craig Woods

Craig Woods
Editor

CW:ks

P.S. <u>Back to the Chinese proverb that opened this letter</u> -- a reminder that you've already taken your <u>first</u> step. Take the next one <u>now</u>. Mail the order card today and receive your FREE TRIAL ISSUE (with no obligation to purchase or subscribe). The next thousand miles are going to be fantastic! Act now!

TWM

FIGURE 8–9   (Continued)

Put some spring in your step...

and a smile on your face. Get more out of life and more out of living...

FIGURE 8–9 (Continued)

Introducing # THE WALKING MAGAZINE

The new magazine for people like you who go their own way—on foot.

Now there's a magazine for the 100 million people across the country who've discovered the low-risk, high-gain benefits of walking. Whether you've already started or you're about to take your first step, The Walking Magazine can help. Here's what you'll find in each exciting issue:

HEALTH Learn how walking helps your heart and lungs. How it increases energy. Tones and firms muscles. Relieves stress. Improves sleep. Lowers blood pressure. Fights osteoporosis. Brightens your mood and mental outlook. It's all in The Walking Magazine.

PEOPLE Meet other walkers from all walks of life. Actors, actresses, athletes, politicians, businessmen and women, newscasters, writers, artists, doctors, lawyers, teachers, stockbrokers, and farmers. Share their experiences. Step in their shoes. Only in The Walking Magazine.

PLACES Discover great walks wherever they may be. From malls to mountains. City streets to country paths. Join us on walks through England's Lake District. Nepal's Everest Grand Circle Expedition. Italy's Chianti region. You'll find it in The Walking Magazine.

POSSIBILITIES See how walking leads to just about anything. Picnics in the mountains. Fishing in a cold stream. Sunning on a secluded beach. Talking to a good friend. Seeing your neighborhood in a whole new light. Learning more about yourself. It starts with The Walking Magazine.

PRODUCTS Keep up with the lastest offerings for walkers like you. Jackets. Sweaters. Shoes. Boots. Walking sticks. Pedometers. Pulse monitors. Hats. Shoulder bags. Backpacks. Socks. Sunscreens. Water jugs. Ointments. And more. All in The Walking Magazine.

ALTERNATIVES Discover new ways to do familiar things. How to plan a family vacation around walking sights. How to organize your shopping routes into walking sights. How to sightsee on foot instead of by car. How to create while you walk. It's in The Walking Magazine.

GUARANTEE As a Charter Subscriber to The Walking Magazine, you'll be paying the low Charter Rate. And your satisfaction is guaranteed. If the magazine ever fails to inform, delight, and inspire, you may cancel for a refund on all issues you've yet to receive. No questions asked. So act now. And welcome to The Walking Magazine.

MAIL TODAY FOR CHARTER PRIVILEGES!

FIGURE 8–9   (Continued)

I'll foot the bill…

Lift Note/Guarantee

NEXT STEP:
- SEND NO MONEY. Just return the order card. We'll send you a free issue to inspect. If you like it, pay our invoice that saves you 44% off the cover price.
- NO OBLICGATION. If you don't like what you see, return the invoice marked "cancel", owe nothing, and keep the free issue. No further obligation. No commitment.
- GUARANTEE. Once you decide to subscribe, your satisfacrtion continues to be guaranteed, or we'll refund your money on all the issues you've yet to receive. No questions asked.

Return portion at right for a free trial issue!

FREE

Send for a Free Trial Issue now!

CHARTER INVITATION
FREE   TRIAL   ISSUE

Please send me a free issue to look over. If I like it I'll pay your invoice for $9.95 for 5 more issues (total of 6), a savings of 44% off the cover price—the low Charter Subscriber rate. If I decide the magazine is not for me, I'll return the invoice marked "cancel", owe nothing, spend nothing, and keep the free issue. SEND NO MONEY!

Cover price $2.95.
Detach and mail today in the postage-paid envelope provided.
THE WALKING MAGAZINE, P.O. Box 56547, Boulder, CO 80321 TWM-CS2

Order Form

Notice how the cover does the job of the outer envelope, while acting as a mini-magazine, complete with cover lines and price. For the right market, the promise is irresistible and sure to get prospects inside. (It's also credible thanks to the photos of the "real" middle-aged women on the cover.)

The first spread carries the letter from the editor in a position where it won't be missed. It rolls off the benefits of the new Rodale book *Age Erasers for Women*. A wrap-around bind-in reply card dramatizes the offer, and the "table of contents" motivates you to move on through. (A clever combination of magazine and direct mail techniques.)

The second spread offers credibility (How did this wondrous book come about?) and medical authority, setting the tone with the large photo.

It is followed by a continual selling dialogue in the left-hand column, reinforced by real people and their testimonials on the right. Knowing the lure of secrets, the writer has broken the story into a series of spreads on "Youth Secrets," "Anti-Aging Secrets," "Body-Mind Secrets," "Beauty Secrets," and "Doctor's Secret Cures."

And what marvelous illustrations on every spread—real people, giving real testimonials that include their ages. (It's easy to see they look younger than their years.) These pictures and testimonials are some of the most impressive aspects of this magalog.

The call to action on the final spread offers a reply card, a 100% guarantee and a referral form to pass along to "your best friend." Spend some time with these spreads before you move on.

It's worth it.

Finished your wine yet? Just in time—because that's the show for now. No more talk about letter writing and direct mail in the chapters that follow.

But please don't forget these great examples by Hank Burnett, Martin Conroy, Bill Jayme, Frank Johnson, Jim Punkre, Ken Scheck, Ken Schneider, and Gene Schwartz—and the other examples that preceded them in Chapter 6 (like those from well-known pros Emily Soell, Linda Wells, and Bob Matheo). Go back to them all when you need inspiration or challenge. Reread them. Enjoy them. Understand what makes them good.

And if, by chance, you say to yourself "Anyone can write like this . . ." then take Frank Johnson's sandhill crane letter for The Nature Conservancy and rewrite it. A humbling exercise, I guarantee you.

There is one thing all these fine writers and others like them share. We talked about it briefly in Chapter 7 when I brought up the intrinsic rewards of writing and all the hard work that goes into it. Good writers actually *enjoy* writing; they love words and word crafting, despite the hard work.

Furthermore, when it comes to polishing and improving, most professional writers quite literally never finish. They can't help

FIGURE 8–10 An Irresistible Magalog

FIGURE 8–10 (Continued)

FIGURE 8–10 (Continued)

1,001 Astonishing Antidotes to Aging!

Medical Experts Tell How to turn back your Aging clock! Announcing . . .

by Mark Bricklin and Pat Fisher

Scientists have finally cracked the mystery of the aging process!

In a major new book, medical experts reveal hundreds of new ways to ERASE many of the most bothersome symptoms of the aging process.

That includes: Age spots. Arthritis. Back trouble. Cellulite. Double chin. Fading eyesight. Fuzzy thinking. Fatigue. Hearing loss. Poor memory. Osteoporosis. Overweight. Thinning hair. Plus many of the other signs of aging.

In almost every instance, doctors and researchers have discovered some uncanny ways to turn back these symptoms of age — and even slow down your body's biological clock so you age SLOWER!

There are literally HUNDREDS of these fabulous "age erasers." Some are as simple as eating a certain food . . . applying a new cream or lotion . . . taking a particular supplement . . . or working under a doctor's care.

Now, the Editors of PREVENTION®, America's leading health magazine, have collected the BEST of these new age-reversing techniques in a fascinating and practical volume that shows you how to **put them to use in your life!**

This new 676-page book promises to be a *smash bestseller*. And this is your chance to see it BEFORE anyone else!

Simply turn this page to learn more about these astonishing AGE ERASERS. Plus how you can take a FREE Sneak-Preview copy of this new book ABSOLUTELY FREE for up to 21 days — with NO risk, NO cost, and NO obligation to buy anything!

(continued on page 6 . . .)

AGE ERASERS for Women

Actions You Can Take Right Now to Look Younger and Feel Great

FREE "SNEAK PREVIEW"

FIGURE 8–10 (Continued)

(continued from page 4)

YOURS FREE FOR 21 DAYS!

Announcing:
1,001 Amazing Secrets For Staying Younger, Longer!

Imagine growing old WITHOUT wrinkles, cataracts, osteoporosis or memory loss. Imagine being able to PREVENT cancer and heart disease indefinitely. Imagine being able to REMAIN active, enthusiastic and young at heart well into your 70s, 80s — even 90s!

And imagine looking years YOUNGER. Picture yourself with a slender figure. With shining, thick hair. With white, even teeth. With a smooth, unlined face. It's all possible. From your clear and sparkling eyes to the tips of your well-groomed toes!

You can look younger, healthier and more attractive. Now, a fascinating book from the PREVENTION® editors entitled AGE ERASERS FOR WOMEN, brings you exciting news of safe and practical ways you can SLOW DOWN the aging process in the human body!

This fabulous volume is filled with HUNDREDS of do-it-yourself techniques you can use RIGHT AWAY. To look younger. Feel livelier. And live longer.

Page after page *actually tells you how* to look and feel younger by putting the brakes on this process of aging. It also brings you medically documented age erasers that can increase your life span and even reverse the damage that bad habits have had on your health.

Erase The Effects Of A Lifetime Of Bad Habits!

No one can turn back the clock. But scientists *have* discovered how to DEFY time and its ravaging effects. What is wrinkled and baggy today can be smooth and firm tomorrow. What's tired and sore can be energized and restored. What is sick can be healed. What is wearing out can be rejuvenated.

Modern medical science has discovered HUNDREDS of astounding ways to ERASE the signs of aging due to poor nutrition . . . a polluted environment . . . even a lifetime of bad habits! Studies at the world's leading medical centers confirm that these symptoms, plus others, can be eased, delayed or reversed. Even those resulting from inherited problems.

This is great news — because it means that for the first time in human history, YOUR GENERATION will be able to live longer . . . look younger . . . stay healthier . . . and remain more mentally fit and productive than any other generation that has ever lived before!

Just think of it: These recent scientific discoveries give you the unprecedented power to turn back your body's aging clock. With less risk of heart attack, cancer, or stroke. More energy and enthusiasm. A more active sex life. A quicker, more productive mind. Better health. Long-term physical fitness and flexibility. And fewer worries about the age-associated ailments that make growing older so unappealing.

(continued on page 8 . . .)

Which Of These TELLTALE AGING SIGNS Would You Like To Erase Right Away?

WEIGHT GAIN: Doctor's trick lets you turn up your "metabolic furnace" and lose weight — even in your sleep! PAGE 256.

CELLULITE: "The best way to reduce cellulite on your body." Described on PAGE 98.

DOUBLE CHIN: Discover the three secret factors that cause double chins. And today's most effective way to get rid of the problem! On PAGE 134.

QUICKNESS: Experts reveal secrets to keeping your reflexes fast and your mind sharp as a tack. PAGE 295.

GREY HAIR: New York hair stylist reveals secrets to hiding gray hair without restoring to hair dyes. See PAGE 181.

OSTEOPOROSIS: How to REVERSE the process of osteoporosis in the female body. See PAGE 271 right away!

MEMORY LOSS: Can't remember ("In all likelihood, you're NOT losing your memory," says Dr. Herman.) Follow his memory-restoring directions, on PAGE 240.

OVERWEIGHT: Easy, NATURAL way to turn up your body's metabolism to a higher rate. (This way you'll burn EXTRA calories — even while you are sleeping or at rest!) See PAGE 256.

SEXUAL PROBLEMS: These secret exercises can help women achieve stronger, easier orgasms. Dr. Cynthia Watson guides you. On PAGE 309.

SKIN: There's a whole new layer of smoother, younger skin beneath those aging lines and splotches. Want to uncover it? Turn to PAGE 607.

WRINKLES: This lotion will gradually peel off the top layers of dead skin. " . . . will make crows' feet and fine wrinkles less visible," says Dr. Elton. PAGE 387.

About the authors:

Mark Bricklin is the Executive Editor of PREVENTION® magazine, America's leading health publication.

For over 44 years PREVENTION has built a reputation on telling readers what doctors, government, and the medical establishment DON'T.

For instance, PREVENTION warned the public of the dangers of chemical additives and preservatives in our food way back in 1957, long before it was a national issue. We alerted our readers to the health hazards of DDT in 1969 a full 10 years BEFORE the government ban. We linked heart disease and cancer to unhealthful foods in the American diet LONG BEFORE doctors saw the connection. And our readers were among the first to discover the cholesterol-lowering effects of fiber foods like oat bran.

Pat Fisher is director of the Rodale Center for Women's Health. Started in early 1993 to focus and direct women's health initiative, the Center sponsors writers and editors who specialize in women's health issues and a Editorial Advisory Panel of the country's top female doctors and experts. The mission of the Rodale Center for Women's Health is to supply women with information to help them take control of their physical, mental and emotional health needs. One of the center's first completed projects is the WOMEN'S HEALTH COMPANION, a complete guide that includes the WOMEN'S ENCYCLOPEDIA OF HEALTH & EMOTIONAL HEALING.

Now, the Center is about to publish one of the most remarkable books in our entire history: AGE ERASERS FOR WOMEN. This is your opportunity to take a FREE 21-day "Sneak Preview" of this amazing 676-page volume of PROVEN age-reversal techniques and ideas. Don't miss it! Mail back the Certificate on PAGE 19 to take a full look.

CAROLE HANS, age 61:
"Old age just isn't *natural.* Most of it is brought on by the thing we do to ourselves that ACCELERATE the aging process. But there is so much we can do to *slow it down.* This book really shows you how!"

FIGURE 8–10 (Continued)

FIGURE 8–10 (Continued)

YOURS FREE FOR 21 DAYS!

(continued from page 8)

ANTI-AGING SECRETS!

An Exciting New Discovery About Aging:

Scientific detectives have made an exciting new discovery about what causes aging in the human body!

They've pinned the crime on a class of rogue molecules roaming throughout the human body and causing destruction and deterioration wherever they go. Scientists call these molecules "free radicals." And their presence actually seems to SPEED UP the aging process by harming cells and contributing to the formation of cancer, heart disease, and other forms of physical breakdown.

These rogue molecules occur elsewhere in nature: They are what causes iron to rust. Why a cut apple turns brown. Why unrefrigerated butter goes rancid. And why untreated rubber becomes hard. In each instance, free radical reactions are responsible. What causes these unsavory reactions? The one-word answer is "oxidation."

Bandits In Your Bloodstream That Steal Your Youth!

Just as this oxidation process can transform a healthy piece of steel into rust, it also can erode healthy molecules in your body, thus encouraging disease.

But there is now good news! Researchers have discovered certain vitamins which seem to BLOCK the damage done by these age bandits. These anti-aging nutrients, called "antioxidants," seem to help DEACTIVATE free radicals and prevent them from attacking your cells.

In your body, these antioxidants act similarly to the way we protect industrial agents from deterioration. Our cars are rustproofed. Paper is treated to keep from yellowing. Special antioxidant compounds on leather and rubber products prevent them from deteriorating. Now, researchers have discovered a class of vitamins and nutrients to help keep the free radicals in line from harming human cells.

"Rust-Proof" Your Body With The New Anti-Aging Vitamins:

To slow down the aging process in the human body we need something like these rustproofing agents for our cells. And it looks like scientists have discovered some effective ones! Increasing scientific evidence shows that certain nutrients, such as beta carotene and vitamins C & E, help protect cells against free radical damage and the aging process.

Recent studies have shown how high intakes of antioxidant vitamins may also help reduce the risk of heart disease, breast and cervical cancers! Be sure to read all about the good news, starting on PAGE 420 of AGE ERASERS FOR WOMEN.

(continued on page 12 . . .)

•10•

Brighten Your Memory!

New research shows how these two trace minerals (zinc and boron) can REVIVE your memory. Dr. Penland explains. PAGE 244.

Chase The Blues!

Dr. Gersten's amazing NATURAL cure for depression. *"It cranks up your brain activity and can reverse the effects of even a MAJOR depression."* Described, on PAGE 118.

Halt Joint Pain!

Patients reported DRAMATIC improvements in their arthritis within one month after beginning the easy diet described on PAGE 40.

Lose More!

Hidden emotions and psychological triggers that FOOL you into believing you are hungry. Dr. Foreyt tells how to disarm these urges to eat. On PAGE 280.

Prevent Osteoporosis!

This anti-osteoporosis exercise actually stimulates your cells to BUILD MORE BONE — particularly in your back and hips where women most need it. Dr. Allen guides you. On PAGE 273.

PLUS:

•**Vitamins that protect your eyes** against cataracts. From a Harvard study. See PAGE 379.

•**Anti-aging foods** that contain a substance that *"literally scours your bloodstream."* PAGE 478.

•**Female mid-life crisis!** Dr. Goldstein tells how to come through it feeling more alive and YOUNGER. See PAGE 261.

•**"Secret way snoring (your own or your mate's) ages you!** How to halt it! On PAGE 325.

•**Even this much television viewing** (see PAGE 344) dulls and ages your mind! From medical evidence. Don't miss this.

•**Why Type A women had a 50% HIGHER risk of heart attack!** From a Harvard Medical School study. How to change. See PAGE 353.

•**Age-erasing benefits of this aerobic exercise!** (It DOUBLES your protection against coronary heart disease.) The full story, on PAGE 401.

OVER 1,001 SECRETS IN ALL! YOURS ABSOLUTELY FREE FOR 21 DAYS!

SUZANNE CARNES AT 57:
"A big part of looking young is FEELING young. And that comes from thinking younger. Taking risks. Accepting new challenges. Breaking old habits and patterns. I do feel EXCITED about my life these days. And I know I'm headline for it!"

•11•

FIGURE 8–10 (Continued)

YOURS FREE FOR 21 DAYS!
(continued from page 10)

BODY-MIND SECRETS!

The Secret Connection Between Your Youth And Your Mind!

There is a lot of scientific truth for the old expression, "You're as young as you think and feel."

Recent scientific research has linked certain attitudes, emotions, and thoughts to health problems like heart disease, arthritis, cancer, and a weak immune system. They also have found that mental states like worry, depression, resentment, and low self-esteem can make you look and act years older than your chronological age.

Now, in AGE ERASERS FOR WOMEN, you'll read about the uncanny connection between your body and mind. And how you can change how you look and feel, simply by changing your mind!

"Studies show how HIGH self-confidence and self-esteem make you look, feel and carry yourself like a much younger woman. You beam with inner strength and positive energy." Page 457.

AGE ERASERS FOR WOMEN brings you page after page of startling new revelations that give you unprecedented power to look, feel, and actually BE younger. For instance, you'll see ...

• **Secret way resentment AGES you.** *"It causes depression and anxiety ... wrinkles, heart disease, depression and other physical problems,"* says Dr. Jampolsky. The good news is, you can REVERSE the damage done. See how, on PAGE 487.

• **These healthy beliefs** (described on PAGE 585) actually boost your emotional health — and decrease your risk of heart disease, cancer and depression, according to medical researchers. Don't miss this!

• **These positive affirmations** (examples, on PAGE 410) can COUNTERACT your negative inner critic. *"You can feel inner tension disappear immediately,"* reports Dr. Jeffers.

And that's just the beginning! You'll find HUNDREDS of other exciting new body-mind discoveries just like these.

Don't miss the opportunity to take a FREE 21-day "Sneak Preview" of AGE ERASERS FOR WOMEN. Remember: there's no obligation to buy the book. And think of the wealth of wonderful anti-aging information you'll gain just by looking!

(continued on page 14 ...)

Instant Relaxation!
Press these secret acupressure points at the base of the skull to TRIGGER total relaxation. How to do it? Simply put two tennis balls in a sock ... and follow Dr. DeIulio's directions, on PAGE 564.

Sleep Yourself Younger!
These sleep habits actually REVERSE these signs of aging. See why doctors call SLEEP "the secret youth enhancer." See on PAGE 608.

Helping Is Good Medicine!
Medical researchers PROVE that helping other people helps YOU live longer! Dr. Andrews describes the best ways, on PAGE 416.

OVER 1,001 SECRETS IN ALL! YOURS ABSOLUTELY FREE FOR 21 DAYS!

The Healing Power of Sex!
Medical researchers reveal how to use SEX to keep yourself and your partner feeling younger. Instructions, on PAGE 596.

Pet Lovers Live Longer!
How a pet keeps you younger (and healthier). One study showed that pet owners had lower blood pressure and cholesterol — *even if they smoked or ate a high-fat diet!* See PAGE 494.

PLUS:

• **People with these religious beliefs** had the LOWEST rates of cancer! See PAGE 588.

• **How to make yourself more likable.** Dr. Wassmer reveals his tips to make yourself instantly liked when you meet strangers, WITHOUT being phony. See PAGE 493.

• **This exercise can IMPROVE a woman's sex drive** and performance! Dr. Crenshaw tells how. On PAGE 597.

• **Secret warning signs of low self-esteem.** Take the quick quiz, on PAGE 461.

• **Dr. Tufto tells how to NEUTRALIZE** certain common self-defeating thought patterns that can "shatter" your self-confidence. See PAGE 458.

WINNIE ...DFIELD, age 72:
Modern science is amazing! I had no idea doctors and researchers could exercise so much CONTROL over the aging process until I read AGE ERASERS FOR WOMEN. What I learned is truly astounding.

•12• •13•

FIGURE 8–10 (Continued)

BEAUTY SECRETS!

Uncanny Water Cure!

Doctors reveal how to use ordinary water to maintain YOUTHFUL skin and firm muscle tone. See PAGE 483.

Youthful Eyes!

Do your eyes droop at the corners, making you look sad and old? Fix this flaw by applying eye shadow at a 45-degree angle up toward the brow at the outside corner of the eye. Your eyes will look YOUNGER! Follow directions on PAGE 553.

How To Hide A Double Chin!

This makeup secret makes a double-chin much LESS noticeable. Use blush and foundation in the clever way described on PAGE 135.

Incredible Bean Facial!

Astounding new home facial treatment! If you have a package of dry red beans, a food processor and a few simple ingredients, you can easily treat yourself to a luxurious home facial. Here's how on PAGE 605.

More Youthful Posture!

These four yoga positions keep your body younger and more limber. Corrects poor posture, too! See PAGES 640-642 for complete instructions.

New Facelift Technique!

New surgical techniques offer gratifyingly, NATURAL, results. "In the past, they'd tighten only the skin, which gave that 'mask' look," says Dr. Maturasso. "Now we hardly pull the skin, and just work underneath, removing fat, and tightening the layers of muscle." Complete description, on PAGE 470.

OVER 1,000 SECRETS IN ALL! YOURS ABSOLUTELY FREE FOR 21 DAYS!

LORI WRENN, age 55: "They say beauty is as beauty does,' and they're right. There is so much that can be done to make a woman look younger and more attractive. It's absolutely ASTONISHING what's possible today. Take a look at AGE ERASERS FOR WOMEN and see yourself!"

·15·

·14·

YOURS FREE FOR 21 DAYS!

(continued from page 12)

A New Generation of Beauty Secrets!

Oh, yes! The science of beauty has been keeping pace with all these new medical discoveries about turning back the aging process.

Now, in AGE ERASERS FOR WOMEN, you'll read about the latest developments in skin care . . . hair care . . . make-up . . . cosmetology . . . weight loss . . . and cosmetic surgery. Many of these techniques are new techniques you probably have not heard about — but they are ready NOW for your use and benefit. For example . . .

* **Secret trick with eye shadow** corrects the features you DON'T LIKE about your eyes. See PAGE 552.

* **Make your skin younger** with this amazing wonder product! It can improve the yellowed appearance of the skin and make it more pink. (But its greatest improvement is on wrinkles and age spots!) See PAGE 607.

* **Camouflage cellulite on legs** with this tanning cream. Incredible! PAGE 99.

* **Fiber foods** that make weight loss a lot easier. (They fill you up without fat or extra calories!) See PAGES 480-481.

* **Restore youthful breasts** WITHOUT implants! Doctor describes how he tightens muscle and removes excess skin in this new procedure. Read PAGE 439.

* **New cosmetic surgery technique** gets RID of deep wrinkles, a punchy jawline, a sagging neck, or baggy eyelids. PAGE 469.

* **Are you a good candidate** for cosmetic surgery? Here's how to tell, on PAGE 468.

Plus HUNDREDS of Others — See Them All — ABSOLUTELY FREE!

You MUST see these fabulous beauty secrets and age-erasing techniques. Each holds the power to BANISH flaws in your beauty and ELIMINATE many of the telltale signs of aging. Best of all, you can begin using them RIGHT AWAY — to help you feel better about your appearance.

To see all 1,001 of these amazing youth-restoring secrets, simply mail back the "Sneak Preview" certificate (on PAGE 19) right away. We'll send you a copy of AGE ERASERS FOR WOMEN as soon as it rolls off the press for a FREE 21-day examination. But there is absolutely **no obligation to buy!**

Don't miss this opportunity to be among the first to see this smash best-seller BEFORE it hits the bookstores. Remember: there's no risk, no cost, no hidden obligations. Here's all you have to do to get your FREE "Sneak-Preview" copy . . .

(continued on page 16 . . .)

FIGURE 8–10 (Continued)

YOURS FREE FOR 21 DAYS!

(continued from page 14)

Doctor's Secret Health Cures For Women! For Example . . .

Don't Miss This Opportunity For A FREE 21-Day "Sneak Preview!"

Now, before your local bookstore has a chance to announce that it has "sold out" of AGE ERASERS FOR WOMEN, we invite you to "Sneak Preview" this new book as soon as it comes off the press. The enclosed reply card (see PAGE 19) will deliver a brand-new copy to your door — *without cost* — for a FREE examination of all 1,001 of these amazing techniques.

I urge you to mail it now, before we are sold out, too. So you can begin benefiting from these astounding age-proofing techniques as soon as possible.

There is absolutely no charge for this free trial.

And if you do not agree that this is the most helpful, hopeful book you've ever seen, we are giving you the *return postage* (label on PAGE 19), so you may send your copy of AGE ERASERS FOR WOMEN back at the end of the trial period at our expense!

To be among the first readers anywhere to preview AGE ERASERS FOR WOMEN, just mail back the enclosed Acceptance Card.

What you will see is sure to raise your eyebrows, your hopes, and — if heeded — your life expectancy, too.

Two Free Bonus Gifts Just For Looking!

If you respond soon, you'll also receive two valuable Bonus Gifts which are yours to keep with our compliments. Keep them even if you return your copy of AGE ERASERS FOR WOMEN.

Gift #1 is a free copy of our new guide to *Home Remedies Just for Women*. This marvelous home handbook contains a wealth of effective remedies and self-treatments for health complaints that nag women.

Now — BEFORE you turn to your doctor or druggist — you can turn here for safe, proven relief for many female health problems.

This guide is all-new and will NOT be available in any bookstore. But we'll send you a copy ABSOLUTELY FREE when you take a no-risk "Sneak Preview" of AGE ERASERS FOR WOMEN.

(continued on page 18 . . .)

Home Remedies *Just for* Women

Doctor Proven

Tips & Tech

Everyday He

FREE BONUS GIFT!

- **These herbal teas** — available at most health food stores — are BEST for relieving breast tenderness in woman. See PAGE 3.
- **Press these acupressure points** to STOP endometriosis pain. To locate the spots, see PAGE 4.
- **Best thing to take once you get a herpes outbreak.** Follow Dr. Stanberry's advice. On PAGE 5.
- **Yes, it is possible to pass the herpes virus** to other parts of your body with your fingers! Take these important precautions, on PAGE 5.
- **Secret trick with vitamin E** EASES hot flashes. See PAGE 6.
- **BEST pain reliever** for menstrual cramps. Listed on PAGE 6.
- **How to use calcium** to STOP leg cramps and pain. Dr. Susan Lark tells how. On PAGE 7.
- **How sugar can CAUSE chronic yeast infections!** What you MUST do. On PAGE 10.

- **How to use yogurt** as the natural HEALER of yeast infections. (Just don't make the common mistake, described on PAGE 8.)
- **Secret way to COOL heartburn** with ordinary water. Works as well as antacids! Directions, on PAGE 15.
- **What to do when you feel faint.** PAGE 16 tells how to keep from losing consciousness.
- **Panic attacks?** Dr. Levine tells how to HALT the most distressing symptoms. On PAGE 23.
- **Acne.** "The best over-the-counter medications you can use," says Dr. Bondi. On PAGE 36.
- **Secret trick for pimples!** Use an ice cube on blemishes as directed after washing makes them less noticeable. Dr. Goodman guides you. On PAGE 36.
- **Secret nutrient (called biotin)** THICKENS nails to help prevent splitting and cracking. See PAGE 37.
- **Eyestrain.** "Take a towel and soak it in brewed eyebright tea." Follow advice on PAGE 16.

- **Uncanny treatment for oily skin.** Steam your face using some Swiss Kriss herbal laxative (sold in many health food stores). Dr. Burke swears by it. PAGE 40.
- **Secret bean diet helps you lose MORE weight** — and you'll lose it FASTER. Dr. Simonson tells why. PAGE 42.
- **Dr. Blackburn's water secret** stops "food cravings" cold. See PAGE 42.
- **How to fade or completely ELIMINATE stretch marks!** Don't miss PAGE 43.

Special Section On Healthy Herbs For Women! Including:

- **This herbal tea** works best on menstrual cramps. See PAGE 45.
- **This herb** (in shampoos and rinses) keeps blond hair at its golden best. PAGE 46.
- **Queasy stomach?** Reach for this herb. (It prevents motion sickness and other forms of nausea, too!) Listen to Dr. Mowrey, on PAGE 47.
- **Best herbal tea to calm a cough.** See PAGE 47.
- **"Treat vaginal yeast infection with this herb,"** says Dr. Mowrey. Directions, on PAGE 48.
- **How to STOP a backache:** *"Lie on a hard surface and position the tennis ball under you so that it is pressing against a tender spot. Roll onto the ball gradually, utilizing your body weight until the pain and tenderness subside." Complete directions, on PAGE 30.*

•16•   •17•

FIGURE 8–10 (Continued)

themselves. Right up to the last second of the final deadline they'll be working away, adding finishing touches. This is not because the copy's late or incomplete, but simply because the writer, never quite satisfied, feels compelled to make just one more tiny change or alteration—much like the great chef finishing a *piece de resistance*, the composer after the final chord is written, the painter as the canvas is finished.

Poor or mediocre writers will not understand this; they will be easily satisfied with far less, handing in their work while the professional writer continues to struggle, rework, and rewrite.

The Joy Factor

A while back when I had my own agency, my copy supervisor was reporting to me on the progress of a junior writer. The supervisor was a very sensitive writer with great talent, and she was troubled by the junior writer's attitude. She said, "He takes no joy in his writing. He never feels compelled to polish or rework for the sake of his craft. For him, it's just pure punishment."

I've always remembered her comment because for me this Joy Factor so clearly distinguishes between the true creative professional and the hack. Those who work quickly and resist reworking their copy and perfecting their art are almost always lacking in the Joy Factor. They'll never be good direct response advertising creators. They can't take the hard work, because writing gives them no satisfaction, no pleasure.

So look for the Joy Factor in yourself, and in those creative people who work for you and with you. Without the Joy Factor, fame, recognition, and wealth are unattainable. Where the Joy Factor exists, you have a writer! And that in itself is a big reward.

Note

1. *The Letters of Henry James, Vol. IV, 1895–1916*, Leon Edel, ed. (Cambridge, MA.: The Belknap Press of Harvard University Press, 1985).

CHAPTER NINE

HOW TO CREATE WINNING PRINT ADS

Up to now we've given short shrift to all forms of direct response advertising except direct mail, because direct mail is the learning ground for *all* direct response (and interactive, as you'll see in the next chapter). Now it's time for you to move on to print. If you haven't been there before, you'll want a little briefing on some of its technicalities and terms.

Let's start with a few basic questions: First, "Why print?" At the rate we're moving into an electronic interactive future you may well wonder about the future of print. Trust me, it will survive—for a good long while. And even if you're *never* called on to "do" print, it's such a logical extension of direct mail (as you'll see) that it would be a shame to not segue into it here.

How is print advertising used in direct marketing? In business-to-business direct response print is used primarily to generate inquiries (for more information or a sales call) and to acquire prospect names. In consumer direct response it's used 1) to generate inquiries on large ticket products and services, 2) to make a sale, to get a "member" or subscriber, 3) to acquire names of qualified prospects (catalog requests), and 4) to test a new product or service.

Print is used in much the same way as direct mail, except for the name gathering. Direct mail is too costly for this activity. (Print is often positioned as "cheaper than direct mail with better quality prospects than broadcast." Since broadcast prospects are at the bottom of the quality scale, you can see where print takes you.)

"How about all those ads for more information with an 800 number at the bottom or ads with redeemable coupons?" Frankly, *any* print ad that asks for a response (be it inquiry or order) can be called "response advertising." It only becomes *direct response* or *direct marketing* when the prospect or customer name and address are captured by the company computer for database tracking, evaluation, and future cultivation.

"What constitutes a print ad?" As if you didn't know. But can you name three or four *different types* of direct response print ads? Try this.

1. Large space (one page—or a spread even—in a magazine) with coupon
2. Small space (half or third of a magazine page, one column or less) with coupon
3. One page or a spread with bind-in reply card (for easy response)
4. One-page insert (a preprinted page bound into a publication)
5. Two or three or four-page magazine bind-ins with perforated reply card (or an entire catalog bound into the magazine!)
6. Even a full spread with coupon and 800 toll-free option with tipped-on plastic card!
7. Advertising supplement, preprinted newspaper insert, or free-standing insert
8. Newspaper run of press (ROP). This print ad goes anywhere the paper puts it, usually up front in the black and white news pages

There are some general rules of thumb for direct response print ads:

- The best quality response usually comes from the good old-fashioned coupon ad, because it takes some effort ("just fill out below," clip, then address an envelope, get a stamp, etc.).
- A bind-in or perforated reply card offers slightly less qualified respondents (no stamp, no cut out, no envelope to address).
- An 800 number respondent is also *less* qualified than the coupon clipper (it's easier still to call).
- The use of a separate bind-in card in a magazine should more than double response. (It generally doubles cost, too.)
- The price and value of magazine inserts varies tremendously and is hard to evaluate. (It's best to start your testing in simple one-page ads before expanding to these.)

Choosing Print for Direct Response Advertising

Direct response ads may seem to run everywhere in all sorts of media. The fact is, certain media have better reputations for bringing in good customers—or for just bringing in customers—than others.

As with all direct response advertising, direct marketers put a lot of emphasis on the "quality" of the respondent or the *backend* performance. How well does the prospect or customer *perform* over the months—even years—ahead? Does the prospect purchase? What? How often? Does the customer pay his or her bills? Or is this just a looker or a freeloader?

Customer quality is estimated as the *lifetime value of a customer*. Using lifetime value calculations, you learn that some media (in this case certain print formats) perform better than others, providing quantity *and* quality response that prove out over time. Good media people work hard to recognize and track this.

Good media people also work to match your customer profile to the right publication in business and consumer print advertising, just as you do with lists in direct mail.

Basically, although the consumer market covers women's publications, men's publications, youth publications, dual-audience or general publications, and special-interest publications, some publications in each of these groups have a natural affinity for mail order and direct response; others don't. Just to give you an idea, here are a few of the more popular publications right now (but remember, things are always changing):

Parade (Sunday newspaper supplement)

USA Weekend (Sunday newspaper supplement)

TV Guide

The National Enquirer (tabloid)

Smithsonian

Good Housekeeping

GQ

Cosmopolitan

Self

Esquire

Allure

Architectural Digest

While the special-interest magazines enable you to reach defined markets that share one specific interest (fitness, hunting, tennis, fast cars), most mass consumer magazines are now segmented to allow advertisers to reach special groups of subscribers *within* their circulation, such as educators or doctors or students or blue-chip business executives.

In business there are such general publications as the *Wall Street Journal, Business Week, Forbes*, and *Fortune* plus specific trade or special-interest publications for just about every industry or field of endeavor.

Print as a Test Medium

Most print also offers cost-effective opportunities for testing. Print testing can take the following forms:

New product or concept testing has long been carried out in *small space* by some astute practitioners. One mail order professional tested every potential new product in small space first, using newspapers such as the *Christian Science Monitor* or the *Wall Street Journal* or national tabloids like the *Star* or the *Enquirer.* If response hit certain levels in this space, he could reliably project he had a winner that would pull significantly in large print ads in magazines and newspapers across the country.

A/B split testing is one of the most popular forms of testing. It means simply that the magazine publisher allows advertisers (for a premium) to alternate two different ads in the same space in a specific issue. It literally "splits" the magazine run equally so that every other copy carries ad B, while the remaining copies carry ad A. This is recommended for major creative and offer tests when you run only *one* test against your established control.

In *regional testing*, publications with broad national readership offer advertisers "regional editions." Although this is an expensive media purchase (because of the costs of segmentation), regionals give excellent opportunities to test more than one creative concept or aspect of a direct response ad in the same medium. Most important, they allow you broad hypothesis testing. (Ads for one such test are shown in the Exercises at the end of this chapter.)

And then there's *selective binding*, one of the newest forms of testing. In its finest form, it can literally personalize an ad with the name of the magazine subscriber. In its most popular use, it divides up issues of a magazine into special-interest groups and enables you to test or to target both editorial and advertising to those groups in their specially formatted issues. *Farm Journal* was one of the first publications to make extensive use of selective binding back in 1982, and today it has over 9,000 personalized editions of each issue. For example, their personalized issues might be targeted to hog farmers in the northeast, corn growers in the north central, cattle raisers in the northwest, and wheat farmers in the south central regions. (See Figure 9–1.)

Why Use Print When You Have Direct Mail?

You may wonder if space advertising is needed at all when direct mail can be used. Good question. And, as with so many questions, the answer is largely based on economics. Print makes sense in the following situations:

- When you're starting out with a new product or service and have a market that is not clearly targeted. (For example, with minimum investment, you want to know how your product or service will appeal to business executives as a whole. You

FIGURE 9–1 Two Spreads from One Issue of *Farm Journal* Targeted to Different Geographic Regions

need a show of hands to determine if you *have* a market, *where* you have a market, *what* your market's potential may be.)

- When you have a market that isn't reachable by direct mail lists. (For example, you want a specific level of executive but no lists offer you a clean break-out with names, titles, and addresses.)

- When you want to generate as many inquiries as possible, efficiently and inexpensively. (Maybe to build your "house list"—to gather lists of your own prospects and customers into your database.)

- When you've used all productive direct mail lists and you need ideas for new lists—more prospect names you can get at a reasonable CPM (cost per thousand). So you scout around in print.

There is an important interrelation between some publications and some lists (I touched on this in Chapter 2 in the section on research). Lists that work—mail order buyer lists and publication subscriber lists—can indicate publications that will work. For example, *Business Week*'s lists work for you, *Business Week* should work for your ad—and maybe the *Wall Street Journal* or *Forbes* or *Fortune* will, too.

If you know the product or publication's source of customers, this can offer you even more print and list opportunities. For example: If X product's customer lists work well for your direct mail promotions, and they advertise for customers in Y magazine, Y magazine may work for you, too. So may similar magazines.

You may (I hope) be shaking your head at this point, saying that I haven't answered the question fully. Good for you. You're right. How do you know which to use—direct mail or space? Economics, I repeat. After all, what's the difference between testing 5,000 or 10,000 names from a subscriber list, or running an ad in the subscriber magazine? The cost. The answer to whether direct mail or print advertising is better is different for every product or service. Only testing gives you the economics (read "answer") for your product or service. For example:

- Some prospects may respond better to print or space advertising than to direct mail (and vice versa).

- Some products and services require the expansive formats of direct mail. Some don't.

- Some products want the privacy of direct mail—others want the publicity of space (and its secondary rub-off benefits, like broader product recognition, corporate image building—"If it's in *GQ,* it's gotta be good!").

- Some space ads produce a poorer quality prospect than does direct mail.
- Some lists or groups of lists are too expensive (read inefficient) for your product, so you can substitute space in publications whose market demographics are the same as or similar to the lists.

Clearer? (If your R.Q. is still high, read Chapter 17 in Bob Stone's *Successful Direct Marketing Methods, Fifth Edition* or Chapter 6 in Ed Nash's *Direct Marketing/Strategy, Planning, Execution.)*

Ultimately, space is the best way to "find out." It is not only an inexpensive way to uncover new prospects (and new list opportunities) it is also a good creative test medium. Use it to test which hypothesis is best in your creative strategy—which approach, which graphics. (I'll show you how to do this in a minute.) Enough of the background; now on to the fun.

Applying What You've Already Learned

At some point as a creative person, you may be asked to do an ad, or a series of ads (a campaign) for a product or service. When this happens, you can apply your normal (by now, I hope) procedures:

- Research
- Proposition testing
- Feature listing and benefit extraction
- Hypothesis development
- Creative strategy outline

SOME QUESTIONS TO ASK FIRST (OR HOW TO GET INTO THE MARKETING PLANNING)

Before you start planning a print ad or campaign, protect yourself and make sure you have answers to the obvious big-picture questions: Why is print chosen as opposed to other media (direct mail, broadcast)? What kinds of ads are to run? What is their purpose? What's the media plan? Is print being used alone or in conjunction with other media?

You can't carry out your research or test your proposition without these answers. You must be comfortable with the market *and the media for reaching the market* as well as the product and offer. This harks back to your format planning—see the discussion of the use of one-step versus two-step direct response in Chapter 5.

Format planning involves *basic objectives and budget* and all the discussions between the marketers, product managers, and powers that be that occurred *before* you came on the scene. How many ads are planned? How large can they be? Is this a campaign? Are these ads planned to test several hypotheses? To test format (size, bind-in versus no bind-in)? To test a series of ads or a single ad? To generate inquiries or sell right off the page? What's the timing?

All space ads are not alike, nor do they attempt to accomplish the same thing. I've divided them into three simple categories here: the workhorse ad, the thoroughbred ad, and the thoroughbred workhorse.

The Workhorse Ad. Any ad that must sell off the page and take an order (firm commitment) on its coupon, card, or 800 number, has a tremendous job to do. It toils. Every inch of it strategizes and strains to set the information down, to hold the prospect, to involve, to motivate, and to answer all questions. (See Figure 9–2.)

In most cases, unless the product or service or sponsor is universally known, your illustrations will be very important. Workhorse ads do especially well for book clubs, magazines, and educational services—in situations where cash with order is not essential.

FIGURE 9–2   A Pure Workhorse Ad from the *Wall Street Journal*

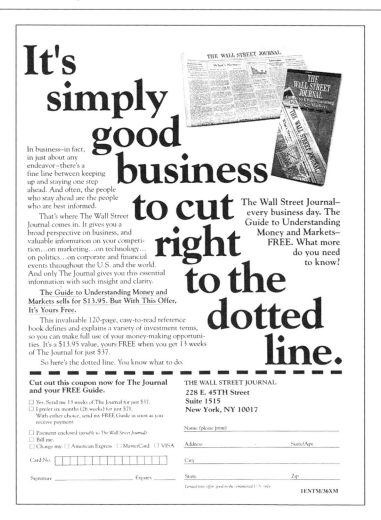

Size or format is also crucial to you. You can't sell many major products and services on less than one page of a magazine; two pages is better still. If you get less space, it may be the time to push for format testing.

Testing for workhorse ads often involves hypothesis testing as well. When your copy strategy gets going, try to develop three to four good hypotheses to see if it's worth a test.

The Thoroughbred Ad. This category, which generates an inquiry (request for more information, request for someone to call, etc.) is called the thoroughbred ad because, compared to the workhorse, it can afford the space to be elegant; it can move in a leisurely fashion. Its job is to involve and motivate, but also to qualify or screen prospects. (See Figure 9–3.)

FIGURE 9–3   A Thoroughbred Ad That Buries the Response Device

Thoroughbred ads are predominantly ads for business and large-ticket consumer products or services. You may need less space for thoroughbreds as their requirements are lighter; they like to travel in groups, too, so you might also want to consider a group or "campaign" of thoroughbreds.

The Thoroughbred Workhorse. There are print ads today that do double duty by both selling products and obtaining a request for more information (a catalog). The sale may be an up-front purchase or simply a qualifier (which is credited against future purchases), or both. The qualifier is a set sum (usually around $3 to $5) that is "refunded" in the form of a bonus coupon against future purchases. These offers are used predominately by catalog companies looking for new customers.

THREE HANDY HABITS TO DEVELOP IN FORMULATING YOUR CREATIVE STRATEGY

1. *Balance the "media buy" (and format) with objectives.* You asked the right questions. You understand the big picture. You've tested your proposition and you're comfortable. Your objective tells you whether it's a workhorse or a thoroughbred. Now—what do you need and what can you have? What are the reasonable assumptions you can make based on the maximum allowable cost per order? Can you have full magazine spreads? Bind-ins? Single page? How about color? Can you test three to four hypotheses? Should you consider a series of two to three ads? What makes financial and creative sense?

2. *Use teamwork for mutual agreement on hypothesis development.* Creative strategy, as you know, can be a solo thing or a team effort. Hypothesis development, as part of this, makes up the very heart and soul of your ad, be it workhorse or thoroughbred. Your headlines and leads, combined with your approach and the graphics, will make or break your ads. But your hypotheses form the foundation that determines your success or failure. Your planning will be much easier with print ads if you have accord and cooperation on this from the start.

3. *Introduce graphic considerations up front.* Your artist was important in direct mail. Your artist is even more important now. Don't go it alone. You'll need all the visual reinforcement you can get for hypothesis exposition, approach, benefit dramatization, and credibility. Again, use teamwork from the start.

YOUR RULES AND FORMULAS

When it comes to space there will be considerable creative baggage that you'll want to bring along. Some you can check at the gate, but keep the big four: credibility, involvement, offer, and motivation.

AIDA as a formula or superstructure works particularly well with print ads.

A—Attention

I—Interest

D—Desire

A—Action

What you *won't* have are a lot of stamps, tokens, and peel-offs. You won't have to worry about computer personalization and package components. You also lose your letters and your spokesperson or specific point of view—unless, of course, you do an ad from the credible spokesperson direct to the prospect: "How I developed this fitness course for you," or "What my new book can do for you . . . ," or unless you use a strong customer testimonial.

How to Create a Print Ad

An ad is the direct mail outer, letter, brochure, and reply card all in one.

You could say that the headline is the outer envelope and the letter lead, the body copy is the brochure, and the coupon is the reply card. Back in Chapters 4 and 7 we talked about the purpose of each of these components, which you write first.

Now these components are combined, often on one magazine page or less and sometimes in space that hardly allows more than a headline, an offer, and a response address. But there is an organization—a creative procedure.

1. *From hypothesis to hook:* Just as in direct mail, you have the all-important hypothesis. But there's no outer envelope to start it, no brochure to support it, no letter lead to introduce it. So? Put it into deathless terms in your headline, and follow it through in your lead sentence. Here's where you hook your prospect! The headline is 75 to 80 percent of the ad.

2. *Approach:* In presenting your hypothesis, will you approach your prospect with a story? An invitation? A question or questions? A problem and solution? A fantasy? Or a straightforward generic announcement of the big benefit?

3. *Graphics:* What graphics best illustrate the hypothesis? And the approach? How many benefits can it show? How much space does it require?

4. *Body copy:* Organize your benefits and features. Keep it tight and theme their presentation according to your approach. Your first job is to *attract attention.* Your next job is to *qualify* your prospect, and it's best to do both at the same time. You may not be fighting a group of envelopes in a mailbox, but you have pages of print—editorial and advertising—to compete with. And you don't know your prospect very well.

Your big headline, often with the help of graphics, pulls it off. It is your outer envelope and letter wrapped in one. It introduces your hypothesis and it states it in glowing, compelling terms.

Many workhorse ads use the Generic Approach with the big benefit. (Save $150 . . . Never worry about money again . . . Be Your Own Boss, etc.) But you'll find that the Question and Story Approaches have been almost as popular. Many also combine these with the Problem/Solution Approach, which recognizes a problem or sets up a problem based on wants, needs, and aspirations, then moves quickly to solve it. Let's take a famous oldie as an example:

Hypothesis: Many people fear that they will lose business and social standing because of their poor command of conversational English.

Headline: Do You Make These Mistakes in English?

Approach: The Question Approach with Problem/Solution.

Try this headline with the Generic or Story Approach. Is it as strong?

Here are other classic workhorse examples.

Hypothesis: During certain periods of physical development, young people have complexion problems that embarrass them and make them feel socially inferior.

Headline: Now—get rid of ugly skin blemishes fast!

Approach: The Generic Approach with Problem/Solution.

Hypothesis: Many people feel that they are not well-read, but new books are often expensive and difficult to obtain.

Headline: Enjoy current bestsellers. Choose any three for just $4 (with membership).

Approach: The Generic Approach with Problem/Solution.

Hypothesis: Most people worry about money and want the security that wealth brings. This book on finance can help people build and maintain their fortune.

Headlines: Never Worry About Money Again (Generic Approach) Money Worries Got You Down? (*Question Approach*) How I Made a Million in Six Months (Story or Testimonial Approach)

Then, of course, there are the problem/solution headlines that go with self-improvement correspondence courses—the Story Approach with the old (and still valid) before-and-after examples. A classic muscle development and fitness course used a series of cartoon frames showing a "97-pound weakling" before and after the Charles Atlas course. To paraphrase the ad, it claimed "They won't insult you and take your girl away if you take this course." You also have the famous John Caples ad that began "They Laughed When I Sat Down At the Piano. But When I Started to Play!—" and the ever-popular before/after testimonial diet ads, "How I lost 75 pounds . . . ."

These headlines are all over 40 years old, but you can see how compelling they were and are—even today! (The same hypothesis may go on and on.) Your greatest challenge will be developing compelling, qualifying headlines that are as timely as these. Your creative methodology should follow along these lines: 1) Determine what specific hypothesis embodies the most appealing or strongest benefit(s); 2) decide which headline and approach give it the most strength; and 3) see how your graphics can help.

Notice that when the hypothesis recognizes a problem (Many people are afraid that . . . "), the primary approach can easily slip into problem/solution. Too loosely applied, problem/solution can become the basis for all hypotheses and all headlines.

THE ROLE OF GRAPHICS

A few great ads have been successful without illustrations (See Figure 9–4). In most cases, however, you'll need graphics along with your headline. Good graphics can be used to attract attention and qualify. Graphics support your hypothesis and approach and can even supplant some copy. (See Figure 9-5.) Graphics also provide quick credibility (a picture of "the founder," for example) and product recognition. (See Figure 9–6.) In some space, you can't really "sell" without the illustration. For example, book clubs and collectibles absolutely require pictures.

In the case of the finance book, let's say you decided on the generic headline, "Never Worry About Money Again." How can graphics be used to attract attention, qualify, and enlarge benefits? If it shows benefits, which benefit illustrations will most people relate to? Or with a headline that promises so much, should you perhaps concentrate on establishing credibility instead with illustrated testimonials? Here you might institute a three-way graphics-combined-with-approach test:

1. Combine the Generic with the Testimonial Approach for credibility (testimonials with pictures of the people themselves).

2. Combine Generic with Fantasy visuals for broad benefit appeal (illustrations of the wealthy life—symbols of money: furs, limousines, jewels, mansions, yachts).

3. Combine the Generic with Identification visuals to show intrinsic benefits of wealth—happy, confident families enjoying the good things.

**FIGURE 9–4   Catchy Headlines Like This One Often Stand
Out Best Without Competing Graphics**

See companies naked.

Xerox Learning Systems has created an exciting, innovative approach to learning for people who need to quickly and surely evaluate financial reading matter.

Called "Reading and Evaluating Financial Reports" this remarkable learning system has only recently been offered to individuals. It can help you learn the ins and outs of high finance in a way you'll never forget.

The material is easy and *fun* to take. Xerox Learning Systems believes that learning is a pleasurable experience. Our idea is to offer you the chance to enjoy yourself as you obtain information you really need.

"Reading and Evaluating Financial Reports" is designed so that when you do read a financial report you will, in effect, see the company naked. You'll know what there is to know (including vital information you might otherwise have overlooked).

Every investor, stockbroker, indeed any conscientious executive who must evaluate companies and their financial statements will benefit from learning how to cut through the special vocabulary of high finance.

You take "Reading and Evaluating Financial Reports" on your own—at home or in the office. The materials are mailed to you complete. You teach yourself; you test yourself. So you will probably find that you are getting far more out of each minute of study than you ever have before. You go at your own speed—and in just a few hours you will have acquired a significant new expertise at quickly and surely reading and evaluating financial reports.

It should be obvious that such knowledge could very well save or earn you or your company considerable sums.

This exciting breakthrough in learning has been proved out by thousands. Investors, brokers, chief financial officers and managers report it fills a real need. Further, Xerox Learning Systems guarantees your complete satisfaction or your money back.

To order "Reading and Evaluating Financial Reports", simply call us, toll free, at:

1-800-453-4002

Major credit cards accepted or send check for $49.95 plus $4.75 shipping and handling to Xerox Learning Systems, 6 Commercial St., P.O. Box 944, Department REFR-R9JWE, Hicksville, N.Y. 11802. In many cases this learning system may be tax deductible.

XEROX

Xerox Learning Systems

**FIGURE 9–5   A Strong Photo Used to Attract Attention and Support
the Hypothesis**

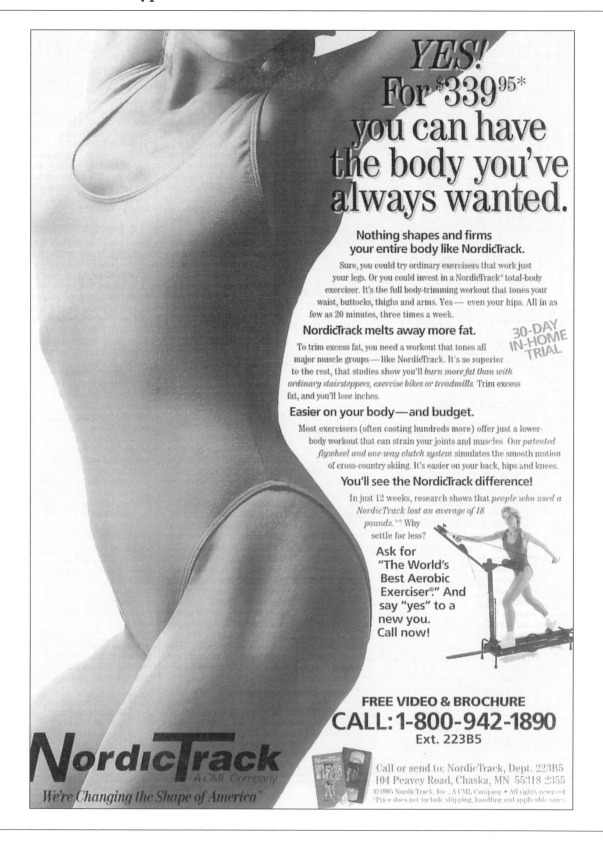

FIGURE 9–6   Graphics Provide Credibility and Illustrate Benefits in This Ad

Train at Home for One of These 58 Career Opportunities

Send for free facts about Career Diplomas and Degrees

Sally Struthers,
Star of Movies and Television says...

66 I know how important training is to having a successful career—without it, trying to find a good job is almost impossible. With ICS, you can train in your own home for a better job, more money, and greater job security. 99

Many courses contain exciting lessons, tools and materials like these.

Send for free facts and color brochure!
If you want more money, more security and a better way of life, now you can train in your spare time—at home—for a diploma or even a degree to help you get a better job.

You learn from specialists... the adult way!
Our staff of educators, consultants, administrators, authors and distinguished instructors guides you step by step. And all courses include the necessary tools, instruments, and materials for your training.

An ideal way to learn!
No need to change your daily routine or take time from your job or family.

Get your Degree without attending college!
The ICS Center for Degree Studies offers an Associate in Specialized Business (ASB) Degree in 6 top business and management fields, and an Associate in Specialized Technology (AST)

Degree in 5 areas of engineering and technology. If you have previous college experience, you may be entitled to advanced standing.

Could a Career Diploma or Degree be worth thousands of dollars to you?
Specialized training in any of these fields, or a Specialized Associate Degree in Business or Technology, could make a giant difference in your lifetime earnings. For more information at no cost, check the career that interests you most and mail the postage-paid reply card today, or call us toll free.

MAIL POST-PAID CARD FOR FREE FACTS OR CALL TOLL FREE
1-800-596-5505 Ext. 8192
CALL ANYTIME—24 hours a day, 7 days a week
If the card is missing, check the name of the course you're most interested in on the coupon at the right and mail it today!

---- If card is missing, mail coupon to: ----
ICS SINCE 1890
International Correspondence Schools, Dept. PVKS75S
925 Oak Street, Scranton, PA 18515
Please send free facts on how I can train at home for the career I have chosen. No obligation. No salesman will visit. **CHECK ONE ONLY.**

ASSOCIATE IN SPECIALIZED BUSINESS DEGREE PROGRAMS
- [ ] Business Management
- [ ] Accounting
- [ ] Business Management with option in Marketing
- [ ] Business Management with option in Finance
- [ ] Applied Computer Science
- [ ] Hospitality Management

ASSOCIATE IN SPECIALIZED TECHNOLOGY DEGREE PROGRAMS
- [ ] Mechanical Engineering Technology
- [ ] Civil Engineering Technology
- [ ] Electrical Engineering Tech
- [ ] Industrial Engineering Technology
- [ ] Electronics Technology

CAREER DIPLOMA COURSES
- [ ] Computer Programming
- [ ] Computer Programming/COBOL
- [ ] Personal Computer Specialist
- [ ] Computer-Assisted Bookkeeping
- [ ] PC Repair
- [ ] Desktop Publishing & Design
- [ ] Secretary with Computer
- [ ] High School
- [ ] Catering/Gourmet Cooking
- [ ] Medical Office Assistant
- [ ] Dental Office Assistant
- [ ] Auto Mechanics
- [ ] Bookkeeping
- [ ] Hotel/Restaurant Management
- [ ] Drafting

- [ ] Animal Care Specialist
- [ ] Electronics
- [ ] Air Conditioning & Refrigeration
- [ ] Secretary
- [ ] Electrician
- [ ] Police Sciences
- [ ] Private Security Officer
- [ ] Art
- [ ] Small Business Mgmt
- [ ] Interior Decorating
- [ ] Wildlife/Forestry Conservation
- [ ] Legal Secretary
- [ ] Gun Repair
- [ ] Fashion Merchandising

- [ ] Motorcycle Repair
- [ ] Surveying & Mapping
- [ ] Fitness & Nutrition
- [ ] TV/VCR Repair
- [ ] Legal Assistant
- [ ] Photography
- [ ] Dressmaking & Design
- [ ] Journalism/Short Story Writing
- [ ] Florist
- [ ] Teacher Aide
- [ ] Medical Transcriptionist
- [ ] Real Estate Appraiser
- [ ] Home Inspector
- [ ] Professional Locksmithing
- [ ] Appliance Repair

Name_____ Age_____
Address_____ Apt. #_____
City/State_____ Zip_____
Phone (   )_____

Let's take another example, a genuine pearl necklace. *Hypothesis:* Women will want this product for social confidence, for the security of an investment, for enhanced self-esteem, for pure enjoyment and because it is a bargain. Which of these needs or wants is most important? (And wouldn't it be nice to emphasize *all* of them?) Here's where basic hypothesis/approach testing is important; graphics are important as well.

Say you decide on a Generic ("value/bargain") Approach because it covers all bases—safely. (Everyone wants a bargain, everyone who wants a pearl necklace wants to buy one at a bargain price. Some of these people want the necklace for pure enjoyment. Others want it as an investment, or to impress friends.)

Headline: Own the Pearl Necklace of Your Dreams and Save $150!

Now with your graphics show an attractive, pleased woman surrounded by friends. She is showing her new necklace to friends. She is proud of the necklace. Friends admire it. All of this implies value and peer approval. (This also introduces the idea of gift giving.)

Your picture has attracted attention, qualified the prospect, introduced the main and secondary benefits. (Properly used, graphics solve problems this way.) And your headline has set down the big benefit (and reason to act).

O.K. You have offer, involvement, and motivation going for you. Next? I hope you said *credibility*. What qualifies you to make this offer? How do you justify the price? Need to add a close-up inset picture of the pearls? Got a guarantee? You're on your way!

Some Rule-Breakers

You understand by now that a print headline, like a letter lead or outer envelope copy, should offer the big benefit. You know it must attract attention and qualify and involve the prospect as well—just like an outer envelope does. And just like the outer envelope, headlines must promise something or arouse curiosity. Headlines can be short (one word) or long, two lines, or even three lines. As John Caples claims, in *Tested Advertising Methods,* "Long headlines that say something are more effective than short headlines that say nothing."[1]

When it comes down to the act of writing headlines, leads, and broad appeals, no one can give you better advice than the late dean of direct response advertising, John Caples. His advice is based on hard data and testing—facts, not opinion. However, it is good to remember that our markets are always changing and as they change, tested appeals may change with them. The strongest, most powerful appeals of 1950 or 1980 or today may be less appealing, less attractive to the markets of tomorrow.

If you've been following these guidelines closely, you may be a little puzzled. I have *not* been describing a lot of the direct response ads you see today.

- How many ads have you noticed with teasing headlines—headlines that certainly don't set forth any hypothesis, but merely hint at one to come?

- How about the softer-selling workhorses that don't put "you" in the headline?

- How about the ones with big pictures and little copy—not even a list of benefits?

- How about the ads with no coupon at all—only an 800 number?

There are several reasons for these rule-breaking ads.

First, up to now, I've been describing primarily the solid, old-fashioned workhorse ad; the classic on which the mail order business was started. (Some of these early ads were pretty cluttered and pretty tacky—*and* pretty effective.)

There's a lot to be learned from these classics. And chances are good that if you do any print for book clubs, book programs, magazines and correspondence courses, you'll need to use this classic format, a format where "you" is always stated up front or clearly understood.

This doesn't mean there's no room for good teasing workhorses or highly qualifying workhorses that talk product and product benefit without the "you" up front. (See Figure 9–7.) Remember, a major rule to get the envelope opened is "arouse significant curiosity." If you have a teaser or a big benefit headline that really does this well—go for it.

Thoroughbred ads don't have to sell off the page and therefore allow you more leverage. They are primarily intended to qualify prospects. They also work to create an image. To do this, they are designed to impress you with their company and their products in general, their qualifications, their credibiity. A good tease is particularly O.K. here.

Such thoroughbreds cannot win their races if they remove the "you" completely, however. Ads that forget "you, you, you" will receive weak response compared to the more compelling "you" copy of the old workhorse. What's more, clever headlines can flop. (A lot of those you see—once—may be flops.)

You can afford to play around a little if you're in friendly, familiar (tested) media, or talking to your own customers. Don't take chances in unfamiliar territory or with strangers, however. And always test.

The second reason that you see a lot of nonconforming direct response ads is that, simply, there *are* a lot of rule-breaking ads that

FIGURE 9–7   A Strong Pre-Qualifying Ad

A Superb Garden Catalogue

WITH PLANTS AND SERVICE TO MATCH

For 46 years, knowledgeable gardeners have selected their annuals, perennials, shrubs, and bulbs from our extensive offering because we travel widely to gather the best ornamental plants from around the world. Each variety is subjected to extensive trials on our nursery before being turned over to our growers for commercial production. This traditional practice is both slow and costly, but it ensures our customers will receive plants that look as good in the garden as they do in our photos.

This spring, we are pleased to announce more than 100 new varieties, many of them in two important new areas:

WATER PLANTS—We've created several complete water gardens, which include plants, containers, and accessories, to allow you to enjoy the astonishing beauty of water plants in a country pond or on a city porch or terrace. The plants we ship are blooming-size specimens of the best varieties, and they are guaranteed to put on a glorious performance this summer.

SOUTHERN PLANTS—With the help of experts from all over the South, we've improved our Southern performance ratings throughout the catalogue and have added more than 20 varieties especially selected to thrive in Zones 6–8. To ensure suc-

cess, we've altered our shipping schedules to allow early delivery, so plants can establish themselves before the heat. While we still have more to learn, our aim is to do full justice to the needs of Southern gardeners.

Of course, there's more to successful gardening than fine varieties. At White Flower Farm, we're plantsmen first and merchants second, and our years of experience allow us to deliver top-quality plants in prime condition for growing at the proper time for planting. Because we grow the plants we sell, we can promise a grade that is larger and stronger than the industry norm, which assures better results for beginners and experts alike. Naturally, every shipment is accompanied by detailed instructions and covered by an unequivocal guarantee.

We'd be delighted to send you a FREE copy of our spring catalogue, called *The Garden Book*. It offers more than 700 varieties of plants in 140 pages of glorious color photos, plus thousands of words of practical how-to-garden information. To receive your copy, please complete and mail the postcard adjoining this page. If the card is missing, you may write to the address below or call 1-800-503-9624. Catalogues will be mailed in late December, and we'd like yours to be among them.

Sincerely, Amos Pettingill

White Flower Farm

PLANTSMEN
PO Box 50, Litchfield 60906, Connecticut 06759-0050

are tried, tested, *and* successful these days, particularly in the areas of mail order soft goods and business lead-getting. (We'll get to these in a minute.)

The third reason: perhaps some general advertising agency just took a standard ad and stuck an 800 number on it (and called it direct response. It happens all the time!

Creative Reasoning Makes the Difference

It's important for you to understand *what* the headline must do as well as *how* to do it. Understand why the headline and the graphics work together. Once you've got the rules down, you can experiment. For example, let your graphics attract attention and qualify the prospect. Use your headline as a teaser that leads into the copy. Or play with your approach; make a question out of your headline and an answer with your graphics—or vice versa. If you understand *why* you do what you do, you're safe. If you do it because it sounds tricky or looks flashy, forget it.

You already know how to check research, test your proposition, set up the format, execute the creative strategy, and pull a hot hypothesis or two (Chapter 5). You know how to use your hypothesis, your approach, and graphics to set up your headline. You're *equipped* to experiment. Work at it. Be confident! And test.

Notice how quickly you can move through AIDA with a good headline and strong approach . . . how you can attract attention and qualify your prospect with the right visuals . . . how you state your hypothesis and create involvement with major benefits—all through headline, copy approach, and graphics.

Is it easy? No. The simpler the result, the harder it is to achieve. Because your headline is 75 to 80 percent of your ad, it had better be good—it had better work hard. So will you before you get to the small print.

Body Copy: Features and Benefits

With small space ads or one-pagers in magazines, there's hardly any room for copy. Book club advertising is a classic example of this. Graphics of book covers are prominent (the more book choices, the better the ad), and offer terms are relatively long and complex. This frequently leaves only a sentence or two for the lead-in paragraph. The rest is headline, graphics, and offer.

At the other end of the spectrum, of course, is the newspaper advertising supplement of four to eight pages of copy with illustrations. Many variations fall in between.

How do you treat the copy, this "body of information"? Here is a suggestion: In establishing your hypothesis, you had to set up a hierarchy of benefits. Before you could do this, you had to list all the features. Take all of this information and organize it a little like a brochure (see Chapter 4).

In ordering and organizing you may want to apply one of several methods. A lot will depend on your overall approach. For example: If you're telling a story, your benefits may unfold sequentially as your story progresses.

In the Question Approach, you can present benefits and features in the form of questions and answers. ("What kind of books can you expect to receive every month?")

If you use a Fantasy Approach, you may want to build all the benefits into the dream. ("Imagine that you're . . . then picture your . . . ") With a straight Generic Approach you could employ the old countdown, listing the benefits and features in descending order, biggest first, smallest last. ("First, you'll have . . . , then . . . , next . . . ")

In many cases, when your space is limited, you might consider the *Cluster Effect*, where you take each benefit separately (usually in descending order) and surround it with the features that produce the benefit. ("You'll enjoy the sheer beauty of your necklace. Each individual pearl is matched perfectly to the next. The color of the pearls together gives a pure, soft white glow." or "Be conversant in all areas of current thought. Every month you'll choose from a wide variety of new nonfiction books on subjects like conversation, politics, history, scientific advances . . . .")

In severely restricted space, you can always try the *Clothesline* or the *Stew* presentation. With the Clothesline treatment, benefits and features are strung out and hung (again, in descending order) from the lead, looping back and forth across the page until they dribble off and get tacked down just before your final wrap-up and call to action. The Stew is similar except it just indiscriminately shoves a jumble of benefits and features into a cramped pot of type lying between the lead and the close, often running benefits or features back to back with no sentence structure.

DON'T FORGET THE MAGIC WORDS

We've talked a lot about the value of "you" (the most magic word we have) and "FREE" (nearly the most magic word we have). If you can justify it, use both liberally. John Caples also pointed out that "new" or giving news is important.

We have a lot of action words (like Now, Here, Hurry, Today) that convey a sense of newness, importance, and urgency—fast. (Now for the first time . . . Do it now!) You'll need these, especially in small space. The action words are also right for exit lines and offers, described in the next section.

YOUR EXIT LINES AND
OFFERS

You will of course wrap up your copy with the traditional call to action and ordering instructions. Make it easy to order, give the options, set out a coupon with the same care as you do your direct mail order form. Where you have a coupon or order form, make sure it states the offer in full so that it can stand alone if it gets clipped and set aside.

When space is very tight, you don't have to repeat the offer in your wrap-up if you have a coupon that clearly states the offer. But coupon ads, once the coupon is clipped, are no good to you or anyone else unless the full offer is stated in the unclipped portion, with an ordering address.

Old proverb says: Interdependent coupon separated from interdependent ad produces two worthless pieces of paper!

Planning a print ad takes time, but not as much time as direct mail planning and execution, unless you're doing a series. By the time you have your creative strategies down, you should be more than halfway finished.

John Caples once said "Now, I spend hours on headlines—days if necessary. And when I get a good headline, I know that my task is nearly finished. Writing the copy can usually be done in a short time if necessary."[2]

Winning Ads and What You Can Learn From Them

In many ways, direct marketers are gradually capitalizing on what standard advertisers have always worked for: good, strong advertising that can build a company's image and make prospects aware of the company and its products. Direct marketers have carried this one step further. They intend that good, strong advertising can build a company's image and create awareness while it is also gathering prospects and/or garnering sales. (And I say, "God Bless Direct Marketers for It!")

They have an ear for the tempo of the times, as well. Just as direct marketers are bringing out new products and services for today's markets, so they are accompanying these with new graphics, strong visuals, and sound copy (without the hoopla of the circus barker).

They understand that the big new markets of tomorrow will take "plastic," the telephone and ultimately the computer for granted. They know the power of pictures. And they are finding that often a greater space and/or time investment up front pays off with quality prospects in the long run in all mass media. (You'll find some prime examples of this on the pages that follow.)

As the costs of direct mail (and postage!) continue to rise, space or print advertising offers one good alternative. Learn to use space well. Make it work for you. You'll be a hero! (Figures 9–11 through 9–30 are fine examples of this.)

14 POINTS FROM DAVID OGILVY[3]

[In the following article you'll find some valid suggestions from an advertising legend on increasing readership of long body copy in print ads. This can help you as you block out your body copy. It can also help your art director.]

Magazine editors have discovered that people read the explanatory captions under photographs more than they read the text of articles; and the same thing is true of advertisements. When we analyzed Starch data on advertisements in *Life*, we found that on the average *twice* as many people read the captions as read the body copy. Thus captions offer you twice the audience you get for body copy. It follows that you should never use a photograph without putting a caption under it, and each caption should be a miniature advertisement, complete with brand name and promise.

If you can keep your body copy down to 170 words, you should set it in the form of a caption under your photograph, as we have done in our magazine advertisements for Tetley Tea.

If you need very long copy, there are several devices which are known to increase its readership:

1. A display subhead of two or three lines, between your headline and your body copy, will heighten the reader's appetite for the feast to come.

2. If you start your body copy with a large initial letter, you will increase readership by an average of 13 percent.

3. Keep your opening paragraph down to a maximum of eleven words. A long first paragraph frightens readers away. All your paragraphs should be as short as possible; long paragraphs are fatiguing.

4. After two or three inches of copy, insert your first cross-head, and thereafter pepper cross-heads throughout. They keep the reader marching forward. Make some of them interrogative, to excite curiosity in the next run of copy. An ingenious sequence of boldly displayed cross-heads can deliver the substance of your entire pitch to glancers who are too lazy to wade through the text.

5. Set your copy in columns not more than forty characters wide. Most people acquire their reading habits from newspapers, which use columns of about twenty-six characters. The wider the measure, the fewer the readers.

6. Type smaller than 9-point is difficult for most people to read. . . .

7. Serif type . . . is easier to read than sans serif type . . . . The Bauhaus brigade is not aware of this fact.

8. When I was a boy it was fashionable to make copywriters square up every paragraph. Since then it has been discovered that "widows" increase readership, except at the bottom of a column, where they make it too easy for the reader to quit.

9. Break up the monotony of long copy by setting key paragraphs in boldface or italic.

10. Insert illustrations from time to time.

11. Help the reader into your paragraphs with arrowheads, bullets, asterisks, and marginal marks.

12. If you have a lot of unrelated facts to recite, don't try to relate them with cumbersome connectives; simply number them, as I am doing here.

13. Never set your copy in reverse (white type on a black background), and never set it over a gray or colored tint. The old school of art directors believed that these devices forced people to read the copy; we now know that they make reading physically impossible.

14. If you use leading between paragraphs, you increase readership by an average of 12 percent.

Testing the Hypotheses in Print Advertising

Figures 9–8 to 9–12 illustrate five ads developed for *Prevention* magazine about 10 years ago and tested in *Reader's Digest, TV Guide,* and *Parade.*

They are all exceptionally good ads, and each has a strong, very clear hypothesis of its own. But one of them beats the others hands down. Study them closely. Identify the hypotheses. Then rank them. (You'll find the rankings at the end of the chapter, but don't peek until you've ranked them all!)

FIGURE 9–8   What Is the Hypothesis for This Ad?

Subscribe to a health magazine. Even if it isn't ours.

We're not philanthropists. And we're not crazy.

Why, then, are we urging you to subscribe to any one of the many health and fitness magazines flooding the nation's newsstands and mailboxes these days?

Because we believe health magazines — many of them, not just ours — have made important contributions to the tremendously reassuring events on the American health scene today.

Cardiovascular-disease deaths have dropped dramatically in the past 15 years. ...A USDA survey indicates that more than 60% of American households are switching to healthier eating habits ... And infants born today can expect to live about 30 years longer than 1900's newborn!

Does credit for all these remarkable gains belong to the health magazines? Of course not.

But it does belong, in many cases, to the people who *read* these magazines.

They were among the first to realize that achieving good health is often up to the individual.

They made the decision to take control of their own lives; to *help themselves* to feel better.

And so they were the ones who went looking for information about the basic sources of health — authoritative guidance, clearly and interestingly written, about tested techniques and new discoveries they could use.

They found it in health magazines! And, for many of them, it made a big difference in their lives.

It could do the same for you — and that's why we hope you'll start reading a health magazine regularly.

Naturally, we'd like it to be *Prevention* magazine. Moreover, we think there's a very good reason why it should be:

Of all the health and fitness magazines, *Prevention* has by far the largest number of readers. And we don't think it could continue to be the largest if it hadn't helped so many people over the years.

Indeed, we're so sure that you'll like *Prevention* — and benefit from it — that we're ready to offer this special "try us" opportunity.

Take a free examination copy *and* three free booklets— we'll take the risk.

We'll send you the current issue of *Prevention* to examine, as well as your personal copies of the three booklets described in the box. If you decide *Prevention*'s not for you, just cancel...keep the booklets without obligation...and owe nothing.

That's our promise. So, subscribe to ours — or subscribe to theirs. But we urge you to find out, now, how millions of people are adding new dimensions of vitality, productivity, and enjoyment to their lives. With a health magazine.

In every issue of *Prevention*, you'll find helpful articles like these...

- A consumer's guide to over-the-counter drugs
- Health rating America's favorite new foods
- Nutrition vs. Cancer more good news
- 12 ways to feel better without doing anything
- Best and worst occupations for good health
- B vitamins can chase a baby's blues away
- Foods that keep cholesterol honest
- A simple way to fall asleep faster
- Sex and nutrition — a perfect marriage
- The best exercises for your back
- The Top 25 "Superfoods"
- And many others

THESE THREE BOOKLETS YOURS **FREE** WHEN YOU TRY *PREVENTION*

21 Surefire Stress Releasers — This 55-page guide is packed with sound ideas for transforming stress from a killer into a health motivator.

How to Live It Up and Live Longer — Tells about nutrients that help increase your functional lifespan by 5 to 10 extra years and much more in its 40 pages.

Herbs for Health — This 46-page report explains the uses of 70 healing plants and herbs — many available at little or no cost.

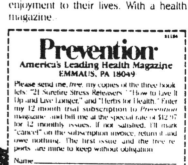

Prevention

America's Leading Health Magazine
EMMAUS, PA 18049

Please send me, *free*, my copies of the three booklets: "21 Surefire Stress Releasers," "How to Live It Up and Live Longer," and "Herbs for Health." Enter my 12 month trial subscription to *Prevention* magazine, and bill me at the special rate of $12.97 for 12 monthly issues. If not satisfied, I'll mark "cancel" on the subscription invoice, return it and owe nothing. The first issue and the free reports are mine to keep without obligation.

Name _____

Address _____ Apt. # _____

City _____

State _____ Zip _____

FIGURE 9–9   What Is the Hypothesis for This Ad?

THE 20 MOST IMPORTANT STEPS YOU CAN TAKE TO LIVE LONGER.

"Comply with only *one*...and your chances of living longer and avoiding illness or injury go up."
—R. Barker Bausell, Ph.D., University of Maryland*

Your hopes for reaching a ripe old age—and then some—do not necessarily depend on luck.

Nor even on your genes.

But your longevity may well depend on whether or not you know such vital facts as these:

• *What is the single factor experts consider most significant in affecting health?*

• *Is it more important to get lots of sleep or to eat breakfast daily?*

• *Do you fit into one of the categories of people most likely to engage in good preventive health behavior?*

• *What do 81% of all Americans fail to do, even though experts call it the third most crucial health-promoting behavior?*

Most important...and most encouraging...you only have to take one of the twenty steps cited by the experts—any one!—to increase your chances of enjoying a longer life. Less illness-prone, more injury-free.

Now available—a breakthrough guide to better health.

All of these important insights—and much, much more—are presented for the first time in a special report recently released by Louis Harris and Associates, world-famous researchers. Based on a study conducted for the Prevention Research Center, the report is called, "20 Important Steps to Better Health."

In their innovative probe, Harris researchers interviewed 103 recognized health experts. They also interviewed more than 1,254 private citizens in a scientifically selected random sampling of the U.S. population.

The result: a fascinating, first-time overview of what highly respected authorities think you should be doing to help yourself to better health...insights

into your fellow Americans' health habits...and an opportunity to determine how you measure up to the general standards.

The report can be yours—free— with a low-cost, no-risk subscription to America's largest health magazine.

To receive a copy of this unprecedented and revealing report, *free*, you need only try a money-saving subscription to *Prevention* magazine at the introductory rate of $12.97 for twelve monthly issues.

And with the magazine comes our promise that it will cost you nothing if you're not completely satisfied. Simply cancel your subscription and you keep the special report, with our compliments.

For it *is* a report you will want to keep.

Like *Prevention* itself, "20 Important Steps to Better Health" aims to give you information that can make a big difference in your life—*if you know about it.*

Every month, *Prevention*—the largest health magazine in America—gives over 7 million readers a wide range of stimulating health ideas on nutrition, insomnia, backaches, allergies, fitness, depression, stress, beauty hints, and much more.

You, too, are likely to find each issue of *Prevention* a rewarding, enriching experience. So, mail the coupon today—and find out how much healthier and more productive your life can be!

FREE.

Read the startlingly innovative research by Louis Harris and Associates revealing what experts think you should be doing to help yourself live longer ...how well you measure up to these standards...and how you compare with other Americans. *20 Important Steps To Better Health* is yours—without charge—just for trying *Prevention* at a low, introductory rate.

Prevention
America's Leading Health Magazine
EMMAUS, PA 18049

Please send me my *free* copy of "20 Important Steps to Better Health;" enter my 12-month trial subscription to *Prevention* and bill me at the special rate of $12.97 for 12 monthly issues. If not satisfied, I'll mark "cancel" on the subscription invoice, return it and owe nothing. The first issue—and the free report—are mine to keep without obligation.   81128

Name_____

Address_____Apt. #____

City_____

State_____Zip_____

*Affiliation noted for identification only.

FIGURE 9–10   What Is the Hypothesis for This Ad?

"LIFE EXTENDERS" $3.95 PAPERBACK –YOURS FREE!

If you love life enough to want five, ten, possibly 20 *extra years of it*, mail the coupon below. It will bring you a FREE COPY of our popular book on "life extenders" filled with news of *the 10 best ways to live longer*, according to a long-term scientific study.

This popular paperback edition sells for $3.95 in bookstores, but *you won't pay a cent*. Yet, you may agree with so many others who call it the most valuable health book they own.

You may be startled by what you read. Like why health experts consider a typical Swedish man of 90 to be healthier than the average 60-year-old American. Why we are falling so far behind in the longevity statistics. And just what we are doing to ourselves that cuts life short.

You'll also be intrigued. By reports of how our bodies *could* give us 120 or more years of service—and how we don't let it. You'll discover why some people seem to age "faster" than others. And you'll learn the single best thing you can do, experts say, to slow down your own aging process!

Frankly, some of what you'll read will amaze you. Like the list of the 25 best foods you can eat—so totally healthful they're being called "super-foods." And the diet that scientists say can actually decrease your chances of heart disease, cancer, high blood pressure and other life-shortening ailments. And even how you can *prevent accidents*—the single greatest cause of hospitalization in America today!

But most of what you'll find in this free book will be inspiring. You'll see the results of a remarkable study that showed how men and women added at least *seven extra years to their lives* by practicing these simple life-extending techniques. You'll discover the nine easy ways you can re-duce the stress in your life for more happiness. Plus you'll learn of the medically documented weight-loss technique (not a diet) that has been called *the most effective way to lose weight permanently!* And much more.

The "life extenders" book is yours as a *free gift* just for trying PREVENTION, America's most popular feel better, live longer magazine. The place where over three million readers find "life-extenders" like these every month.

We're offering it because if you love life enough to want extra years of it, we're betting you'll want to read PREVENTION magazine regularly too. Because it's the best way to keep up with all the very latest better health and natural healing discoveries.

How about you? Ready to add extra years and better health to your life?

The coupon below is your ticket. Mail it back to us right away for your free book and free look at PREVENTION, the most popular better health magazine in America.

10 Ways to Live Longer

Prevention · AMERICA'S LEADING HEALTH MAGAZINE

NUTRITION VS. CANCER: MORE GOOD NEWS

THE BEST EXERCISES FOR YOUR BACK

NATURAL HEALING FORMULAS

HERE'S YOUR FREE BOOK!

YES! Please send me my *free* copy of "10 Ways to Live Longer," and enter my 12-month *trial* subscription to PREVENTION. Please bill me at the special rate of $12.97 for 12 monthly issues. If not satisfied, I'll mark "cancel" on the subscription bill, return it to you and owe nothing. The first issue—and the free book—are mine to keep without obligation.

NAME _____

ADDRESS _____ APT. # _____

CITY _____ STATE _____ ZIP _____

Mail to: PREVENTION®
EMMAUS, PA 18049

FIGURE 9–11   What Is the Hypothesis for This Ad?

279c

How many of these medical myths do you still subscribe to?

If you still believe in any of these medical myths, PREVENTION—America's most popular better health magazine—would like to offer you a second opinion. Because an ounce of information now, could save you a ton of trouble later.

Illness is a natural part of growing older.

NOT SO. Sure, sickness *does* occur, but that doesn't mean it *has* to. In fact, the latest scientific thinking indicates that *we create most of our* health problems. By eating and doing what we shouldn't. And by ignoring things that could help. Research clearly shows that *the majority of illness can be prevented or can be avoided altogether.*

How?

For over 40 years, the pages of PREVENTION have been filled with medical reports that show people how to keep their health longer. These days, PREVENTION is reporting on the very newest health discoveries. Like what you can do to prevent stroke. How you can bring down high blood pressure without drugs. Plus a way of eating that offers the best-known protection against cancer. So if you're missing PREVENTION, you're missing a lot.

If I eat well enough, I won't need vitamins.

SORRY. Researchers have found that the foods we eat today are so processed that many won't even support laboratory life. In fact, experts *blame* our poor diet for many of today's serious health problems. This, they report, plus our extra stress, requires that we strengthen ourselves with vitamins to be optimally healthy.

But which vitamins do what? And how much do you need? And what are the best sources?

In PREVENTION magazine, you'll read about vitamins that give extra energy. The vitamin that banishes depression and perks up memory, according to a medical study. The vitamin shown to build a stronger heart. Plus ten ways to heal with vitamin C, many of them new. When it comes to vitamins, PREVENTION is the most reliable source of information in print today.

The doctor knows best.

NOT ANYMORE. As helpful as doctors are, they don't have all the answers. And the good ones will be the first to admit it. Nearly 20% of all hospital patients *get sick as a result of their medical treatment.* As high as 25% of all surgery may be unnecessary, it is estimated.

Who knows best?

You should. Because you just can't afford to depend on your doctor for health, no matter how good he or she may be.

That's why PREVENTION magazine brings you news of how to take better care of your health yourself, so you can have it longer. You'll see how to rate your physician—and important questions to ask. Plus a list of the most addictive and sickening prescription drugs. And how to tell if your x-rays, tests, and surgery are really necessary.

These days, it's easy to make a medical mistake. Or *become* one.

Take better care of yourself.

MAIL THE COUPON BELOW TODAY for a *free examination* of the latest issue of PREVENTION and see why nearly three million health-loving Americans subscribe to its natural advice.

FREE BOOK BONUS! Mail the coupon today and receive a free copy of "How to Live It Up and Live Longer." In it you will discover little known ways to add perhaps 5 to 10 extra years to your life . . . find more energy . . . relieve stress . . . plus so much more. Send for your free copy right away.

FREE COPY! YES! Please send me my free copy of "How to Live It Up and Live Longer," enter my 12-month trial subscription to PREVENTION magazine and please bill me at the special rate of $12.97 for 12 monthly issues. If not satisfied, I'll mark "cancel" on the subscription bill, return it to you and owe nothing. The first issue—and the free book—are mine to keep without obligation.

NAME _____

ADDRESS _____ APT. # ___

CITY _____

STATE _____ ZIP _____

Clip and Mail to: PREVENTION.® Emmaus, PA 18049

FIGURE 9–12   What Is the Hypothesis for This Ad?

Answers to *Prevention* Hypotheses Rankings

1. *Illness Isn't Natural (almost twice as effective as 2!)*
2. *Medical Myths*
3. *Life Extensions*
4. *20 Steps*
5. *Subscribe to a Health Magazine*

Notes

1. John Caples, *Tested Advertising Methods*, 4th ed. (Englewood Cliffs, NJ: Prentice-Hall, 1977), p. 19.

2. Ibid.

3. David Ogilvy, excerpted from *Confessions of an Advertising Man.* Copyright © 1963 David Ogilvy. Reprinted with the permission of the author.

AT LAST—CREATING FOR BROADCAST AND DIGITAL INTERACTIVE MEDIA

You're finally here where all the action is—electronic interaction. You may have been wondering when we were going to get down to something really glamorous. Well now's the time and, although I don't want to deglamorize it for you, I hope you remember that telephoning is electronic interaction. So is faxing, and all forms of broadcast from networks and cable, 60s and 120s to infomercials and online Net communication. And you're about to discover that creatively they're all very similar to print and direct mail.

So it's most appropriate to start this chapter with a quote from John Yeck, founding partner of Yeck Brothers, Dayton, Ohio, and chairman of the Direct Marketing Association's Educational Foundation from 1967 through 1998:

> The Information Superhighway is a super medium; but only a medium, 21st century smoke and drums . . . without taking away a bit of the magic of this dramatic technology, all of us are smart enough to know deep in our guts that *what* we communicate is far more important than *how* we communicate.
>
> For the medium is *not* the message. It shapes the delivery of the message but the message is still the *message* . . .
>
> Of course, the highway will deliver all sorts of messages, from entertainment to statistics. Marketers will use it to persuade others to change their minds: *to get them to do what the marketer wants them to do.* To take action through back and forth messages; to interact.
>
> For that's the marketer's purpose.

Persuasion consists of getting a message into someone else's mind—effectively, in order to change it. Advertisers will have to develop some new techniques to fit new opportunities, just as they did for radio, television and card packs, but the *fundamentals of persuasive communications stay the same.*

Amen to that! Now on with those fundamentals . . .

New Horizons in Broadcast and Interactive Media

With broadcast you may get to take part in casting, go "on location," visit a studio, or sit in a darkened editing room, but you'll find the thrill wears off pretty fast. It's hard work—and hard waiting. You'll get pretty bored standing around the set or location all day between takes (see "terms" at the end of this chapter). You'll also understand why everyone working on location seems to carry a book or magazine.

Before we get into the creative part, let me give you a little background. Television (the national networks and cable) is undisputedly the largest, most far-reaching medium that direct marketers use right now. It works fast. It can generate a lot of heat in the form of orders, inquiries, and awareness. On the downside, however, it doesn't deliver the quality that print—and especially direct mail—can. And it will prove totally inefficient for some highly specialized markets.

The Internet's World Wide Web promises to have every bit the reach that television now provides plus the advantage of interaction, targeting (and self-selection), instant response and instant measurement. Once its measurements are indeed available (research) and its markets are clearly defined (major numbers of participators), there can be no doubt that this will be a most powerful medium.

But we are reminded in a recent *Forbes* article that "The truth about cyberspace is this: New technologies go through three phases—mania, bankruptcies, rebirth. Right now it's mania time on the Internet."[1]

As early as 1970, everyone was excited about the more specialized capabilities of cable TV and satellite communications, and about the possibility of interactive video. The Direct Marketing Association even themed its annual conference around the video future that year. Many prophets were certain that in a decade or so, mail and print would bow to the video medium. It has been far longer in coming that any gurus imagined. And it hasn't happened quite the way many thought it would.

Cable TV finally arrived in the eighties when it reached a circulation of over 30 million homes. This opened special-interest channels to direct marketers—sports channels, music channels, travel channels, ethnic channels, financial and news channels. It also opened opportunities to test new commercial forms such as infomercials and home shopping channels.

Direct response video services expanded to include support TV for direct response print as well as 60 second and 120 second spots with 800 numbers. Then home shopping became still another form of direct response with some of the most energetic salespeople ever.

Infomercials took the direct response salesperson to new highs: in 30-minute segments with production costs of $100,000 to $200,000 to $500,000, personalities such as Victoria Principal, Dionne Warwick, Joan Rivers, and Dick Cavett became winning presenters . . . exercise trainers joined them and became celebrities . . . then evangelists and faith healers, psychics and psychologists, trainers of all kinds in half-hour infomercials for mental and physical self-improvement and wealth-building hit the air, mostly cable. And it paid. It often stirred up retail demand for its products. Eventually, infomercials even moved into corporate image-building. They became respectable.

Watch a few of the infomercials that "sell." Analyze them and you'll find they start with attention getters, move to heavy dramatization of benefits, then testimonials for credibility, then involvement with more benefits and big, big offers and calls to action—sound familiar? (More on this later.)

The World Wide Web's arrival shifted the focus as every company made plans for a home page. Interactive operations became hot new businesses, *Wired* magazine was started for those who were or wanted to be "wired." Advertising agencies established special "Interactive Agencies" under their umbrellas.

Some direct marketers milled at the starting gate, waiting for the race to begin and waiting to see their place in it. Occasionally, someone sprinted forward. Ultimately, most experimented and learned.

Once the Net's head counts were verified, it was clear that a substantial, growing market was forming and more and more direct marketers began to claim success—thousands of responses, hundreds of new customers at the lowest cost per order of any medium. And, although such experimental efforts were clouded by questions of privacy and security, we were off and running!

What You Should Know about Interactive Media Today for Tomorrow

Let me be candid with you for a moment regarding this glamorous digital medium and your place on it. Although all far-seeing professionals acknowledge that we are certainly moving fast into exciting electronic technologies, it will be a while before pure, secure electronic interaction arrives on a commercial level that enables us to base major marketing decisions on it.

Technologically, right this minute it's possible for you to view a video sales message on your computer, respond within seconds, and have your order processed within 24 hours. But even though you and your kids may be ready, easy-to-use, mass-priced technology still isn't quite ready for the big markets.

Smart direct marketers believe in a bright electronic interactive future and that's why they've spent and are spending money experimenting and learning. And well they might because we—you—as direct marketers are unusually well-qualified to lead once the customer tells us it's O.K.

There are four basics that qualify direct marketers for leadership in interactive marketing:

> First, our early recognition of the importance of the role of the customer, and our role of listening to the customer. Which, in turn, is testing, of course. And this gives us

> Second, the tested techniques of creative persuasion. Our rules and direct response technique.

> Third, our reliance and understanding of database and its role in effective marketing and good relationships.

> Fourth, the absolute necessity for establishing a relationship of trust and credibility with our customers by giving full value.

Caveat: If you want to move into direct response to do interactive Web stuff—congratulations on your foresight. But don't do it without full direct marketing knowledge and practice. Direct marketing basics will give you a sound grounding in the use of interactive dialogue and relationship marketing for interactive digital marketing success.

Although it's changing almost every day, direct marketers using the World Wide Web for interactive selling are already combining new digital technologies with sound direct marketing principles. Good direct mailers (read "those who test") like Rodale Press and the Meredith Corporation and top catalogers like L.L. Bean and Lands' End still use the basic rule of AIDA (Attract *A*ttention . . . Arouse *I*nterest . . . Stimulate *D*esire . . . Call for *A*ction) in planning their Web sites.

As they have always done, they lure the prospect in with strong headline promises and graphics, they involve the prospect with benefits and motivators, they give value and reinforce with credibility, they call the prospect to act and make it easy to order.

Some say the prospect is "in control" on the Internet, that the prospect will browse at his or her leisure and pick and choose at will or on impulse. Perhaps, but this should not imply that a Web site simply "sits" there passively.

Although it allows prospects to browse, drop out or completely ignore our marketers at will—the World Wide Web is no different from any other direct response medium that is properly used. The prospect may feel he/she is in control, but the good direct marketer knows better.

A creative grounding in direct-response broadcast couldn't hurt either, as it will continue to function for us despite the World Wide Web's appeal and it offers you a fine learning experience.

Broadcast Basics

Let me tell you what to expect in broadcast. First, guidelines are called for. And, as with the Web, there are two kinds of guidelines.

The first kind are those that grow from what you've been learning all along here. The second kind of guidelines are those technical rules and formulas indigenous to a specific medium, be it broadcast or radio or the Internet.

I'm going to cover only the creative aspects of broadcast advertising here. For a good technical overview, read Al Eicoff's book, *Direct Marketing through Broadcast Media,* or read *Direct Response Television, The Authoritative Guide* by Frank R. Brady and J. Angel Vasquez. Then talk to a video producer and an editor and learn all you can about basic television production and editing capabilities before you start creating commercials. Also read carefully our experts' advice at the end of this chapter.

Some formulas or structures are set forth here to help you understand the creative process, and that's what you and I are going to concentrate on for now. We'll start with some broad-brush economics: TV commercials are expensive. The cheapest ones (practically home movies) start around $10,000 to $15,000, and they go up from there to $90,000 or so for a respectable production, then on up for the more impressive jobs with large casts and expensive locations.

Once a commercial is produced, you spend still more for testing on air. If it works—hallelujah! If it doesn't, you're out a bundle. Point: This is no place for amateurs.

Next, please keep this in mind as we move through the chapter: *Broadcast is linear while digital (the World Wide Web) transmissions are, in fact, circular or repeatable. In broadcast you start at a given point and move straight through to the end. The prospect cannot go back to reread, check a fact, get a phone number, or examine a drawing. Your promotion makes it on the first pass or it doesn't make it at all!*

There are three kinds of direct response broadcast commercials in radio and television, apart from infomercials.

1. *Support commercials:* This is the announcement that tells you to "watch your mail" or to look for something in print that's about to come your way. It can be used much as the announcement postcard is used, or even in conjunction with it. It can be used with local billboards, too, or newspapers, or any other medium. It's used with direct mail as a segment of a multimedia program.

This national television support, however, is limited to mass-appeal products such as Time-Life videos or *Reader's Digest* or big magazine subscription agents like Publisher's Clearing House and American Family Publishers. For anything less, it is costly and inefficient. Radio, on the other hand, is more flexible and can be employed on both a local and national basis.

Television support can increase response from 10 to 50 percent or more. That's respectable. So it's certainly worth testing if you qualify as a big mailer with a mass-appeal product.

2. *Lead generation:* Television and radio are pet media for such broad lead gatherers as the armed services, public services, financial services, tourist boards of many countries, and job training schools.

You can compare this use to thoroughbred print ads in terms of objectives, but the quality of the broadcast leads (particularly TV) will seldom measure up to those you get from print. That means your marketing chiefs will give special consideration in broadcast to stringent qualification, extra follow-up conversion steps, and careful testing and tracking.

3. *Selling:* The commercials that make an offer and actually call for orders are the workhorses of broadcast, and you probably visualize exercise machines, kitchen appliances, and self-help programs when you think about them. Tabletop demonstrations and "talking heads" in front of blue curtains—that's the way it used to be and still is in many infomercials. And just like our hard sell print ads, these talking heads and tabletop demonstrations get orders. Lots of them.

But you and I both know that's not the only style that works. Thanks to Time-Life Books, *U.S. News & World Report, The Wall Street Journal,* Rodale, National Liberty, Ryder Trucks, and many others, we have commercials that look great, sound good, and also get orders—the kind of commercials you wish *you* had done.

These commercials (also called *commercial spots,* or just *spots*) come in three sizes: 30 seconds, 60 seconds, and 120 seconds. The 30s are always support; 60s and 120s are generally relegated to selling products—especially products that are good TV actors. This means lots of moving parts and demonstrable benefits.

Television sells dreams, too. And it's known to do a good job on some magazines and recordings, club programs, and book and video continuity series. (Remember the joining offers with premiums from Chapter 3? Those are the kinds of offers that work best.)

Magazine subscriptions and continuity programs use the 120 commercial successfully. But all workhorse commercials should test at both 60 and 120.

The following chart shows the basic elements of each type of commercial, along with the recommended—or, dare we say, traditional—length. The number of seconds generally allotted to each element is also shown.

Classic 60-Second Support Commercial

1. Dramatization of proposition (10 to 30 seconds)
2. Facts about the primary medium (30 to 50 seconds)

Classic 30-Second Lead-Gathering Commercial

1. Statement of benefit or a problem (5 to 10 seconds)
2. Dramatization (10 to 20 seconds)
3. Telephone number and/or address (10 to 15 seconds)

Classic 60-Second Direct Response Commercial

1. Attention-getting opening (about 5 seconds)
2. Promise and/or mention of premium (up to 15 seconds)
3. Product display, possibly with premium (30 seconds)
4. Ordering information and telephone number (15 seconds)

Classic 120-Second Continuity Commercial

1. Opening and premise (5 to 10 seconds)
2. Introduction of series (15 seconds)
3. Dramatization of series (40 seconds)
4. First installment display (20 seconds)
5. Premiums, if any (position variable—10 seconds)
6. Terms of offer, ordering instructions, telephone number (20 seconds)[2]

Although such structures can be helpful to you for starters, please remember that television as a whole is always in the testing stage. Direct marketers are still learning and trying and changing. Smart marketers challenge and test such things as

- Do I really need 60 seconds on my support . . . let's test 30 seconds against this (or—are ten 30-second supports better or worse than five 60-second ones)?

- Can I get my product message across in 60 seconds? Will I need 120 seconds instead?

- How about lead generation—isn't 60 more effective than 30? Can we afford it?

When such questions of length arise, you'll find that marketers may ask you to do the longer commercial in such a way that they can merely lift out or pull out the shorter version. The shorter commercial is, in effect, an edited or cut version of the longer one. (This way, you get two commercials for the price of one—almost.)

Look again at the four commercial structures on page 355. You'll find several familiar refrains in terms of technique.

The two "selling" commercials, or video workhorses, incorporate AIDA. They have to work very fast, but their first job is to attract attention (opening); their last job is to call to action (ordering instructions). The lead-gathering commercial usually starts with a big benefit or a Problem/Solution Approach, followed by a dramatization and a call to action. This could be easily compared to the thoroughbred print ad.

The Basic Law—Does this make sense?—applies at all times. How do the commercial structures relate to the big four from Chapter 3—involvement, offer, credibility, and motivation?

Involvement: All the good commercials use the "you," just like your print ads and direct mail.

Offer: Without a strong offer, no TV spot can make it today. This usually means a premium of one kind or another and a 100 percent guarantee. If your offer doesn't have both, find out why.

Motivation: Thanks to a strong offer, and heavy emphasis on ordering instructions, good television utilizes the same kind of motivators and motivating language that you'll find in good workhorse and thoroughbred ads. And it promises almost instant gratification with its 800 response number.

Credibility: I've saved this one for last. Although the basics of credibility don't change (Who are you? Why are you qualified to make this offer?), two factors are unique to television. Let's look at them.

1. Most products and services using television do so because of broad appeal and/or broad recognition. There is less need (and less time) to establish the "who" and "why."

2. Credibility is most often established for a company (particularly a service company in a competitive situation), by the choice of spokesperson.

Some products and services do this by

- Celebrity presenters (from Deion Sanders to Ed McMahon, Arnold Schwarzenegger to Willard Scott, Kenny Rogers to Michael Jordan)

- Real-life testimonials (with real people)

- Dramatizations that demonstrate effective, reliable services

- Actors, cast as logical presenters to convey a sense of solid reliability and honesty

In addition to AIDA and the big four, your creative concept development and all that goes into it—your research, your hypothesis, big benefits and the approach—will also work for you with commercials. It must work to enable you to develop a sound foundation for your creative work, the actual planning and writing of the commercial.

Try this analogy: In your commercial, your opening is like the direct mail outer envelope (or headline/graphics in a print ad). The spokesperson and approach from your letter become the audio dialogue of your commercial. The brochure becomes your audiovisual story with dramatization of benefits and exposition of features. Your nuts 'n' bolts, the order card or coupon, becomes your ordering information at the end.

Magic words and action words (FREE, You, Here, Now, New, Act Today) are just as important as ever. Repetition is also important—even more important in the case of ordering instructions. (Response commercials not only show the 800 number, but they repeat it several times.) As with small space, you have to get it all across quickly and efficiently.

Feel comfortable with the analogy? Good. Because now I want to underline the differences for you. And they are big—so big from a creative point of view that some competent direct response writers will just never do good commercials (not you, I hope—but some).

How to Determine If You Have the Right Stuff

In addition to all the basics we've talked about, there are really two major creative qualities that you need to pass muster. These are directly related to those wonderful abilities that you honed and developed in Chapter 1 (your curiosity and your imagination). First is the ability to visualize well. Second is the ability to write good dialogue. They go together, but I'm going to take them on one at a time.

YOUR ABILITY TO VISUALIZE WELL

This requirement should come as no shock to you. You've been encouraged to do this with every print ad, every direct mail package, alone and in conjunction with the art director.

Do I hear you crying "Foul" out there? Not the same thing, you say? Stay with me a minute. We're doing a logical progression.

In a direct mail package your brochure's job is to dramatize your benefits and show all the features. Your print ad's graphics carry a heavy visual burden because they have a lot to accomplish (attract attention, qualify prospects, and introduce a benefit or two). Now what do the visuals in a commercial have to accomplish?

- Attract attention
- Qualify the prospect
- Dramatize benefits
- Show the features

However, and this is a big HOWEVER, to do it well you need a well-fed creative imagination combined with a technical (or production) knowledge of what makes up good (creative, compelling, and cost-conscious) visualization within a tight time frame. Some mouthful. But a very important mouthful.

You'll have new and exciting digital tools and you'll have to keep up-to-date on them—digital tools that enable you to blend live action with special effects seamlessly (including programmed shots, morphing, motion control). It'll be digital everything—digital manipulation, digital music, digital actors.

You also need to apply the Basic Law—will this make sense? Even in a video fantasy, it can make sense if the viewer actively suspends disbelief. (Translation: You make viewers want to believe, even though they know it's not real.)

Let me give you an example: Say your product is a magazine for car lovers. Your offer is a one-year subscription with a "car evaluation" premium. Your creative strategy meetings have kicked out a hypothesis that says, "People who appreciate new cars, fast cars, sports cars will identify with this publication and be motivated to subscribe when they learn about the premium."

Now you're sitting down with the artist for the first time. And since we're doing a commercial, let's even put this example in a script form to get you used to it. (First, you will need to know a few terms: *Storyboards* are a series of pictures that follow the script, giving illustration to every changing visual and camera move. These pictures show scenes (indoor and outdoor), details of the scenes, people, their dress, facial expressions, hands. The storyboard frames serve as a guide for the director, camera operator, producer, set designer, editor—everyone who will be involved in producing the commercial. Storyboards are the layouts or final comprehensives of video advertising. The *script* is your copy. It records every word, sound, action, and setting in your commercial.

Scenario 1

VIDEO	AUDIO
A conference room with two creative individuals. One has a beard and wears a rumpled shirt and jeans—this is the artist. The other, is the well-dressed writer—*you!*	
Both are sitting at a conference table surrounded by papers. There are two half-empty coffee cups.	

VIDEO	AUDIO
The artist has a storyboard pad in front of him.	ARTIST (tone, self-assured and slightly overbearing): Here's how I see it. We'll need race track. A lot of really classy sports cars parked next to the track. Then, if we can get this guy that won the Indy 500, shoot him racing . . . then he drives right up to the camera and holds up a copy of the magazine. We CU on it, then dissolve to someone like Tom Brokaw telling the viewer. . . .
The artist sits opposite the writer. Both seem somewhat rigid, uptight.	
The writer frowns.	
The writer shifts nervously.	
Finally the writer can't hold back. Writer stands up and interrupts.	WRITER (voice high-pitched and agitated): I don't see it that way, Harry. I think we ought to theme the whole thing as a dream sequence. All the new cars featured on the premium should sort of float across the screen with these elegant models standing around. At the back we'll have a symphony orchestra with Michael Douglas conducting and . . .
Artist squirms and stares out the nearest window, all but ignoring the writer.	

CUT!

Scenario 2 (Same as Scenario 1)

VIDEO	AUDIO
Artist and writer are hunched over a pile of papers at the end of a long conference table. They are friends and you get a sense of real collaboration.	ARTIST (warm voice but concerned): I think this is going to be tough. We only have $45,000. That sort of zaps out the celebrity spokesman. WRITER (thoughtful, intelligent): Yup. And if we have to shoot in December, we can't even afford to do a location.

VIDEO	**AUDIO**
	ARTIST (energetic and optimistic): California would have been nice. Well, let's switch to digital. (reads slowly from list) race track and race . . . classic car show . . . antique car race . . .
	WRITER (interrupting thoughtfully): You know, we could do something nice here, and still have the money for a real race driver presenter!
Artist begins to sketch. Camera moves in to CU of paper	ARTIST (speaks with slight humor): I take it you're not planning on a cast of hot-shot characters?
	WRITER (thoughtful as always): One really good actor should do it—unless we can find a real live race star. Willing and cheap.
As the two of them work you can see the excitement build.	ARTIST (with enthusiasm): We've also got all those beautiful spreads from the magazine!
	WRITER (nodding and looking thoughtfully at papers): Yes—and the premium. Wow! I'm running short on time already.
First the artist jumps up, then the writer. The two walk toward the door together, completely absorbed in their conversation.	ARTIST (with enthusiasm): I'll check out the stock footage. And see what the chances are on a big star.
	WRITER (with determination): Good. Meanwhile, I'm going to play with a couple of approaches.
	ARTIST (hopefully): Will you have something by next week?

VIDEO	**AUDIO**
	WRITER (resignedly): Sure. I guess so. Damn—I wish this was shooting in June!

CUT!

Now which is the right scenario? And who said this is a glamorous business?

You haven't even begun to draw on your creative imagination and already you're dramatically limited by the budget. What's more, you desperately want this commercial to win. A tough assignment. But it's not unusual. And it gives you a good idea of the many production elements to be considered long before you get your good idea.

Start with budget and production requirements; gain a firm knowledge of what things cost *before* you start spinning your creative wheels. Otherwise, you'll walk in with a great visual idea that's either totally or way out of the bounds of your budget. To understand the creative possibilities, you need some technical grounding in

- The cost of location work
- Studio and set costs, lighting options
- Costs of talent (and residuals)
- Ballpark costs on big names
- Capabilities and costs of digital editing
- Advantages and limitations of tape

Once you have this technical grounding, let your creative imagination go for a strong visual image that can dramatize the benefits within the bounds of the budget and the restrictions of time. In creating your spot, never forget your objective—to get a response (and a customer)—NOW!

YOUR ABILITY TO WRITE GOOD DIALOGUE

This is a second essential and you won't even get past your creative supervisor if you can't handle this one well. All along we've been discussing dialogue marketing, one-on-one, and "talking" to your market as you talk to one individual. By now you know every direct mail letter needs a logical spokesperson, and that your role as a writer includes the skills of both actor and salesperson. You take on these roles primarily to establish a dialogue with the prospect. Like your letters, your commercial will talk directly to the prospect. Right?

But this, this is the real thing, you may say. It's—well—audio. Right again! How it *sounds* is every bit as important as how it reads.

When you write broadcast, you write in the sound of tinkling glass, a footstep . . . a deep, authoritative tone . . . a hesitant, weak reply . . . the clock ticks, the door slams, the announcer talks on, the music rises. And you must *hear* it all. Then record it, on paper or your computer.

How inadequate. Paper and pencil. To record something so alive, so vibrant. But someone, many people (director, actors, actresses) will need a map to follow and that's what your copy—your script—will give them.

Imagine this for a moment. You've started visualizing, digging around for a really keen idea that can work within your budget and your time frame. Now who are your actors? Who is your logical spokesperson? Is this a simple one-on-one (one announcer to one viewer)? Or are you doing a dramatization for the viewer? Or both? Do you want to hear and see your announcer? Or just a voice? And how do you get started?

Starting out may be the toughest part for you. But think for a minute. How have we been starting all along? By choosing an approach.

1. Put down your hypothesis.

2. Choose your spokesperson (don't forget credibility!)

    *   disembodied (but credible) voiceover

    *   dialogue between two people

    *   a presenter (on camera)

    *   a celebrity presenter

3. Now go for your approach. What works best with your big visual?

Many television spots just drop the viewer right into a dramatization for starters. You can do this, too. Viewers are used to it . . . thirty seconds in someone's bathroom . . . fifteen seconds in a strange kitchen or a speeding car. (Think how many commercials do this to you every time you watch TV.)

O.K. Back to first base. How do you get a strong fast start? Answers:

1. Lead with a hot dramatization and voiceover—or a dramatization in which the primary figure becomes the spokesperson.

2. Lead with a standard presenter on camera and a simple "Hello." Then move right into your headline—your strong lead that attracts attention and qualifies the prospect ("Hello. How'd you like to win a million dollars? You can. Listen carefully.")

3. Lead with a celebrity presenter on camera. Go for instant identification, then move right into the lead. ("Hi, I'm Thistle Braithwaite. Have you ever seen the pain in a hungry child's smile?")

Close your eyes and go over your big visual. Now choose your approach or approaches:

- *Problem/Solution*: "Make sure your white shirts never look gray and dingy."
- *Question*: "How many times have you made this same mistake?"
- *Testimonial*: "Boy, I never thought I'd be a winner."
- *Story*: "There we were, 100 miles from nowhere with a flat."
- *Fantasy*: "How'd you like to be Queen for a Day!"
- *If/Assumptive*: "If you're tired of coming home to dirty dishes . . . ."
- *Generic*: "Now, for the first time, enjoy exercising at home. . . ."

And so on.

"GET IT DOWN" TIME

Think of your customer. Put the customer in front of you. Listen to the dialogue in your head. Follow your big visual. Use your approach. Remember your structure. Write it all down! Then go back and fix it up.

Suggestion: Block out the action. Overlay your rough timing: for example, your opener—5 seconds, your offer—15 seconds, your dramatization—25 seconds, your wrap-up and order information—15 seconds.

Then make sure your dialogue builds on the visuals and moves you logically into the sales message, through the visuals and out at the end to your call to action. Your TV spot is a stage, and every segment of your drama must flow into the next with continuity. Don't worry about the details (like sound effects) until you develop the dialogue. And don't step out of character. Hear your characters speak as you write. Keep the spoken words short, clear, direct.

- "Christmas . . . Crisp, cool mornings and warm memories. . . ."
- "Designed by skilled Florentine craftsmen . . . ."
- "What a lovely gift idea!"
- "This amazing little knife even grates cheese . . . ."
- "The lion—if it's hungry, it will eat you."
- "Enjoy it all, every month, in the pages of . . . ."
- ". . . and it's all yours for only $19.98!"
- "Here's how to order . . . ."

Caveat: Here's one of the biggest mistakes you may make as you start out. *Don't use dialogue to repeat the visual.* Let the camera do a lot of your talking. See it. Then use words to complete and expand the visual. For example: A dirty, tired man sitting on a kitchen stoop.

No: "Boy, am I dirty and tired . . . ."

Yes: "Boy—I'm going to think twice before I try to clean the cellar again."

Next, what kind of sounds will you have? And how about your stage instruction? Listen. Listen to your dialogue. Voice sounds, room sounds, outdoor sounds. Hear the footsteps, hear the floor creak while you see the door opening. Hear the sounds of a cup connecting gently with its saucer as the woman moves it aside.

Now listen to her. You know what you want her to say. But you must also make her warm and credible and authoritative and clear and convincing. In 20 seconds. Every word counts.

How about adding music? It can set your mood and enhance it, and it can move you along.

Consider the details of the scene:

- You want a couple discussing the pros of the product. How do you get them on? How do you position them and make them real?

- You want the gentle touch of a child—a brief comment from a small boy. Justify him. Can you get him on and off in 15 seconds? What editing techniques might you apply?

- You plan to have a man and a woman presenter. Who should they be? Why are they qualified? Orchestrate the sound and pitch of their voices mentally. Who's the heavy? Does it work?

- What's the dialogue structure between the two actors—question and answer? A countdown list? Point and counterpoint? Any humor? You have 40 seconds.

- You're going to tell a story with only an announcer's voiceover to carry it along. How do you finish? Should the announcer come on camera? You have only 20 seconds for the order information.

Once you've gone through "Get it down!" and "Do it over," and put in all your sound instructions and staging, get yourself a stopwatch and start timing and cutting. It's time to polish it up.

And remember, budget enough time for polishing. (You probably recognize this as the same set of guidelines you've had all along. But now you also have to see and hear and orchestrate it all together in your script within your allotted time.)

The best way to cut and polish—the only way I can see doing it—is *out loud* with your stopwatch. (People will think you're going crazy after a while, so close your door.) Visualize, read out loud, act, change, improve. Time it. Visualize, act out with emphasis, change, improve. Time it. And on.

By the way, when you get those technically correct writers doing commercials, you're liable to hear what I call a lot of "audio hype." And it really does sound like a circus barker. This goes hand in hand with those old-fashioned talking heads. There is a place for this, I guess, but try to avoid audio hype. Use your creative imagination along with your acting ability to create warm, friendly, credible dialogue. Play it straight. Keep it simple. (Remember small space ads!)

How Others Figure in with You

1. *The Artist or Art Director:* By now you've probably guessed what I'm going to say. Yes, call in your art director *early*—especially if you have worked as a team through the creative strategy development. (Remember, artists have a reputation for thinking visually.) Keep the collaboration going right through your creative presentation (you with the script, the art director with the storyboards). (Note that artists working on commercials are almost always called "art directors.")

2. *The Casting Director or Supervisor:* After all the approvals are in and the script is finalized, a production house is chosen and the casting begins. If you can stay with it (if they'll let you), don't abandon your baby! Try to sit in on the casting, make your opinions known. After all, you heard that voice when you wrote the script. You *saw* that face. Now shouldn't you have a say in making the selection? I think you should.

3. *The Director:* Once your final script is approved, the director takes over. I hope you can go along. There's only one caveat. At some point, your baby also becomes the director's baby. You can't be a tyrant or fight to protect your creation here. Work closely with the director—he or she is in charge. Watch and listen.

4. *The Editor:* If you felt you could help with casting, imagine what you can add to editing. Here they'll be cutting and combining footage, adding sound effects (SFX) and special effects (DISS, RIP, FREEZE, SLOMO, FADE, WIPE, S.S., SUPER). Be there if you can! You saw it and heard it first. It was your concept. See it through. (This goes for the artist or art director, too.)

Your contribution to production and editing will depend a lot on the director's relation to you and on the rest of the production and postproduction group. If it's a loose operation and you know your film business, you may be part of the filming or taping and work directly with the editors. In some rare cases the director may not want you on the premises. I hope this doesn't happen. You'll learn more about creating good commercials when you know all the magic things a director and an editor can do. By the way, you'll grow to love good editors. They're the miracle workers, the problem solvers, the edge-smoothers who will give your commercial a professional shine.

Bet You Thought I Forgot Radio

I have not focused on radio up to now, but I haven't forgotten it, and I hope you don't either. Radio is a thoroughly delightful place to learn, practice, and apply dialogue principles without having to worry about visuals. It's easier to script, it's easier to cast, no artist is needed, and in a pinch, you can even double as the director (unless, of course, it's a big production with personality talent teams and tailor-made jingles).

Radio experience can also give you an entree to TV. Radio spots come in about the same sizes and shapes as TV spots: they're used the same way. But the budgets are miles apart. You write it, bid it out (to a sound studio), cast it, rehearse it, tape it, and edit it. And often you can come in under a few thousand dollars and get more than one commercial. Of course, where original music or top personalities are involved, costs can go much higher. But on the simpler commercials, your cost (the cost of creating the script) is probably the biggest number in the budget.

Does radio work? I don't think anyone knows the big answer to this. Some people use it regularly because it works for them—on a small scale. There are even a few cases where the "right" station with the right product and right commercials at just the right time has put a small company in business. Radio also pops up frequently as part of a media mix. But no one has done any heavy research on response and radio. Consequently it languishes.

You won't find much support radio in direct response marketing, either. On a national basis, the big support users prefer television, and when radio is used on a local basis, nobody seems to bother to test such a low-budget investment. With no measurements you have no success story—and no big popularity.

Radio ranks well below television as a selling medium because it lacks visual credibility. Overall, radio has a pretty tough time attracting and holding attention and getting someone to pick up a pencil or a phone, unless the product is already known to the audience and the spot is run frequently.

Magazines have done well with 60-second spots for subscription sales, but this can be directly attributed to good media buys where the market already knows the product. Radio can work for lead getting with a premium. But this is part of a mix. For your purposes, just know that radio is not a primary medium.

Radio, however, could be good news for you. If you do get a radio assignment, try to avoid radio's equivalent of the talking head. Think about it. It's bad on TV, but doubly bad (boring) on radio! There are two alternatives to a blaring monologue floating without root or reason on the airwaves: 1) Get the local announcer to do it (and take your chances), or 2) Do a peppy dialogue between two people.

Either alternative can be effective. Both offer easy on-stage/off-stage possibilities. The dialogue can be a lot of fun for you, and fun for the listener, especially if you're out for pure support. It's one place where there's room for levity—a little, anyway. But make sure it's ho-ho-ho, not ho-hum. Do your timing and your reading out loud just like TV. Give yourself enough time, too—just like TV.

The big difference: With radio you don't augment the video. You've got dialogue, but no one can see, so your dialogue builds the picture. No lines like, "What are you doing here?" Instead, "What are you doing in the basement?" For the man on the stoop, back to, "I've never felt so dirty and tired . . . ." Your words build the visual.

I'd like to be able to tell you that radio is making a big comeback today. It deserves to. Perhaps it is. Watch for it. And write for it when you can. It's a delightful experience every time.

Your Media Mix

Most broadcast is part of a media mix or part of an advertising campaign rather than a primary medium all on its own. Because of this, your work in most electronic media, be it television, radio or the Internet, must also *integrate*—tie in with the campaign, reinforce its offers, incorporate its themes. Your big visual may come directly from the print ads . . . your radio may reproduce and reinforce the TV spot's audio (same jingle, same slogans) . . . your support spot may tell the viewer not only to watch for the mail, but also how to respond to the mail to get an extra premium. ("Check the empty box on the reply card for an additional free gift.") This sort of thing gives you a solid measure of the effectiveness of your electronic support. All such media planning is usually done at one time up front, well-coordinated and timed, part of the big picture.

You may run into the mix often these days as direct marketers are becoming more and more involved with multimedia programs. They are learning to make the media work together for image building and awareness as well as for selling. Even though true measurements on the value of each individual medium have been nearly impossible to achieve, the overall impact, both immediate and long-range, can often more than justify the overall expense.

Wisdom from the Pros

TOP TV WINNERS DISCUSS THEIR SPOTS

I'd like to enrich your background a little here with some pertinent experience from two top award-winners for direct response television (those 120s and 60s). Both Bob Dodd, executive creative director at Time-Life Video, and Bob Cesiro, senior vice president, group creative director at FCB Direct, contributed heavy creative direction for commercials in the early 1990s that received the Direct Marketing Association's highest awards.

Bob Dodd's winning "Predators of the Wild" was a series of exciting, fast-moving videocassettes with animals, birds—even insects—

that preyed on other living things for food. Bob had an unusual situation because the selling power of the product—the actual film footage—was available to him. But how to organize and plan . . . how to make this a story that did the job without going too far, but just far enough!

Here are the steps that Bob and his team followed, from their creative preproduction planning through the shoot:

1. The Positioning Statement was written in committee during a three-meeting process with the marketing staff, followed by the final formulation by Bob and his creative partners.

2. The Customer Promise was the creative translation of the marketing positioning and the first step in the *Creative Work Plan* that Bob then developed. Notice that this plan includes such subtle guides as "Sensations" and "Negatives," as well as Benefits, Features, Hot Buttons (visual input based on research and available footage), Tone, Look, Music, Possible Supers, plus specs and offers. (See Figure 10–1).

3. Since the body of the Predator commercials would come from the actual cassette footage, artwork and design were confined to the framing—beginnings, end, and in between. Both computer composition and actual drawings were used in this stage of development. (See Figure 10–2.)

4. The script prior to shooting offers screen instructions for both clips and offer plus full audio. But note the changes in this script during the shoot. Compare the initial script shown in Figure 10–3 with the final script shown in Figure 10–4.[3]

Now here's sound advice from Bob Cesiro, who explains what he learned from creating commercials that both generate awareness for the client's product and produce measurable response:

> I do not believe in rigidly following rules or structures, but always use them for guidance, as David Ogilvy once recommended . . . . I believe it's more important to learn why something works. People often make fun of a Ginsu-knife commercial, or other typical late-night TV offers that follow a formula, but it's critical to learn and understand why those things work. In short, be creative—manipulate the formula to the unexpected, but make sure it works.
>
> With DRTV [direct response TV] there are many basic truths that are really things that are simple and practical. For example, much has been discussed and written about how long the phone number should appear. It is always better to err by having it appear too much, rather than too little. When possible, the number should be heard as well as seen, simply because it's easier to remember.
>
> *Make sure the reply card fits into the reply envelope*—What are we talking about? This was supposed to be television. Having done a great deal of direct mail before I ever worked on television, I learned that many principles of direct marketing transcend the media. In mail, if the reply card doesn't fit the reply envelope, less

FIGURE 10–1   Creative Work Plan for "Predators of the Wild" Commercial

Something caught his eye or ear, he got the feeling he had something very weird and true here, his thumb paused on the remote control. He can surf away any time, he was curious, "what is this?"

Ooo, this is very cool stuff. Dark and deadly, chilling. You can feel the hunt. Hey, I wanted to see more of that, but this is weird, too. God, I wouldn't want to run into that—wait a second, I wanted more. I didn't know there were still places and things like that—I didn't know there were things like that. Where's the phone?

While he was waiting for the operator and started his transaction, Steve filled up his head with the pieces of facts he heard, the weird places and the deadly creatures, their powers and abilities—all the cool things he was going to have to talk about.

Customer Promise

Confront living nightmares and discover the true facts of their deadly powers with *Predators of the Wild* from Time-Life Video.

Reasons Why

- You'll see amazing, true things that are beyond belief (real facts about the strangest creatures, the weirdest places).

- You'll see the most deadly and horrifying creatures on the Earth—and only them (no pretty, harmless creatures here, except for prey).

- You'll feel squeamy confronting the scariest, creepiest creatures on earth (and charged by sitting there and facing it).

- This is not your usual NATURE VIDEO. It's just the coolest, and only the coolest, nature stuff.

Collection Benefits

- You see things you won't believe—a giant tarantula killing a lethal snake, a tiger attacking an elephant, tribesmen eating roasted spiders, vicious hyenas and more.

- Discover why these creatures are so feared, hear the myths and see the facts about their remarkable instincts and powers, their amazing tactics and behavior.

- Explore the deepest, darkest, most dangerous places on the earth, and watch its murderous everyday life unfold.

- Rare, up-close and personal footage of the creepiest, scariest, most deadly creatures on the earth. Creatures you usually don't see *anything* about—now you can understand *everything* about them.

FIGURE 10–1   (Continued)

- *Predators* is full of stories and interesting facts you'll be able to share with friends.

- Sharp, handsome and compelling packaging, each conveniently featuring its own deadly creature.

- You'll get new insights into human interaction by watching the hunting behavior of these creatures.

- You won't see anything that's fuzzy and gentle and cute—unless one of the *Predators* is killing it.

- This is a must for any serious nature video collector—a specified, in-depth look at the most interesting and compelling creatures in wildlife, with more details and more facts about snakes and tarantulas and the other real-life monsters in the natural world.

Hot Buttons

Things that the prospect really gets excited about.
(Explanatory subhead on old TLV CWP form)

Okay, I'll go with that. So, rather than bullet compelling shots that are actually on the tape, or images related to the product that are already in the pop culture and should be exploited (which are the two ways we've been approaching it), this time I'll list the kinds of imagery that would best work against this positioning and work plan. Let's see how this old-fashioned "conceptual" listing works as a guide to our actual shot selection.

- Eyes glaring through foliage, targeting.

- The intense, building suspense of the hunt: waiting, stalking, then the sudden, vicious attack.

- Facts and details they've never heard before; angles and views of horrific creatures they've never seen before.

- The uneven, vicious combat of two creatures, the animal that doesn't stand a chance putting up a great, noble fight.

- Deadly creatures lunging out of nowhere right into your face.

- A sense that the cameraman is in actual danger.

- The beauty of slow-motion—the intricacy of any *Predator*'s strike at a pace that you can see it.

Negatives

- Ultimately this is a nature film, to ignore that fact would be a huge negative. It would be like marketing football without the running game—everybody would think you're selling Arena Football again and not want to watch.

FIGURE 10–1   (Continued)

- Boring, intoning British voices saying predictable, overly-dramatic phrases.
- Too much of any one kind of action—Johnny One-Noting.
- Giving away the store—showing too much of any one thing.

Tone Of Commercial

Promising. Threatening. Masculine. Insinuating.

Look Of Commercial

Suspenseful. Vicious. "In your face." Suggestive.

Music

Dramatic, suspenseful, deadly.

Possible Supers

Now on Home Video
No Club to Join
Delivered to Your Home
Phones Open 24 Hours
Satisfaction Guaranteed
Cancel Any Time
Call Now

Plus price and terms; the necessary copyrights and logos; and anything else that comes out of the script that will help the sale.

Required Specs.

- :120, :90 & :60 for each spot in the test
- Additional voice-over piece stating $5.00 higher price point (e.g. $14.99 & $24.99) for possible Canadian versions.
- *A list of phone number placements (in and out points) in frame-specific time code covering all versions.*

Offer(s)

First Tape $9.99 plus $3.23 S&H
Following tapes $19.99 plus $3.23 S&H each

FIGURE 10–2   Art Used to Frame Video Clips

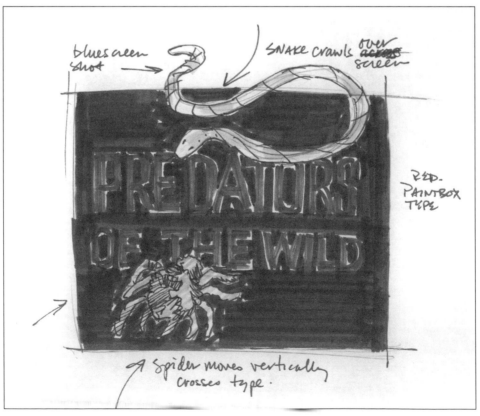

FIGURE 10–3   Initial Script for "Predators of the Wild" Commercial

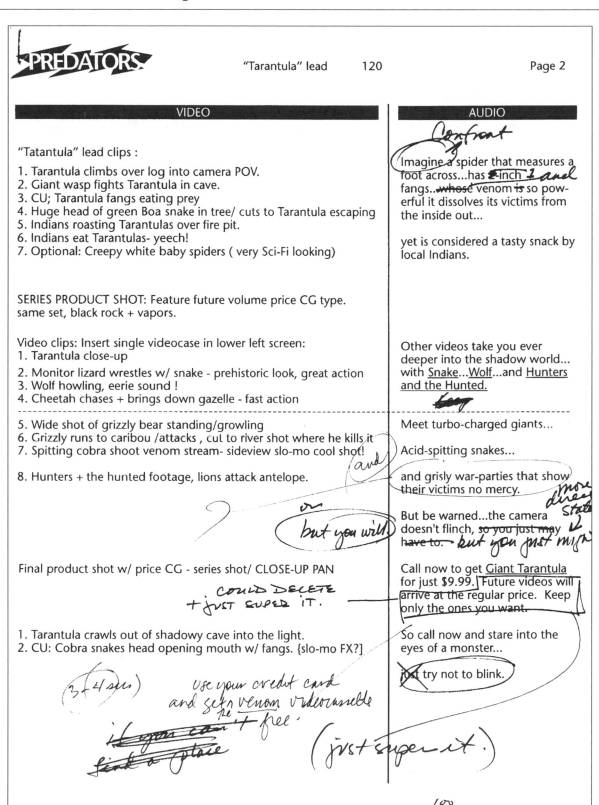

"PREDATORS   "Tarantula" lead   120   Page 2

VIDEO	AUDIO

"Tatantula" lead clips :

1. Tarantula climbs over log into camera POV.
2. Giant wasp fights Tarantula in cave.
3. CU; Tarantula fangs eating prey
4. Huge head of green Boa snake in tree/ cuts to Tarantula escaping
5. Indians roasting Tarantulas over fire pit.
6. Indians eat Tarantulas- yeech!
7. Optional: Creepy white baby spiders (very Sci-Fi looking)

Confront
Imagine a spider that measures a foot across...has 2-inch *1 and* fangs..~~whose~~ venom ~~is~~ so powerful it dissolves its victims from the inside out...

yet is considered a tasty snack by local Indians.

SERIES PRODUCT SHOT: Feature future volume price CG type. same set, black rock + vapors.

Video clips: Insert single videocase in lower left screen:
1. Tarantula close-up

2. Monitor lizard wrestles w/ snake - prehistoric look, great action
3. Wolf howling, eerie sound !
4. Cheetah chases + brings down gazelle - fast action

Other videos take you ever deeper into the shadow world... with <u>Snake</u>...<u>Wolf</u>...and <u>Hunters and the Hunted.</u>

5. Wide shot of grizzly bear standing/growling
6. Grizzly runs to caribou /attacks , cut to river shot where he kills it
7. Spitting cobra shoot venom stream- sideview slo-mo cool shot!

8. Hunters + the hunted footage, lions attack antelope.

and

Meet turbo-charged giants...

Acid-spitting snakes...

and grisly war-parties that show their victims no mercy.

more direct state

But be warned...the camera doesn't flinch, ~~so you just may have to.~~ *but you just might*

on

but you will

Final product shot w/ price CG - series shot/ CLOSE-UP PAN

COULD DELETE + just SUPER IT.

1. Tarantula crawls out of shadowy cave into the light.
2. CU: Cobra snakes head opening mouth w/ fangs. {slo-mo FX?}

Call now to get <u>Giant Tarantula</u> for just $9.99. Future videos will arrive at the regular price. Keep only the ones you want.

So call now and stare into the eyes of a monster...

~~just~~ try not to blink.

(3-4 secs)

Use your credit card and get a venom videocassette free.

if you can't

(just super it.)

100

FIGURE 10–3   (Continued)

Bob Dodd comments in blue

PREDATORS   "Tarantula" lead $9.99/:120   9/93

VIDEO	AUDIO

VIDEO

Opening clips: Nightime oriented shots - eerie

1. Camera POV: rushing thru the jungle at ground level- fast
2. CU: rattlesnake attacks camera
3. ~~Shark rises from water surface/ flashs teeth~~
4. Wolves fighting w/ each other at night
5. Leopards face w/ glowing green eyes at night
6. ~~Tarantulas crawling at night~~
7. Tiger ~~hunts at night, stalking thru the leaves~~ of trees/sideview.
   (Above video clips will be edited w/ some "negative" FX
   to accentuate night time/terror look + feel)

Cut to Full screen super of series title w/ live snake +tarantula crawling over the image. Followed by FIRST PRODUCT SHOT: series shot
on black rock/ mountain surface w/ dry ice vapors at ground level +
red/purple gel lighting FX.

Series clips: action oriented

1.CU: Snake headw/ fangs
2. Tarantula fights snake in cave
[2.A:] Infared view of mouse(snake prey)- snakes sense heat of prey
3. Great white shark swims on surface opens mouth full 'o' teeth
4. Violent thrashing mako shark eats fish chunk, close-up view
5. Hyena walks with zebra leg in mouth!
6. Two lions pull down bison, (from opening trailer section)
7. CU: wolf snarls at camera w/ shining eyes - scary!
8. Sideview of tiger stalking thru dense jungle/trees
9. Tiger grabs monkey in jungle, swings it in the air violently.

LEAD PRODUCT SHOT: "GREAT TARANTULAS"
   w/same set, black rock + vapors.

AUDIO

You're in a

Annc: ~~Imagine a~~ nightmare...
...filled with monsters that bite...
   that crawl...
   that kill.

A nightmare more terrifying,
because it's real.
Welcome to nature's dark side...

Welcome to Predators of the Wild
-- an intense journey through a
real-life chamber of horrors --
only from Time-Life Video.

Face creatures so fearsome only
the brave dare get close enough
to film them.
Lightning-fast fangs...
· Spiders that launch missiles...
· Bone-crushing jaws...
· Lethal weapons in an ancient war
  of survival...

Seen so close...they will make
your skin crawl.

Call this toll-free number now
and begin your journey to the
shadow world with Giant
Tarantula --yours for just $9.99.

FIGURE 10–4   Final Script for "Predators of the Wild" Commercial

N:120

YOU'RE IN A NIGHTMARE...
...FILLED WITH MONSTERS THAT BITE...
    THAT CRAWL...
    THAT KILL.

A NIGHTMARE MORE TERRIFYING, BECAUSE IT'S REAL.
WELCOME TO NATURE'S DARK SIDE...

WELCOME TO PREDATORS OF THE WILD -- AN INTENSE JOURNEY
THROUGH A REAL-LIFE CHAMBER OF HORRORS -- FROM TIME-LIFE
VIDEO.

FACE CREATURES SO FEARSOME ONLY THE BRAVE DARE GET CLOSE
ENOUGH TO FILM THEM.

LIGHTNING-FAST FANGS...

SPIDERS THAT LAUNCH MISSILES...

BONE-CRUSHING JAWS...

LETHAL WEAPONS IN AN ANCIENT WAR OF SURVIVAL...

SEEN SO CLOSE...THEY WILL MAKE YOUR SKIN CRAWL.

"Now on Home Video"

CALL THIS TOLL-FREE NUMBER NOW AND BEGIN YOUR JOURNEY TO
THE SHADOW WORLD WITH GIANT TARANTULA -- YOURS FOR JUST
$9.99.

CONFRONT A SPIDER THAT MEASURES A FOOT ACROSS...HAS 1-INCH
FANGS...AND VENOM SO POWERFUL IT DISSOLVES ITS VICTIMS FROM
THE INSIDE OUT...

YET IS CONSIDERED A TASTY SNACK BY LOCAL INDIANS.

OTHER VIDEOS TAKE YOU DEEPER INTO THE SHADOW WORLD... WITH
SNAKE...WOLF...AND HUNTERS AND THE HUNTED.

MEET TURBO-CHARGED GIANTS...

ACID-SPITTING SNAKES...

AND GRISLY WAR-PARTIES THAT SHOW THEIR VICTIMS NO MERCY.

BUT BE WARNED...THE CAMERA DOESN'T FLINCH, BUT YOU PROBABLY
WILL.

Call Now

CALL NOW TO GET GIANT TARANTULA FOR JUST $9.99. KEEP ONLY
THE TAPES YOU WANT. THERE'S NEVER A COMMITTMENT TO BUY.

SO CALL NOW AND STARE INTO THE EYES OF A MONSTER...

AND TRY NOT TO BLINK.

people will respond . . . . Fit is important. For television, comfortable fit is key. I've noticed that many people new to DRTV (and even those with experience) tend to overwrite or put too much in a television commercial. Copy usually should not be wall-to-wall sound. More time than originally planned is often needed for an image to convey a message, or to set a pace or mood, or to alleviate the drone of a two-minute announcer . . . beware when constructing a spot; things fit on paper much easier than in reality.

You have a much harder job to do with a DR spot compared to a brand or straight spot. You have to make somone get off the sofa and make a phone call, which is harder than it sounds. Inertia will hold the prospect back, even if he's interested.

One of the reasons DRTV spots say "operators are standing by" and often show a telemarketer is to reinforce that you can call right now.

I prefer doing simple sketches when doing a story board, especially when people are involved. Sometimes clients react to the style of the sketch . . . . if it looks too finished they may get caught up in how pretty or colorful the picture is or how someone looks.

This commercial (see Figure 10–5) was an idea we presented to AT&T to explain local toll calling. It's a very complex problem when you consider that people have no time to listen to explanations of calling patterns, intra-latas, etc. (Research showed people responded to the simplest explanation possible, using known locations for reference.)

Use as many or few frames as needed to clearly express the idea. This board does not have video instructions. The on-camera man in the spot is supposed to be a football coach writing on his chalkboard—it's an image that is easy for anyone to visualize. The title cards are meant to be graphically similar to the bold chalk lines on a blackboard, as the coach explains the problem he's having when he calls one of his plays.

This is about the simplest way to do a board and it's the quickest and most economical. I've presented boards like this with music playing in the background while the script is read, or with a soundtrack that has all the dialogue and voiceovers recorded.

Obviously, more detailed boards are often needed depending on the situation . . . special effects, complexity of the image . . . The best way to present and create boards depends on the creative, you and the client. I've presented scripts and key visuals that were developed on a napkin.

With technology, there are more tools available. "Steal-A Matics" or work done from sample film footage can be done faster than ever before with computers. The danger is that more variations and changes can occur because the technology makes it easier to do. The AVID equipment that lets editors do remarkable things quickly on line is a deterrent to the creative when used the wrong way. The industry joke is that AVID really stands for Another Version Instead of Decision.

Soon more of this technology will be available at your desktop. Recognize when it's getting in the way of your ideas. Go back to the napkin at regular intervals.[4]

FIGURE 10–5   Storyboard for an AT&T Commercial

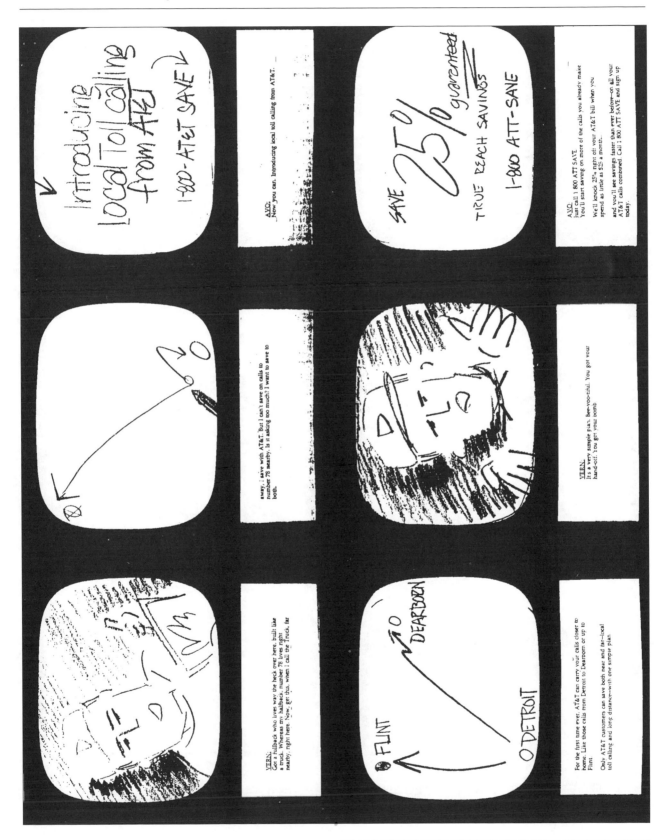

FIGURE 10–5   (Continued)

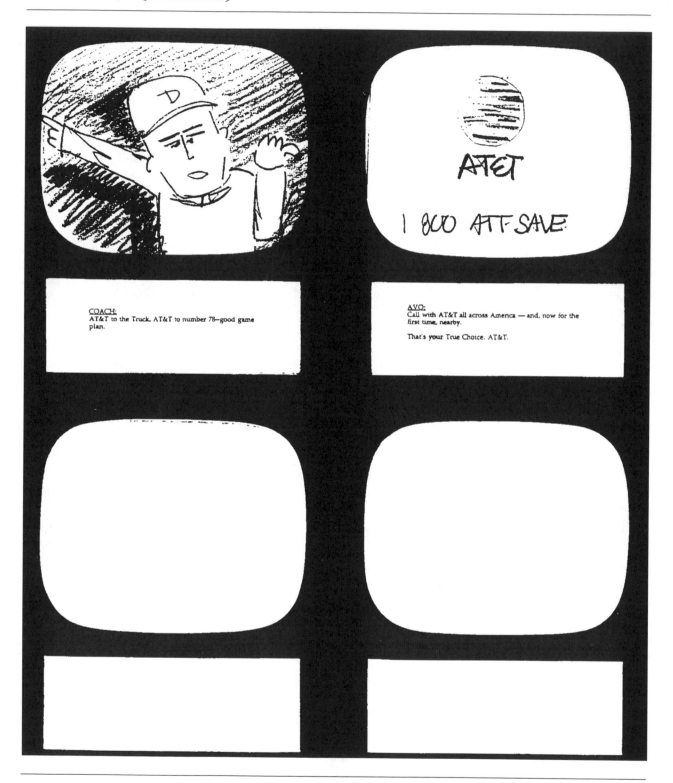

You can see here that traditional formats and storyboard structures (with dialogue and visuals blocked out, SFX and timing) are no longer a strict tradition. Bob Cesiro keeps it loose, depending on the project and the client, while Bob Dodd adjusts to the use of existing footage, carefully cut and manipulated for a truly dramatic effect.

More flexibility is the word for the future of video creative—which, I suspect, will ultimately become a pure digital desktop function.

An Inside Look at Infomercials

Next I want to add a little special inside input from leading creative people and companies that are making those half-hour infomercial winners. Rated among the top producers are Guthy-Renker Corporation in Palm Desert, California, and Time-Life Video in Alexandria, Virginia. They have provided some advice for you along with helpful examples.

If you watch cable (and I certainly hope you do), you've seen Guthy-Renker and Time-Life Video infomercials many times. Guthy-Renker developed and produced such early winners as Victoria Principal's "Principal Secret," Vanna White's "Perfect Smile," Bruce and Kris Jenner's "Power Trainer," Fran Tarkenton's "Power Rider," and Anthony Robbins' "Personal Power."

Time-Life Video got its experience with 60s and 120s, as you've already seen. The jump into winning infomercials was a logical one for their video and audio cassette series. So let's pick up where the 120s left off. Here's what the pros thought you should know.

INFOMERCIAL GUIDELINES FROM GUTHY-RENKER

The financial constraints of 30-minute infomercials are significantly different than those of a 120-second spot. Simply said, products that sell well in 120 seconds are frequently unable to generate the revenue needed to succeed in a longer format.

Since infomercial products are traditionally higher priced than their short form direct response counterparts, they frequently have unique characteristics. Here is a brief list.

Infomercial products should:

1. Possess tremendous margins
2. Confer an immediate benefit
3. Have few substitute products (little or no competition)
4. Have continuity potential
5. Be hard to duplicate
6. Offer mass market appeal
7. Be easy to explain

Here are some suggestions on how to develop successful supporting copy.

- Create three stand-alone creative features called "pods." Each pod is approximately eight minutes in length and is followed by a two-minute "commercial" that summarizes the offer and presents the price. A pod should explain in full the product, the benefits it confers and why it is an exceptional value.

  Why eight-minutes pods? Relatively few people see an infomercial in its entirety. Research indicates people may see pieces of an infomercial five or six times before making a purchase.

  Since people see only bits and pieces of your marketing material, you must make sure they can still get the full message. This is why infomercials are divided into three short (more digestible) pieces.

- Infomercial copy should appeal to the fact the DRTV customers are impulse buyers looking for products that provide immediate benefits (lose weight, gain wealth, etc.).

  Copywriters should keep in mind that infomercial customers are looking for immediate satisfaction. The copy in an infomercial should be constructed with this in mind.

  Because of it, prevention products (fire extinguishers, stop smoking programs, etc.) have a harder time realizing positive revenue.

- Infomercial copy should highlight the importance of buying the product immediately. (This product is not sold in stores.)

- Infomercial copy should convey that different groups (men/women, young/mature) find the product appealing and enjoyable to use for maximum appeal.

  This does not mean that the positioning of the product should change. Successful direct response copy is centered around a benefit that is described through the product's features and illustrated through testimonials from different "groups." The key is to slam home the product's immediate benefit.

- Justify the price point.

- Use testimonials. The home shopping networks have proven that sales increase when sincere testimonials are integrated into the pitch. Testimonials can also expand the demographic profile of a product without diluting its positioning.

The Offer and call to action should come at the end of each pod. Therefore, at the end of each eight-minute sales presentation, copywriters should include a separate 120-second "commercial" to announce the offer.

Since the call to action only comes every eight minutes or so, do two things throughout the show:

1. Make sure the viewer knows this is an infomercial—good story telling is important, but the goal is to sell the product.

2. Interest and involve the viewer, encouraging him/her to stay tuned until the offer is displayed.

The Presenter is very important. Only match a presenter with a product he/she can actively enjoy and support. A good presenter can confer additional features on a product. This can immediately translate into improved benefits in the minds of the consumer. The wrong presenter can strip a good product of its benefits.[5]

AN INFOMERCIAL TREATMENT FROM TIME-LIFE VIDEO

Time-Life Video has an infomercial "treatment" for you, taken from one of its most successful infomercials, Dick Clark's Rock 'n' Roll Era music program. This program broke all previous Time-Life sales records and grossed over 26 million dollars. The product consisted of seven albums (cassettes or CDs) with some 140 songs popular from 1957 to 1964.

The treatment that follows demonstrates how you get started in planning your infomercial, long before writing the dialogue. It covers all bases (market, sets, presenters, and creative strategy as well as taking you through the action). This treatment was developed by the creative directors in the teamwork stage and serves as a guideline for the final meetings before actual copy is written.

You'll notice that this infomercial was planned so that a number of "historial clips" could be inserted; it was framed by a nostalgic diner set—a diner right out of the 50s.

I've included most of the treatment verbatim because it so clearly illustrates the thought process and rationales involved—a process that you may someday want to emulate!

How to Do a Story Treatment for a Winner

The purpose of this treatment is to produce a baseline of thinking so that all parties may begin to move ahead with the process of putting the infomercial on track with our schedule. It is meant to provoke discussion . . . not to end it. It should allow us to get a handle on our direction, structure, and technique. No words herein are copy . . . and no ideas are set in stone.

Primary Audience. While core market is still those men and women aged 50 to 60 who were young adults in the '54 to '59 musical era, we want to broaden our focus to other, younger adults—say 35 and up—who are sixties or seventies classic rock fans.

The older group is, of course, familiar with the music—but perhaps more in a nostalgic sense—as background music to their growing up. The younger group has also heard much of this music throughout their lives . . . but has never before been able to place it in a musical/historical context.

For both of these groups, the product's Unique Selling Proposition is the same; *this is the first collection that takes the era seriously* . . . that takes you behind the bubble gum and bobby socks exterior to re-introduce you to some of the hottest music of the century.

Creative Strategy. In order to make that USP work for the audience we've designed, I believe that the infomercial has to say three very important things about the product:

1. *That we are respecting the era.* People call the fifties shallow and superficial. Some people think of the era's music as saccharine and sentimental. We want to give the Rock 'n' Roll era—and the people who lived through it—the place in history they've always deserved.

2. *That this is more than a weepy nostalgia sell.* We've picked these 5–6 years because they were critical in the musical history of Rock 'n' Roll—not to mention in the history of American culture. You may have heard these songs before . . . but they've never seemed so hot, so exciting, so musically important.

3. *That this music has really stood the test of time.* Think this music sounds dated? Then why is it the hottest ad soundtrack commodity around? Think it's tame? Take a look at Little Richard's Tutti Frutti.

A Note on the Set. Our concept is to use Mel's Diner at Universal Studios as a location for at least the opening and closing segments of the show. There might be some extras in 1990s dress walking behind. In any case, this "busy" environment would be used only top and bottom in the show. Thereafter, we would find a more serene environment within the diner or elsewhere in which the host can do in-show commercials and throws.

I think a set like this works for a couple of reasons: First, because it provides a physical space in which the show can take place, thereby lending it some credibility as an actual television "event." Much in the same way that a single opening sequence in the Rolling Stone offices established the rest of the show as the real thing.

Second, because it reinforces our central premise . . . that this is the first '50s Rock 'n' Roll collection that brings the era of the fifties to life through its music.

Third, it's a visually exciting environment for shooting. This is particularly important in the case of this show because so much of the footage we'll be showing is black and white. In addition, the diner seems like a natural environment for testimonials, if we choose to do them. And the "clarity of CD sound" pitch would really work well when contrasted with an in-booth jukebox or a vintage car radio.

A Note on Dick Clark. Needless to say, the quality of Dick Clark's footage is invaluable to the show. And a straight-out testimonial from Dick would undoubtedly also add a lot to the credibility of the product.

I also believe, however, that we can tap into another, equally powerful advantage that Dick's endorsement can give us. He, after all, has a personal, emotional connection to the music and the footage that we are going to see. He was there. He met Chuck Berry and Little Richard. He can give a personal insight when introducing the clips that no one else can replicate.

Further, I think Dick's presence on the set will add to the power of the show. Even if his role is limited to the top and bottom of the show, performing that role in the same environment as the host gives that host credibility, as well as adding some star power to the show as a whole.

I believe that one of the strongest attractions to the show will have to be that rare footage we promise. I think that promise will have a stronger impact if Dick makes it as part of the show, rather than through a paid testimonial "wrap."

The Show. Here's a rough outline of how the show might run. The particulars are—needless to say—dependent upon dozens of undecided factors, the paper track chief among them.

Introduction—I feel strongly that Dick Clark should be the first person that we see on the screen. This is both because he has the highest likelihood of attracting attention, and because he can best do the tease for the rare footage in the show (Figure 10–6A).

FIGURE 10–6A

Again, I would like to see him out in front of the diner . . . neon lights and vintage cars behind. He reminds us of how exciting and how revolutionary a time the fifties really were. He promises us that the show will give us a vision of the era we've never before had. New, remastered versions of the greatest rock songs in history. Footage so rare . . . you haven't seen it in decades . . . if at all.

All the while, the camera follows Clark past the cars . . . under the neon . . . and through the doors of the diner, where he intros the host—the person who's going to take us through this journey. The host says hi . . . and asks us to stay tuned to hear the greatest collection of fifties music ever made . . . in Time-Life's Rock 'n' Roll Era.

FIGURE 10–6B

Product Introduction—Product is introduced through a graphics-filled sequence that features the history-making moments of early Rock 'n' Roll. And particularly features the great Rock'n Roll moments we will show (Figure 10–6B).

First host throw—Host, now in a sedate environment within the diner, begins our journey through the Rock 'n' Roll era. The year is 1954, Pat Boone and Doris Day are at the top of the charts . . . when all at once, something different turns up on the radio.

FIGURE 10–6C

FIGURE 10–6D

FIGURE 10–6E

FIGURE 10–6F

FIGURE 10–6G

FIGURE 10–6H

First set of clips—Addressing (I would assume) several early acts from the era. We might intersperse some lifestyle footage of cars . . . clothes . . . kitchens . . . power images of the era, together with the synch footage. We could slow down and/or manipulate the footage somewhat in post-production to give an emotional feel to the era (Figure 10–6C).

CD Sound demo—At the time, who would have thought that the music would sound so great 40 years later. And the digital clarity of CD sound is one reason that it does.

We should do this segment with one of the table juke boxes in the diner . . . or, if that's not possible, with a Wurlitzer juke box. The opportunity to use one of the icons of the era seems too good to let pass.

First commercial (Figures 10–6D and E)

Second set of clips—Now we see clips from the great performers in Rock 'n' Roll's heyday. It would be great if Dick Clark could add a certain retrospective element to some of these clips. I can imagine a montage of clips that show young Clark with some of the acts on American Bandstand. Either way, it would be good to use some of Dick's reminiscences to personalize the artists we show in the clips. Perhaps he can tell a story about how many letters he got after one act was on the show. Or how another singer did something else unexpected (Figure 10–6F).

Whatever the story . . . this can add to the message that the music and clips we are seeing are both hot musically and important historically. Dick Clark helps us put the music in context.

Testimonials—while not always a part of music infomercials—testimonials may help us send an important nonverbal message in this case. If we show a wise range of age groups grokking on music of the late '50s . . . it says that this music really is cool—no matter how old you are. It also gives us a chance to throw in a pinch of nostalgia to the sell . . . which couldn't hurt.

Second commercial (Figure 10–6G)

Final host throw—Host introduces the last set of clips by telling us how Rock 'n' Roll exploded in the latter part of the fifties . . . and how it moved from being outlaw to mainstream in the public mind.

Final set of clips—Bands from '58–'60 (Some of them in color?). Could have some lifestyle footage of the times a'changin to bring the whole thing full circle.

Host wrap-up—Never before had the country witnessed music this hot . . . this powerful . . . this sexually-charged. Never before could you hear the music as it was meant to be heard. Year by year in digitally-crisp CD sound. Only in Time-Life's Rock 'n' Roll Era.

Final commercial (Figure 10–6H)[6]

Our experts have spoken, and now—I hope you can see why I believe you can move neatly from a direct mail package on to commercials and even infomercials!

Something to Come Away With

Film biz is funny biz and fun, too. When you're on the outside, you want to be a star. But once on the inside you'll find all the insiders (stars included) want to be directors.

After you've scripted a few commercials, I'm betting you'll want to direct, too. It's a normal longing, especially if you care about your baby.

The job of this chapter is to pass on to you what I call creative perspective. With it comes confidence, gained through understanding. If you understand why you do what you do, there's no mystery, no mystique to put you down. It frees you to do your best work. It gives you the ability to analyze and judge your own work and that of others because you understand what makes good work tick.

Understand, too, that our creative process—the process of persuasion—really changes very little from one medium to another. Once you're secure with this, you can tackle just about anything, and do it well (including the Internet). That's my wish for you. I also hope you turn out to be a stellar visualizer and dialogue writer. And get some good chances to prove it! (Keep eavesdropping and exploring! Keep that imagination going!)

Some Basic TV Terms

Here are a few film terms and lingo that will help you communicate as you visualize and write your script.

Close Up (CU): A shot in which a subject is very large, filling the screen.

Dolly: The camera itself changes position (back or forth, from one side to the other), as you move your body.

In synch: Abbreviation for *In Synchronization.* Sound effects or dialogue that coincide with the proper or correct action. It's also used to signify lip synchronization—the movements of the lips matching the words spoken on the sound track. It also means in the same mode with someone; to agree with someone is to be "in synch" with that person.

In the can: This is the equivalent of "the shoot's over." It implies that the film has been used and is in the can, ready for development.

Limbo: A shot in which the product appears to be floating in air without any spatial relations.

Location: The site for a film or taping outside of a studio. (You are "on location" while you work there.) Location is chosen for greater realism—and when the cost of reproducing the setting in the studio is impractical.

Pan/Tilt: The camera's eye moves from one side to the other and up and down just like your eyes when you move your head from side to side or up and down.

Point of view (POV): Exactly what the camera should see at the precise angle from which you want it seen.

Set: The setting, usually indoors. It is set up, actually, for the shoot.

Set-up: The arrangement of lights and camera to make an individual shot.

Shoot: What a camera does when it films or tapes.

Shooting or *the Shoot:* Filming or taping, the filming or the taping.

Slice of life: A commercial dramatization usually involving a common, or popular, situation (family meal, two women shopping, woman doing laundry, a car and mechanic).

Studio: Where you go when you don't shoot on location. Studio shooting is usually done for better control and efficiency.

Tabletop: A term used to describe a demonstration commercial where most of the action is limited to a flat, tablelike surface.

Take: The director breaks the script into scenes or takes, then shoots only one scene (or take) at a time.

Talking head: The good old head-and-shoulders, face-on stationary presenter. Usually shot only from one POV.

Voiceover (VO): A voice without a visual on the screen. Usually the announcer.

Zoom: What a Zoom lens does—moves out and back easily and allows you to bring an image closer or move it farther away without moving the camera.

Now, try your hand at planning a few TV commercials (and, this time, don't worry about your budget!).

1. The first product is a broad-appeal health and fitness magazine. Let's just call it *Gym*. The offer is one year for $19.97 plus a large exercise and diet chart as a premium.

The hypothesis you've chosen is: *People generally want to be more fit today, but lack of discipline and motivation causes them to neglect exercise or slack off.* (A major benefit is the promise that the magazine can motivate the reader to plan and act and keep him or her enthusiastic.) You have 60 seconds.

What's your approach? (Question? Story? Testimonial? Fantasy? Problem/Solution? A combination?)

Who's your spokesperson? (A voiceover with dramatization? A fitness training instructor? A celebrity athlete? An average guy?)

What's your strong visual? (A fitness center in action? A runner? A before-and-after drama? Color pictures from the magazine? A dramatization of organizing and planning your own fitness program with the help of the magazine?)

Block it out on the time frame: 5 seconds for openers to attract attention (big benefit), 10 seconds for the premise and offer, 30 seconds for product and premium display, 15 seconds for ordering information.

2. The next product is a continuity book plan with instructions, recipes, and illustrations for gourmet cooking. It's called *Secrets of the Gourmet Chef.* There are twelve volumes. The lead (or first book sent) is *French Cuisine.* A new book will follow automatically every month thereafter until the customer cancels. (Each book costs $29.95, and each is shipped with its own invoice.)

When the customer signs on, he or she will be sent volume 1, *French Cuisine*, plus a special premium book on growing, buying, and using herbs and spices.

The hypothesis you've chosen states that although women in general spend less time cooking for the family today, more time is spent planning and cooking elaborate, sophisticated meals for special occasions, parties, and holidays. (The major benefit of the series is its promise to make readers into gourmet cooks—to impress their guests and gain the rewards of self-expression through entertaining.) You have 120 seconds.

What's your approach?

Who's your spokesperson?

What's your strong visual?

Block it out on the time frame.

3. The Smith Credit Corporation is looking for homeowners who might consider a second mortgage. They would like interested homeowners to write or call and they'll send out further information and application forms (leadgetting).

The hypothesis is: *Many people need extra cash for good reasons. If they qualify, they can take a second mortgage on their home and get that cash.* (The big benefit here is one of security and enjoyment—you can send your kids to college or put an addition on your home this way.) You have 60 seconds.

What's your approach?

Who's your spokesperson?

What's your strong visual?

Block it out on the time frame.

WRITING DIALOGUE

How about some dialogue practice? Try your hand at this 60-second radio support. (Remember, your prospects can only *hear.*)

Marcia and John are out to alert the radio audience to an exciting direct mail package that arrives next week. The package announces a sweepstakes with a $1,000,000 grand prize and 7,000 additional prizes of rainbow umbrellas. The mailing consists of a bright red outer envelope, sweepstakes entry certificate, and opportunities to subscribe to 60 top magazines all at cut-rate prices.

Who's your spokesperson? Who are John and Marcia anyway? Nameless voices in limbo? Mail deliverers? Husband and wife?

What's your approach? How are they going to start—with a Problem/Solution? A Question? A Generic statement? A Testimonial? A Story? A Fantasy? How will you play them off to give your dialogue cadence and variety? (Balance your speakers. Don't give one more time than the other.)

Block it out on the time frame. Then fill in with dialogue—and have fun. (If you enjoy this exercise, chances are you'll do well with dialogue.)

Notes

1. David Churbuck, "Where's the Money?" *Forbes*, January 30, 1995, pp. 100–108.

2. John Witek, *Response Television: Combat Advertising of the 1980's* (Lincolnwood, IL: Crain Books, an imprint of National Textbook Company, 1981), pp. 24–37.

3. Courtesy Bob Dodd, Executive Creative Director, Time Life, Time-Life Books Inc., Alexandria, VA 22314.

4. Courtesy Bob Cesiro, Senior Vice President, Group Creative Director, FCB Direct, New York, NY.

5. Courtesy David Mutter, Guthy-Renker Corporation, 41-550 Eclectic, Palm Desert, CA 92260.

6. Courtesy Bob Walter, Creative Director Broadcast, Time Life Marketing, Time-Life Books Inc., Alexandria, VA 22314.

CHAPTER ELEVEN

RELATIONSHIP MARKETING—A CRITICALLY IMPORTANT CREATIVE AREA

While you've been out generating all those prospects, subscribers, and customers through direct mail, print ads, broadcast, and electronic interactive media of all sorts, perhaps you wondered: Who is going to pick up the ball and continue the dialogue? Who is going to promote those inquiries, renew the subscribers, sell to all the customers?

The glamour creative jobs bring in the prospects and customers through our national media, whether it's mail, print, or electronic. This is where the recognition lies and the awards are made. The stars work here. The agencies fight to get this business.

But who continues the dialogue? You just paid six dollars in promotional costs to get a customer on television or fifteen dollars in the mail. Who's going to make that customer pay off? And how?

Sure—good product and good service are critical to retaining a customer, but along with them, who continues the dialogue?

- Who encourages the club member to purchase and purchase more? With every member mailing?

- Who convinces the catalog recipient that everything in the catalog store is wonderfully appealing? Each time?

- Who reminds the magazine subscriber to renew the subscription? Every year or so?

- When the prospect inquires, who tells him or her all about the product or service? Then goes on from there?

Many direct marketing creative people used to get their initial training right here. It's a wonderful place to begin, because it teaches the basic workings of dialogue, its value and its importance.

It's not a bad place to work in any event, wherever you are now—especially today because today the spotlight's moving over to this area. It's big business. We've even given it a name, *Relationship Marketing.*

As customer acquisition costs continued to rise year after year, direct marketers began to turn their attention to their house files, their current database, and discovered that customer *segmentation and cultivation* paid a lot better than just letting customers fend for themselves. What's more, without attention many customers fell away, while marketers paid through the nose to replace them. So it's "love thy customer" for very good reasons. (Back to the Premises of the Basic Law in Chapter 2.)

The Basic Law for Relationship Marketing

Unlike the retailer, direct marketers go out to people uninvited and, in most cases, have to convince a stranger to order something that stranger doesn't even know he or she wants! It takes a lot of promises for us to achieve this. And considerable trust on the part of the stranger.

I think that sometimes we focus so hard on this initial act, this bells-and-whistles magic of prospecting, that often we give too much attention to our promise and too little attention to fulfilling that promise.

Think about your own experience. I'll bet you can remember buying something through direct marketing . . . opening the package with great anticipation and excitement, then feeling the disappointment as you saw that the product or service was not all you'd expected or hoped or imagined.

There's a secret here. And all the successful and growing direct marketing companies know it. When they use it, it works like magic. But it takes guts, because it means they can't pinch pennies, cut back, squeeze for profits, or be the least bit greedy.

It means they have to trust their prospects and customers; they have to invest, go out on a limb and give more.

Jerry Hardy, one of our great direct marketers and founder of Time-Life Books, insisted that you must give people a little more value than they can reasonably expect for the money.

For direct marketers, particularly, this is our absolute key to success, the basis of our relationship marketing.

Jerry demonstrated this by publishing and selling beautifully illustrated books of the finest quality for less than such books were ordinarily offered at retail. And millions flocked to buy these books in series of 12, 15, 20—even more—on an open-ended 'til forbid basis. Because each book was so much more than the customer could reasonably expect, virtually no one even asked how many books were in a series! And Time-Life Books has never had to tell them in its direct response promotions!

The more we give value (not the more we promise) determines our customer relationship and the success of our relationship marketing.

In relationship marketing, by the way, giving value can go far beyond just the value in the products or services you sell. It can also mean something as simple as sending a birthday card, or a regular "customer" newsletter relating to the service you give them, or a note asking them how you're doing so you can serve them better, or a small unsolicited, non-self-serving gift.

Say you send out a no-strings wild flower and herb chart to your garden magazine subscribers some two months before you ask them to renew. Is it any surprise that this group renews unusually well in the months that follow?

Or how about a rose? That's what Kurt Medina did when he headed National Liberty's Senior Service Division. They prospected with a Medicare supplement insurance policy that offered a month's worth of coverage for $1. This was followed by full information on the policy plus a bill for the next month.

Within two or three days after receipt of the informational package, they tested adding a long cardboard tube. (It couldn't possibly be missed in the mailbox.) Inside was a single silk red rose along with a note thanking the respondent for becoming a member of the Secure Care Family.

No further selling was done, but renewals increased immediately by 10 percent. In fact, the rose generated over $1 million in incremental premiums over the first year it was used. (See Figure 11–1.)

FIGURE 11–1   A Thank-you Gift That Boosted Renewals

Having a year-round program that does this sort of thing in addition to giving value where it was promised—that's relationship marketing, and I hope you have a chance to both plan and execute it. It can prove to be a wonderful experience in pure, first-rate dialogue marketing for you.

If You Have a Chance to Be Creative with a Catalog

What an opportunity! Don't let it get by you. Grab it! Catalog specialists, by the way, often complain about classifying catalogs as backend. Technically, they're correct. Catalogs are both backend and frontend. They are, in fact, total "relationship" vehicles because their primary job is to keep up the dialogue that they start.

So don't be fooled by catalogs. They are a lot more than product pictures and descriptions; at least, good catalogs are. Let me give you a little background first.

Catalogs were "in," hot, *the* thing in the 1980s. A busy mail order buyer could receive as many as 150 or more catalogs in September, October, and November combined, and around 40 or more in January! That's a lot of merchandise. And a lot of paper!

Experts were worried that it was far more than even a serious mail order market could use. Although the pie itself has been growing as more buyers enter the mail order market every year, rising costs of postage and paper continue to cut heavily into profits. The results? Many new catalogs have come and gone over the past 10 years. And some of the older catalogs have been sold, combined, modified, or discontinued.

But how about the many that continue on, despite smaller profit margins? The smart ones are already experimenting with new media like CD-ROM catalogs and online digital selling. Some are even adding new catalogs for special markets within their markets.

Why will one catalog fail and another one survive tough times? Not because of any mail orderer's pie. Three basic areas are important to a catalog's success. And the winners know this.

First, the merchandise selection. The best catalog people are just natural-born merchants. Lillian Vernon, founder of Lillian Vernon, is one of these. She'll select an article out of dozens of possible products and say, "This is good. I'll take it." She knows what her customers want. She finds it for them. She has been phenomenally successful. Richard Thalheimer, President of Sharper Image, is another superlative buyer. He, too, has a nose for his market's tastes.

Smart new merchandisers select their products to fill certain needs and desires that are not being filled for a substantial market segment. They look for a niche, an exclusive segment to carve out for themselves.

One of the best examples of niche marketing that I've seen lately is called "Rent Mother Nature." Primarily an ecologically oriented catalog, it offers products from all over the Americas. You don't exactly buy the product, however; you rent the product producers instead. You rent the cows or the sheep, the coffee bushes or rice plants, the beehives or maple trees. Then you enjoy great progress reports with an educational slant while you wait for your cheese, wool blanket, coffee, rice, honey, or maple syrup. It goes without saying that these make wonderful gifts! (See Figure 11–2.)

FIGURE 11–2 A Niche Market Catalog

FIGURE 11–2   (Continued)

The second area that's critical to success is fulfillment and customer service. Poor order processing, poor record keeping, slow delivery, and difficult returns and exchanges lose customers rapidly. Smart mail order companies are doing everything possible to create a strong feeling of bona fide personal customer service.

The third area (and most important from your creative point of view) is the catalog image-identity-personality. With today's catalog glut, many catalogs tend to look and sound alike. Bad sign. Even more important, they go out to the prospects' homes without explaining *who* they are or *why* they are qualified to offer the enclosed products. *They lack credibility.* What right do they have to go into a strange home and sell? Why should a prospect use them?

How can you, the creative person, contribute? Let's hope your catalog has carved out a market niche, has good merchandising and fulfillment, and is working to establish an image. (If any of these brings a resounding "No!" be prepared for a short-lived relationship.)

Assuming all systems are "go"—what is your creative role? How do you know to what extent the catalog is sound? Or where and how creative comes in? Or how much you will be able to help?

TAKING THE CREATIVE MEASURE OF YOUR CATALOG

Here's where you go back to your basics and apply the Basic Law. Look at your proposition. Based on the objectives and the market definition, does this product (this catalog) make sense?

Pretend you never heard of it. If you received the catalog in the mail would you try it out in preference to a known retail store? If so, why? If not, why not? Ultimately, the catalog's job is to establish confidence and trust and maintain a dialogue. Is it going to do this?

Work your benefits to develop a hypothesis. "This catalog was planned for X market in the belief that this market would be receptive to Y products because . . . "

Next take your four sales guidelines (Involvement, Credibility, Motivation, Offer) and a formula like AIDA (Attention, Interest, Desire, Action) and overlay them on your catalog, then ask these questions:

1. What makes this catalog look distinctive, different from other catalogs, easily identifiable? Does it have its own tone or sound? Just like people, catalogs should look and sound (or read) distinctive. (Both Eddie Bauer and L.L. Bean are nationally famous outdoor and sports gear catalogs. You could never confuse one with the other, however. Aside from the format and the layouts, the copy tone and copy treatment are totally distinct in each.)

2. As you consider the graphics and tone, ask who's speaking. From whom is your catalog coming? Where did the tone come from and is it sustained throughout? In other words, who's the logical spokesperson?

Who's Speaking? A good catalog comes *from someone credible* (owner, president, manager, or a team—Harry and David—or a family, even) who speaks out, usually up front or on the order form, to explain *why* the catalog is there (if it's new) and why and how the spokesperson is qualified to do the speaking.

Generally these are statements of commitment or newsy, friendly communications that directly or indirectly reinforce credibility and qualifications to do business with the customer. (Like the helpful salesperson who always remembers your name or your friendly neighborhood grocer.)

They also help to establish a dialogue. This is the catalog's answer to the letter and many times statements of commitment are presented in letter form up front. (Note: Many, if not most, department store catalogs neglect the upfront note or letter from the logical spokesperson. This could be an outgrowth of the old traffic-building catalog concept. All of these companies started as retailers, not direct marketers. Since people came to them, they probably just never picked up the habit, or the logic, of credibility. They just assumed everyone already knew them!)

Figures 11–3, 11–4, and 11–5 offer you good examples of successful catalog spokespersons and credibility. *Country Curtains'* inside front page (Figure 11–3) introduces you to the founders and updates you on their family. They explain how the catalog got started and why, then move on to help the prospect understand how to use "country" decorating.

Robert Redford speaks for his *Sundance* catalog—and most of us are delighted to listen. In addition to sending messages about the nature of his products, he sends messages about ecology and preservation, our land and the effect of modern society on it.

Other catalogs use a variety of personal touches. Richard Thalheimer plays an active role in his catalog, *Sharper Image*, with a message on the new products he's collected in the current catalog, talk about the cover feature, plus (where appropriate) a special bind-in letter with a discount offer to encourage "dormant" customers to resume purchasing.

FIGURE 11–3   Country Curtains Catalog

FIGURE 11–4   Sunnyland Farms Catalog

Jane and Harry Willson

Sunnyland Farms, Inc.
**WILLSON ROAD AT PECAN CITY
ALBANY, GEORGIA 31706-8200**

Our Office
1-912-883-3085

Dear Friend,

What a pleasure to be greeting our old friends and meeting new friends as we begin our 47th year. How could the time have passed so quickly? It seems only a short while ago since 1948 when we packed pecans from the Willson family orchard for Jane's college alumnae club.

That successful project convinced us to make these fresh delicious pecans available to more folks through the convenience of mail. We placed a couple of small ads in magazines, sent a mimeographed letter to a few companies and so started Sunnyland Farms mail order.

Pecans in-the-shell and pecan halves were our only offerings then. Gradually we added more good foods as more and more people learned that Sunnyland products were the freshest and prettiest they could get anywhere. Now the catalog has grown to 48 pages and lists many, many popular and tasty Sunnyland Farms products, including those first two pecan items which got us started. They're still a hit today!

At first the two of us did most everything at home. We opened mail, typed orders, packed boxes and took them to the Post Office in our pickup truck.

Because you great folks who are loyal customers kept ordering and telling your friends how to get the best nuts by mail, we outgrew the home kitchen. We moved our work to a building right here in the middle of the orchard and began bringing in other people to help us keep up with the growing number of orders. You'll meet many of these folks in this catalog. And of course, a bigger truck replaced the pickup.

As you look through the catalog you'll enjoy learning how we grow and process pecans and how the fine people at Sunnyland Farms make sure that you receive only the best. And as always, there's an update on our four children who grew up with the mail order business. Many of you tell us your own family update when you order. We love it!

To you our many loyal customers who have ordered over the years, we say a heartfelt "Thank you" for allowing us to become friends and serve you in past seasons. We are truly grateful for "old" friends like you and are anxious to hear from you again soon.

To you who are new to us, we extend a hearty Sunnyland Farms welcome. We hope that you will like what you see in our catalog and give us an opportunity to serve you too with our wonderful Sunnyland products.

Sincerely,

Jane & Harry

DIRECT FROM OUR GROVE TO YOU AND YOUR FRIENDS

OUR GUARANTEE TO YOU

We fully and unconditionally guarantee each package and its contents. If a package is lost or damaged, or if you are not satisfied for any reason whatsoever, we will either replace the package or refund your purchase price by return mail – and you keep the box.

NO SHIPPING CHARGES TO ADD

We pay regular ground shipping, all handling and insurance charges to the 49 Continental United States. To Hawaii we ship only by Post Office Airmail; add 30%. We do not ship overseas and we do not ship to Canada. For Airmail, see pg. 47.

Order by Mail , by FAX or by our "800" phone service **1-800-999-2488**. See Page 47.

A big welcome to Sunnyland Farms from all of us. We're six miles from Albany "The World's Greatest Pecan Center"- according to the local Chamber. Pecan City, a whistle-stop on the railroad, is well named. There are trees everywhere.

This photo shows a few of the 14,000 trees in the Willson Orchard.

2

FIGURE 11–4   Sunnyland Farms Page "Banners"

Visit S. GA too. There is lots to see.

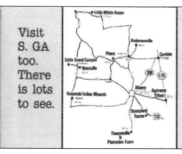

The Chehaw National Indian Festival is a colorful celebration of Native American heritage. Tribes from all over the U.S. come to Albany each year

1996 dates

May 17-19

5

At Clint Murphy's (23 yrs) computer shop your orders are key punched. Shipping labels and acknowledgment cards are printed.

With Linda Haning (1 yr) in charge, the folks in Lancaster, OH, take your orders on our 800 number and modem them to us 4 times a day. Fast, accurate service.

9

---

news every year for Christmas.
e you order Sunnyland Cashews,
won't buy from anyone else."
Irs. Naomi Parks, Indianapolis, IN

No. 9161	Case of 9 No. 161 to one address . **$161.30***
No. 6362	Case of 6 No. 362 to one address . **$137.60***
	HOME BOXES
No. 162	Home Box Net wt. 2 lb. 8 oz...... **$ 24.65***
No. 163	Home Box Net wt. 4 lb. 12 oz. . . . **$ 38.75***
No. 164	Home Box Net wt. 6 lb. .... **$ 46.50***
No. 165	Big Economy Box Net wt. 12 lb. . . **$ 83.60***
No. 4162	Case of 4 No. 162 to one address . **$ 86.30***
No. 9162	Case of 9 No. 162 to one address . **$178.70***
No. 3163	Case of 3 No. 163 to one address . **$106.20***

Toasted NOT Salted Jumbo Cashews

On April 22 we had our third annual "Family Day" - the best yet. Light clouds kept it cool. Nearly 670 people came.

| Good food and plenty of it. | The playground stayed busy. | Bounce House always has a line waiting. | Everyone wanted a balloon hat. |

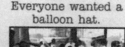

38

All four of our children and their spouses and our five grandchildren were here for Family Day. We are mighty proud.

40

The front spread in *The Vermont Country Store* gives a full history of the company from Lyman Orton, the son of the founder, plus current Vermont news, a guest editorial on Vermont, and an invitation to visit the original store.

But *Sunnyland Farms'* Jane and Harry Willson (Figure 11–4) outdo them all by including not only a letter but a narrative with lots of pictures that run across the bottom of every page. In a friendly humorous tone it explains what's going on at the farm, what specific employees are doing, all the celebrations they've had over the year, how the nuts are grown, harvested, and shipped, what's going on in the neighborhood, and news about the Willson family, its children, and grandchildren. They invite you to visit, tell you when it's best and how to get there. One can't ask for more.

3. Does your catalog offer extra, editorial commentary? Catalogs with unusual products or product lines that have interesting stories can give the reader educational and anecdotal information in addition to straight product copy. Informative and entertaining, these stories increase involvement.

Tell Stories. The J. Peterman Company catalog (Figure 11–5), for example, is filled with wonderful short stories about the products. Nothing beats these for flights of imagination with a smattering of fact:

> "Men invented the sport of fox hunting. (It prepared you for the cavalry, you know. Possibly even marriage.) Men consequently awarded themselves all the serious duties, like directing the hounds, blowing the bugle, as well as wearing the most dashing attire. Prime example: the famous "pink coat," named not after the color, which is scarlet, but Mr. Pinque, the tailor who designed it . . . "

> "There are dresses *like* this. They are fine. If you don't mind arriving at Orly looking like you've been on a charter from Auckland. This is the correct version, in uncrushable denim. Roll it up like a pair of jeans, shake it out and go anywhere. You won't need one of those little irons. (I know you only take one bag anyway) . . . "

> "For a long weekend. The beach before breakfast. Cups and Cups of fresh Blue Mountain decaf, fresh huckleberries, fresh trout. Rowing across the sedge pond. Dinner outdoors at twilight. Sleeping in. The first time in how long? And that's just Saturday . . . "

Few catalogs sell clothes with drawings instead of photographs. But with this copy, who needs photographs? Notice the 800# box; it appears on almost every spread.

The White Flower Farm catalog (Figure 11–6) is also well-known for fine copy—in this case, geared to the serious gardener. It is a pleasure to read and certainly greatly increases involvement. It

FIGURE 11–5   A Catalog Using the Story Approach

Haidée's Caftan.

She looks at me with large, dark eyes, smiling just slightly. Puzzlement flickers somewhere between her eyebrows.

Well, I must admit to her that no, I haven't ever been to a nine-hour-long Indonesian shadow-puppet play, but it sounds like an idea, I hear myself saying.

Haidée can be very persuasive.

Born in England, commutes between London and Yogyakarta. Knows where the good stuff is.

This caftan, for instance. A flattering vertical floral batik in Navy and tan, each color in two tones. More depth that way.

A person can wear it through an all-night performance of wayang kulit (followed by spicy coconut fried chicken for breakfast) and keep on looking great, feeling comfortable and free the rest of the day.

(Women in Java don't fit the subdued-Asian-female stereotype. The island is mostly Muslim, but you'll never see a veil.)

All graceful floor-length cotton. One size fits most.

Haidée's Caftan (Nº. 38B2657). Price: $42. Imported.

(I don't know how you've managed to get along without something this graceful and comfortable, but you don't have to anymore.)

47

The Sighting of a Fox.

Men invented the sport of fox hunting. (It prepared you for the cavalry, you know. Possibly even marriage.)

Men consequently awarded themselves all the serious duties, like directing the hounds, blowing the bugle, as well as wearing the most dashing attire.

Prime example: the famous "pink coat," named not after the color, which is scarlet, but Mr. Pinque, the tailor who designed it.

(The old hunting prints show the Field Master and first-rank huntsmen leading the charge in resplendent pinks, while the somberly dressed ladies lag behind.)

Today, of course, there is no reason on earth why a woman can't wear a pink wherever she pleases, although some will try to think of reasons.

And there's no better pink than our Classic Pink Coat, in 100% wool cavalry twill. Long flowing darts. Special buttons hand cast by jewelers, two in front and one per cuff. Two-button belt and inverted pleat in back. The definition of panache.

Where? When? With what? Whom? Make it up as you go along.

Color: Field Master's face if he'd seen you in one a century ago.

Women's even sizes: 4 through 16.

Classic Riding Jacket (Nº. 38B1153). Price: $295.

Stock. The slightly grim utilitarian reason for wearing a stock for ascot) collar while fox hunting: if you fall, that long length of fabric can be used as a sling.

On the bright side, there's no limit to the nifty bows and knots you can fashion under your hunting coat (see diagram). Wear with anything, as long as you're defying tradition. A blazer. A vest, slacks, jeans, skirt.

Authentic Stock Blouse in 100% cotton. A must in equestrian circles since 1800. This one has a straight back yoke. French front, six antiqued white buttons. And shirttail hem with discreet side slits. Nicely fitted. Women's even sizes: 4 through 16. Color: Natural. Stock Blouse (Nº. 38B1127). Price: $85.

Fox Hunting Etiquette: 1. Always be punctual. 2. Be neat and clean. 3. Never kick a hound or ride on seeded land. 4. Do not leave a gate open, letting livestock escape. 5. Be sure to put a ribbon in your horse's tail if it kicks.

To order toll free
800-231-7341
7AM to 1AM (ET)
24-hour FAX orders: 800-346-3081
Overseas FAX: 606-254-1112
Overseas phone orders: 606-254-5444

48

---

regales the gardener with current anecdotes and friendly news from the neighborhood. It has even been known to include a first-rate "fish" story. Read this typical copy and see if you can sense the Down East tone of Amos Pettingill, their spokesman.

Patagonia active sportswear (Figure 11–7) is known for its strong environmental stance, as well as its authentic photos of *customers* in wild places wearing its gear. This lends a wonderful aura to everything in the catalog. Wear Patagonia and be a true adventurer who loves and cares for Planet Earth! It's adventure, involvement, credibility, and the basis for a stellar kind of relationship all in one!

FIGURE 11–6   White Flower Farm Catalog

White Flower Farm
THE GARDEN BOOK
FALL 1995

VER...LIGHTLY

your hands ing suspen- it properly, ged to think creatively and write compellingly about gardening in the fall just when our spirit is eagerly responding to the first clear signals of spring. For you, the challenge is to direct your attention to next year's garden at the very peak of this year's bloom, looking past the miracle that is before your eyes to imagine a still greater miracle of your own creation. The process is not without challenges for both of us, but when it works, the result is pure delight.

The point, you see, is that gardening is a process containing many elements, not all of which take place in the garden. At its most obvious level, it is, of course, about the marvelous and evanescent beauty of flowers and the pleasure to be had from their presence in our lives. This is a strictly seasonal experience for most of us, and there are plenty of perfectly reasonable folks for whom a reliable explosion of June color is all they want or need from their garden. This can be easily accomplished with a modest investment of energy and foresight

(money is, of course, an alternative approach), leaving hands and minds free for golf, sailing, and the occasional Meyers and tonic. We understand people who feel this way, because that's how we started too, and we try to accommodate them with suggestions for easy and essentially foolproof plants (among which the very finest are spring-flowering bulbs).

At some point, however, a previously hidden genetic flaw may reveal itself and the gardener begins to think about gardening, rather than simply having a garden. This is a dangerous moment that threatens to contradict many widely held assumptions of our culture, including the following:

• If it can't be done quickly, it can't be worth doing.

• Taking the trouble to learn about something is likely to spoil the fun.

• Things that are not obviously expensive are probably not valuable.

• Humans can manage nature.

Over time, the combination of intelligence and experience produces wisdom, from which grows the understanding that what goes on in

FRONT COVER

NARCISSUS FOR CONNOISSEURS 84315.

Take a look at the Daffodils in your garden, or in your neighborhood. Do they all look the same? That's because local garden centers, with only a dozen slots on their shelves for Narcissus, inevitably sell only the reliable and familiar yellow Trumpets that everyone knows. Yes, they are lovely, and durable, and free from pests, but enough's enough. There are, in the world of Daffodils, dozens of exotic and entrancing characters in colors and forms you'd scarcely expect from this well-loved genus. Some are demure, others flamboyant, and a few are so stunningly beautiful that even Orchids will shrink before them. We know this crowd because we have spent dozens of years wandering the breeders' fields in Holland, and have seen the best the gene pool has to offer.

Now it's your turn, because we've assembled a mixture of the most extraordinary Daffodils on the market. Their beauty and diversity are beyond compare and they will bring joy to your entire neighborhood. Because these exquisite beauties are recently introduced varieties, this mix is more expensive than our other mixtures, but take one look and you'll recognize a fabulous value. There's nothing remotely like this in the trade. The mixture offers 50 bulbs from no less than 10 varieties. Hardy in Zones 3–8.

50 bulbs $39.95, 100 bulbs $75.95, 200 bulbs $146.95

FIGURE 11–7   Patagonia Catalog

4. Does your catalog present its products dramatically, clearly, and with compelling copy? Just giving a list of product features and a price is not enough. Each product should be treated like the subject of a small space workhorse. The product picture is your valuable graphic that works with your headline.

Many catalogs rely only on the illustration and a flat-out single line product description (like "Miniature Garden Seat" . . . "Doorman's Giant Umbrella" . . . "The Deli Meat Slicer" . . . "Cashmere Cardigan" . . . "Cotton Camp Shirt" . . . "Solid Maple Display Table" . . . "Luggage Rack") for the headline. When the descriptive copy that follows is filled with promises (benefits to you) and features, they seem to get on fine.

But how much stronger, in a competitive market, to use such headlines as

File of rich oak. A friendly alternative to cold steel.

Flexible fins. A new power source for swimmers.

From beans to brew while you sleep. (The Sharper Image)

A silken touch of bedtime luxury.

You'll love how you look in a Felt Crusher!

The last watch you'll ever need to buy (Early Winters)

Lift Your Toast Before It Roasts . . . .

Our quiet little box fan moves heat from room to room . . . .

Bring the tang of Vermont Pine and Balsam woods into your home. (Vermont Country Store)

Or even longer ones likes these:

Lands' End "Ultimate" sweats. Not flimsy or fashiony but heavy-duty like the kind college teams work out in. More expensive than imitations, but worth it for long wear and superior performance in action.

Some think we sell more pinpoint oxfords than anyone else because of our lower price—$29.50. Maybe. Lands' End Quality Specialists, who compare our pinpoints to others, tell us we sell more because it's the best pinpoint on the market. (Lands' End Direct Merchants)

Or wonderful lead-ins like the two here from J. Peterman Company:

Your father had one of these. Your grandfather, too. But where is it? How can a silver belt buckle just vanish? (We can't solve the mystery, but we can remedy the situation; no questions asked.)

The classic Irish sauntering hat. I snapped up Jonathan Richards' entire year's production . . . . When you wear it, people will assume you know great stories. Even if you don't say a word. . . .

Fine starters, all. And in all cases they're followed by equally fine description. Notice, too, that each group from each catalog has a consistent and distinctly different tone (or approach), suited to its image.

5. Does your catalog have a strong offer? Is there a carefully worded 100 percent guarantee? Does it use deadlines, discounts, or bonus coupons? Are instructions clear? Does it have a competitive credit policy? Is the order form easy to use? Are there assurances of active customer service, fast delivery (specific times), and a good return policy? Do you use testimonials from satisfied customers? Is the 800 number in clear view? Do you ask for referrals?

You can learn a lot from our top catalog companies in this area. Copy heavily from the best of them, if you can. For example:

- Most top catalogs have two-day service and next-day UPS or Federal Express (for an extra charge).

- Sunnyland Farms offers free recipes next to the order form.

- Many catalogs such as Lands' End, Sturbridge Yankee Workshop, Orvis, and Breck's feature their service staff and fulfillment operations.

- Most catalogs offer small impulse items on their order forms for add-on sales.

- Every one of them provides a prominent airtight guarantee and toll-free telephone service.

- Good catalogs also offer toll-free calling for *customer service.*

- There are lots of ways to incentivize customers who have stopped buying. For example: discounts and specials. J. Crew does it very well with a catalog wrap-around. (See Figure 11–8.)

Study the order forms of Lands' End and Breck's, shown in Figures 11–9 and 11–10; both have an excellent reputation with their customers. And this is where it starts. Remember, lack of clarity in ordering creates inertia!

NOW GO FOR IT!

Once you've asked your questions and made your comparisons, make your contribution by being sure the overall catalog image or personality gets through to the customer loud and clear. (Who are you? Why are you qualified? Why is the product important to your prospect? What do you "believe in"? How do you intend to conduct your relationship with your customer?) Strengthen the image with

FIGURE 11–8   A Catalog Wrap-Around Aimed at Lapsed Customers

You've been missed here at J.Crew. Matter of fact, it's been so long since we've heard from you that we assume we let you down, one way or another.

We apologize for any disappointment and hope you'll give us another chance to show that we can satisfy the most discerning requirements in style and service.

To help make amends for any past mistakes, here's a credit of $20 on an order of $80 or more. When phoning your order just cite "code RX6" and our operator will give you the $20 credit (it's good till August 1).

$20   J.CREW   **$20**

This coupon can be applied as $20 toward a purchase of $80 or more.

Just enclose this coupon with a mail order, or simply cite "code RX6" when ordering by phone. One coupon per customer. Valid through August 1.

- A logical spokesperson with commitment and credibility
- An explanation and demonstration of how and why the owners and the company are particularly well-qualified to bring the products to the customer
- Anecdotes, stories, examples, history of how this was achieved
- A look at the operation today, the people who serve the customers now
- Quotations from real customers in praise of the catalog (with their pictures, if possible)
- Invitations to visit the store(s)
- Lots of good operations pictures to build credibility

FIGURE 11–9   Lands' End Order Form

↓ Please fold and tear along perforated line ↓

LANDS' END
DIRECT MERCHANTS
Lands' End, Inc., 1 Lands' End Lane
Dodgeville, WI USA 53595

Call us toll-free 24 hours a day, 7 days a week to charge your order: 1-800-356-4444
FAX: 1-800-332-0103

Ordered by:

C D25B 6B2B 6   L95530
JOAN THEROL NORTON
PO BOX 453
POUND RIDGE   NY 10576-0453

IMPORTANT: If this is not your own name and address, please cross it out and correct it above.

Daytime phone (   )_____ Evenings (   )_____ Ask for _____

Ship to: (Only if different from "Ordered by".)

Name _____
Address _____
City _____ State/Prov. _____ Zip/Postal Code _____
Country _____
Gift card message _____
From _____

Item Number	Page No.	Description	Size	Shirt sleeve length	Pants inseam length	Cuffs?	Color	Alternate Color Choice (if first color choice is not available)	*Monogramming—see page 3 of order form ($5 each or $10 for towel sets) First initial	Middle initial	Last initial	Word/Name w/punctuation	Style No.	Gift Box $5	Qty.	Price Total
9 9 9 9–9 9 9 9	7	100% Cotton Oxford	15	34			White	Pink	J	R	B		4	✓	1	Example

Method of Payment:
All prices stated in US dollars.

Please include credit card number and expiration date with charge orders!

☐ Charge to my *(circle one)*:
Discover   Visa
MasterCard
American Express

Expiration Date: Month / Year

X _____ Signature (as shown on credit card)
Happy Holidays

☐ Check or Money Order Enclosed

Page 1

*1995, Lands' End, Inc.

Charges below are for first "Ship to" address.

Total Price of Items	Shipping, Packing and Handling charge
$0-30.00	$4.25
$30.01-70.00	$5.75
$70.01+	$6.95

Shipping to each additional address add $4.25.

We make it our business to ship your order using the most efficient method (see instructions on page 2). If you have a preference, please check below.

☐ UPS   ☐ Parcel Post
☐ UPS Next Day Air $6 (additional) to Alaska or Hawaii $16 (additional)

** WI residents of Iowa, Dane, Sauk and Milwaukee counties, please add an additional ½ sales tax.

Total price of items	
*Monogram ($5 each, $10 set) or Gift Box ($5 each)	
Delivery in IL, add 6¾% sales tax; in IA 5%	
USA Shipping, Packing and Handling (see chart at left)	
UPS Next Day Air	
Shipping to each additional address ($4.25 each)	
Canadian/International Shipping (see reverse side)	
Total	
**For delivery in Wisconsin, add 5% sales tax to total	
Total—Wisconsin deliveries	

LI November

↓ Please fold and tear along perforated line ↓

We make holiday shopping easy.

Ever since we started doing business back in 1963, selling racing sailboat hardware, we've done our level best to satisfy our customers. So you can be sure that whenever you call, we'll do whatever we can to help you shop, in our friendly Wisconsin way.

WE'RE ALWAYS OPEN.
1-800-356-4444
You can order from us toll-free 24 hours a day, 7 days a week, 364 days a year. (We're closed on Christmas Day.)

UNITED STATES/CANADA
PHONE: 1-800-356-4444
FAX: 1-800-332-0103

INTERNATIONAL
PHONE: 1-608-935-6170
FAX: 1-608-935-4000

TDD SERVICE
(PHONE DEVICE FOR HEARING IMPAIRED)
1-800-541-3459 6 AM-MIDNIGHT WEEKDAYS, 6 AM-10 PM WEEKENDS AND HOLIDAYS.

INTERNET
Windows users interested in receiving our electronic order blank
E-mail: sendwineob@landsend.com

Speedy shipping without the express charge!

We usually fill your order within 24 hours. (Monogramming or inseaming adds an extra day or two.) Then we deliver it almost anywhere via UPS just two business days later. Cost is $4.25, $5.75 or $6.95, based on the amount you order. See chart on page 1 of order form.

(We ship orders to Alaska and Hawaii via Airmail, usually in 2-3 business days.) If an item is backordered, it will be shipped as soon as it becomes available via regular UPS.

UPS Next Day Air service will get your order to you by 5 p.m. one business day after we ship it. Cost is an additional $6 per shipment for Continental U.S. and $16 per shipment to Alaska and Hawaii. Not available to APO/FPO addresses, P.O. boxes, and some rural areas.

Canada: We'll take care of clearing packages through customs and arrange delivery to you. Call for details.

International: Taxes and applicable duty charges paid by recipient. (All pricing in U.S. funds.) Specify Surface, Airmail, or UPS. See shipping instruction sheet in catalog for rates and delivery time estimates.

Guaranteed. Period.®

If you're not satisfied with any item, return it to us at any time for an exchange or a refund of its purchase price.

Any comments?

Don't be shy. Please let us know what's on your mind regarding our catalog, product, service or prices—anything. Call or write with your comments or E-mail us via Internet at: mailbox@landsend.com.

Ordering by phone:

Before you call, please fill out our order form, and have your credit card and expiration date handy. Credit cards only; sorry, no C.O.D.'s.

Ordering by mail or fax:

Mail orders can be placed with a personal check, bank draft (drawn on U.S. banks only), money order or by credit card. Fax orders must be placed with a credit card only. Please SIGN the order form where indicated and enter your card number and expiration date. In the U.S. and Canada dial 1-800-332-0103. International customers dial 1-608-935-4000.

Page 2

FIGURE 11–9 (Continued)

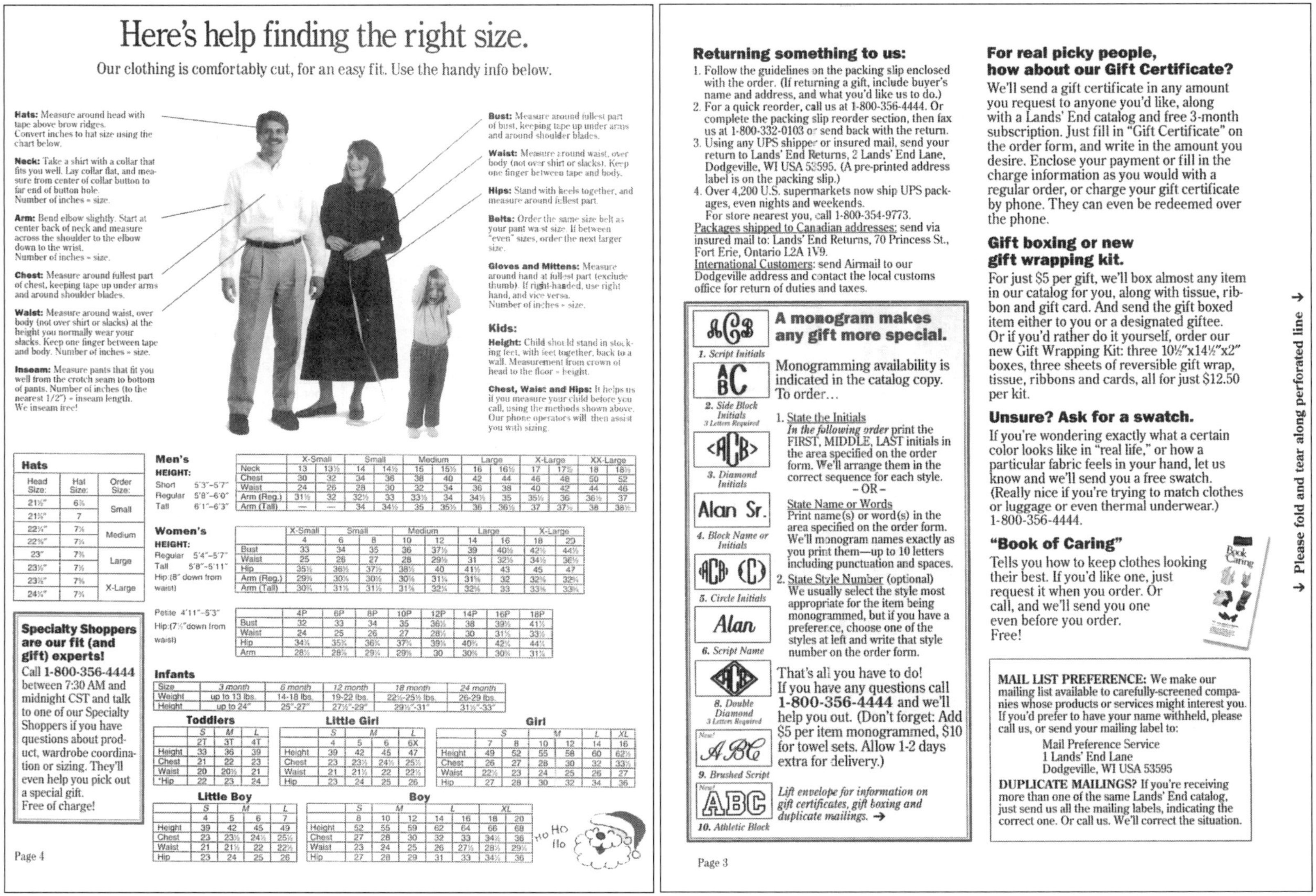

↑ Please fold and tear along perforated line ↑

For real picky people, how about our Gift Certificate?

We'll send a gift certificate in any amount you request to anyone you'd like, along with a Lands' End catalog and free 3-month subscription. Just fill in "Gift Certificate" on the order form, and write in the amount you desire. Enclose your payment or fill in the charge information as you would with a regular order, or charge your gift certificate by phone. They can even be redeemed over the phone.

Gift boxing or new gift wrapping kit.

For just $5 per gift, we'll box almost any item in our catalog for you, along with tissue, ribbon and gift card. And send the gift boxed item either to you or a designated giftee. Or if you'd rather do it yourself, order our new Gift Wrapping Kit: three 10½"x14½"x2" boxes, three sheets of reversible gift wrap, tissue, ribbons and cards, all for just $12.50 per kit.

Unsure? Ask for a swatch.

If you're wondering exactly what a certain color looks like in "real life," or how a particular fabric feels in your hand, let us know and we'll send you a free swatch. (Really nice if you're trying to match clothes or luggage or even thermal underwear.) 1-800-356-4444.

"Book of Caring"

Tells you how to keep clothes looking their best. If you'd like one, just request it when you order. Or call, and we'll send you one even before you order. Free!

MAIL LIST PREFERENCE: We make our mailing list available to carefully-screened companies whose products or services might interest you. If you'd prefer to have your name withheld, please call us, or send your mailing label to:
Mail Preference Service
1 Lands' End Lane
Dodgeville, WI USA 53595
DUPLICATE MAILINGS? If you're receiving more than one of the same Lands' End catalog, just send us all the mailing labels, indicating the correct one. Or call us. We'll correct the situation.

Returning something to us:

1. Follow the guidelines on the packing slip enclosed with the order. (If returning a gift, include buyer's name and address, and what you'd like us to do.)
2. For a quick reorder, call us at 1-800-356-4444. Or complete the packing slip reorder section, then fax us at 1-800-332-0103 or send back with the return.
3. Using any UPS shipper or insured mail, send your return to Lands' End Returns, 2 Lands' End Lane, Dodgeville, WI USA 53595. (A pre-printed address label is on the packing slip.)
4. Over 4,200 U.S. supermarkets now ship UPS packages, even nights and weekends. For store nearest you, call 1-800-354-9773.

Packages shipped to Canadian addresses: send via insured mail to: Lands' End Returns, 70 Princess St., Fort Erie, Ontario L2A 1V9.
International Customers: send Airmail to our Dodgeville address and contact the local customs office for return of duties and taxes.

A monogram makes any gift more special.

Monogramming availability is indicated in the catalog copy. To order...

1. **State the Initials**
In the *following order* print the FIRST, MIDDLE, LAST initials in the area specified on the order form. We'll arrange them in the correct sequence for each style.
– OR –
2. **State Name or Words**
Print name(s) or word(s) in the area specified on the order form. We'll monogram names exactly as you print them—up to 10 letters including punctuation and spaces.
3. **State Style Number** (optional)
We usually select the style most appropriate for the item being monogrammed, but if you have a preference, choose one of the styles at left and write that style number on the order form.

That's all you have to do!
If you have any questions call 1-800-356-4444 and we'll help you out. (Don't forget: Add $5 per item monogrammed, $10 for towel sets. Allow 1-2 days extra for delivery.)

Lift envelope for information on gift certificates, gift boxing and duplicate mailings. →

Monogram styles:
1. Script Initials
2. Side Block Initials (3 Letters Required)
3. Diamond Initials
4. Block Name or Initials
5. Circle Initials
6. Script Name
8. Double Diamond (3 Letters Required)
9. Brushed Script
10. Athletic Block

Page 3

Here's help finding the right size.

Our clothing is comfortably cut, for an easy fit. Use the handy info below.

Hats: Measure around head with tape above brow ridges. Convert inches to hat size using the chart below.

Neck: Take a shirt with a collar that fits you well. Lay collar flat, and measure from center of collar button to far end of button hole. Number of inches = size.

Arm: Bend elbow slightly. Start at center back of neck and measure across the shoulder to the elbow down to the wrist. Number of inches = size.

Chest: Measure around fullest part of chest, keeping tape up under arms and around shoulder blades.

Waist: Measure around waist, over body (not over shirt or slacks) at the height you normally wear your slacks. Keep one finger between tape and body. Number of inches = size.

Inseam: Measure pants that fit you well from the crotch seam to bottom of pants. Number of inches (to the nearest 1/2") = inseam length. We inseam free!

Bust: Measure around fullest part of bust, keeping tape up under arms and around shoulder blades.

Waist: Measure around waist, over body (not over shirt or slacks). Keep one finger between tape and body.

Hips: Stand with heels together, and measure around fullest part.

Belts: Order the same size belt as your pant waist size. If between "even" sizes, order the next larger size.

Gloves and Mittens: Measure around hand at fullest part (exclude thumb). If right-handed, use right hand, and vice versa. Number of inches = size.

Kids:

Height: Child should stand in stocking feet, with feet together, back to a wall. Measure from crown of head to the floor = height.

Chest, Waist and Hips: It helps us if you measure your child before you call, using the methods shown above. Our phone operators will then assist you with sizing.

Hats

Head Size	Hat Size	Order Size
21⅜"	6⅞	Small
21½"	7	
22⅛"	7⅛	Medium
22½"	7¼	
22⅞"	7⅜	Large
23¼"	7½	
23⅝"	7⅝	X-Large
24⅛"	7¾	

Specialty Shoppers are our fit (and gift) experts!
Call 1-800-356-4444 between 7:30 AM and midnight CST and talk to one of our Specialty Shoppers if you have questions about product, wardrobe coordination or sizing. They'll even help you pick out a special gift. Free of charge!

Page 4

Men's HEIGHT:

Short	5'3"-5'6"
Regular	5'8"-6'0"
Tall	6'1"-6'3"

Women's HEIGHT:

Regular	5'4"-5'7"
Tall	5'8"-5'11" (8" down from waist)
Petite	4'11"-5'3" (7" down from waist)

FIGURE 11–10 Breck's Order Form

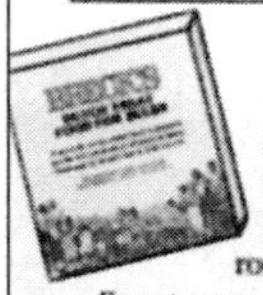

Reinforce that image with merchandise presentations in a tone and a format that support the image, while doing the job of small workhorse space ads (with strong involving headlines). Extend the image right onto the order form and make sure your company is a paragon of customer service virtues.

All right, you know how to evaluate your catalog. You know what to look for. You know how to approach and analyze your catalog assignment. You know why certain things are needed to bring the customer into the dialogue. You know how to use AIDA and other formulas, and to keep an eye out for Involvement, Credibility, Offer, and Motivation. You have all the tools you need whether you are creating a paper or a video catalog.

Let's hope you also know you can't do all of this alone. Who's missing? You're right; just as before—just as always—your artist, or art director, or designer. Your words are important, but equally important is the look, the design and layout of the catalog. The two of you should work closely from the beginning.

What more do you need? Well, if I were you and about to get a catalog assignment, I'd rush off and order 10 to 15 of the country's top catalogs. You can't find better teachers, or better sources of new ideas. I've made up a list for you here. It includes many of the newer catalogs as well as some classics. Newcomers have to fight harder to develop an image, so they may be particularly helpful to you.

A CELEBRATION OF THE CATALOG

Browsing through catalogs makes one realize what wonderful experiences these are! What a joy to shop them, meet their people, learn about new products and improvements and all sorts of intriguing things from the story of European goose down to exploring the rapids of the Andes, from browsing for fresh Hawaiian orchids to buying an outfit like the one Countess Blixen wore in the untamed Africa of the early 1930s.

I wish you a good experience with catalogs, particularly with those that can use your help. You have the equipment to provide this help. Use it. Not many people know how to examine the creative elements of a catalog analytically. You do and can.

Send in for your catalogs; enjoy them and learn from them! Order from them! You'll find it's irresistible!

SEND AWAY FOR THESE CATALOGS

The J. Peterman Company
1318 Russell Cave Road
Lexington, KY 40505

Lillian Vernon
Virginia Beach, VA 23479-0002

Lands' End Direct Merchants
Lands' End, Inc.
1 Lands' End Lane
Dodgeville, WI 53595

The Sharper Image
650 Davis Street
San Francisco, CA 94111

Williams-Sonoma
P.O. Box 7456
San Francisco, CA 94120-7456

Breck's
U.S. Reservation Center
6523 North Galena Road
Peoria, IL 61632

Patagonia Mail Order
1609 W, Babcock St.
Bozeman, MT 59715

Eddie Bauer
Fifth & Union
P.O. Box 3700
Seattle, WA 98124-3700

J. Crew
One Ivy Crescent
Lynchburg, VA 24513-1001

L.L. Bean
Freeport, ME 04033

The Ben Silver Collection
149 King Street
Charleston, SC 29401

The Vermont Country Store
P.O. Box 3000
Manchester Center, VT
   05255-3000

Sundance Catalog
1909 South 4250 West
Salt Lake City, UT 84104

Neiman Marcus by Mail
P.O. Box 650589
Dallas, TX 75265-0589

Rent Mother Nature
52 New Street, P.O. Box 193
Cambridge, MA 02238

White Flower Farm
P.O. Box 50
Litchfield, CT 06759-0050

Buy from one or two or more, and sooner or later, everyone will have your name! Enjoy!

What to Do with All Those Subscribers

There is only one answer because a direct marketer has only one objective for subscribers—renew them! Or if they're first-time subscribers—convert them! This is called circulation promotion. It's part of direct response because it enables you to continue the dialogue you began with your initial prospecting for new subscribers to magazines, newspapers, newsletters, and trade journals.

Over the years, circulation (the distribution of a publication via the mails) has become increasingly sophisticated. In the 1950s and 1960s most magazine publishers merely sent out a series of notices or letters informing new and old subscribers alike that their subscriptions would soon run out.

Human beings, being human, frequently postponed renewing and let their subscriptions lapse, so publishers and circulation directors decided to give subscribers more time to respond by moving up the notices and increasing the number of efforts. They also began offering incentives and special rates to spur subscribers to act.

Being good direct marketers—some of our first relationship marketers, in fact—the publishers and circulation directors also tracked, tested, and measured. They found that the earlier they started, the more direct mail efforts they sent, the greater the response—particularly if later messages became more urgent in tone.

Ultimately, they also tested expired or lapsed subscribers and found that, if offered special low prices, many of these people could be returned to the fold or reinstated.

In a few cases, all of this testing and trying resulted in renewal series of ten to fifteen or more mailings. In most cases, only five to seven efforts were profitable. And sometimes a phone call around the fifth effort paid off.

Whether five or fifteen, renewal notices always seemed terribly wasteful and irritating to outsiders, but productive to the inside professionals, as no effort was maintained that couldn't pull its own weight in subscriber response. (For example, if an effort cost $350 per thousand to mail, it had to bring in at least that much in renewed subscriptions.)

A standard series (a series format that works for most monthly publishers) evolved.

First notice—four months prior to expiration

Second notice—three months prior to expiration

Third notice—two months prior to expiration

Fourth notice (last chance)—one month prior to expiration

Fifth notice—two weeks or a month after expiration

Sixth and final notice (optional)—two months after expiration

In addition to careful testing, magazine circulation people also led the movement for good database planning. By the 1960s, thanks to the computer and its ability to develop and maintain extensive subscriber records, circulation directors knew where a subscriber came from (source), how long a subscriber had been on the books (first time renewal or regular), the kind of offer the subscriber responded to up front (full price, half price, premium, or sweepstakes). They were then able to study subscriber actions as groups, based on their source.

When you begin to learn all these things about your customers (or subscribers) you also begin to see that not all new subscribers behave the same way. And, ultimately, to maximize response, maybe they should be treated differently, according to source.

Situation: Those obtained from TV had a very low first renewal or conversion rate. Those from direct mail consistently did well.

Solution: Concentrate on direct mail-acquired subscribers. Convert television-acquired subscribers with special price or offer.

Situation: Those new subscribers acquired through an up-front offer that included a premium did not convert (or first renew) as well as new subscribers acquired with a standard offer without premium.

Solution: Offer premium-acquired subscribers premiums with first conversion.

Situation: Subscribers acquired through agents that used big national sweepstakes converted poorly, often taking an agent's new sweepstakes offer and starting a new subscription rather than converting as a regular subscriber through the publisher.

Solution: Send these subscribers a *very early* conversion opportunity loaded with extras such as a publisher's sweepstakes offer or multiple premiums.

From all this "sourcing" several things became apparent, and they now form the basis of the kind of renewal planning you'll encounter today.

1. Direct mail is the best and strongest source of new subscribers. Even the direct mail *format* can predetermine the future profitablity of the subscriber. (A double postcard is weak. Direct mail or even a magalog is strong. Conclusion: the more description, benefits and features, the better the "customer.")

2. In all groups, subscribers who *plan* to renew will do so in early efforts (one and two). Later efforts must become more promotional to encourage the fence sitters.

3. Sweepstakes-sold or premium-sold new customers require like or similar offers to respond well in conversions (premium sold equals premium renewed).

4. It is cost-efficient to promote weak source groups with only three to five efforts, while stronger, direct-mail sold sources may go profitably for six to twelve or more efforts. Each publication must determine its own exact pattern through testing.

5. A promotional "Early Bird" offer (sent some six months prior to expiration and two months prior to the first regular renewal) can hype upfront renewal response considerably. Sometimes, however, it is merely robbing Peter to pay Paul; the renewal series *overall* response ends up about the same in both test groups when this is split tested. Only cash flow is altered.

6. All conversion and renewal efforts seek to upgrade the subscriber to full renewal rates. This can be done quickly with some sources (direct mail) or it may take a couple of years (for some cut-rate and agent-sold subscribers).

7. Net sub value—or the lifetime value of a subscriber—is determined by tracking and costing source groups over a period of years. (Don't worry, there are computer models for this.)

As you may guess, today's renewal planning is no simple thing. A publication can have as many as six or seven sources for new subscribers. Most source group renewal series will vary in length. Some will have varying offers. And offers within any one group may change as expire time approaches and passes. Not to mention a seeming endless year after year run of publisher rate-up testing.

To further complicate this, circulation directors are also testing formats. Many are using the magazine itself as a vehicle for expiration notices through cover wraps or (depending on who you talk to) "outserts" or "onserts." ("*This* is your last issue!") and bind-in cards and pages ("Yes, renew my subscription.").

Sound complicated? Just wait. You're only getting started. Let's review, however, before we jump ahead.

1. Your basic renewals are keyed or broken out into two kinds of renewals—first time (or conversions) and regular. Some publishers, by the way, even break regular renewals into "first regular" and "regular." (Oh, never mind.)

2. Each conversion group is broken out by source: direct mail sold, insert card obtained, agent sold, TV, print ads, and unknowns or write-ins, called *white mail.* (Sourcing is carried in the customer record for many years to track the overall net worth of the subscriber group during its lifetime. But for renewal purposes, it is used only to break out promotional planning in the conversions.)

3. The offer is composed of price and term (number of days, weeks, or months in the subscription), plus any specials such as premiums or sweepstakes. (There are audit control bureaus that limit or supervise price setting and offers, one for consumer publications, one for business publications.)

4. Offer, term, and price structures are carefully overlaid (and frequently tested) on all *conversion* source groups to determine the most effective offer structure for each group. Within each group, offer variations will be tested as well. By comparison, regular renewal groups are subjected to very little offer testing.

5. Length of series also varies by source among the conversion groups (when does the first effort mail, how many efforts are to be used).

6. Renewal format testing on the entire series is very popular today. Some publishers test wraps and bind-ins in conjunction with direct mail; others, to replace direct mail. Results are uneven here;

quite a few publishers have had success with a pure wrap series on the four issues prior to expiration, others have had more success with a standard series of direct mail efforts *plus* a wrap or cover on the last issue prior to expiration ("Your next to last issue") and on the expiration issue ("Your LAST issue"). Some publishers also find that telephone renewing is helpful around the fifth effort.

In short, wow—it can be complicated. Be prepared; research; ask questions; take notes. And remember the Basic Law. Your series has got to make sense to the subscriber to be effective!

WHY I AM TELLING YOU THIS

First, you won't find this information so easily anywhere else. Unless you know enough to start those questions coming.

Second, you need this information to understand how creative development takes place in a highly personalized, very instructive segment of direct response dialogue.

Third, circulation promotion is an excellent learning ground for direct marketing creative people and if you have the chance, you might want to do something here. It is not simple, but this chapter will help you dig in and understand what it entails.

Finally, it's a great place to work in applying the Basic Law—over and over. As you might already imagine, circulation directors and publishers get so caught up in segmentation and number crunching that the forest-and-trees syndrome sets in! They're out there in the woods. You must stay back and look at the forest.

Your new subscribers are *people*. How is all of this going to sound to them? Remember how you can destroy credibility by crying "wolf" too often? You do the same thing by telling the relatively new subscriber that the subscription is running out a full six months before expiration! Or by saying that this is absolutely, positively the last chance when it isn't.

Here are two wonderful tools to help you make sense to your subscribers and still be creative in planning and dealing with all the offers, source groups, and formats.

TIMING AND PACING— THE TOOLS TO SEE YOU THROUGH

Let's take timing first as you'll be hanging your pacing from it. Timing? Isn't that the distance between efforts? Like four weeks or a month? Right you are. That's part of it. By the way, do you know *why* we leave four weeks between most efforts instead of three or seven? Because that's the time it takes to get an effort or mailing out (via third-class mail) and back by first class, with a little time at the end for updating your customer files as to who answered and who didn't. Mail any closer, and you'll suffer huge doses of "crossed in the mail." This irritates customers and creates extra trouble for you.

So why not mail six weeks apart and really update the file before your next mailing? Nope. Four weeks. *If* you want to maximize overall response with as many efforts as are reasonably possible prior to the subscription expiration date of each expire group while *also* minimizing "crossed in the mail" complaints for those you didn't catch in the computer update—it's got to be four weeks.

Timing in terms of spacing between efforts is only half the story however. This half helps you convey creatively to your customer or subscriber just exactly what is happening, has happened, and will happen to his or her subscription in real time.

If it is well done, you'll have a socko series; if badly done—confusion, irritation, and inaction on the part of your subscribers. That's how important it is!

Consider, for example, these badly timed situations:

Situation 1: You send a notice saying "your final issue of *Black Snail* is on its way to you. This is absolutely your last chance to renew without a break in service." This notice is followed by two more issues.

Situation 2: You send a notice in *March* telling the subscriber that "your subscription is about to run out." The computer renewal form shows a July expiration date.

Situation 3: You use a wrap for the last subscription issue. It says "this is your last issue of *Black Snail*" but your last-chance letter, which states "your *next* issue is your last," follows this issue-with-wrap by a day or two.

Subscription service, unfortunately, is not run on a four-week cycle. The subscriber file has to be updated in the computer and this is done on a set date. Last-minute renewals can't always promise that the customer won't miss an issue, and expired subscriptions are not always cleaned out immediately, but often sent an extra issue or two. What's more, subscriber copies are mailed out on a specific day every week or month. Some publications are received in a day or two, others may take as much as a week or more to arrive.

All of these factors will affect your renewal credibility negatively if you don't take them into account in your planning. To do this you must understand expire policy. How and when subscribers will be dropped, held, and reinstated, when the customer file is updated, when the issues mail each month or each week, when they are 90 to 95 percent received.

You must *overlay all of this* on your timing—whether you have a basic five or six part series, a shorter or a longer one. For example: A renewal effort stating "the issue you have just received is your last" is a powerful statement if indeed the last issue has just landed on my desk a few days ago. If, on the other hand, I receive such notice two weeks later or—heaven forbid—two weeks earlier, it is ineffectual, confusing, and irritating.

Good timing that takes all of this into consideration is the first step in formulating a solid renewal series or improving an existing one. The proof of the pudding of course is always "Will this make sense to the subscriber?"

PACING AND YOUR
CREATIVE STRATEGIES

Circulation does not use the good old sequence of proposition, benefits, hypothesis, and approach you've been following all along with customer/subscriber *acquisition.* If your publication has done its job, you are primarily providing an easy opportunity for satisfied current customers to continue. Those who didn't get the value or involvement they expected are largely lost causes and will fall away *regardless of what you say or do.* (No publication ever hit the dust due to a weak renewal series!)

Your real work is to convince all those waverers and doubters. Those who may or might—or might not—or just don't want to think about it yet.

Your hypothesis still revolves around the benefits of the publication. But instead of throwing all of this into one big direct mail offering, you develop a group or string of efforts paced to tease, coax, and convince—and there is a pattern.

You cull out the happy subscribers up front with your first two efforts; you become more urgent and pull in a few more; then just in time to renew without missing an issue, you hit them hard with "Last Chance." This is the high point in your pacing. After expiration you offer a quick reinstate (still time), then at the end either a poignant, involving "how-can-we-serve-you-better/where-did-we-go-wrong" or a hard-hitting, one-time only, last chance price break.

Here's a standard creative theme outline that may be helpful; assuming you overlay real time, this is paced to build to Effort 4.

> Effort #1: *Time to Renew* (Editorial preview—all the great things ahead. Now's no time to be without *Black Snail* . . .)
>
> Effort #2: *Reminder* (Don't forget—time to renew) short effort.
>
> Effort #3: *Hurry Up* (Possible edit review of all the past good things or involvement questions; time is running out.)
>
> Effort #4: *Last Chance* (Urgent notice that you are about to get your last issue. A break in service is imminent.)
>
> Effort #5: *Expire!* (Still time to reinstate your lapsed subscription; won't you think it over quickly?)
>
> Effort #6: *If Part We Must* (One last opportunity. How might we have served you better? Or an absolutely one-time chance for the lowest rates we can offer you. Or both.)

How you handle your pacing depends on your publication (consumer or business magazine, trade paper, or newsletter) and its policies (when it runs the updating, its procedures regarding final issues), its frequency or timing (weekly, monthly, six times a year), and its renewal rate structures.

Consumer publications usually treat their "worst" or hardest-to-convince subscribers *best*, offering the lowest rates at the end of the series. This doesn't seem fair, somehow, but believe me, a few publishers have reversed this, trying to inject fairness. They warned laggards that the best rates were only for the early renewers. Humans, being what they are, continued to hold out, and the series as a whole fell flat on its face.

WHO'S TALKING?

The next step in your renewal planning is your choice of spokesperson. A series written by the circulation director and/or the publisher is totally suitable. There are, however, other opportunities for creativity (and more fun for you) if you vary your spokesperson.

After all, who might logical spokepersons be for a magazine? The editor is obvious when you do an editorial sell or a "preview." The editor or publisher is best on a final "If Part We Must," credibly inquiring how to serve the subscriber better—while all the time reselling the product. (Crafty, eh?)

The circulation director is good on Last Chance because seeing that subscribers get subscription service is his or her logical role. Then all sorts of other staff can be brought in—if you find a logical reason (researchers, writers, photographers—even news bureau chiefs, well-known experts who contribute to the publication, even the corporate president or founder as long as each one is credible in his or her role). Check the masthead and use your imagination.

YOUR TONE AND STYLE

Traditionally, the tone and style of every renewal series should reflect the publication. If it is a serious, thoughtful publication, its renewal efforts should be serious and thoughtful. If it is raucous and irreverent, its renewals should reflect this. A business publication requires a businesslike renewal series—one that matches its style and tone as well.

Your pacing, of course, should be overlaid on your style. For example: Effort 4 for a business publication would be businesslike and urgent . . . for a consumer humor magazine it would be light but urgent . . . for a sports magazine it might incorporate sports competition—use the symbolism of the race—to show urgency . . . for a drama magazine it could imply that the curtain was falling on the last act, and so on.

Here are two good examples of style and tone, one from the *Wall Street Journal* (Figure 11–11), the other, one effort from a series used for *Parents* magazine (Figure 11–12). Notice the appropriate

FIGURE 11–11 A Renewal Letter for a Business Publication

THE WALL STREET JOURNAL.

World Financial Center, 200 Liberty Street, New York, NY 10281

It is evening. The building is quiet.
The last secretary left an hour ago.
You are alone in your office.

You look out into the parking lot. Only
a few cars are left. It's starting to rain.

You call home to tell them you're on the
way. You slip one more report into your
briefcase and walk toward the door.

The phone rings.

Dear Reader:

Do you let it ring or do you answer it?

If I'm right, you answered it.

Why? You could call it curiosity, but it's something more.
It's simply the way you do business. Whole-heartedly. From
beginning to end.

You honestly enjoy every minute of a business day. You thrive
on the challenge. The involvement. The responsibility. And the
personal satisfaction.

There are times when you still find your business utterly
new and exhilarating. And, to be sure, there are times when you
find it equally demanding and frustrating. But you never find
it boring.

That's the mark of a Wall Street Journal reader. You've been
a Journal subscriber before so you know what I mean. Journal
readers demand a news source that shares their unfailing enthusiasm,
interest, and concern for the events of business. The Wall Street
Journal meets that demand.

The Wall Street Journal is one daily which doesn't relegate
business to the back page. Every page of The Journal is business.

The Wall Street Journal is your daily
briefing for the challenge of change.

Your success -- and your company's -- depends on how well
you meet and conquer change. Change is the one constant of

(over, please)

business. It's what happens after the budgets are prepared and
the marketing plans are made. It's the real world.

It's the world you confront every business day. It's the
world The Wall Street Journal illuminates. Every business day.

Only a business news-gathering organization with the depth,
speed, and experience of The Journal can keep pace. The Journal
provides more information, more facts, more figures and more
insight about business than any other source.

Only The Journal makes it so easy for you to pinpoint the
news you need. Together, The Journal's three daily sections
provide an unmatched breadth of key business intelligence, comprehensive economic analysis and unrivalled statistical reporting.

The Journal's first section focuses on current business
and financial news -- events which will shape the future of the
economy, your industry and your business. Then, in Marketplace
The Journal's second section, you'll keep up-to-the-minute with
those trends, technological developments, marketing strategies
and legal decisions which could be important to your company
and invaluable to your career.

Finally, Money & Investing, The Journal's third section,
is your complete guide to the financial markets with the day's
pivotal market stories, equity, futures, and options quotations,
credit market reports, statistical charts, and key market
indicators.

A Special "Welcome Back" Offer

If you act now, you can again make The Journal part of
your daily planning for change. You can receive 13 weeks of
The Journal for just $29.75. That's the next 65 issues delivered
to your home or office for less than you'd pay if you had to take
time out to pick up The Journal at your local newsstand.

Or you may wish to take advantage of one of our longer-term
subscriptions for old friends. An annual subscription for $119
saves you $8 off The Journal's cover price. Our best buy, two
years for $208, saves you a full $46!

So don't delay. Just tell us the term you prefer on the
enclosed order card and mail it in the envelope provided. The
postage is already paid!

Sincerely yours,

Peter R. Kann
Executive Vice President/
Associate Publisher

PRK:cw
Encs.

P.S. The cost of your Journal subscription may be tax deductible.
Ask your tax advisor.

FIGURE 11–12 A Renewal Series for a Consumer Publication

You won't want to miss this opportunity!

Although your subscription still has a little way to go, we're opening up an unusually fine renewal opportunity if you act now.

This is a special renewal price, lower than our regular rates and a significant savings over the newsstand cost of PARENTS Magazine.

To take advantage of it, just return the enclosed form. No need to send payment now, we'll bill you later.

The Parents at PARENTS

Dear Subscriber and Fellow Parent:

   Aside from all the other things you do, we appreciate the fact that your job as a parent is one of the most important and possibly the most difficult jobs in the world.

   Our job at PARENTS Magazine is to help you do it right in every way we can.

   Being a modern parent takes a lot more than love. It also means keeping up and ahead on the little and the big things that help you be the kind of parent you want to be - loving <u>and</u> knowing.

   That's where we come in. To help you be the best possible parent when it comes to knowing.

   So I hope you plan to continue your most important journey with us. There is still much

difference in tone, yet both are friendly. Notice, too, the *Parents* series use of pacing and timing, voice, and graphic unity (with pictures from the magazine itself).

YOU AND THE ARTIST—
STILL WORKING TOGETHER

Just as you work your timing and pacing into the theme along with the style and tone of your publication, so you'll want graphic development that gives you the appropriate visual pacing and theming. For example: Should your Last Chance outer shout? Should it be solid red? Should your second effort *look* like a reminder—a memo copy? Should art work or photography be used? Should the overall feeling be conservative? Want to change the format of the fourth effort? Want to test a postcard on the final effort?

SHOULD YOU USE A
GENERIC RENEWAL SERIES?

You may come across publishers (usually ones with a stable of special interest magazines) who use what I call a *generic series*.

A generic series follows the standard five-to-six effort theme and pacing *without* style or tone. It is basic, informative and—if the timing is fine-tuned—efficient. And one series can be used for all magazines, with a simple change of logotype on the letterhead.

In some cases (largely business and trade publications), renewals even run under a generic letterhead like "Subscription Services" or "Circulation Services." (If the reader sees his or her publication listed in the group at the top under these heads, the reader can assume that's the product they're talking about.)

Such series are indeed economical. They lower renewal costs considerably. But they eliminate editorial reselling, previews of features to come, reviews of past highlights, reminders of benefits—all the things that attracted the subscriber in the first place. They eliminate a good part of the dialogue in fact—the relationship-building dialogue.

You, by now, have come to understand that the more direct, the more personal a promotional communication can be, the more effective it will be. The best direct mail efforts are those that know their prospects well and capitalize on this.

And, although renewals and conversions are selling efforts, or efforts to resell customers—most of whom believe they are either going to renew or not going to renew before receiving a single effort—there are still a lot of fencesitters to deal with.

How can the response be as strong, then, when we treat the customer like a stranger and use only a portion of the knowledge we have? I like to think that generic renewals can't possibly lower promotion costs enough to make up for the subscribers they lose.

Some Helpful Pointers on Other Backend Areas

IF YOU'RE ASKED TO DO A BILLING SERIES ON THE SIDE

"Charge it" traditionally increases mail order response by a minimum of 30 percent and sometimes by much more. House accounts, however, are a rarity and publications are the big exception. (The advantages far outweigh the risks for publications, as service can be suspended after a few issues are sent.) Because of this, nearly all publishers offer "bill me" options, and over 80 percent of all subscribers opt to be billed. This creates a massive dunning situation for every publication, and most of them are handled in much the same way.

You may be called upon to do a dunning series, or to improve an existing one. Please remember, *this is not the same thing as renewals.* Not at all. Don't try to be flamboyantly creative here. Billing has its structure—usually five to seven efforts (four weeks apart) with an extra week thrown in between the last two efforts.

Some series are longer (if it pays to continue); others are shorter. All start politely and end up strong—as strong as you can make it without offending or inviting legal action. Always apply the Basic Law and stick to the facts.

Your series should run something like this (but there are many variations).

> Effort 1: Welcome or "thank you," and, by the way, your invoice is enclosed (possibly with an opportunity to take a longer term at an even greater saving. Circulation people call this "Renewal at birth.").
>
> Effort 2 (4 weeks later): Reminder.
>
> Effort 3 (4 weeks later): Second reminder. Is something wrong? Please let us know or take care of this matter now. (Concern and puzzlement.)
>
> Effort 4 (4 weeks later): This is the fourth notice we have sent and still no word from you (mild threat of discontinuing service).
>
> Effort 5 (4 weeks later): Strong threat, usually with time limit on service cutoff.
>
> Effort 6 (5 to 7 weeks later): Last chance—final opportunity to pay and have service reinstated (sometimes with threat of turning unpaid bill over to a collection agency).

Many publishers and circulation directors have tried to improve (or lower) their bad pay by adding style and tone to their copy to coax their recalcitrants. No good. They've added humor and editorial resell. It doesn't work either. On the other hand, most publishers hesitate to get too strong and alienate a prospect for a few dollars.

This is not benefits-to-you time. Billing or dunning is not selling. It's serious stuff. Nobody's interested in talk. The bill's primary job is to gain attention and to impress or motivate the recipient to act—now.

Remember, up front you're talking to prime customers. After the second bill, in most cases you're working a group of deadbeats. So make it look and sound serious—official even, as you move along. Use the comptroller or treasurer as spokesperson for final efforts. But not *too* harsh . . . here's your chance to play kindly bill collector. And even that can be fun.

Happily, the bad pay percentage in almost every direct marketing business or service never runs much above 2 to 3 percent. (And if it does, this often indicates a deeper, more serious problem with the offer, product, or service.)

MEMBER MAILINGS

Like magazine circulation, book clubs have been known as good training grounds for aspiring direct response writers. It's a fine place to start, because book club relationship marketing consists of regular member communications (a package every month, or every 26 days or so). You have a chance to do the equivalent of small space ads for books—or for whatever else your club is offering. And you may have a chance at a small catalog as well.

Each club has its own procedures for handling members (and rules) which you will learn. But here's something to bring to it, whatever the club: Go back to the Basic Law. In customer dialogue, remember—*something has gone before and something will follow.* Does your assignment fit in and make sense with the big picture—the customer continuity?

Step out of context and *be* a customer. Make sure you're on the mailing list. Is it all clear, positive, and promotional? Does the club have a *welcome mailing* for new members? Does it project a good image? Does it have an image to project? If so, sustain and strengthen it. If not, see if you can start to develop one (and don't forget your art director).

The book clubs have a job to do, like the catalogs: repeat business, satisfied customers. Your job is to seek, examine, question. You know how. You may, in fact, be surprised at how much you know and how few of your fellow workers question established formats and procedures. Don't let that slow you down.

Figure 11–13 shows one of the best "Welcome Packages" I've seen. It not only made the new Quality Paperback Book Club member feel important with a membership card but it made him or her feel good about having chosen to join; then it went on to answer all possible questions that might come up during the course of membership. The exanples in Figure 11–14 represent wise efforts from other companies to promise good, honest treatment.

Magazine circulation and book club member mailings are excellent training grounds for relationship marketing. They teach you to plan ahead for months or a year in advance. They show you the

FIGURE 11–13 A "Welcome Package" for a Book Club

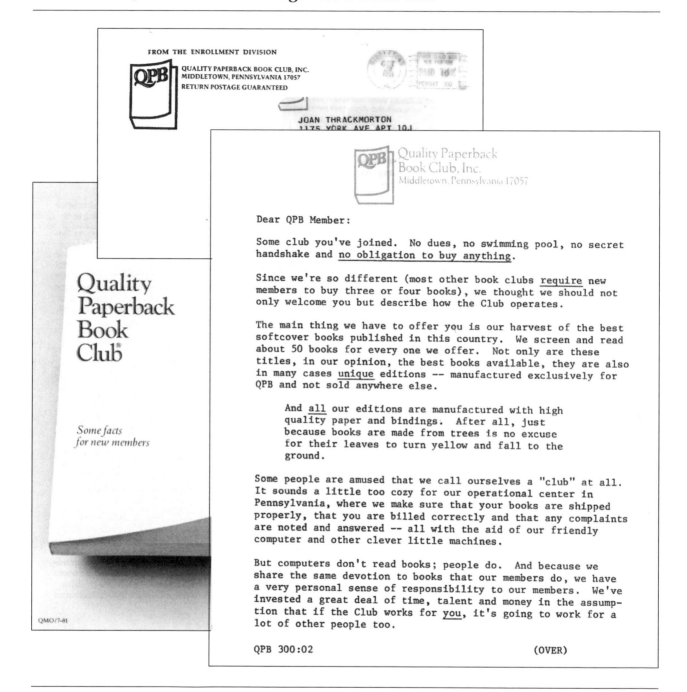

FROM THE ENROLLMENT DIVISION

QUALITY PAPERBACK BOOK CLUB, INC.
MIDDLETOWN, PENNSYLVANIA 17057
RETURN POSTAGE GUARANTEED

JOAN THRACKMORTON
1175 YORK AVE APT 10J

Quality Paperback
Book Club, Inc.
Middletown, Pennsylvania 17057

Quality
Paperback
Book
Club®

Some facts
for new members

QMO/7-81

Dear QPB Member:

Some club you've joined. No dues, no swimming pool, no secret handshake and no obligation to buy anything.

Since we're so different (most other book clubs require new members to buy three or four books), we thought we should not only welcome you but describe how the Club operates.

The main thing we have to offer you is our harvest of the best softcover books published in this country. We screen and read about 50 books for every one we offer. Not only are these titles, in our opinion, the best books available, they are also in many cases unique editions -- manufactured exclusively for QPB and not sold anywhere else.

    And all our editions are manufactured with high
    quality paper and bindings. After all, just
    because books are made from trees is no excuse
    for their leaves to turn yellow and fall to the
    ground.

Some people are amused that we call ourselves a "club" at all. It sounds a little too cozy for our operational center in Pennsylvania, where we make sure that your books are shipped properly, that you are billed correctly and that any complaints are noted and answered -- all with the aid of our friendly computer and other clever little machines.

But computers don't read books; people do. And because we share the same devotion to books that our members do, we have a very personal sense of responsibility to our members. We've invested a great deal of time, talent and money in the assumption that if the Club works for you, it's going to work for a lot of other people too.

QPB 300:02   (OVER)

importance of addressing a member as "member" or subscriber as "subscriber" (or customer as "customer") and treating him or her differently from the riff-raff out there . . . they train you to work with an eye to pacing and timing and to pleasing the customer at every opportunity. They also remind you that customers respond, say "yes" or "no" to you in a dialogue that can indeed go on and on if you work at it. That's good relationship marketing.

FIGURE 11–14 Promises to Customers

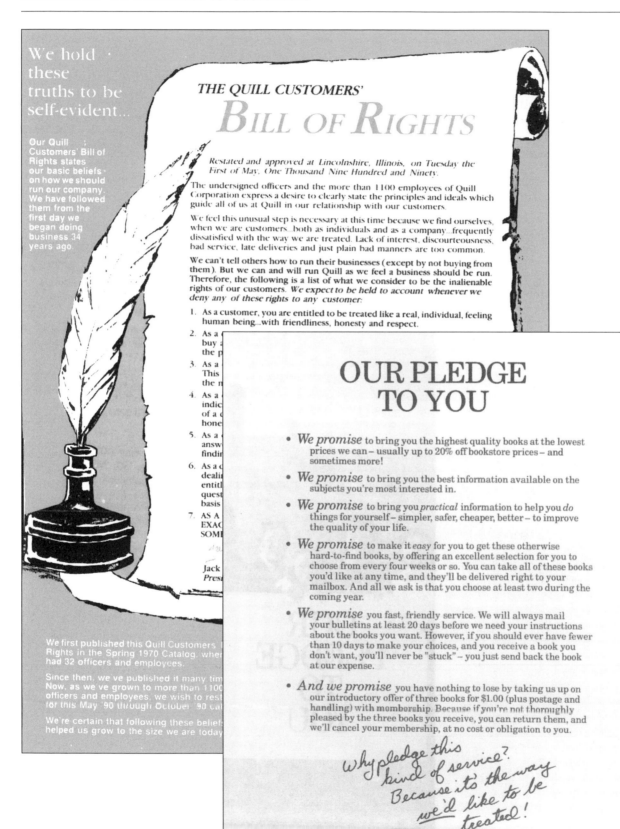

INQUIRY FULFILLMENT—
ANOTHER OPPORTUNITY

This is also a good place to get your feet wet because it's very much like direct mail prospecting, except that the door has already been opened by an inquiry of one kind or another.

In other words, you have a friendly audience. And that's nice. After all, with a good lead-getting program, think of what you know about your prospect! Your first step is to find out, of course, who these prospects are and what you do know. Request a copy of the direct response promotion that produced the inquiry. From this you will get the basic data for your fulfillment approach.

Once you determine exactly what you know about your prospects, utilize this information as fully as you can. For example:

- Although you know he or she is interested in the product or service, what is the extent of the interest? This will be determined by the qualification factors in the promotion. (Was it a freeloader's paradise or did it qualify prospects with a tight offer and highly related premium?)

- You now have a correct name and address. If this is a business inquiry, let's hope you also have a title. (Good personalization!)

- Did you get a phone number? They're great for "next steps." ("John Smith, our sales representative in Houston, will call you in a few days.")

- Any other data given? Size of company? Type of service desired? Monies available? Size of investment or loan considered? Effective inquiry fulfillment will utilize such data in a covering letter along with any promised collateral or premiums.

Now plan for the next step. Unfortunately, many marketers spend fortunes acquiring leads, yet treat these valuable prospects like second-class citizens when they arrive. Little provision (budget) is made for follow-up and even less good planning for continuing the dialogue! (If, thanks to bad planning, it takes weeks even to get an answer out in the mail, you can forget it, because the prospects have, too, by then.)

It's almost as bad to add "Just call if you have any further questions." (Further questions? Who's selling whom?) Of course it's better than nothing. Or is it? You put all the responsibility on the prospect's shoulders. And some inquiry fulfillment does just this.

Wouldn't it be better to continue the dialogue—to move the relationship to another level? Sure, you shouldn't have to be thinking of this. Some marketer somewhere has it all worked out. He or she surely knows.

Don't accept this! If and when such dead-end situations occur, ask for the objectives. (Ask anyway, just to be sure you're doing your part.) Then see if you can find a way to keep the dialogue going.

Will a salesperson call for an appointment? Do you want the prospect to come in to the salesperson and if so, why should he or she? How about getting the prospect to request more specific information? Or outright asking for the order?

If you know the next step—or the basic objectives—you can help work toward this by using response motivators or door openers for the next round. For example:

- Enclose a fill-out-and-return analysis form so that "our local sales representative can call and deliver the completed profit analysis directly to you within two weeks . . ."

- Add an invitation to come in "to our local loan offices with the enclosed certificate for an immediate credit evaluation . . . "

- Ask the prospect to choose a free book on whichever machine they indicate as best suited to their operation requirements. "We'll send an engineer as well, if you wish. Just look over the preliminary specifications and availabilities here and . . . "

- Enclose a "key" token to take down to their local Maxi dealer today. "Enjoy a test drive of the new Maxi and a free first aid kit for your car—on the house . . . "

Two more things (they may seem pretty obvious to you by now, but not to a lot of those other people involved in inquiry fulfillment): 1) Get the envelope opened; and 2) include a letter.

Under the absolutely worst of circumstances (no budget), you can capitalize on the inquiry request to maximize your direct mail impact very simply. Merely put "Enclosed, the materials you requested" on your outer. This is no secret. Nor can I believe it's any secret to you as to why it works, every time.

Even with a minimal budget, push for a brief letter. You should be able to develop excellent letter formats that can accommodate all the data from each inquiry and start a dialogue.

If the response device in the original promotion was looking for several kinds of inquiry responses, you'll need an equal number of letter versions (one for the large equipment interests, as opposed to the small equipment; one for the bond investors and one for the stock investors; one for the health insurance group and one for the life insurance; and so on).

Remember, it has to make sense, preserve continuity, and embody as much personalization as you can give it. Don't use the too familiar, lazy "Here's the information—thanks—goodbye."

The Heart of Relationship Marketing

Effective relationship marketing isn't a one-shot thing or something you plan as you go along. *It's the way you treat your customers*, with every contact planned ahead, keeping the dialogue open with frequent mailings—all logical and involving to the customer.

Unlike prospecting, always announce your company up front. Also, wherever possible, lead on the outer with a member-subscriber-customer "special." (Never include current customers in your new prospect mailings.)

Always treat your customers just a tad better than anyone else.

Thank them for ordering. Even send them a thank-you gift. (See Figure 11–15.)

FIGURE 11–15 Thank-you Gifts and a Customer Questionnaire

Customer Research Questionnaire

Since you are among the very first to buy and use <u>Deneuve</u> and since <u>Deneuve</u> is available only by mail, we want to give you the best service possible. We would be grateful if you would take a couple of minutes to answer the questions below.

	YES	NO	
1.	☐	☐	Would you like us to continue to send you convenient reorder notices?
2.	☐	☐	If it were possible, would you like to have reorders shipped to you automatically on a fixed schedule?

3. What other <u>Deneuve</u> products would you like us to develop?
☐ *body creme*
☐ *environmental room fragrancer*
☐ *bath soap*
☐ *body lotion*
☐ *purse spray*
☐ *dusting powder*
☐ *other*_____

Your Personal Comments on <u>Deneuve</u> (we'd very much like to share your experience with our new fragrance): _____
_____
_____
_____

Be sure to check your mailing label, and make any changes necessary to insure prompt delivery.

Deneuve

Essex VT 05451

Thank You

NOW A GIFT FOR YOU

990 DIVIDEND CHECK

One Dollar and Thirty Seven cents   *** 1.37 ***

VALID ANYTIME TOWARDS PRODUCT PURCHASE

Carole A. Ziter, President

Non-negotiable

Ask their opinion on ways you might serve them better, new ideas for products and services. Make sure these are carefully planned to make it easy for them to answer (their time is valuable) and to put the information in a format you can use.

Ask them for positive comments or stories on their experiences with your company. See if you can use these in your prospecting (enhanced credibility).

Urge them to call with question or ideas (see Figure 11–16). Invite them to visit your factory, offices, or showrooms.

FIGURE 11–16 A Winning Letter, Thanks to Its "Caring" Lead

Colonial Penn Auto Insurance

JOHN E. HOEY
Senior Vice President

Dear Experienced Driver:

A few days ago, I closed my office door to interruptions, sat down and put myself in your place...to try and figure out:

Why we haven't convinced you to look into
our low priced Auto Insurance.

This Colonial Penn Auto Insurance program was specifically designed to give you low rates by cutting the cost of coverage for drivers who have distinguished themselves by their good driving record. In fact, Colonial Penn spent many long months building into this program the lower rates and special privileges we felt safe drivers had earned. That's why...

More than one-half million drivers have
changed to Colonial Penn.

And I just don't understand why you haven't at least given us a chance to quote you our low rates. After all, I'm not asking you to commit to anything...I'm only asking you to compare with no strings.

So, putting myself in your place, I decided we just hadn't answered all your questions yet. I tried to think of the toughest questions I could...questions a driver like yourself would want straightforward answers to before making a decision to change insurance companies.

First off, you're probably thinking...

Why have you contacted me for
this special program?

Over the past few years, auto insurance rates have continued to increase...by nearly 43% between 1980 and 1984 in many areas of the country. That means year after year your insurance rates have probably gone up...no matter how careful a driver you have been...or how long you've stayed accident free.

(over, please)

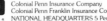

Colonial Penn Insurance Company
Colonial Penn Franklin Insurance Company
NATIONAL HEADQUARTERS 5 Penn Center Plaza/Philadelphia, Pennsylvania 19181

Make sure your database is current and allows you easy access to that magic *20 percent of your customers who buy 80 percent of your products and services.* (Do this if you do nothing else!)

Then structure special levels of service with rewards for your customers: Gold Card customers (with special privileges), Silver Card customers, etc. Hey—why not give them a newsletter? (See Figure 11–17.)

FIGURE 11–17 Customer Newsletters Add Value to the Relationship

Develop a special program to reactivate customers who have fallen away and haven't purchased from you recently.

And always remember that all opportunities to talk to customers should make sense and should be handled with loving care. None of this "Yah—they're old friends; no fancy stuff, just give 'em letter #22." And acknowledge *their* responses to *your* requests.

Direct marketers have learned that their current customers are indeed their best friends. These customers are crucial to direct marketing success because that's where the profits come from. Yet some marketers still spend heavily on the glamorous front end, acquiring prospects and customers, then scrimp with little thought or planning on the real profit center, the backend. How foolish.

When you start at the backend, you learn to nurture and respect the customers who make your job possible. Maximize sales with those customers by dealing productively on a continuing basis and giving good value and good service. Develop a feeling for the continuing dialogue that's possible thanks to our computer abilities and customer records; see how you can use this to build a customer relationship that's far more personal and more caring and more effective than any relationship in today's retail arena.

That's direct marketing. Nothing else comes close to it.

RELATIONSHIP MARKETING AND THE SELF-PERPETUATING MACHINE

Figure 11–18 is a sort of Rube Goldberg sausage machine that illustrates the importance of relationship marketing and how it works. The object is to illustrate the continuing process of

- Bringing on new prospects from a wide variety of media efforts

- Converting prospects to customers via direct mail, telephone, an office visit—even the Internet—or combinations of these (losing as few as possible to bad pay, poor service, general inertia, or nonresponse)

- Motivating customers to purchase more often and in larger quantities

At all times, while you are upgrading some customers, you will be losing others, but many of them (old or inactive customers) can be activated by repromotion or reinstatement efforts.

Just imagine that everything is moving in this diagram—up, down, across. Nothing stays the same. Customers and prospects come on up front and immediately start to fall away due to failure to pay bills or nonresponse to new promotions or poor customer relations. At the same time, other customers are buying—each time more and more.

This is a continuing process, for all business and consumer prospecting via direct response, all mail order catalogs, publication

FIGURE 11-18 The Self-Perpetuating Direct Marketing Machine

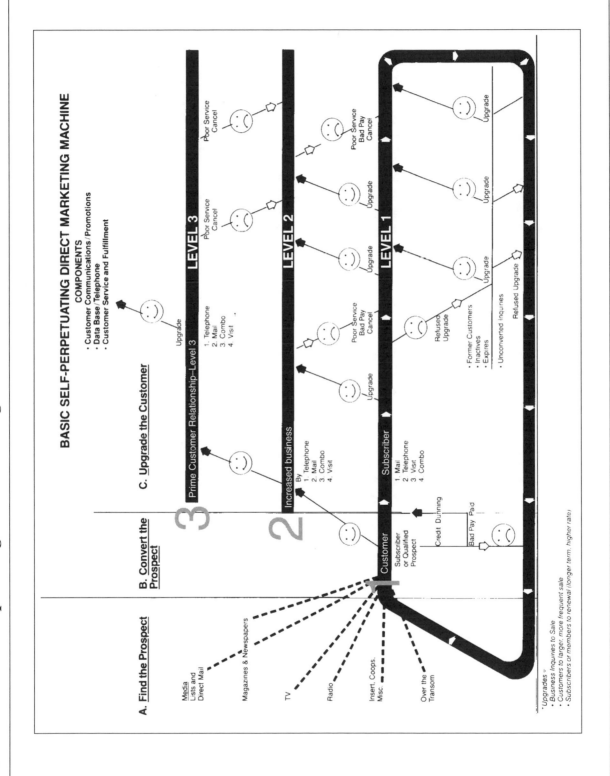

subscriptions, and book club memberships. It employs all the media and direct response methodologies to prospect, convert, upgrade, reinstate, repromote and, ultimately, to recycle. Not much is wasted in a good sausage machine. Same goes here!

CHAPTER TWELVE

YOU MOVE ON

Well, here we are at the last chapter. We've been through a lot, you and I, and now it's time for you to graduate—to go it alone. You've probably already guessed that the purpose of this whole thing is to give you the confidence and the ability to make creative judgments, starting with basic common sense—the Basic Law.

Your ability to apply creative reasoning to your assignments will enable you to make the sound decisions that save you from failed work. Your ability to work with others and develop creative strategies, applying the appropriate formulas and rules, will ensure that your work will be competent and effective. You will plan well and test intelligently.

Your ability to write, be it a letter, small space, broadcast, or other forms of interactive electronic media will be enhanced if you follow the procedures and guidelines set down for you.

The ingredients that no one can give you are personal style and creative genius. The way your writing sounds is your personal style. Writers inject their personalities into their work, whomever they write for, whatever role they act out. They still sound like themselves beneath it all. It's their own particular way of developing dialogue—not necessarily better, just different.

As for style and genius, I suggest you read a small gem called *Becoming a Writer* by Dorothea Brande, published by J. P. Tarcher, Inc., Los Angeles, California. In the foreword the late John Gardner promises:

> The root problems . . . are problems of confidence, self-respect, freedom: The writer's demon is imprisoned by the various ghosts in the unconscious.

Ms. Brande points out—with the delightful wit we find everywhere in her book—that for the writer suffering from uncertainty and self-doubt, writing teachers and books about writing, not to mention symposia of famous authors, do to the young (or old) struggling writer just about the worst thing they could do: "In the opening lecture, within the first few pages of his book, within a sentence or two of his authors' symposium, he will be told rather shortly that 'genius cannot be taught'; and there goes his hope glimmering. For whether he knows it or not, he is in search of the very thing that is denied him in that dismissive sentence." Ms. Brande's purpose in *Becoming a Writer* is to make available to the writer the very thing usually denied.

She is right that genius can be taught (once the secret emptiness of that phrase is understood) because in fact genius is as common as old shoes . . . .[1]

If writing is self-expression for you, if you take joy in creative development, and polishing your work is second nature, the odds are strongly in your favor. You'll be a writer all right. Just believe and keep working at it. You'll find all the "genius" you need.

Your Future in Direct Marketing

Now before you leave, I'd like to give you an idea of where direct marketing is taking you, if you choose to join it and if you plan to stay with it.

These can be exciting times for you. Many of the futurists in direct marketing claim that it is an expanding form of marketing, and will gradually encompass all goods and services, regardless of size or cost.

There is a growing focus on the customer and the importance of proactive customer care. Many giant companies have begun serious database building and will offer customers a diversity of interrelated products and services—merchandise services, financial services, medical services, even.

The irony is, direct marketing pretty well achieved this back in 1909! (But people forget.) That was the year Sears Roebuck and Co. first introduced its *mail order homes*.

At the time Sears already had a highly personalized customer service operation. Individual telephone reps were assigned to catalog customer groups. Each rep kept a full file on every assigned family in a manual card catalog in a shoe box; the cards recorded ages and numbers of children, birthdays, anniversaries, and the like. The reps used the data to make outgoing calls to these customers with seasonal offers and to remind them of special occasions.

Sears sold its 100,000 mail order homes (ranging in price from $595 to $5,000) between 1909 and 1937, largely through newspaper advertising. There were two-bedroom cottages, three-story houses, and even a mansion with Gothic columns, curving staircase, and servants' quarters. The prices were good and the materials were "quality." And many of these homes are still lived in today, cherished collectors' items.

According to an article in the *Wall Street Journal,*

> The pieces for the houses arrived by train, complete with everything required, including the kitchen sink. Rail deliveries were arranged so that each shipment arrived at just the right time in the construction schedule. The lumber for the frame came first, already cut, notched and mitered, and with each piece numbered to identify its place in the house. Then came shipments of window frames, plaster, plumbing, wiring, trim, glass, red cedar shingles and, finally, enough paint and varnish for three good coatings. Even the nails came from Sears. And the floor plans were marked to show where an extra Sears sofa or Sears piano might be placed. Financing was also provided by Sears. Monthly payments on a $2500 home might come to about $30—and Sears would even lend $500 in cash to help meet the cost of construction.
>
> The instructions were bound in leather and bore the new homeowner's name in gold. Creativity was discouraged. "Do not take anyone's advice as to how your building should be erected," the manual said. "This causes more difficulty than all other things put together."
>
> Possible pitfalls were highlighted. The instructions warned, for example, that "there are mistakes made in the erection of chimneys which are too numerous to mention." And it called for extra care in the construction of the porch, since "this part of your house is seen first and last!"

"In a 1929 newsletter," the *Wall Street Journal* continues, Sears had even personified its houses and given them a soothing voice:

> To all in the family, I guarantee contentment, a new sense of stability and independence, and the knowledge that regardless of any vicissitudes of fortune, you will always have one of the prime essentials of civilized life—comfortable, substantial shelter.
>
> After all the philosophies of the ages are condensed, one thing alone remains—the desire for happiness. And, in the final analysis of my offerings, it is Happiness that I present.[2]

Is this direct marketing—or is this direct marketing! 1909—not 2000! And a model for today.

Sadly, the Great Depression finished Sears' modern-homes department in the 1930s, but it remains one of the best mail order examples on record—*the* big sale (perhaps bigger than any like it today), *plus* financing and a clear-cut effort for add-on product in home furnishings. An ongoing dialogue, solid backend efforts, and an outstanding hypothesis are all contained in this example.

A Major Problem Ahead

We may not be as original today as we think we are, and that leads us to a big problem. Everyone wants to try the "newly discovered" direct marketing. It's future marketing. It's chic. But as we rush forward, some people are indeed forgetting the lessons of the past (if they ever learned them). And knowledgeable direct marketers are expressing concern.

Direct marketing has been exceeding its bounds while practitioners jostle to define the bulging bounds themselves. The expansionists want direct marketing to be all-encompassing, and often self-interest pushes them to stretch their definitions to any form of advertising that receives a measured response! (All sorts of clients today are asking for "accountability.")

Some of these expansionists also claim that it's impossible (or unnecessary) to test—that direct response should go into a vast national campaign, a media mix, all of which must "break" (or reach the market) in time and in tune with general advertising.

The purists (among whom I stand firmly) recognize direct marketing as *measured* response combined with the establishment (and use) of a *database*—dialogue marketing (see Chapter 2)—*and testing*. All the rest is whatever else you choose to call it—sales promotion or response advertising. It is not direct marketing.

What difference does the definition make, you ask? Here's the difference. With the lack of a clear, mutually acceptable definition, direct marketing will become diluted and diffuse. It will gradually lose its careful practitioners and stern requirements to test and implement and "roll out," to measure and learn and improve and project. It will cease to work to define and acquire a customer, then to establish a dialogue and cultivate that customer.

It will lose its rules and guidelines, while it goes for the megabucks of packaged goods and mass sampling instead. As it does this, it will become nothing—nothing more than a promotional tool, a coupon that's counted, a "vote" on a national toll-free number, a faceless wave of response or rejection, mass advertising's child.

That's why it is important for you to understand *what power and authority testing and accountability bring to the practice of direct marketing and how it can continue to be the force that it is—if you and others like you help keep it pure.*

What Response Rate Do You Need?

Aside from these threats of dilution and diffusion, there are other challenges to face. For example, if you hang around in direct marketing for a while you're bound to wonder about "the other 98 percent." Some direct marketers have been tossing 2 percent around as an acceptable direct mail response for a long time: "Hey, Joe—what do you think we ought to get from this mailing?" "Oh, I guess you could get 2 percent all right."

The real question here is, *What do you need?* Are your expectations realistic? After all, if you're selling a Mercedes or Sears' houses, you don't even need 2 percent response to make a fortune. If, on the other hand, you have a $10 silk scarf, you'd better hustle and get at least 10 percent to turn a profit (and *that* may not be a realistic expectation).

Whether it's 2 percent, or 1 percent, or 5 percent, or more, the question still remains: "What happened to the 98 percent, the 99 percent or the 95 percent that never responded? How do we get them to respond?" Put another way, can you continue to advertise in markets where over 90 percent of your expensive promotion is a dud?

With electronic interaction this is a question that will be getting increasing attention in the years ahead—and it will affect you. In search of an answer, you may be asked to come up with new ways of pulling in or qualifying some of that 98 percent that isn't answering, using highly sophisticated interactive online techniques.

You will be given more and more data about your prospects, as marketers use ever more sophisticated techniques of segmentation and market selection to reduce the 98 percent. Databases will allow you to know far more about your customers. How you use this data to strengthen your hypothesis and personalize your copy can provide an important contribution.

Privacy—Keep an Eye on It

This brings us to another challenge coming up. The more you know about your market, the more effective your advertising will be in this customer-driven form of marketing. But there are bounds and limitations to how much any of us should know about the other guy (without the other guy's permission). There is such a thing as privacy—and if you overstep the bounds of good taste you risk offending and irritating your prospect. Just what these bounds should be, and what the individual has to say about it, has become a national issue with a capital P—*Privacy.*

The growing computer information network that helps direct marketers be personal and caring and highly service oriented can also become a weapon to be used against them if it is abused. Be careful how, and to what extent, you use personal data. Use it to enhance the relevance of your message without showing off how much you know. (You want to make friends but don't be impudent. It's still a customer/business relationship. You're not one of the family.)

It's the old story: If we don't police ourselves here, someone else steps in and does it for us. And Privacy looks like one cause that every state and federal legislator has his or her eye on. Keep your eye on it, too.

Play by the Rules— Your Best Protection

Every so often bright, young creative people, or older creative people trying to sound bright and young, deplore the state of the art. They call to task the direct marketing industry for using tired formulas and rules that don't work, employing "hack" writers and weak graphics. Self-examination by the profession can be productive, but consider the improbability of such statements. If you are in a customer-driven business and if testing is its basis, how can the feelings, desires, and preferences of the market be ignored? And how can your rules and formulas not work, *if* you constantly test them? Can these critics possibly be suggesting that we're advertising without the moral imperative of a well-constructed hypothesis—or (worse still) that we've *stopped testing?*

On the other hand, why not ask, "If there is good advertising, why can't there be better advertising?" And right you are! I think you can see from many of the examples in your mailbox, in magazines, on television, and in this book that we do some very good direct response advertising, and it's getting better.

One major aspect of creativity is changing—and that is the role of the art director, designer, or artist.

The "Age of the Art Director" is truly upon us. Neglected for too long, subordinated to the copywriter in the creative process, the art director is now beginning to come into the limelight.

More often than not these days, the art director or designer is in at the start—and I hope that by now I don't have to spell out the advantages of this. But why? Why are designers becoming more important? Are we making up for years of artistic suppression? Nope. Business—and particularly advertising—just doesn't work that way.

Look at the market for your answers. The customer drives, remember? Is it not possible that our society today is somewhat more visually oriented than the societies of the past? (See Chapter 4.) Twenty years ago when you wanted news, you read a newspaper or listened to a radio. Today over 65 percent of the American people take their news by screen. We are far more visually alert or visually oriented than we've ever been. All-type ads used to be popular. Now there are few markets or media that can support pure type.

Such type ads still do best in magazines and newspapers that they resemble, those designed for serious readers. But even our literati, when they look for a new car, like to see it from all angles, and most of our larger market segments require dramatic new graphics to attract and hold the prospect's attention (the glutted mailbox, remember?). We are getting more sophisticated graphically. Or perhaps I should say, "more visually-oriented."

Why We Are Reactive, Not Proactive

Because we are customer-driven, direct marketers tend to be reactive; we do not lead. We follow the tastes and dictates of the customer as they may have been established or developed by other forms of advertising and communications that are proactive. In other words, we test.

Thanks to modern advertising, art, and design, thanks to the computer, thanks to video-oriented customers, we have new opportunities. How we use these opportunities to develop our own exciting graphics is something else again.

That's why the designer (or graphic "technician") is coming into the picture in a big way. Copywriters can no longer do their best work without an artist or designer by their side. The good copywriters readily acknowledge this. Unfortunately, good art directors are just as rare as good copywriters.

With our growing digital sophistication and capabilities for desktop work from the Macintosh, everyone has become a designer. Good? Not necessarily. Sometimes bad—very, very bad. Computer "designers" have sprung up overnight in print, and some of them do have talent. Many, however, understand little if anything about direct mail or direct response advertising. Or about readable copy, for that matter.

Which brings us to the next point. If direct marketing survives diffusion and dissolution and graphic sophistication and lack of talent—will it survive in the form or in the media we know today? What about the telephone?

Let's dispense with the telephone quickly. It's here—a permanent part of the mix, one of the fastest-growing aspects of direct marketing. It serves our prospects and customers, it works with every other medium, but it seldom stands alone as an effective prospecting medium. It stands on its own as a medium for customer relationship development and as an efficient order-taker. Why mail or write when you can call? The 800 number is instant gratification, order verification, credible communication all in one. It increases response. It can also increase order size.

As the telephone, the fax in direct marketing serves largely to facilitate direct response orders for products and services that require sender "records." Consumers occasionally use it when ordering "lists" of products (such as plants or flower seeds and bulbs). Some businesses use it for sending large orders as well. However, the fax is not proving to be a marketing tool for us any more than the telephone. It is invasive and comes into offices (and homes) as unwanted as "cold calling" on the telephone—those phone calls that ask us to support a charity or take out a mortgage every time we sit down to our evening meals.

What about CD-ROM, the Internet, digital video programming and interactive television or virtual reality? Will these change everything? In a word, "yes." But gradually.

Sure, business is already enmeshing itself in the Net. And here's where our new digital designers and technicians are really taking over. The computer revolution started in the 1950s. The video revolution started in the 1970s. We're entering another new phase today!

To help you evaluate for yourself as you go along, here's a valid rule of thumb. Once a well-measured (read "accurately-measured") consumer market tops one-third market penetration—it's a "go." So catch your breath. There's time. And remember, history shows that all media can continue to coexist together.

Forbes magazine said it best back in January 1995:

> Railroads changed the world in the 19th century, but many of the early railroad companies went broke. So did many of the pioneer auto companies. Three decades ago, it was predicted that IBM, General Electric, RCA, and Control Data would dominate the computer age. Only IBM actually made it. Several of today's leading players, including Compaq and Apple, were created only when the computer era was already 30 years old.
>
> Few of the pioneers in TV have even survived—remember Dr. Allen DuMont, his manufacturing company and his network? The movie companies, once thought to be victims of TV, turned out to be among the biggest winners.
>
> In short, the triumph of technology is foreseeable; what direction it will take and how society will use it is not predictable.
>
> So it may be with the Internet."[3]

More words of comfort for you: smart direct marketers are the conservative advertisers. They test the water and wait until the market is ready. They use the medium, the form of advertising, that is *most comfortable for the customer.* They are not trying to change the customer, but to *accommodate* him or her. Their first job is to coax response and listen carefully.

It was not until the 1980s that direct marketers began to use space advertising to do more than produce a measured response. They never seriously considered the extra benefits of multimedia efforts until the 1980s either. The effect of one medium on another in multimedia campaigns was virtually ignored because this was hard to measure—and expensive. What's more, few direct marketers had multimedia programs. This has all changed today.

If there is any one area where you will see changes in the years immediately ahead, it is in the growing use of more than one medium—the media mix. Direct marketers are learning how to carry successful creative efforts from one medium to another, how to plan multimedia campaigns and use the media to create awareness and build image while it also returns a measured response. (Yes, we *can* do product branding and do it well in conjunction with our benefit selling!)

These will be the newer trends or movements facing you, not the demise of direct mail or print, or an all video future. As Peter Francese, President and Founder of *American Demographics* says, "The endgame of this process will come when businesses market to individuals rather than to consumer segments."[4] Add to this John Yeck's keen reminder that the medium is *not* the message and— sounds like direct marketing to me.

Of course, we change with the times. But it has been said that within the past we find the seeds of our future. Are the mail order homes of Sears Roebuck and Company from 1909, with real estate and financing, furnishing and insurance, and the promise of family "happiness" so very different from our concepts for tomorrow?

As to predicting our future, no one does it better than Lester Wunderman, as he ably demonstrated in this excerpt from his article in *DM News*, May 9, 1994:

> The final and most critical change in our future will result from the interactive technologies now being developed and made ready for test.
>
> Interactivity isn't an invention—it's an ongoing process that began in the Post-Industrial Revolution and will continue to grow as new technologies that best serve the consumer's needs continue to develop. It will make possible a whole new dimension of relationship-building.
>
> Until now, we alone have been the architects of the connective link between manufacturers, consumers and media. For the near future we will have to remain so. But before the end of this century and the beginning of the next millennium, we shall become the partners of manufacturers, retailers and consumers who will use our skills to express and transact their needs and services with one another. I believe we have already begun to see the grand design of that future."[5]

Advice for Direct Marketing Beginners

If you are not already gainfully employed in direct marketing—and most particularly as a direct response creative person—here are some tips on getting started.

Originally, I promised you fame, wealth, and power if you mastered the techniques and strategies for creating winning direct response advertising. Let's say you're ready to start practicing in earnest and accumulating a little of that fame, wealth, and power. How do you convince others that you've arrived?

Whether you use an employment agency or the local paper, much will depend on where you start. Pickings will be slim in small towns, of course. Cities like New York, Atlanta, San Francisco,

Boston, Chicago, Kansas City, and Dallas offer the most opportunities. Geography will also determine your selection of *types* of direct response. New York and Chicago have a range of direct response agencies, book publishing operations, and magazine circulation departments—a wide variety of direct response entry possibilities.

If you like your local neighborhood and it's not New York, Chicago, Boston, or some other city with a variety of opportunities, research your own area. Look into local publishing operations or catalog companies or regular advertising agencies that may be planning to set up a direct response arm. (I've found lots of these in places around cities like Philadelphia, Charlotte, Atlanta, Phoenix, or Ft. Lauderdale or Miami.)

What to Look for in Your First Job

There's a lot of dabbling in direct marketing or *faux* direct marketing procedures going on in companies that are convinced it's fashionable. Some of the larger ones even set up "direct marketing" in their sales promotion or merchandising areas. A few general agencies put in instant direct marketing departments when their clients ask for it.

If you can help it, don't get involved with these people. They may need you, but you've little to learn from them. Here are a few questions to ask to help determine how suitable and serious a company is:

1. Does the company really understand direct marketing? Is it honestly committed to it? A brief investigation on two points can give you an answer here. First: Is the management committed to testing? From top down, do they allow time, planning, and budget for it? If it's an agency or other service company, do they insist their clients test? Second: Are they committed to building and maintaining a database? Note: No one will deny this. (It's like saying you don't believe in God, or forming clouds that spell out S-E-X in a Disney-animated sky.) Ask, instead, if they have pinpointed the 20 percent of their customers who purchase 80 percent of their products or services . . . then ask to see the special program they've developed for these special people!

2. Who's in charge of direct response advertising? Is there at least one major corporate executive working full-time on direct marketing? Is the executive experienced in direct marketing? What kind of staff is there? How much space does it have? What facilities are available to it? (If everything's in the planning stage or "about to be," watch out.)

3. Does the company have a direct response training program? Sadly, this is a toughie to get a "yes" on. Not many will.

4. Does it offer its creative people classes or seminars outside the company?

5. Is it a member of local direct marketing groups? Or the national organization, the Direct Marketing Association? If not, they ought to have a *very* good reason why not.

If the company got poor marks (especially on 1 and 2), beware.

How to Get Hired and Avoid Creative Catch-22

Let's say you've found some honest-to-goodness openings. They need a creative person, and you want them to want you. Now how do you go about it? The best answer is that everything helps— resume, references, samples, perseverance.

Let's start with the resume. If you have direct mail or direct marketing experience, flaunt it—whatever it may be. If you have creative experience, flaunt that, too. If the best you can say is that you've worked and you're willing, then show what you've done and tie it in, if you can, with the job's requirements. Last, but not least—what about your education? Did you major in advertising? Have you taken special courses in writing or direct marketing?

Next, samples. From day one every writer and artist starts compiling a book of samples. If you already have your collection started, organize your materials so that those showing qualities and executions most important to the job predominate. If you have direct response samples, these will be of primary importance.

What if you have no samples? Should you make up examples— rough copy and layouts for imaginary assignments? It's like chicken soup: It can't hurt if you're willing to work hard and make a professional presentation. But some interviewers aren't impressed with this. They only want to see what you can do by looking at examples of what you've done. Reasonable enough if you have just what they want. Otherwise it's creative Catch-22: "Show us that you have done it and we'll give you the job." "Give me the job and I'll show you what I can do."

This happens primarily 1) when you're moving from general advertising to direct response advertising; 2) when you're moving from one kind of direct response advertising to another (remember financial writers or consumer writers versus business-to-business writers in Chapter 2?); or 3) when you're just starting out and have no samples at all.

To overcome the problems, offer to take on a small assignment for them. Act as a free-lancer. Ask your questions, get samples, do your research, draw up your creative strategy, hypothesis, and approach. Do the work professionally, complete with copywriter's dummy or rough. It is not unreasonable to ask them to pay you for the work *if they use it*, particularly if you've been doing direct response copy.

This kind of offer shows two things: your interest and enthusiasm for the job, and your willingness to prove yourself to them. If they are sincere and interested in you, most prospective employers will take you up on the offer because it gives them a chance to see how you work, what questions you ask, how you relate to others (creative director, artist), how you take responsibility, how your mind functions as you develop creative concepts, how you meet deadlines, how you present, and how you receive criticism.

One point I mentioned deserves special emphasis. Regardless of your experience, your samples and your resume, your *interest in and enthusiasm for the job* can override a lot of shortcomings.

If you're sincerely excited about the products and services you'll be dealing with, if you're bursting with enthusiasm over the opportunity to do direct response advertising, you'll rack up high marks on attitude. What's more, if you're sincere (and I trust you will be), the odds are strong that you *will* do good work.

Something to Keep with You

Once you're hired and settled in, in no time at all you'll remember Tom Collins' words, "Advertising is hard!" You do have to do your homework, plan carefully, write hard, then rewrite and polish, polish, polish, but don't be discouraged. You've also got to keep the Joy Factor going. Otherwise, two things may happen to you that happen to potentially good writers all the time as they grow their wings:

First, you may freeze out all creative fun by the fear of making a fool of yourself. You stick close to the rules and cancel out your own creative emotions with a fearful "That might sound dumb."

Second, you can try too hard. This may sound silly coming from me, but you can work so hard to excel that you completely lose your perspective. Your work may even become convoluted and obscure. You will see distant reasons and grand, universal patterns behind your thinking, but you will have left the effective, simple solutions behind—along with most of us, sitting back on earth confused and unimpressed.

Don't let these things happen to you. If you continue to be shy or tense, here's a suggestion that's worked for some of my students. Their creativity is alive and well on assignments or exercises that aren't judged by a supervisor or creative director. All right, take a real assignment and do it two ways—the way you think is more "acceptable" and the way you'd like to see it go.

Present both to your creative supervisors and explain what you're doing. Enlist their help. They'll appreciate it. Listen. Learn to channel your creative ideas into acceptable formats. Or maybe—just maybe—you'll prove to the world what a genius you are right from the start!

Remember, you are a creative, reasoning human being. You have talent. You can use it wisely. Despite the rules and formulas and strategies, you have the ability to be unique. Don't be afraid. Relax. Concentrate. Now—get lost in the challenge and fun of your project!

It's your turn now. Time to gather your samples, update your resume and go out and shake up the direct response advertising business. Direct response needs your talent! So go for it! And good luck.

Just put this book on the shelf for now. It will be waiting should you ever need a little reinforcement or friendly support. But don't let it get dusty.

Notes

1. John Gardner, "Foreword" to *Becoming a Writer* by Dorothea Brand. Copyright © 1981 by J. P. Tarcher, Inc. Reprinted by permission of Houghton Mifflin Company and J. P. Tarcher, Inc.

2. Reprinted by permission of The Wall Street Journal, © Dow Jones & Company, Inc. 1985. All Rights Reserved.

3. "Where's the Money?" David C. Churbuck *Forbes* magazine, January 30, 1995 pp. 100–108.

4. *American Demographics*, September, 1995, p. 63.

5. "Electronic Media and Market Demassification" Lester Wunderman, *DM News*, May 9, 1994.

INDEX

TITLES OF INTEREST IN
ADVERTISING, SALES PROMOTION, AND PUBLIC RELATIONS

For further information or a current catalog, write:
NTC Business Books
a division of *NTC Publishing Group*
4255 West Touhy Avenue
Lincolnwood, Illinois 60646–1975